THE WIDOW TRADITIONS IN LUKE-ACTS
A Feminist-Critical Scrutiny

SOCIETY
OF BIBLICAL
LITERATURE

DISSERTATION SERIES
Michael V. Fox, Old Testament Editor
Pheme Perkins, New Testament Editor

Number 155

THE WIDOW TRADITIONS IN LUKE-ACTS
A Feminist-Critical Scrutiny

by
Robert M. Price

Robert M. Price

THE WIDOW TRADITIONS IN LUKE-ACTS
A Feminist-Critical Scrutiny

Scholars Press
Atlanta, Georgia

THE WIDOW TRADITIONS IN LUKE-ACTS
A Feminist-Critical Scrutiny

Robert M. Price

© 1997
The Society of Biblical Literature

Library of Congress Cataloging in Publication Data
Price, Robert M., 1954–
    The widow traditions in Luke-Acts : a feminist-critical scrutiny/
Robert M. Price.
        p.   cm. — (Dissertation series ; no. 155)
    Includes bibliographical references.
    ISBN 0-7885-0224-7 (cloth : alk. paper)
    1. Widows in the Bible. 2. Bible. N.T. Luke—Feminist criticism.
3. Bible. N.T. Acts—Feminist criticism.   I. Title.
II. Series: Dissertation series (Society of Biblical Literature) ;
no. 155.
BS2589.6.W43P75 1997
226.4'06—dc21   96-53453
                                                 CIP

Printed in the United States of America
on acid-free paper

Dedicated to the Memory of
the Reverend Pat Wickham,
Virgin and Martyr.

Contents

Introduction:
Ascetical Women and Apocryphal Traditions

Widow Traditions

It is a commonplace in the study of Luke-Acts that its author, more than any other in the New Testament, has a pronounced interest in women. A bit less often it is noted that Luke has a surprising number of stories and sayings dealing specifically with widows.[1] Where did he come by these materials? And what did he mean to do with them? To answer these two questions is the goal of this dissertation.

I intend to extend the recent theories of Ross S. Kraemer, Stevan L. Davies, Dennis Ronald MacDonald, and Virginia Burrus to the study of Luke-Acts. These works have in common the contention that the Apocryphal Acts of the Apostles incorporate stories of celibate women and that these stories stem from circles of women story-tellers who are to be identified with the charismatic widows of the early church.[2] I mean to show that the various widow traditions of the canonical Acts, with its companion Gospel, stem from the same milieu. Further, I aim to show that this supposition casts much new light on the tradition-history of the sayings and stories in question. In it we will begin to perceive some surprising things about the role of women in the dawn age of the Christian faith. The life and faith of the early church, like those of any religious movement, form an organic whole, and the recovery of the role of women in the early church cannot help but reveal other things as well, other aspects of early Christianity that have been long obscured along with its egalitarianism.

Ross S. Kraemer ("The Conversion of Women to Ascetic

---

1. Neal M. Flanagan, "The Position of Women in the Writings of St. Luke," *Marianum* 40 (1978): 293; E. D. Freed, "The Parable of the Judge and the Widow," *New Testament Studies* 33 (1987): 44-45; Michael D. Goulder, *Luke, A New Paradigm*, Journal for the Study of the New Testament Supplement Series, ed. Stanley E. Porter, 20 (Sheffield: JSOT Press, 1989), 661.
2. Virginia Burrus, *Chastity as Autonomy: Women in the Stories of Apocryphal Acts*, Studies in Women and Religion, vol. 23 (Lewiston & Queenston: Edwin Mellen Press, 1987), 68-72.

Forms of Christianity," 1980)[3] noted the recurrence throughout the Apocryphal Acts of episodes in which women hear the preaching of an apostle of ascetic, encratite[4] Christianity and immediately abandon home, parents, and husband to convert and follow the apostle. This striking pattern implied the presence of a whole cycle of oral traditions or legends which originated among ascetic women and functioned to summon other women to flee traditional domesticity and join them.

Stevan L. Davies (*The Revolt of the Widows: The Social World of the Apocryphal Acts*, 1980)[5] argued a kindred thesis independently in a study published the same year. He focused on much of the same material in the same texts. Noting the apparent predominance of women's concerns and the preference for female characters, often even at the expense of the eponymous apostles, in the Acts, he, too, suggested the origin of the stories among communities of ascetic women, the widows of the church. The main difference from Kraemer's theory was that Davies took the Acts as literary wholes to be the work of women. This conclusion was in large measure prompted by the widely held theory that the Apocryphal Acts as a genre represent a Christian mutation of the genre of the Hellenistic novel[6] as well as the supplementary assumption of Erwin Rohde[7] that the Hellenistic novels were chiefly written for women. If for, why not by?

Davies's attribution of the Acts as wholes to early Christian women paid insufficient attention either to the ancient ascription of the Hellenistic novels to male authors (Achilles Tatius, Longus, Chariton, Heliodorus, Xenophon of Ephesus, Apuleius)[8] or to the ancient ascriptions of the *Acts of Paul* by Tertullian to a presbyter

3. Ross S. Kraemer, "The Conversion of Women to Ascetic Forms of Christianity," *Signs: Journal of Women in Culture and Society* 6 (Winter 1980): 298-307.
4. James Strahan, "Encratites," in *Encyclopaedia of Religion and Ethics*, 1981. I refrain from capitalizing the term where it refers to the broad classification of ascetic, celibate piety, as opposed to the sect supposedly headed by Tatian. I capitalize the latter.
5. Stevan L. Davies, *The Revolt of the Widows: The Social World of the Apocryphal Acts* (Carbondale & Edwardsville: Southern Illinois University Press; London & Amsterdam: Feffer & Simons, 1980).
6. Rosa Söder, *Die Apokryphen Geschichten und die romanhafte Literatur der Antike*, Würzburger Studien zur Altertumswissenschaft 3 (Stuttgart: Kohlhammer Verlag, 1932).
7. Erwin Rohde, *Der griechische Roman und seine Vorläufer* (Hildescheim: Olms Verlag, 1960, reprint of 1876 ed.).

of Asia or of the corpus of five major Acts to one Leucius, apostate disciple of John.[9] However, elsewhere Davies made a case that it was not the *Acts of Paul* that Tertullian was condemning, but rather a pseudonymous epistle.[10] In this case we would not after all have an ascription of the *Acts of Paul* to a male author.

Davies's theory was embraced with more or less conviction by Joyce E. Salisbury,[11] Jo Ann McNamara,[12] and Gail Paterson Corrington.[13] Dennis Ronald MacDonald ("The Role of Women in the Production of the Apocryphal Acts," 1984)[14] and Virginia Burrus (*Chastity as Autonomy: Women in the Stories of Apocryphal Acts*, 1987)[15] rejected Davies's ascription of literary origin. MacDonald pointed out that to base the authorship of the Acts on the conjecture of female authorship of the Hellenistic novels was to build on sand, while the female viewpoint and agenda evident in particular stories, such as that of Thecla in the *Acts of Paul*, were not demonstrably present throughout the texts as we might expect had they been written by women in their entirety.[16]

Burrus, on the other hand, challenged Davies at a more fundamental level, rejecting the notion that the novels were the progenitors of the Acts after all. That there were certain broad thematic commonalities, notably the motif of devotion between the protagonists that could withstand any trial, she did not doubt. But, she argued, their presence made more sense as the result of both genres drawing on the same folklore sources. In

8. Dennis Ronald MacDonald, "The Role of Women in the Production of the Apocryphal Acts of the Apostles," *Iliff Review* 41 (1984): 22.

9. Devon H. Wiens, review of *The Revolt of the Widows: The Social World of the Apocryphal Acts*, by Stevan L. Davies, in *Journal of Biblical Literature* 101 (1982): 471.

10. Stevan L. Davies, "Women, Tertullian, and the Acts of Paul," *Semeia* 38 (1986): 139-143.

11. Joyce E. Salisbury, *Church Fathers, Independent Virgins* (New York: Verso, 1991), 4.

12. Jo Ann McNamara, *A New Song: Celibate Women in the First Three Christian Centuries*, Women in History Series, ed. Eleanor S. Riemer (Institute for Research in History and Haworth Press, 1983), 78.

13. Gail Paterson Corrington, *Her Image of Salvation: Female Saviors and Formative Christianity*, Gender and the Biblical Tradition, eds. Ross S. Kraemer, Carol Meyers, and Sharon H. Ringe (Atlanta: Westminster/John Knox Press, 1992), 185-186.

14. MacDonald, "Role of Women," passim.

15. Burrus, *Chastity as Autonomy*, passim.

16. MacDonald, "Role of Women," 23-24.

this argument the folktale studies of Vladimir Propp served her in good stead.[17]

It may be that the chief significance (for my purposes, anyway) of Burrus's book lay in its drawing together and refinement of Kraemer's delineation of the stories of female ascetical conversion and the work of Kraemer, Elizabeth A. Clark, Elizabeth Castelli, and others on the socially liberating function of asceticism as providing the one possible avenue of freedom from the restrictions of the traditional domestic role.[18] With great acuity Burrus traced out the constituent features of the "chastity story" form sketched in broad outline by Kraemer. This important contribution to form criticism will be of great concern to us later on.

Both MacDonald and Burrus agreed with Davies that at least many significant traditions/stories stemming from the telling of groups of celibate ascetic women had been preserved in the Apocryphal Acts. Willy Rordorf[19] had independently come to the same conclusion.

It was Dennis MacDonald's great contribution to extend the search for ascetic women's traditions into the canonical New Testament (*The Legend and the Apostle: The Battle for Paul in Story and Canon*, 1983).[20] He examined four sections of the *Acts of Paul* (the story of Thecla, the death and resurrection of Nero's cup-bearer Patroclus, the meeting of Paul and the baptized lion in the arena, and the martyrdom of Paul), showing how each section bore the marks of oral formation and subsequent commitment to paper. MacDonald showed how very few of the Patristic allusions to the events of these stories need be taken to denote the writers' familiarity with the text of the *Acts of Paul;* more likely they referred to well known oral traditions.

17. Burrus, *Chastity as Autonomy*, 44-60.
18. Rosemary Radford Ruether, "Mothers of the Church: Ascetic Women in the Late Patristic Age," in *Women of Spirit*, eds. Rosemary Ruether and Eleanor Commo McLaughlin (New York: Simon & Schuster, 1979), 72-98; Elizabeth A. Clark, *Ascetic Piety and Women's Faith: Essays in Late Ancient Christianity*, Studies in Women and Religion, vol. 20 (Queenston & Lewiston: Edwin Mellen Press, 1986); Elizabeth Castelli, "Virginity and Its Meaning for Women's Sexuality in Early Christianity," *Journal of Feminist Studies in Religion* 2 (1986), 61-88; Kraemer, "Conversion of Women." passim.
19. Willy Rordorf, "Tradition and Composition in the *Acts of Paul and Thecla:* The State of the Question," *Semeia* 38 (1986): 92.
20. Dennis Ronald MacDonald, *The Legend and the Apostle: The Battle for Paul in Story and Canon* (Philadelphia: Westminster Press, 1983).

These contentions enabled him to take a new look at the long-standing debate over the relation between the *Acts of Paul* and the Pastoral Epistles. Both sources seem to be aware of certain names (e.g., Demas, the household of Onesiphorus) and story allusions (sufferings at Iconium, a trial before Nero, the abandonment of Paul by cowardly or greedy disciples). Did the Pastorals lift the material from the *Acts of Paul?* Or did the *Acts of Paul* depend at these points on the Pastorals? Without rehearsing his whole case here, suffice it to say that MacDonald demonstrated the likelihood that, since the *Acts of Paul* was apparently a composition from oral tradition, the Pastorals and the Acts had independently drawn on the same oral sources.

Focusing on the ascetic, radical, and female viewpoint implicit or explicit in the Thecla story, MacDonald recalled that Tertullian opposed the reading of the *Acts of Paul* because of the appeal made to the Thecla story by women who claimed the right to teach and baptize. Then he argued that in a slightly earlier period the writer of the Pastorals was responding to a similar polemical use of the Paul and Thecla traditions by the very storytellers who composed them. His is an earlier, though a less friendly, use of the same traditions than that we see in the *Acts of Paul.*

The compiler of the *Acts* was either quite friendly with the agenda of the Paul and Thecla traditions (MacDonald connected him with the contemporary Montanist movement, though this suggestion did not go unchallenged)[21] or oblivious or indifferent to their implications. But the Pastor regarded as pernicious libels the tales of Paul preaching mandatory celibacy, breaking up marriages, eating only vegetables, etc., all marks of the ascetic movements of Asia Minor where both the *Acts of Paul* and the Pastorals were written. So, writing in the name of Paul, he sought to co-opt the implied history of the tales (hence the references to Onesiphorus, Iconium, etc.) but pretending to set the reader straight as to the real facts of the Pauline preaching and ethic.

He condemned the doctrines of encratism (1 Timothy 4:13), vegetarianism,[22] and teetotalism (5:23). And for good measure he tried to cut off the subversive oral traditions at their source by

21. David Rensberger, review of *The Legend and the Apostle: The Battle for Paul in Story and Canon,* by Dennis Ronald MacDonald, in *Journal of Biblical Literature* 104 (1985): 364.
22. Ibid.

severely restricting the church organization of widows, making it into a simple geriatric relief charity, and eliminating both the membership of younger, never-married women and the teaching function of widows (5:9; 2:11-12). (I will give further attention to MacDonald's sketch of the state of the widow communities and their restriction by the Pastor a little further on, as I present my own scenario for use through the rest of the dissertation.)

So MacDonald has pursued the trajectory of celibate women's oral traditions into the New Testament itself. But only so far. Now three other scholarly developments have convinced me that it is time to pursue the trajectory a crucial step farther, into the canonical Acts and its twin, Luke's Gospel. In so doing, of course, I am seeking to follow the path marked out by Helmut Koester and James M. Robinson in their ground-breaking collection of studies *Trajectories Through Early Christianity* (1971).[23] They showed that it may be that developments seen full-blown in the second century and beyond occur in seed form (or in the form of largely erased vestiges) in the New Testament documents, and that we can only recognize them as such from the perspective of the later phenomena. The splendid studies of Kraemer, Davies, MacDonald, and Burrus have blazed a trail that I propose to follow back into Luke-Acts and even earlier.

Apocryphal and Canonical

The first of these developments is to be found in the work of Richard I. Pervo (*Profit with Delight: The Literary Genre of the Acts of the Apostles*, 1987).[24] He is principally concerned to place Acts in the genre of the ancient novel. Along the way, building on the apparent kinship of the Acts genre with the novel genre (and even on Burrus's reading, some kind of kinship exists, even if the two genres are cousins rather than siblings), Pervo has occasion to challenge the venerable scholarly supposition that a wide gulf yawns between the apocryphal and the canonical Acts.

Taking the arguments of Schneemelcher and his congeners one by one, Pervo shows quite effectively that the differences are more apparent, nay, more imaginary, than real. For example, we have been assured that the Apocryphal Acts are essentially non-

---

23. James M. Robinson and Helmut Koester, eds., *Trajectories Through Early Christianity* (Philadelphia: Fortress Press, 1971).
24. Richard I. Pervo, *Profit with Delight: The Literary Genre of the Acts of the Apostles* (Philadelphia: Fortress Press, 1987).

theological, while Luke's Acts is a theological document through and through. The latter judgment no doubt exaggerates what theological interest there is in Acts, betraying the logocentric bias of Protestant scholars who often sought to squeeze theological blood out of a good, solid narrative stone. But the writer of Acts certainly does display certain, at least rudimentary, beliefs about Christ, the Spirit, etc. And so do the Apocryphal Acts! How can one read the repeated discussions of encratite spirituality and of docetic Christology and come away with the conclusion that their authors had no theological thoughts to share? They even tend to share them in much the same way Luke does, through apostolic speeches and inset letters.[25]

Are the Apocryphal Acts taken up with shameless and credulous miracle-mongering? Indeed they are, but let us not forget too quickly the fondness of Luke for Peter's therapeutic shadow and Paul's thaumaturgical handkerchiefs! With no reference at all to the Apocryphal Acts, James D. G. Dunn has characterized Luke as too reliant on the unsophisticated strategy of convincement by miracle,[26] and Haenchen and others (including Mac-Donald) have drawn almost precisely the same line between the Pauline Epistles, with their theology of the cross, and Acts with its triumphalistic theology of glory.[27] As MacDonald has shown, the triumphalism of the Lukan portrait of Paul has much more in common with the *theios aner* manner of the Corinthian *huperlian apostoloi* than with Paul who opposed them.[28]

In such a contrast Luke's Acts seems to fall in more readily with its black-sheep relatives the Apocryphal Acts. It seems in retrospect as if the long-held scholarly disdain for the Apocryphal Acts has functioned primarily as a subtle apologetic for the

25. Ibid., 125.
26. James D. G. Dunn, *Jesus and the Spirit: A Study of the Religious and Charismatic Experience of Jesus and the First Christians as Reflected in the New Testament* (Philadelphia: Westminster Press, 1975), 192-195.
27. Ernst Haenchen, *The Acts of the Apostles: A Commentary*, trans. Robert McL. Wilson; trans. rev. Bernard Noble, Gerald Shinn, Hugh Anderson (Philadelphia: Westminster Press, 1971), 113-114; Dennis Ronald MacDonald, "Apocryphal and Canonical Narratives about Paul," in *Paul and the Legacies of Paul*, ed. William S. Babcock (Dallas: Southern Methodist University Press, 1990), 63-69.
28. MacDonald, "Apocryphal and Canonical," 69; cf. Pervo, *Profit with Delight*, 24.

boundaries of the canon.

It seems that, again, we must place a New Testament work in the context of the developments after the canon if we are to understand it rightly. And, though I cannot pursue it here, allow me to register the opinion that, based on Pervo's observations, Luke's Acts ought to be placed within an already-extant genre of self-sufficient Acts. There is no indication that any of the extant Apocryphal Acts was intended as a sequel to any gospel, canonical or apocryphal, much less as a continuation of the canonical Acts. All these Acts are self-contained, each a gospel, so to speak, of its particular apostle, who in large measure usurps the central role of Jesus as divine epiphany and object of devotion.[29]

I see no evidence that the other Acts, which differ from each other as well as from Luke's at many points, were conceived in dependance on Luke's model. The extravagant martyr accounts in the Apocryphal Acts are certainly poles removed from the martyrological reserve of Luke and are thus not imitations of it. Thus I see no reason to suppose that Luke's Acts is the first, though it may be earlier than the other surviving members of its genre.

Was Luke an innovator? He is often said to have broken new ground by continuing the gospel story of Jesus with his story of the apostles and the church, and I would agree, provided what we mean is that he was the first to whom it occurred to write a specimen of each genre and to follow the one with the other.

At any rate, Pervo's observations that the canonical Acts is so similar in many ways to its apocryphal fellows must make us ask with renewed urgency whether it is not like them in another respect also: does it employ oral traditions stemming from communities of ascetic widows?

Luke and Women

The second development that concerns us is a great shift of

---

29. Francis Bovon and Eric Junod, "Reading the Apocryphal Acts of the Apostles," *Semeia* 38 (1986): 168; Paul J. Achtemaier, "Jesus and the Disciples as Miracle-Workers in the Apocryphal New Testament," in *Aspects of Religious Propaganda in Judaism and Early Christianity*, ed. Elisabeth Schüssler Fiorenza, University of Notre Dame Center for the Study of Judaism and Christianity in Antiquity, no. 2 (Notre Dame: University of Notre Dame Press, 1976), 162, 174; MacDonald, "Apocryphal and Canonical," 61-63.

exegetical opinion *vis à vis* Luke's treatment of women. From an earlier sentimentalism that made Luke's gospel "the gospel of womanhood"[30] more recent scholarship, eyes opened to new questions by the dawning of feminist consciousness in Europe and America, began to reexamine the nature of Luke-Acts' relevance to women. Prompted, perhaps, by the sheer fact of the number of women in Luke-Acts, some scholars characterized Luke as egalitarian. Helmut Flender may be cited as representative of this view. For Luke "man and woman stand together and side by side before God. They are equal in honor and grace, they are endowed with the same gifts and have the same responsibilities (cf. Gal. 3.28)."[31] Constance F. Parvey likewise notes, with an eye toward the social setting of Luke and Acts, "both of these works may have been compiled in a Hellenistic setting and may well reflect the more emancipated attitudes toward women in that setting."[32] William Willimon suggests in the same vein that "Perhaps Luke gives prominence to the role of women like Lydia to reassure Theophilus' church—a church which may have regressed to more traditional cultural mores regarding the status of women—that the leadership of women had apostolic precedent."[33]

Dennis M. Sweetland congratulates Luke for "suggesting that an equality exists between men and women." He is thus "more progressive than his Jewish or Greco-Roman contemporaries."[34]

E. Jane Via suggests that "For Luke, the patriarchal oppres-

---

30. Alfred Plummer, *A Critical and Exegetical Commentary on the Gospel According to St. Luke*, International Critical Commentary, eds. Charles Augustus Briggs, Samuel Rolles Driver, and Alfred Plummer (New York: Charles Scribner's Sons, 1906), 528; F. W. Ferrar, *The Gospel According to Luke*, Cambridge Greek Testament for Schools and Colleges, ed. A. Carr (Cambridge: Cambridge University Press, 1912), xxxv; cf. John R. W. Stott, *Basic Introduction to the New Testament* (Downers Grove, IL: InterVarsity Press, 1964), 32; Henry J. Cadbury, *The Making of Luke-Acts* (London: SPCK, 1958), 263-264; Vincent Taylor, *Behind the Third Gospel: A Study of the Proto-Luke Hypothesis* (Oxford: Clarendon Press, 1926), 214.

31. Helmut Flender, *St. Luke Theologian of Redemptive History*, trans. Reginald H. Fuller and Ilse Fuller (London: SPCK, 1967), 10.

32. Constance F. Parvey, "The Theology and Leadership of Women in the New Testament," in *Religion and Sexism*, ed. Rosemary Radford Ruether (New York: Simon & Schuster, 1974), 138.

33. William H. Willimon, *Acts*, Interpretation series, ed. James Luther Mays (Atlanta: John Knox Press, 1988), 137.

sion of women, evident in the restrictions on her presence and
participation in worship at both synagogue and Temple, is itself a
cause of the divine wrath acted out on Jerusalem and the Temple,
the heart of unbending religious authority."[35]

Other exegetes have come instead to see Luke as part of the
problem, not part of the solution. Elisabeth Schüssler Fiorenza
lines up the New Testament materials (much as F. C. Baur once
did with a different issue in view) along both sides of the debate
over the role and status of women in the Christian community.
Romans 16, with its list of Pauline female co-workers, including
the apostle Junia, and the baptismal formula quoted in Galatians
3:28 weigh in on the side of early Christian egalitarianism. But
"The other side of the debate emerges through, for instance . . .
the construction of early Christian beginnings by Luke-Acts."[36]

Elisabeth Meier Tetlow agrees:

> It would seem that women had an important and
> active role in Luke's own late first-century community.
> This was such that he could not ignore the importance
> of women altogether, but, reacting negatively to their
> present active role, he could, through the theology of
> his gospel, attempt to argue for the restriction of wom-
> en's role in the Church of his day.[37]

So Jane Schaberg:

> Luke restricts the roles of women to what is acceptable
> to the conventions of the imperial world. . . . Moti-
> vated by the desire that Christian leaders and wit-
> nesses be acceptable in the public forum of the empire,
> the world of men, Luke blurs traditional and historical

---

34. Dennis M. Sweetland, "Luke the Christian," in *New Views on Luke and
Acts*, ed. Earl Richard (Collegeville, MN: Liturgical Press, 1990), 60.
35. E. Jane Via, "Women in the Gospel of Luke," in *Women in the World's
Religions, Past and Present*, ed. Ursula King (New York: Paragon House,
1987), 45; cf. E. Jane Via, "Women, the Discipleship of Service, and the
Early Christian Ritual Meal in the Gospel of Luke," *St. Luke's Journal of
Theology* 29 (1985), 43.
36. Elisabeth Schüssler Fiorenza, *But She Said: Feminist Practices of Biblical
Interpretation* (Boston: Beacon Press, 1992), 95.
37. Elisabeth Meier Tetlow, *Women and Ministry in the New Testament:
Called to Serve* (New York: Paulist Press, 1980); reprinted as College The-
ology Society Reprints in Religion 1 (New York: University Press of
America, 1983), 101.

traces of women's leadership and exaggerates the
leadership by men.[38]

Gail R. O'Day echoes the same assessment: "Luke ignores
the leadership roles held by women in the church. This amounts
to a *de facto* silencing of those women."[39] Mary Rose DAngelo
admits that "Luke does increase the number of stories about
women in the Gospel," but it is no less clear, she reminds us, that
"the roles in which women appear are more restricted by what is
acceptable to the convention of the imperial world than are the
roles of women in Mark or John."[40]

My observations will certainly tend to corroborate the conclusions of this last group of scholars. Before proceeding, however, one must ask why the phenomena cited by these scholars
(to be discussed throughout the dissertation) were so nearly
invisible to the earlier, feminist or feminist-sympathetic, generation of researchers. Schüssler Fiorenza labels the exegesis typical
of that wave of scholarship the "feminist apologetic" approach.[41]
I believe she is correct.

That is, no matter how sophisticated one's critical approach,
as long as a scholar remains within the traditional community of
faith, there is an instinctive bias to expect the Bible to teach that
which the reader believes to be the truth. Similarly, there is the
hope that the Bible will prove to be an ally in any intrachurch
debate. And once it became evident that Luke did have a special
interest in women, it was natural to hasten to count him as an ally
in the struggle. One neither wanted nor expected to see the biblical text as a foe.

If such it proved to be, and, to my mind, has now proven to
be, then the stakes of the battle are different. The line of defense
(or perhaps of attack) lengthens considerably once the Bible is

---

38. Jane Schaberg, "Luke," in *The Women's Bible Commentary*, eds. Carol
A. Newsom and Sharon H. Ringe (Louisville: Westminster/John Knox
Press, 1992), 279.
39. Gail R. O'Day, "Acts," in *The Women's Bible Commentary*, 312.
40. Mary Rose D'Angelo, "Women in Luke-Acts: A Redactional View,"
Journal of Biblical Literature 109 (1990): 442.
41. Elisabeth Schüssler Fiorenza, "Theological Criteria and Historical
Reconstruction: Martha and Mary: Luke 10:38-42," in *Protocol of the Fifty-
Third Colloquy: 10 April 1986* by the Center for Hermeneutical Studies in
Hellenistic and Modern Culture (Berkeley: Graduate Theological Union
& University of California), 5.

seen to be not a weapon in one's own arsenal, nor even a level though neutral playing field, but rather part of the phallocentric citadel against which one wars.

Luke and the Pastor

The apologetic stance of Luke-Acts as described by many of these scholars, though most do not expressly call attention to the fact, reminds one of the sensitivity to decorum before a Roman public that we meet with everywhere in the Pastoral Epistles. Schüssler Fiorenza, however, does several times note the illuminating similarity between Luke's handling of women's questions and that in the Pastorals:

> Luke's redactional interest is remarkably similar to that of the Pastoral epistles which also distinguish between ministers who labor "in preaching and teaching" (1 Tim. 5:17) and those who "serve" (1 Tim. 3:8ff). . . . While the Pastorals explicitly prohibit women from teaching men, the Lucan work fails to tell us stories about women preachers, missionaries, prophets, and founders of house churches. While the Pastorals silence our speech, Acts deforms our historical consciousness and imagination.[42]

At one point she muses

> one has to face, of course, the problem that we don't know where the Lucan work is to be situated geographically. For example, it would be much easier if one could situate Acts in Asia Minor. Then one could clearly situate the story within the context of the ecclesial struggles in Asia Minor which still can be traced in the post-pauline rhetoric for the patriarchal ordering of Christian household and community.[43]

Given the similarity between Luke's general stance toward women and that of the Pastorals, we should not be surprised to discover that the use of widow/ascetic women traditions in Luke-Acts parallels the use made of them, as MacDonald describes it, in the Pastorals. Luke-Acts' redaction of widow traditions might be expected to stand closer to that of the Pastorals

42. Ibid., 8; also see 49, 57.
43. Ibid., 49.

than to that of the *Acts of Paul*.

And we are thus brought to the third scholarly development which causes us to press our question. We have seen that since Luke's work has other affinities with the Apocryphal Acts it might be expected that it, too, would use the stories of celibate women. We have also seen that, given the similarity between its general treatment of women and that of the Pastorals, we would not be surprised to find Luke-Acts using women's traditions in a manner similar to the use made of them by the Pastorals. The probability of this being the case increases still further if, as some scholars have argued, Luke is the author of the Pastoral Epistles.

C. F. D. Moule argued for the identity of the two writers on the basis of several pronounced similarities, especially but not exclusively lexical. He noted a number of previous studies of the common vocabulary of Luke-Acts and the Pastorals, all of which he took to be encouraging though not decisive to the case for single authorship. But Moule judges several instances of shared vocabulary to be especially suggestive. For example, "Luke and the Pastorals almost possess a monopoly within the New Testament, of the word group *euseb-*, denoting piety or godliness: *eusebeia*, outside Acts iii. 12 and the Pastorals, only occurs in 2 Peter (ii. 9); *eusebos* comes only at 2 Timothy iii. 12 and Titus ii. 12."[44] So with various other words and compounds. An especially interesting one, for our purposes, is the Lukan-Pastoral corner on the market for the word *tima* used to denote a monetary honorarium, in Acts 28:10 and 1 Timothy 5:17.

To this Moule adds a number of striking coincidences of turns of phrase and image, uncommon in or absent from the rest of the New Testament. For example, 1 Timothy warns good Christians to eschew the love of money (*philarguria*) in 6:10 and haughtiness (*me hupsélophronein*) in v. 17, while over in Luke 16:14-15 Luke condemns the Pharisees as "lovers of money" (*philarguroi*) who hold as highly estimable (*hupsélon*) what God hates. Otherwise, *philarguros* appears only in 1 Timothy 3:2; its opposite, *aphilarguros*, appears only in 1 Timothy 3:3 and Hebrews 13:5.

I would add another interesting parallel, that between the discipleship paradigm in Luke 9:62, where we read that "No one who sets his hand to the plow and looks back is fit for the king-

---

44. C. F. D. Moule, "The Problem of the Pastoral Epistles: A Reappraisal," *Bulletin of the John Rylands Library* 47 (1964-1965): 442.

dom of God" and the advice of the Pastor to his reader to "Plow a
straight furrow with the word of truth" (2 Timothy 2:15), exactly
the point, one would think, of not turning one's head while plow-
ing.

I think it safe to say that many critical scholars have found
themselves unable to take Moule's case seriously at least partly
because of his admitted use of the theory as something in the
nature of an apologetic to connect the Pastorals with Paul. He
could not evade the force of the arguments of P. N. Harrison and
others that these Epistles simply could not have come direct from
the pen of the Apostle. But neither could he bring himself to
admit they were pious forgeries. So his expedient was, first, to
identify the writer of Luke-Acts with Luke the beloved physician,
companion of Paul according to 2 Timothy 4:11 and Colossians
4:14. Of course, this was the traditional ascription of authorship,
and Moule was trying to stay as traditional as he could. So he
suggested that Luke was Paul's amanuensis for the Pastorals, and
that he acted with a rather free hand. I dare say most scholars
today regard this as a half-measure, an uneasy transition to critical exegesis by a scholar who could not make a clean break with
an older paradigm.

But Moule's case for the identity of the writers of Luke-Acts
and the Pastorals in no way depends on traditions or guesses
about who that author may have been. And since Moule's day
the case has been made again, and more strongly, by those who
would not tie either Luke or the Pastor to the historical Paul.

Stephen G. Wilson (*Luke and the Pastoral Epistles*, 1979)[45] does
not think for a moment that either the Third Evangelist or the
Pastor was the companion of Paul, but he does judge them to
have been the same man. Wilson begins with the linguistic evidence garnered by Moule and A. Stroebel, who had also argued
for Luke as the Pastor,[46] concentrating on Stroebel, whose tabula-
tions were more recent and more comprehensive than Moule's.
Here is his summary.

> Stroebel notes that the Pastorals have a total vocabu-
> lary of 850 words (excluding names) including 175
> *hapax legomena*, and that an almost exclusive sharing of

---

45. Stephen G. Wilson, *Luke and the Pastoral Epistles* (London: SPCK,
1979).
46. August Stroebel, "Schrieben des Lukas? Zum sprächlichen Problem
der Pastoralbriefe," *New Testament Studies* 15 (1968-1969): 191-120.

> approximately 64 terms with Luke-Acts is remarkable. It is pertinent to observe, for example, that of 540 terms common to Paul and the Pastorals only 50 are typically Pauline, but none of them are shared exclusively with Paul. And in comparison with the 37 terms which the Pastorals share exclusively with Luke-Acts, the next most frequent are 10 shared with Hebrews and 7 with 2 Peter.[47]

Wilson hastens to admit that not all the words common to the two books are always used in the same sense in both, but all in all he finds the statistics quite impressive, though not decisive. Other factors, never adequately surveyed in the previous consideration of the question, push him to near certainty.

The lion's share of the book is taken up with careful comparisons tending to show the close similarity or identity, as far as it can be gauged, between Luke and the Pastor when it comes to the issues of eschatology, soteriology, Christian citizenship, church order and the ministry, Christology, Law/Scripture, and their depiction of Paul.

But may not all this evidence prove no more than a common ecclesiastical *Sitz-im-Leben* for the two sets of writings? May they not just represent two writers who belong in the same kind of church in the same historical period, the similarity one might expect to see between two nineteenth-century Anglo-Catholics, or between two Catholic Modernists?

Wilson's answer, I think, is a good one: we do in fact find such kinship in the similarities between Luke-Acts or the Pastorals on the one hand and 2 Peter, Polycarp, and Hebrews on the other. There is much to place these documents in a common milieu. But precisely such a comparison indicates that the Pastorals and Luke-Acts are much closer than they need to be if this is the only link between them.[48]

Wilson also discusses the option of the two sets of writings stemming from a common "Lukan School" comparable to the Pauline School responsible for Ephesians or the Johannine School responsible for the Fourth Gospel and Epistles, but this reduces to the option just considered, a common milieu of kindred spirits, and we would have to raise the same question: do the writings have to be quite so similar to come from the same school?[49]

---

47. Wilson, *Luke and the Pastoral Epistles*, 9.
48. Ibid., 137.

In what might be called a form-critical or *Gattung*-critical argument, Jerome D. Quinn goes beyond the lexical, stylistic, ecclesiastical and theological arguments of his predecessors and suggests that Luke wrote the Pastorals as a third volume to follow the Gospel and Acts, continuing his narrative by switching over to a different genre entirely, that of the epistle.[50] One need not suppose that the Pastorals and Luke-Acts were intended or published as part of the same work to accept a common authorship for all the writings in question. But it would certainly make an even stronger case for common authorship if it could be shown that the Pastorals would make sense as part three of a Lukan trilogy.

In the first place, as scholars have long noted, Luke's reference in Acts 1:1 to the Gospel as his first book uses the word *proton*, implying first in a series, not *proteron*, implying the former, the first of two. In the Hellenistic period, Quinn admits, *proton* had begun to fade into meaning the same thing as *proteron* but need not have lost all its original precision. By using *proton*, did Luke mean to tantalize the reader with the prospect of another book, one that, alas, he never got around to writing, as some have suggested?[51]

But Quinn says he did write it. Scholars just don't recognize it. As it happens, many books from first-century Hellenism close with an epistle or collection of epistles in the name of the principal character, and sometimes these epistles were later separated to circulate by themselves. Examples include the Hellenistic edition of the Jeremiah canon: Jeremiah, Baruch, Lamentations, Epistle of Jeremy; the fivefold collection we know as 1 Enoch which ends with the Epistle of Enoch; the Syriac Apocalypse of Baruch, ending with a nine-chapter epistle which, circulating by itself, survived the long night of oblivion in which the remainder of this book slept until its rediscovery after twelve hundred years. A dozen of Diogenes Laertius' *Lives of the Eminent Philosophers* con-

---

49. Ibid., 137-138.

50. Jerome D. Quinn, "The Last Volume of Luke: The Relation of Luke-Acts to the Pastoral Epistles," in *Perspectives on Luke-Acts,* ed. Charles H. Talbert, Perspectives in Religious Studies, Special Studies Series, ed. Watson E. Mills, no. 5 (Danville, VA: Association of Baptist Professors of Religion, 1978) passim.

51. See Donald Guthrie, *New Testament Introduction* (Downers, Grove IL: InterVarsity Press, 1973), 342 for a list of scholars who have held this view.

cluded with a letter or group of letters, and that of Epicurus with three long doctrinal letters.

Charles H. Talbert had already shown that Luke-Acts followed the classical pattern of the lives of the philosophers in which was presented, first, the life of the founder of the school, then the story of his followers (shown in such a manner as to vindicate their claims of legitimate succession), followed by a summary of his teaching.[52] The suffixing of the Pastorals onto the end of Acts would approximate this pattern.[53]

If the preface of Acts provides the clue that the reader ought to have expected a third volume, would it not also lead us to expect a preface to that third volume reminiscent of the florid eloquence of the prefaces of Luke and Acts? Quinn suggests that Titus was the first of the Pastorals, despite the order in our Bible, a suggestion that will surprise no one, and that the exceedingly long pseudo-Pauline salutation of Titus 1:1-4 was intended as the opening of the three letters together. Among Paul's letters only the salutations of Romans and Galatians are longer, and so long a preface for so short a letter as Titus, by itself, would seem all out of proportion.[54]

On Quinn's theory, the up-in-the-air character of the "conclusion" of Acts is really a pause leading the reader on to Part Three, the last portion of which will lead us straight back to Paul's imprisonment, providing us with a last testament, reminiscent of that given in the speech to the Ephesian elders (Acts 20:17-38). I must admit that I find the hypotheses of Wilson and Quinn quite plausible, indeed most probable, since otherwise it is all just too close for comfort, too much to qualify as coincidence. I will adopt the theory of the Lukan authorship of the Pastorals (or, more to the point, the Pastoral authorship of Luke-Acts) in what follows. The theory of identity of authorship seems to me both to be reinforced by the kind of convergences between the two noted by Schüssler Fiorenza and implied by O'Day, Schaberg, D'Angelo, and others, and uniquely to explain those correspondences.

However, let me hasten to note that my analysis will not really depend on the theory of Wilson and Quinn. If one were to hesitate at their conclusion and instead choose to regard the Pas-

---

52. Charles H. Talbert, *Reading Luke: A Literary and Theological Commentary on the Third Gospel* (New York: Crossroads Publishing Company, 1982), 2-3.
53. Quinn, "The Last Volume of Luke," 68-69.
54. Ibid., 92.

torals and Luke-Acts as products of the same ecclesiastical-histor-
ical milieu,[55] little would change. But if Wilson and Quinn are
correct, then the present thesis represents the direct continuation
of MacDonald's. I will be asking if the Pastor treated women/
widow traditions the same way in his Gospel and Acts as he did
in his Epistles.

MacDonald himself dismisses Wilson's identification of
Luke with the Pastor, but he does so with no real argumentation
except to notice that Luke-Acts seems to promote celibacy, while
the Pastorals resist it.[56] MacDonald points to Luke 20:34-35 as
denoting Luke's opinion that anyone who hopes to rise from the
dead must qualify now by eschewing marriage, unlike the sinful
"sons of this age" who marry. It will be worth dealing with this
objection, since even apart from the question of the identity of
Luke and the Pastor, it will be important throughout this dissertation to keep in mind at least the general similarity of the ethical
stance of the two authors.

The contrast MacDonald seems to see here is one between
"sons of this age" (as tantamount to "worldlings" as in Luke 16:8)
and "those accounted worthy [here and now, by their manner of
life, including continence] of the resurrection." The one group
marries before the eschaton catches them naked and ashamed,
with some tall explaining to do (cf. Genesis 3:7-13), while the
other are pure, virgins, not having defiled themselves with the
opposite sex (cf. Revelation 14:4).

As S. P. Brock shows, this is certainly how the passage was
understood by Syrian ascetics. Here is how the verse appears in
the Old Syriac, as Brock translates it:

> Those who have become worthy to receive that world
> (i.e. the kingdom) and that resurrection from the dead,
> do not marry, nor can they die, for they have been
> made equal with the angels, (and being) the sons of
> the resurrection (they are) like the sons of God.[57]

Pervo also takes this text, along with others to which I shall
return in a moment, to imply Luke's encratism.[58] But it is far

---

55. P. N. Harrison, *The Problem of the Pastoral Epistles* (Oxford: Oxford
University Press, 1921), 53.
56. MacDonald, *Legend*, 55.
57. Sebastian P. Brock, "Early Syrian Asceticism," *Numen* 20 (1973): 5-6.
58. Pervo, *Profit with Delight*, 181.

from clear to me that the text must be read that way. One can read it equally as well as contrasting human life now in the old age of flesh and then in the future age of spirit: there is marriage now, but that will change in the future age, the resurrection's transformation marking the transition. That is clearly the point of the Synoptic parallels. Luke's version is more cumbersome, perhaps showing itself the result of clumsy harmonizing of two independent versions of the saying. But even in Luke's longer version the additional clauses seem to preserve the same distinction: the not marrying any more is clearly predicated on never dying any more, being a son of God through the resurrection, a sense in which no one is yet a son of God (cf. Romans 8:29-30, where eschatological glorification seems to be paralleled with becoming a son of God in the fullest sense). Not marrying, then, would seem to fall on the far side of the resurrection, along with the undying angelic state on which it is predicated.

Further, I suggest that the heavy-handed Lukan redaction of the tradition represents his attempt to make Jesus' saying apply more directly to the case posed him by the scribes: why had the woman been married at one time or another to all these men? Because one by one each brother died, occasioning the marriage of the woman to the next brother in line. But the question of her marrying any but the original husband becomes irrelevant in a situation where the death of her spouse no longer obtains. She is back to square one, and the reason for her having been married to the other six vanishes. Levirate marriages will be a thing of the past on Resurrection Morn, since there will be no death. And in general, "marrying and giving in marriage," though innocent enough, are restricted to this age (cf. Luke 17:26-27).

If Luke 20: 34-36 does not advocate celibacy as a condition of salvation, a doctrine thrust away by the Pastor as rankest heresy (1 Timothy 4:3), what of the other verses cited by Pervo? Luke adds "I have married a wife" to the excuses barring attendance at the Great Supper (18:29)—or does he? We do not know that this excuse was not present in Q, since Matthew seems to have summarized his source here ("But they . . . went off, one to his farm, another to his business . . ." 22:5). Given the ubiquitous law of threefoldness,[59] we would expect a third excuse; the marriage

---

59. Archibald M. Hunter, *Interpreting the Parables* (Philadelphia: Westminster Press, 1960), 11; Joachim Jeremias, *The Parables of Jesus*, 8th. ed. (New York: Charles Scribner's Sons, 1972), 28.

excuse was omitted by Matthew probably because he has turned the supper itself into a wedding feast and the marriage excuse seemed to clash with this new feature. Thomas knew one man avoided the feast because of marriage, albeit not his own. "My friend is to be married and I am to arrange a dinner" (logion 64). Thomas probably changed it to make the new bridegroom into a calculating caterer in accord with his redactional interest expressed in the terminus of the parable: "Tradesmen and merchants will not enter the places of my Father."

Luke has added "wife" to the commodities to be forsaken in both 14:26 (contrast Matthew 19:29) and 18:29 (contrast Mark 10:22).[60] But perhaps Pervo has missed the point here. Schüssler Fiorenza observes that Luke did not add "wife or husband," but only "wife." Thus his point is not celibacy but to "restrict entrance into the radical discipleship of Jesus to men."[61] Schaberg is equally clear on the point: "Luke's addition of 'wife' (with no corresponding addition of 'husband') to the list of what must be left for the sake of the kingdom of God means that the disciples are imagined as men."[62] Interestingly, as Kraemer points out, Philo did the same thing:

> While much of Philo's general description of contemplatives applies equally to men and women, one particular detail does not. When he lists those whom philosophers abandon to take up the contemplative life, husbands are conspicuous by their absence, while wives are specifically noted.[63]

It would have been quite easy to add "husbands" to the list if it had entered Luke's mind that there might be women disci-

---

60. Pervo, *Profit with Delight*, 181-182; Cadbury, *Making*, 264-265, 272; Wolfgang Stegemann, "The Following of Christ as Solidarity between Rich, Respected Christians and Poor, Despised Christians (Gospel of Luke)," in *Jesus of Nazareth and the Hope of the Poor* by Luise Schottroff and Wolfgang Stegemann, trans. Matthew J. OConnell (Maryknoll NY: Orbis Books, 1986), 83-84.
61. Elisabeth Schüssler Fiorenza, *In Memory of Her: A Feminist Reconstruction of Christian Origins* (New York: Crossroad Publishing Company, 1984), 146.
62. Schaberg, "Luke," 281.
63. Ross S. Kraemer, "Monastic Jewish Women in Greco-Roman Egypt: Philo Judaeus on the Therapeutrides," *Signs: Journal of Women in Culture and Society* 14 (Winter 1989): 351.

ples who would have left them. Joanna the wife of Chuza (Luke 8:3) may come to mind as being just such a solo woman disciple minus husband, but as we will see, her case is that which proves the rule, as a vestige of pre-Lukan tradition (see Chapter 6). How difficult can it have been for Luke to write words like those found in the *Acts of Thomas*, where an ascetic woman disciple prays

> Look upon us Lord, since for your sake we have left our homes and our fathers' goods . . . we have left our own possessions for your sake, that we may obtain you, the possession that cannot be taken away . . . we have left our fathers and mothers and fosterers that we may behold your Father and be satisfied with his divine nourishment . . . for your sake we have left our bodily consorts and our earthly fruits, that we may share in that abiding and true fellowship and bring forth true fruits.[64]

The relevance of these Lukan texts for a reconstruction of his ethic *vis à vis* celibacy is uncertain to say the least, since Luke seems to be aware of the more restricted applicability of such texts to the "wandering charismatics" described by Gerd Theissen, of whose theory I will say more later. It is not so clear that Luke is laying down a law of celibacy for all readers.

True, Thaddée Matura shows that Luke nowhere indicates that in recording these sayings of radical discipleship he is issuing counsels of perfection for the elite among his readers.[65] But then on the other hand neither does Luke explain why it is suddenly all right for the settled communities of the Pauline mission to refrain from letting goods and kindred go. Community of goods seems to vanish from the Lukan church once one steps outside the Jerusalem city limits. All of which is to say that it is going much too far to make Luke a proponent of encratite celibacy as Pervo and MacDonald do, and thus to prevent the identification of Luke as the Pastor.

Hermeneutics of Suspicion

In what follows I will attempt a feminist-critical reconstruction of the widow traditions (by which term I will henceforth

---

64. Kraemer, "Conversion of Women," 301.
65. Thaddée Matura, *Gospel Radicalism: The Hard Sayings of Jesus* (Maryknoll, NY: Orbis Books, 1984), 51, 56, 69, 99, 126, 142.

refer to the stories of celibate women issuing from their communities and advancing their interests) of Luke-Acts. My treatment
will be much in the manner of Elisabeth Schüssler Fiorenza. This
involves the employment of a hermeneutic of suspicion, which
has, as I view it, two basic moments.

First, one sniffs out what appear to be loose ends in the texts,
apparent vestiges of an earlier state of affairs in which women
exercised a greater role and enjoyed a greater freedom than was
normative later in the Christian movement. "Although the canon
preserves only remnants of the nonpatriarchal early Christian
ethos, these remnants still allow us to recognize . . . a glimpse of
the early Christian movements as a discipleship of equals"
(Schüssler Fiorenza).[66] "Even given Luke's particular agenda,
however, glimpses of women's lives and experiences slip into the
story and work against Luke's aims" (Gail R. O'Day).[67]
"[W]omen can develop a hermeneutics of suspicion which recognizes the androcentric ideological construction of reality in . . .
texts. . . . Although we are scripted, contradictions and fissures in
the scripts make a reading 'against the grain' possible" (Schüssler
Fiorenza).[68]

Tamis Hoover Rentería, in an important study of the Elijah
and Elisha stories, many of which concern widows and emanated
from circles that included them,[69] traces out an exactly analogous
process of the co-optation of traditions of the oppressed by the
pro-Monarchic Deuteronomic Historian. She shows, too, that the
original thrust and partisanship of the Elijah and Elisha stories
can still be discerned through the overlay of Deuteronomic
redaction "as a form of counter-hegemonic expression preserved
within the dominant hegemony." It is just such a "counter-hegemonic expression," an expression of Christian women's self-
hegemony surviving in witness against the dominant male hegemony over women, that the feminist-critical method seeks to
uncover in the New Testament texts, in our case Luke-Acts.

---

66. Elisabeth Schüssler Fiorenza, *Bread Not Stone: The Challenge of Feminist
Biblical Interpretation* (Boston: Beacon Press, 1984), 35.
67. O'Day, "Acts," 312.
68. Schüssler Fiorenza, *But She Said*, 90.
69. Tamis Hoover Rentería, "The Elijah/Elisha Stories: A Socio-cultural
Analysis of Prophets and People in Ninth-Century B.C.E. Israel," in *Elijah and Elisha in Socioliterary Perspective*, ed. Robert B. Coote; Society of
Biblical Literature Semeia Studies, ed. Edward L. Greenstein (Atlanta:
Scholars Press, 1992), 113.

The employment of the hermeneutic of suspicion is nothing particularly new. Though feminist scholars apply it anew to women's questions, what we are applying is pretty much what has come to be known as the criterion of dissimilarity. Though the phrase is perhaps most associated with Norman Perrin's work, Perrin himself accurately points out[70] that it is just a name for a methodological tool long employed by form critics and other historical critics as far back, I would add, as Reimarus and Strauss.[71]Perrin had suggested that we could be sure we had authentic Jesus tradition only where it clashed with both contemporary Judaism and the early church. But, as Schüssler Fiorenza employs the criterion, the point is not so much to discover what Jesus himself did or said, but, more modestly, to distinguish between earlier and later stages of the tradition of the early church. Where a pericope clashes with later church practices, we still do not know whether it may not simply represent an earlier phase of church practice rather than the practice of Jesus himself. And where a saying or story refuses to fit the Jewish context, this may only mean it is a Hellenistic Christian anachronism.

The idea is to apply to the biblical text a close reading to disclose tensions and contradictions in the texts, which are then recognized as protruding like bits of masonry from a buried, earlier structure. The critic's imaginative judgment seeks to reconstruct the outlines of the now-hidden structure, using the textual remains as levers, if possible, to pull the larger whole up to the surface for scrutiny.

As any excavator knows, though, there is a danger that whatever has been built atop the old ruins may itself be disrupted, having its foundations shaken by the digging process. Just as the edifice of orthodox dogma and historical apologetics once trembled at the application of the historical-critical method which threatened to expose sand beneath the foundations, so today does the structure of patriarchal Christianity and phallocentric theology resist the application of the feminist-critical

---

70. Norman Perrin, *Rediscovering the Teaching of Jesus* (New York: Harper and Row, Publishers, 1967), 39-43.
71. Hermann Samuel Reimarus, *Reimarus: Fragments*, trans. Ralph S. Fraser; ed. Charles H. Talbert; Lives of Jesus, ed. Leander E. Keck (Philadelphia: Fortress Press, 1970), 80, 101, 109, 117, 127-131, 135; David Friedrich Strauss, *The Life of Jesus Critically Examined*, trans. George Eliot. ed. Peter Hodgson; Lives of Jesus, ed. Leander E. Keck (Philadelphia: Fortress Press, 1972), 302-303.

method to the texts. For if the latter should disclose (as it seems to be doing) an original discipleship of equals, then the lordship of the male God and his Son, held in trust by their vicars, the male hierarchs and theologians of the church, might be threatened. The feminist-critical method, using the hermeneutic of suspicion, then, is engaged in a new struggle, but it is employing a proven weapon forged in past struggles against different enemies.

The second moment of the hermeneutic of suspicion is the differentiation between the descriptive and the prescriptive in biblical texts, and the readiness to recognize that what poses as descriptive may in fact be prescriptive, and thus proscriptive. That is, when a writer says "Widows do not baptize; women do not teach; the role of women is to pray and nothing else," it most likely means the writer is attempting to create such a reality by suppressing a different one he does not like. Else why say it? What is the point of observing what is merely the fact of the matter, the order of the day? And when the writer dons the Esau-mask of an apostle or of Jesus himself in order to say it, we cannot doubt that we have a rewriting of history in order to change someone's role in the present.

Is 1 Timothy 2:12 evidence that women were not teachers in the Pastoral community? Or is it not rather evidence of the opposite? Eventually the Pastor had his way, to be sure, but he would have had no occasion to lay down the law in the manner he did had not women been exercising a prior freedom to teach, which no doubt in certain quarters they continued to do. As Schüssler Fiorenza says,

> especially normative texts often maintain that something is a historical fact and a given reality although the opposite is the case. . . . Androcentric texts and documents do not mirror historical reality, report historical facts, or tell us how it actually was. As androcentric texts our early Christian sources are theological interpretations, arguments, projections, and selections rooted in a patriarchal culture.[72]

I will, in short, be attempting to reconstruct the widow traditions Luke used and co-opted; in the process I will seek to sketch

72. Schüssler Fiorenza, *In Memory of Her*, 60; cf. Schüssler Fiorenza, *Bread Not Stone*, 108-109.

out the fuller religious reality of consecrated women as implied in the hypothetical earlier form of these traditions.

Schüssler Fiorenza is sober, one might even say pessimistic, about the prospect of recovering the treasure of women's history so long and deeply buried in the New Testament textual field: "Many of the traditions and information about the activity of women in early Christianity are probably irretrievable because the androcentric selection or redaction process saw these as either unimportant or threatening."[73]

Luke seems to her a particularly barren field: "We find short references to widows and prophetesses, but Luke does not tell us anything about their activity or function. Luke's conception of history is harmonizing and therefore does not acknowledge a 'woman's problem' in the early church."[74]

Yet I am more optimistic than Schüssler Fiorenza. In fact, I venture to say that a surprising amount of what was lost can be found again, and it will be the aim of this dissertation to find it.

How to do it? Schüssler Fiorenza suggests that "women's actual contribution to the early Christian missionary movement," though "lost," can and "must be rescued through historical imagination as well as in and through a reconstruction of this movement which fills out and contextualizes the fragmentary information still available to us."[75] "Such a feminist critical method could be likened to the work of a detective insofar as it does not rely solely on historical 'facts' nor invents its evidence, but is engaged in an imaginative reconstruction of historical reality."[76] "The task, therefore, involves not so much rediscovering new sources as rereading the available sources in a different key. The goal is an increase in historical imagination."[77]

Feminist Criticism and Historical Criticism

To those unsympathetic with the whole enterprise it may

---

73. Schüssler Fiorenza, *In Memory of Her*, 49.

74. Ibid.

75. Ibid., 167.

76. Ibid., 41.

77. Ibid., xx; cf. Carol P. Christ, *Laughter of Aphrodite, Reflections on a Journey to the Goddess* (San Francisco: Harper & Row, Publishers, 1988), 162; and Bernadette J. Brooten, "Early Christian Women and Their Cultural Context," in *Feminist Perspectives on Biblical Scholarship*, ed. Adela Yarbro Collins, Society of Biblical Literature Centennial Publications (Atlanta: Scholars Press, 1985), 67-68.

seem that Schüssler Fiorenza is advocating some sort of undisciplined fantasy: "We don't have much to go on, so let's just wing it and rewrite history the way we wish it had been," the sort of business about which Winston Smith was engaged in his cubbyhole at the Ministry of Truth. But this would be a caricature. As Collingwood, certainly no axe-grinding feminist, said, the historian always works with a tentative and corrigible model of the past which he or she uses to weigh the probability of any claim or piece of data offered in a document.[78] This picture of the past is in turn based on previous judgments about data. What we have is an ongoing hermeneutical circle. Schüssler Fiorenza is far from denying that the feminist-critical method represents "engaged scholarship,"[79] but is equally far from admitting that this makes it mere special pleading propaganda.

The criterial model for the past which the feminist critic employs to weigh and sift the traditions is itself the product of a reading of data (e.g., Romans 16; Galatians 3:28 as a baptismal formula) which combine to indicate, by their dissimilarity to later patriarchalism, an earlier stratum where egalitarian discipleship was possible. These data contribute to a picture of the Christian past that indicates the "dissimilar" data we can see is the tip of an iceberg we cannot readily see. But we now know where to look, and we may be able to trace out the dimensions of what we can see only in a glass darkly.

Similarly, when Schüssler Fiorenza wants to make the experiences of the outcasts, the marginalized, and the oppressed to function as a hermeneutical lens in evaluating and reconstructing the evidence ("To truly understand the Bible, it is necessary to read it through the eyes of the oppressed . . .to develop a hermeneutics 'from below'"),[80] she is not saying, "Let's read the text through tinted glasses to make it look the way we want." She is rather simply invoking the venerable principle of analogy. We do not know, by and large, how the ancient women and slaves of the biblical stories experienced their roles and lives and sufferings. If we are to hope to gain any insight into their history as they experienced it, we must at least experiment with extrapolating backward from the better known experiences of the oppressed and

---

78. R. G. Collingwood, *The Idea of History* (New York: Galaxy Books, a division of Oxford University Press, 1957), 244-245; cf. Schüssler Fiorenza, *In Memory of Her*, xvii.

79. Schüssler Fiorenza, *In Memory of Her*, xxii.

80. Schüssler Fiorenza, *Bread Not Stone*, 50.

the marginalized nearer to our own time. This may provide us a set of lenses through which hitherto obscure features of the texts will assume a sharper focus. And as F. H. Bradley said, without the assumption of historical analogy and continuity no inference is possible.[81]

Schüssler Fiorenza rightly sees her work as part of a larger paradigm shift from an androcentric to an inclusive framework of research and discourse.[82] She is working on "a new feminist paradigm."[83] Thomas S. Kuhn's work on paradigms has convinced many of us that scholarly and scientific advances have not been occasioned on the whole, as was long assumed, on a succession of new "discoveries," demonstrable improvements or increases in true information. Rather, the history of scholarship is a succession of interpretative paradigms. We construe the data according to a particular conceptual map or model regnant at the time. The conformity of the data to the contours of the explanatory model, the place of phenomena in the schema, determine their meaning for us. A model becomes "outmoded" when sufficient attention is drawn to various data which do not seem naturally to fit into the paradigm's confines. Then someone will propose a model which accounts better for, or is even based on, the hitherto anomalous data.[84]

Kuhn's suggestions have now been widely adopted. But I think that one crucial implication of the new approach has not been quite as evident to some as it ought to be. The nature of verification is subtly changed once we recognize that, in biblical historical reconstructions, we are not discovering the truth so much as experimenting with a new paradigm within which to display the data in a new and striking arrangement. One need not demonstrate in every case that one's individual exegeses are "right" while all previous exegeses were "wrong." One cannot always even banish a previous interpretation as inferior. The data are genuinely susceptible to many viable readings, as the history of New Testament exegesis clearly shows.

The question of verification rather becomes: provided the

81. F. H. Bradley, *The Presuppositions of Critical History,* ed. with an Introduction and Commentary by Lionel Rubinoff (Chicago: Quadrangle Books, 1968), 96.
82. Schüssler Fiorenza, *Bread Not Stone,* 106.
83. Schüssler Fiorenza, *In Memory of Her,* xxi.
84. Thomas S. Kuhn, *The Structure of Scientific Revolutions* (Chicago: University of Chicago Press, 1969), 52-76.

new exegeses are tenable and do not engage in special pleading,
text-twisting, do they *together* make new sense of the data as a
whole, especially the anomalous data that ground like sand in the
gears of the old paradigm? Does the new paradigm tie up the
loose ends without leaving too many of its own? If so, then its
persuasive power lies here, not in some kind of definitive dis-
posal or refutation of all previous views.   Or, as Schüssler
Fiorenza says, "how much has the account reached an optimum
plausible integration of all available historical information?"[85]

The feminist-critical method, really like any version of the
historical-critical method, "reconstructs historical-social 'reality'
not as a 'given fact' but as a plausible subtext to the . . . text."[86]
The past is simply not definitively recoverable. It can never be
known. Any reconstruction of it will be a story of our own devis-
ing. That does not give us the license to make up whatever story
we want, but it is a constant reminder that there are no assured
results of historical criticism.

In the same way, Paul de Man and Harold Bloom warn the
literary interpreter that there can never be a true "reading" of the
text. One can never engage the text and telepathically enter into
it (Schleiermacher notwithstanding) and come away knowing
what the "real meaning" is or was. This means all attempts to
read, to discover meaning in, the text are only stronger or
weaker, more or less plausible, "misreadings" of the text. A
strong misreading is one which is particularly fruitful of subsequent misreadings.[87]

To call all interpretations of the text "misreadings" is not to
abandon any attempt to get at the meaning of the text. A supposed meaning of the text is always kept in view as a goal, albeit
an ever-receding one. But we must remind ourselves that corrigible misreadings, no matter how good they look to us, are all we
poor mortals can ever attain.

Even so, there is no obtainable objective truth of the past.
(There probably never *was*, in one sense, since few observers can

---

85. Schüssler Fiorenza, *Bread Not Stone*, 104.
86. Schüssler Fiorenza, *But She Said*, 96.
87. Harold Bloom, *Kabbalah and Criticism* (New York: Continuum Publishing Company, 1984), 95-126; Jonathan Culler, *On Deconstruction: Theory and Criticism After Structuralism* (Ithaca: Cornell University Press,
1982), 175-179; Christopher Norris, *Deconstruction, Theory and Practice*,
rev. ed. (New York: Routledge, a division of Routledge, Chapman, and
Hall, 1991) 100; Schüssler Fiorenza, *But She Said*, 83, 96.

ever completely agree on the meaning even of current events!) There are only more or less compelling reconstructions, misreadings of it. In that spirit of chastened confidence I will propose to set forth one more misreading of the text, trying to get at the egalitarian subtext hinted at by the "anomalous data" which show a greater role for women in the New Testament churches, especially in those of Luke-Acts.

Schüssler Fiorenza speaks of the necessity to rehabilitate the argument from silence.[88] She claims that the rejection of it in mainstream scholarship is a subtle tool of oppression wielded by androcentric scholarship. The rehabilitation she intends is to

> find ways to "break" the silences of the texts and to read their "silences" as indications of the historical reality of women about which they do not speak directly. Rather than reject the "argument from silence" as a valid historical argument, we must carefully read the clues of the text pointing to a different historical reality and integrate them into a feminist model of historical reconstruction in such a way that we can give voice to their silences and understand them as part of the submerged traditions of the egalitarian early Christian movement.[89]

Walter Bauer, in *Orthodoxy and Heresy in Earliest Christianity*, was following exactly the same procedure. He paid careful attention to what Derrida calls the "counter-signature" of the anti-heresiological literature of the early church and heard the surprising echoes of the voices of "heretics" who had been excommunicated or persecuted, their scriptures burned and their traditions largely obliterated. He was like a rock-climber making slow progress upward by learning to grasp the nearly invisible fissure lines in what others with a less patient glance would have regarded a completely smooth surface. And he made it to the top, at least to a vantage point where he could see much that no one had seen for a long time.

And it is no surprise to read that the objection repeatedly registered against Bauer's unsettling book was that he made too free a use of the argument from silence. According to Georg Strecker's appendix to the English translation of Bauer, "The

---

88. Schüssler Fiorenza, *In Memory of Her*, 41.
89. Schüssler Fiorenza, *Bread Not Stone*, 112.

Reception of the Book," Dibelius, de Zwann, Völker, Strathmann, Simonin, and Lebreton all leveled this charge against Bauer.[90] I cannot help but think that, just as Schüssler Fiorenza charges, such an objection boils down to an attempt to keep the marginalized at the margins. For to accept the Bauer thesis is to place the catholic and apostolic charter of ecumenical orthodoxy in the same dustbin as the Donation of Constantine. I think this apologetic strategy is worth a closer look as I begin my own investigation, since it would seem to invite the same charges.

It seems evident to me that conservative apologists are asking us not only to suppose that, when there is a paucity of evidence, we cannot say exactly what happened, but also to suppose we can be pretty sure that nothing happened, nothing out of the "ordinary." That is, nothing contrary to the ordinance of the received view of the past which legitimates the present of which the apologists are the guardians.

They contend, in effect, that nothing happened if something is not clearly attested. This axiom is to prevail even when what data there are point suggestively in some (unorthodox) direction. As long as there are gaps, as long as there is ambiguity, apologists assure us, we can ignore the seeming implications of the data and go on assuming that nothing untoward ever occurred. The suggestion that something "odd" did happen will be greeted with derisive hoots of "Speculative!"

Yet how are we to account for the presence of these anomalous data at all? If some very early Christians were not adoptionists, how came there to be texts like Acts 2:36; 13:33; Romans 1:3-4? If no such doctrine existed so early, why are there such texts that all require harmonization, though all would seem to make good sense as teaching adoptionism?

If there had really been an unbroken, undeviating progress toward catholic orthodoxy, i.e., no early feminist, Gnostic, adoptionist Christianities, would we not expect to see *no* aberrant evidence? Wouldn't everything pretty much fit? As Bauer showed, early heresiologists seemed to realize this and so sought to late-date the heretics, make them a single line of disciples to one another (not a wide spectrum of diverse options), to retroject the

---

90. Georg Strecker, "The Reception of the Book," rev. by Robert Kraft, Appendix 2 to Walter Bauer, *Orthodoxy and Heresy in Earliest Christianity*, trans. by a team from the Philadelphia Seminar on Christian Origins, eds. Robert Kraft and Gerhard Kroedel (Philadelphia: Fortress Press, 1971), 295.

credentials of catholic orthodoxy with myths of apostolic succession, etc. Damage control strategy: minimize the data.

If, on the other hand, there had been a wild luxuriance of early views and options, with no attempt to stamp them out, we should expect to find a fulsome variety of evidence hard to chart and place in any order. In fact we do find a state of affairs at least approaching this in the second and third centuries, after the canonical books were segregated and purified. There still survive several Gnostic or apocryphal books which escaped the zeal of the book-burners.

If there had been a wide variety of options, doctrines, Christianities, but these had been suppressed at some point, would we not find various oddities, pieces of troublesome data that refuse to fit the orthodox story of origins, square pegs that will not be forced into round holes? This is what we do find, it seems to me: clues that once things were another way. And why do we find only remnants, fossils, vestiges? Because all else was destroyed, all memory suppressed. The stubborn dismissals of the evidence and its implications by apologists seek merely to *keep* it all suppressed. Here is a situation in which "skepticism, as well as credulity, can serve the purpose of maintaining the *status quo*."[91]

It is as if the church were a repressed individual. There are pains and strains the person knows not how to account for. In fact they stem from the repression of an old trauma, in this case early Christian diversity. One might seek relief through analysis: self-knowledge. But one refrains because the cost would be too high: one's life as one now lives it, especially one's sense of purpose, one's security, rests on leaving things just as they are, leaving every stone unturned.

Over against such agnosticism in the service of orthodoxy, I hold to the postulate that where there's smoke, there's fire. Or as the Synoptic Apocalypse puts it, where ever the body is, there the vultures will gather" (Luke 17:37). They don't circle around nothing. The aberrant hints we find must be the few remaining colored stones in a once complete mosaic. The sparseness of them does not cast doubt that there was once a full picture, though admittedly it is going to take some imagination to fill in the gaps.

I am engaged in the excavation of fossils and artifacts from a

91. Daniel Liechty, *Theology in a Postliberal Perspective* (London: SCM Press; Philadelphia: Trinity Press International, 1990), 32.

period of the church that is long lost and obscured under many layers of patriarchal rewriting and reinterpretation. It is no wonder that little evidence from that "Dark Age" survives. In what follows I ask the reader to keep in mind the cautions of Cornford in *The Origin of Attic Comedy:*

> Many literary critics seem to think that an hypothesis about obscure and remote questions of history can be refuted by a simple demand for the production of more evidence than in fact exists.—But the true test of an hypothesis, if it cannot be shown to conflict with known truths, is the number of facts that it correlates, and explains.[92]

The words of E. R. Dodds are also well worth remembering: "Much of this is of course speculation, not certainty or near-certainty; anyone who talks about certainties in this field forgets the enormous gaps in our evidence."[93]

My textual base consists of all those sayings and stories in Luke-Acts involving, explicitly or implicitly, widows and celibate women. I restrict myself to texts that are the exclusive property of Luke-Acts. I do not consider two passages, the widow's mite (Luke 21:1-4) and the woe on those who devour widows' houses (Luke 20:47). These are both taken over from Mark and thus do not fall under consideration as possibly deriving from a special widow source for Luke-Acts (though they may yet have come from similar widow sources). Also, though I suspect there are connections between the celibate women of the early church and Luke's account of Mary of Nazareth, to try to encompass this huge subject would make an already long dissertation altogether unmanageable. For the same reason I restrict myself narrowly to the question of celibate women, leaving aside the larger question of the ministries of other women in the early church and Luke-Acts. Thus, e.g., no treatment of Prisca. But I want by no means to convey the impression that the ministry of consecrated celibate women was the only or the proper role for women in early Christianity.

---

92. Francis MacDonald Cornford, *The Origin of Attic Comedy,* ed. with a Foreword and Additional Notes by Theodor Gaster (Garden City: Anchor Books, a division of Doubleday & Company, 1961), 191.
93. E. R. Dodds, "Maenadism in the *Bacchae,*" *Harvard Theological Review* 33 (July 1940): 176.

The hermeneutical program of Schüssler Fiorenza extends farther than mere historical reconstruction. What I am doing is only preliminary spadework in the larger task of empowering Women-Church today by creating/reconstructing a "usable past," dispelling a historical amnesia imposed on women to keep them subjugated. I salute this agenda but can pursue it no further here. The scope of this dissertation is already broad enough. I will restrict myself to this particular corner of the vineyard, though I hope my results may prove to be fruitful source material for feminist theologians to use in their work. And, though I consider myself a feminist, even a theologian, I am a man; I fear that any attempt by me to do feminist theology would be pretentious and inauthentic.

Finally, a word of warning: it will soon become apparent that I have drunk deep from the wells of the great higher critics of the last century, imbibing not merely substance but style as well. Something of their polemical flare, I confess, has at length permeated my own prose. Some readers, accustomed to the antiseptic restraint of today's academic language, may chafe at this; others may find, as I did reading Baur, Strauss, and Wellhausen, that it spices the stew and makes an otherwise dry meal a bit more enjoyable.

CHAPTER ONE

Virgin Matrix:
The *Sitz-im-Leben* of the Widow Traditions

Widows in the Pastorals

Kraemer, Davies, and MacDonald have identified the matrix of celibate women traditions as communities of widows in the second and following centuries. MacDonald supposes that we may place the existence of such communities already in the time of the Pastorals, which he locates in the second century. I agree with him (and the many other scholars who hold this view). And with many scholars, in the last century and in this one, I also place Luke-Acts in the early to mid-second century, a judgment independent of arguments for common authorship.[1]

So Luke-Acts and the Pastorals are not much earlier than the period for which widows' communities are attested. But I will briefly seek to show the likelihood that they are known in the milieu from which Luke-Acts and the Pastorals emanate. We know there were widows in the communities from which the Pastorals stem and to which they are fictively addressed (as 1 Timothy 5:3-16 makes clear, at least), but was there something like a widows' order, some defined group with set duties, privileges and responsibilities, as later in the history of the church?

Were widows simply one of a number of groups, like the sick and the destitute, for whom care was taken in the community of the Pastorals? On the basis of the regulations regarding them in 1 Timothy 5:3-16, some have answered yes. E. K. Simpson is uneasy with the suggestion that the text might have more than geriatric charity in mind: "This passage has also been identified with the official Church-widows or *presbyterae* of later date and made a ground of suspecting the authenticity of the Epistle; but nothing here specified involves official position."[2]

Here, as so often, a nuance of someone's doctrine of inspiration seems to control exegesis. The widows *cannot* have constituted an official body, given Pauline dating, hence they did not. One rather suspects that this is the hidden agenda behind the judgments of Fee and Guthrie, both of whom withstand the battery of critical arguments to hold onto Pauline authorship at any cost. Guthrie: "While the . . . following passage clearly points to

— 1 —

some kind of register with a specific age qualification, there is not
sufficient data to conclude for an order of widows."[3]

1. I am convinced of the second-century date for Luke-Acts for the following reasons. As Charles H. Talbert shows in *Luke and the Gnostics: An
Examination of the Lucan Purpose* (New York: Abingdon Press, 1966),
Luke-Acts shares in several striking ways the defensive agenda of the
second-century Apologists, trying mightily to secure the pedigree of
authentic Christianity by appeal to what would later be called apostolic
succession, as well as to a definitive tradition of scriptural exegesis
derived from Jesus and the apostles. The worrying over the fleshly character of the resurrection body of Jesus as well as the device of fresh revelations in a post-resurrection period also seem to betray an atmosphere
of debates with the Gnostics. Though Talbert himself, ironically, does
not date Luke-Acts in the second century, everything in his book points
to that conclusion.

Similarly, J. C. O'Neill (*The Theology of Acts in Its Historical Setting*
[London: SPCK, 1961]) shows how the theology of Acts places it comfortably in the age of the Apostolic Fathers and the Apologists. The
Apostolic Decree seems to reflect second-century Christian cultic mores;
the title "servant" for Jesus is paralleled in the *Didache, 1 Clement,* and the
Martyrdom of Polycarp, but nowhere in the New Testament. The natural
theology of chapters 14 and 17 is cut from the same fabric as those of Justin and the Apologists. The notion of a final and definitive rejection of
the gospel by the Jews, everywhere presupposed in Luke-Acts, is too late
for the first century.

Pervo and others have shown the kinship of Acts to both the Hellenistic novels and the Apocryphal Acts, both genres that flourished in the
second century. I would add that Luke also shows clear connections
with the Apocryphal Gospels of the second century. With the *Gospel of
Peter* it shares the trial before Herod Antipas. With several Infancy Gospels it shares the tradition of Jesus the adolescent Wunderkind.

Finally, I would note the surprising parallels between Luke and
Papias, another churchman of the second century. Both mention extant
written gospels with which they are apparently familiar, but both prefer
their own research, derived, supposedly, from those who heard the witness of the original apostles, whom both Luke and Papias admit they did
not themselves hear. Both mention the prophesying daughters of Philip.
Significantly, Luke's is not among the gospels mentioned by Papias,
leading me to suppose that it did not yet exist. Both know of the gro-
tesque legend of Judas Iscariot swelling up and exploding. Both finally
wrote their own gospels, Papias' being called *An Exposition of the Oracles
of Our Lord.* Luke, too, expounded his Lord's oracles, not merely con-
tenting himself with recording them, as he often prefaces a parable with
an explanation of what he supposes Jesus meant by it. I picture Luke
and Papias as kindred churchmen of similar antiquarian tastes. And as
such they are figures of the second century, men looking back on a dim-
ming memory of the apostolic age. I make them contemporaries.

Fee: "Some see this as indicating that there was by this time in the church an official 'order of widows,' who were expected to perform the 'duties' of verse 10 and would in return be cared for by the church. But that seems to ask too much of what is actually said in the text."[4] Yet I should say that at least that much is simply what the text says!

It is true that for a widow to be "enrolled" might mean no more than that she is on a list to receive donations, but some commentators point out that the word in question, *katalegestho*, is the word regularly used for being entered on a list, registered, catalogued, as, for instance, as part of a levied military troop.[5] For Kelly, this "makes it absolutely clear that there was a definite order of widows."[6] Likewise, for Plummer, "she holds an office."[7] As far as Hanson is concerned, "There certainly was some sort of an order for widows in the church which the author knew."[8] Daniélou:

> the interesting point is the enrolment on a register and the conditions it implies, for this makes plain that we are concerned here not with all widows, but with some of their number who constitute a special category of the community. This is the first indication we have of an order of widows, parallel to the other orders.[9]

2. E. K. Simpson, *The Pastoral Epistles: The Greek Text with Introduction and Commentary* (London: Tyndale Press, 1954), 74.

3. Donald Guthrie, *The Pastoral Epistles: An Introduction and Commentary*, Tyndale New Testament Commentaries, ed. R. V. G. Tasker (Leicester: Inter-Varsity Press; Grand Rapids: William B. Eerdmans Publishing Company, 1957), 102.

4. Gordon D. Fee, *1 and 2 Timothy, Titus*, Good News Commentaries, ed. W. Ward Gasque (San Francisco: Harper & Row, Publishers, 1984), 80.

5. Martin Dibelius and Hans Conzelmann, *The Pastoral Epistles*, trans. Philip Buttolph and Adela Yarbro, Hermeneia Series, ed. Helmut Koester (Philadelphia: Fortress Press, 1983), 75; J. N. D. Kelly, *A Commentary on the Pastoral Epistles, Timothy I & II, and Titus*, Harper's New Testament Commentaries, ed. Henry Chadwick (New York: Harper & Row, Publishers, 1960; Peabody MA: Hendrickson Publishers, 1987), 115.

6. Kelly, *Pastoral Epistles*, ibid.

7. Alfred Plummer, *The Pastoral Epistles*, Expositor's Bible, ed. W. Robertson Nicoll (New York: A. C. Armstrong & Son, 1888), 154.

8. Anthony Tyrell Hanson, *The Pastoral Epistles*, New Century Bible Commentary, gen. eds. Ronald E. Clements and Matthew Black (Grand Rapids: William B. Eerdmans Publishing Company, 1982), 96.

The regulations for enrolled widows are more detailed than those for bishops (1 Timothy 3:1-7) or for deacons (vv. 8-13) and resemble them in more than one point, e.g., the stipulation that the enrolled widow have been the wife of one husband (5:9) just as the bishop and deacon must be the husband of one wife (3:2, 12). It surely seems most natural to see here something approaching the semi-clerical order later described in more detail by Tertullian and other writers to whom I will soon refer. Lock even grants that the reference in v. 3 to "honor" may include a "special seat in the meetings and rank in the Church hierarchy," as in later sources.[10]

Were they an order or group given to celibacy? It would seem so, since otherwise the troubled deliberations in the passage over whether some belonging to the group ought to marry seem difficult to explain. If one were simply left alone by the death of a spouse but then had the opportunity to remarry, who would challenge it? It seems clear by contrast that something else is presupposed, if not stated outright, in the passage, namely that the women in question have taken some sort of vow of celibacy that subsequent marriage would violate.

And note, as MacDonald does,[11] that the text says nothing at all about widows remarrying, only about marrying. Surely the implication is that here, as in the Ignatian *Epistle to the Smyrnaeans* 12 and in Tertullian (*On the Veiling of Virgins* 33), at least some of the women under discussion are among the "virgins who are called widows." And if this is so, then we are most definitely talking about a celibate order, even if in an early form. Fee seems to sense the danger to his position here and is willing to go to any length to avoid the implications. For him the proposition is the remarriage of young widows, but since he will not brook anything so nascently catholic as a vow of celibacy in a text from the pen of Paul (or his amanuensis), he must engage in exegetical gymnastics of the worst sort: why on earth would it be a sin for a young widow to marry again given the text's own advice (v. 14) to do precisely that? How would it violate her "pledge" (*pistin*)

9. Jean Daniélou, *The Ministry of Women in the Early Church*, trans. Glyn Simon (London: Faith Press, 1961), 13.

10. Walter Lock, *A Critical and Exegetical Commentary on the Pastoral Epistles (I & II Timothy and Titus)*, The International Critical Commentary, eds. Charles Augustus Briggs, Samuel Rolles Driver, and Alfred Plummer (New York: Charles Scribner's Sons, 1924), 57.

11. MacDonald, *Legend*, 75.

since she cannot have taken one? *Pistin,* then, must not refer to a vow but to her Christian faith. She must not sacrifice her faith or sin against it by marrying an unbeliever. Fee as much as admits he is reading this concern into the text.[12]

The same issue comes up in 1 Corinthians 7, by my reckoning another second-century piece and part of the Pastoral stratum delineated by Winsome Munro.[13] There the writer comes to a somewhat different conclusion but wrangles over the same issue: contrary to the opinion of some, "if a virgin marries, she does not sin" (7:28). Why bother to say such a thing unless there is a special class of consecrated virgins who are never to marry?

Jouette Bassler, Elisabeth Schüssler Fiorenza, and MacDonald all argue that the Pastoral Epistles are far from defining the institution of church widowhood for the first time, as if creating such a thing. Rather, it is clear from the fact that there already exist younger widows whose supposed abuses are known to the writer that he wishes to restrict the age limit so to avoid such scandal in the future.[14] Bassler and Hanson go so far as to doubt the organic unity of the passage as it stands,[15] proposing not that what we read is a textual corruption, but rather that, as Hanson says, "the author is adapting an existing church order source." Thus these widow rules assume earlier ones.

Were the widows of the church subsidized by the church? No one doubts that at least the enrolled widows were. The real question is whether they were receiving a ministerial stipend of some sort. Here the issue hinges on the meaning of the word *tima,* "honor," in v. 3. Hanson notes that virtually all commentators who are not trying to preserve Pauline authorship take the word's appearance in connection with elders in v. 17 to refer to a stipend or honorarium.[16] MacDonald, Schüssler Fiorenza, and Bonnie Bowman Thurston all conclude that the word is used in 1 Timothy 5:3 to denote payment.[17]

12. Fee, *1 and 2 Timothy, Titus,* 81.
13. Winsome Munro, *Authority in Paul and Peter: The Identification of a Pastoral Stratum in the Pauline Corpus and 1 Peter,* Society for New Testament Studies Monograph Series, ed. G. N. Stanton, 45 (New York: Cambridge University Press, 1983), passim.
14. Schüssler Fiorenza, *In Memory of Her,* 310-311; MacDonald, *Legend,* 74-75; Jouette M. Bassler, "The Widow's Tale: A Fresh Look at 1 Tim 5:3-16," *Journal of Biblical Literature* 103 (1984): 34.
15. Bassler; Hanson, *Pastoral Epistles,* 96.
16. Hanson, *Pastoral Epistles,* 100.

I agree. Two arguments seem decisive to me. First, immediately following the advice to render double *times* to elders who rule well, we find the quotation of Deuteronomy 25:4, "You shall not muzzle an ox when it is treading out the grain," a text already applied to compensation of gospel workers in the Pauline tradition (1 Corinthians 9:9), followed by the Lukan (!) saying "The laborer is worthy of his hire" (10:7—the similar Matthew 10:10 has "food" instead of "hire").

Second, as Thurston points out, the author, a reader of the Septuagint, can scarcely have been ignorant of the use of *tima* to mean monetary compensation in Sirach 38:1, "Honor [*tima*] the physician with the honor [*timais*] due him," a formulation closer to 1 Timothy 5:3 than 5:17.[18]

How could it be clearer that *tima* denotes payment in 1 Timothy 5:17? And if it does, what other than phallocentric, chauvinistic bias can prevent us from taking the same word in the same sort of context as meaning the same thing when it is applied to compensation for enrolled widows? I suggest that the reluctance to see a stipend for ministering women here is of a piece with the long-standing refusal to countenance the presence of a woman apostle in Romans 16:7, despite the clear lexical attestation of a female name "Junia" and no male name "Junias."

So as all admit, there were poor widows supported by the church dole, and as I have just argued, there also appear to have been widows compensated by the church for their ministry. Later church history shows us communities and communal houses in which widows lived supported by the generosity of one of themselves, a patroness herself dedicated to celibacy. Clark, Ruether, Brown, and others[19] provide good discussions of the later widow houses and communities known to us from the

---

17. Schüssler Fiorenza, *In Memory of Her*, 310-311; MacDonald, *Legend*, 75; Bonnie Bowman Thurston, *The Widows: A Women's Ministry in the Early Church* (Minneapolis: Fortress Press, 1989), 45.

18. Thurston.

19. Clark, *Ascetic Piety*, 43; Elizabeth A. Clark, ed., *Women in the Early Church*, Message of the Church Fathers Series, 13 (Collegeville, MN: Liturgical Press, 1983), 134-135, 223; Salisbury, *Independent Virgins*, 120-121; Mary Lawrence McKenna, *Women of the Church: Role and Renewal*, with a Foreword by Jean Daniélou (New York: P. J. Kenedy & Sons, 1967), 58; Peter Brown, *The Body and Society: Men, Women, and Sexual Renunciation in Early Christianity* (New York: Columbia University Press, 1988), 264-265; Ruether, "Mothers of the Church," 75-92.

writings of Jerome, Gregory of Nazianzus, Palladius, Theodoret, Gerontius, and the *Testamentum Domini*. But did anything like them exist in the period of the Pastorals and Luke-Acts? This would be quite important as indicating a certain independence of widows and other ascetic women from the provision, and thus of the control, of the churches and those who "ruled" them (1 Timothy 5:17).

In the nearly contemporary writings of Ignatius (probably pseudonymous by my reckoning, but perhaps not much later than the late second century) we have some possible evidence of such living arrangements, as Schüssler Fiorenza points out.[20] In the Ignatian *Epistle to the Smyrnaeans*, we find the writer greeting the "houses of my brothers and wives/women and children and the virgins who are called widows" (13:1a). Here we certainly seem to have both an explicit reference to a well-defined group of consecrated celibate women who were not literally widows (though the literal-metaphorical shift probably moved in both directions, with some women once married adopting the title "virgin" in token of their newfound independence of the control of men)[21] and an implicit reference to households of such women parallel to those containing conventional families. But the evidence in 1 Timothy seems clearer still. In 1 Timothy 5:16 we read, "If any believing woman (*piste*) has widows, let her assist them, and let the church not be burdened, in order that it may be able to assist the real widows." We have already heard exhortations to the effect that a believer ought to take care of his or her own relatives who are widows, and that in no uncertain terms (vv. 4 and 8). Do we meet the same advice here yet again?

Such redundancy ought to make us look for another option. Redundancy is, to be sure, often a mark of amended and interpolated documents, and if Bassler and Hanson are right about the composite character of this section, that could be the reason for the redundancy at this particular point, but I doubt it. Why no less than three versions of the same fairly obvious exhortation in so short a space? Are we to imagine that in the span of thirteen verses we have the loose ends of three separate church orders combined?

Besides, the restriction of the addressees in the earliest texts

---

20. Schüssler Fiorenza, *In Memory of Her*, 313.
21. Sarah B. Pomeroy, *Goddesses, Whores, Wives and Slaves: Women in Classical Antiquity* (New York: Schocken Books, 1975), 6.

to believing women is inexplicable if the command is just another version of vv. 4 and 8. This seeming peculiarity led some scribes to emend the text, changing it to either "any believing man" or "any believing man or believing woman." Modern commentators are just as confused. Guthrie, not knowing quite what to make of the reference to women alone, acquiesces in the "man or woman" emendation,[22] while Fee and Kelly, both partisans of Pauline authorship, seize on the apparent peculiarity of the "believing woman" to buttress their belief that 1 Timothy is an actual personal letter of advice from Paul, not a pseudonymous church order. Paul must have heard of a specific case of an ungrateful woman, most likely one of those suspicious younger widows straying after Satan, neglecting her widowed relatives.[23]

MacDonald is correct, I think, when he says, "The most natural reading of v. 16 is to take the 'believing woman' who has 'widows' as a woman who kept widows in her home and who received financial assistance for doing so from the church. Without doubt, such houses for widows were common in early Christian communities."[24] I would add that we must then take the command of verse 16 to imply the cessation of such church support. "If you want them in your home, pay for them yourself." This would presumably be a difficult transition to make, and one wonders if the goal of the Pastor were not in fact to break up such houses, to force the widows to return to the church dole—and to church supervision. MacDonald and Schüssler Fiorenza both understand certain references in Ignatius to imply that male church hierarchs were becoming worried over teaching, eucharistic activity, or other "unauthorized" ministry outside their oversight.[25] Ignatius warns the bishops of Smyrna that eucharists celebrated without the bishop are invalid and to be stamped out (8:1); and remember, it is Smyrna where Ignatius recognizes households of widows. Can they, Schüssler Fiorenza wonders, be the outlaw celebrants? Ignatius urges Polycarp, "Do not let the widows be neglected. After the Lord, you yourself be their manager. Let nothing be done without your approval" (Ignatius to Polycarp, 4:1). In light of the surprising last sentence, does the preceding mean "keep a close watch on the widows"?

22. D. Guthrie, *Pastoral Epistles*, 104.
23. Fee, *1 and 2 Timothy, and Titus*, 84; Kelly, *Pastoral Epistles*, 121.
24. MacDonald, *Legend*, 75.
25. Ibid., 74; Schüssler Fiorenza, *In Memory of Her*, 313, 314.

Christine Trevett thinks not. She admits that the scenario reconstructed by Schüssler Fiorenza is superficially plausible but objects that sufficient evidence is lacking. Her main objection seems to be that we cannot be sure that the refrain "Let nothing be done without your approval," recurrent in more or less the same words throughout the Ignatian correspondence, is a direct reference to the situation, whatever it was, of the widows.[26] But then why does the advice occur just where it does? Did Ignatius randomly pepper the text with the phrase without regard to where it fell? Even if he did, do we not have the connection suggested by Schüssler Fiorenza already implied in the preceding sentence: "After the Lord you yourself be their manager"? Is not the point to urge that the bishop assume direct administration where perhaps others had fulfilled these responsibilities hitherto? Surely this is the implication in a text that everywhere urges that things not (i.e., no longer) be done outside the radius of monepiscopal supervision.[27]

Against the proposed understanding of the believing woman who has widows (1 Timothy 5:16) as referring to widow patronesses of fellow widows, Kelly protests the impossibility of narrowing down the meaning of "woman" (implied in the feminine *piste*) to "widow."[28] But I wonder if it is he who, with most other commentators, has mistaken the import of *piste* as meaning "believing." Rather, I see this as an analogy to Fee's improbable definition of *pistin* in verse 12 as referring to the Christian "faith." I propose that we take *piste* in v. 16 in light of *pistin* meaning "pledge of celibacy" in v. 12. The *piste* of v. 16 would then mean "woman pledged (i.e., to celibacy)." And then the correspon-

---

26. Christine Trevett, "Ignatius and the Monstrous Regiment of Women," in *Studia Patristica XXI, Papers Presented to the Tenth International Conference on Patristic Studies held in Oxford 1987. Second Century, Tertullian to Nicea in the West, Clement of Alexandria and Origen, Athanasius*, ed. Elizabeth A. Livingstone (Leuven: Peeters Press, 1989), 213-214.
27. Trevett seems more recently to have retreated somewhat from her dismissal of Schüssler Fiorenza's scenario. She admits it looks as if an order of widows was emerging in Smyrna (*A Study of Ignatius of Antioch in Syria and Asia*, Studies in the Bible and Early Christianity, vol. 29 [Lewiston, NY: Edwin Mellen Press, 1992], 53) and that Ignatius did urge Polycarp to exert his authority over widows (ibid., 101). She even quotes the relevant passage of Schüssler Fiorenza, *In Memory of Her*, as if to second Schüssler Fiorenza's suggestion, despite the fact that earlier in the same book (53) she had questioned it.
28. Kelly, *Pastoral Epistles*, 121.

dence with the later living situations of a wealthy widow sup-
porting poorer widows, saving them from helpless dependence
on the church with its Ignatiuses and Pastors, would be complete.

In second-century sources we find the widows seemingly in
charge of certain ministries, especially the care of orphans. Hermas' angelic familiar bids him send a copy of his revelations to
the bishop Clement and another to a woman named Grapte, who
is to use it to "exhort the widows and the orphans" (*Visions* 2.4.3).
Presumably she is a widow herself, given her assumed contact
with them. Also note that she holds some official or semi-official
status analogous to that of Clement, since Hermas is directed to
send a copy of his revelation to each. Grapte is to "exhort the
widows and orphans," as if she ministers to them in some fashion analogous to that of Clement in the rest of the community.
Lucian recounts how widows kept vigil with their darling the
persecuted prophet Peregrinus when he was in jail. And the
widows brought their charges the orphans with them (*The Passing of Peregrinus* 12).

In light of these apparent parallels, it would seem natural to
take the reference to child rearing in 1 Timothy 5:10 as meaning
orphan care, though of course it might be taken to mean that a
widow, to qualify for official enrollment, ought to have raised her
own offspring well. But in the latter case there would seem to be
a tension with the previous requirement that an enrolled widow
must be without children who could support her. If she has
raised her own children in a pious Christian way, where are they
now when she needs them?

I think it more likely that we are dealing with women who
have embraced celibacy and are raising orphan children, perhaps
exposed infants rescued by Christians who found them in the
gutter.[29]

Widows were assigned the ministry of prayer (1 Timothy
5:5), a function often reiterated in church orders and manuals of
later centuries.[30] Two things deserve note here. First, as any
Christian might be expected to "pray without ceasing," a piece of

29. John Boswell, *The Kindness of Strangers: The Abandonment of Children in
Western Europe from Late Antiquity to the Renaissance* (New York: Vintage
Books, a division of Random House, 1990).
30. Carolyn Osiek, "The Widow as Altar: The Rise and Fall of a Symbol,"
Second Century 3 (Fall 1983): 160; Roger Gryson, *The Ministry of Women in
the Early Church*, trans. Jean Laporte and Mary Loise Hall (Collegeville,
MN: Liturgical Press, 1980), 12-13, 24, 37; Thurston, *Widows*, 69, 111.

paraenesis from another late Pauline pseudepigraph, 1 Thessalonians 5:17, I suspect that for someone to have a specially designated ministry of prayer implies that she is recognized as living a contemplative life supported by church funds to compensate her for her prayerful efforts. She is subsidized as one might patronize an artist or a writer, so that she may be absorbed fully in the affairs of the Lord, rather than be distracted with the concerns of an earthly bridegroom, as we read in the roughly contemporary Pastoral stratum of 1 Corinthians (7:32-35). But, as is evident from 1 Timothy chapter 5, as MacDonald suggests, there is a tendency to restrict the number of women eligible for such a desirable position.[31]

Second, I believe I detect a hint of the restriction of widows' ministry to something harmless to the interests of the male church hierarchy. Replying to Celsus' complaint that Christians refused to serve in the Roman army and thus were miserable parasites, Origen protested that Christians performed a far more strategic service for Caesar by praying for the peace of Rome (*Contra Celsum* 8.73). How convenient. Similarly, I suspect that the supposed esteem in which the widows' ministry of prayer was held was a patronizing rationale for the denial of other work they wanted to do and had once done: "But my dear, we've left you the most important work of all, don't you see?"

It didn't matter what the old women were telling the Almighty in their prayers as long as they didn't embarrass the church or spread heresy by what they were telling other people! The third-century church order the *Didascalia* disdainfully reminds the reader that if a widow should try to explain any but the most rudimentary elements of Christian doctrine to outsiders, she would only succeed in making it sound absurd: "they will mock and sneer at it" (3.5). "It is neither right nor necessary therefore that women should be teachers, and especially concerning the name of Christ and the redemption of His passion. For you have not been appointed to this, O women, and especially widows, that you should teach, but that you should pray and entreat the Lord God" (3.6).

Clearly, then, the widows known to the writer(s) of the *Didascalia* were teaching. They are told to stay home and pray instead. Do we not find precisely the same picture in 1 Timothy? There, too, women are not to teach (2:12), and young widows,

---

31. MacDonald, *Legend*, 75-76.

that is, pledged virgins, who make pastoral calls from house to house are viewed with suspicion because of what they will say there (5:13). The church-subsidized leisure they so exercise is scorned as "idleness" (v. 13). Here, as in the later *Didascalia*, "Women are reduced to cloistered ignoramuses who can be trusted with nothing" (Carolyn Osiek).[32]

Apparently someone had grave doubts about women teaching and probably what they were teaching as well. But what was that teaching? MacDonald makes a good case for their having propagated the encratite doctrines that the Pastorals are most concerned to refute.[33] David Rensberger seems not quite to get MacDonald's point when he takes him to mean that the Pastor is narrowly trying to refute the attribution of such notions to Paul. Rensberger says that there are no such explicit refutations ("I never said any such thing!"), hence he rejects what he thinks is MacDonald's thesis.[34] But MacDonald's Pastor is shrewder than that. His is an indirect refutation of the "slander" against Paul; he simply lets the reader hear Paul rejecting the blasphemous doctrines that the widows' stories depicted him advocating. He need not say they are false if he shows they cannot be true.

Yet I think more can be said about the "heretical" teaching of the widows than MacDonald says. Kroeger and Kroeger have shown that a careful scrutiny of 1 Timothy 2:12, especially centering about its use of the rare and ambiguous word *authentein*, indicates that a doctrine parallel to the teaching of the Nag Hammadi text *The Origin of the World* may here be attributed to the widows.[35]

The Gnostic text recounts that the spiritual Power Eve created Adam by taking him from her side. He came to consciousness only subsequently, at which time the despicable Archons approached him with the lie that while he was asleep, the Demiurge had taken from *his* side the woman Eve, whom he had never seen before, so he didn't know any different. Kroeger and Kroeger document that *authentein* can mean "to originate, be the

32. Osiek, "Widow as Altar," 168.
33. MacDonald, *Legend*, 54-77.
34. Rensberger, Review of MacDonald, 365.
35. Catherine Clark Kroeger, "1 Timothy 2:12—A Classicist's View," in *Women, Authority & the Bible*, ed. Alvera Mickelsen (Downers Grove, IL: InterVarsity Press, 1986), 232-237; Richard Clark Kroeger and Catherine Clark Kroeger, *I Suffer Not a Woman: Rethinking 1 Timothy 2:11-15 in Light of Ancient Evidence* (Grand Rapids: Baker Book House, 1992), 117-125.

author of." Indeed our words "author" and "authority" both stem from this word and reflect the multivalences of it.

Can the Pastor be telling women not "to teach to originate (that is, that women originated) man"? Is he arguing instead that "Adam was not deceived" by the Archons, "but the woman, being deceived" by the serpent, "became a transgressor"? If one finds the Kroeger theory compelling, and it is certainly an ingenious option worth serious consideration, one need not choose between it and MacDonald's thesis, as if the Kroeger theory implied switching from encratite radicals to Gnostics as the Pastor's opponents. The *Schwärmerei* of Asia Minor, as MacDonald himself numbers them, included both types of enthusiasts.

I think enough has been said to justify my working hypothesis that in the period of the Pastorals, the same period in which we ought to locate Luke-Acts, there were already communities of consecrated widows who taught and ministered, some of whom lived a contemplative life by the subsidy of the church, though they were finding this privilege being turned against them, turned into a prison. Others preserved a greater measure of independence by their attachment to communal houses subsidized by wealthy widows. These arrangements had been curtailed insofar as the church hierarchy began to withdraw funds once contributed to the houses, hoping to bring the widows back under their closer supervision. If the patronesses were wealthy enough, however, such a strategy would merely result in the loss of any remaining churchly control over them.

We have seen that the names and authority of the apostles were being invoked by the church hierarchs who claimed to be their rightful successors, and in the names of the apostles the patriarchal leaders sought to exercise greater control. This they did in the production of church orders pseudonymously attributed to the apostles. The earliest examples of such documents would include the Pastoral stratum of 1 Corinthians, the Pastoral Epistles, and the *Didache,* but the trend continued with such manuals of discipline as the *Didascalia* and the *Apostolic Constitutions.*

Widows as Story Tellers

It seems that, especially insofar as they include an apostolic figure or Jesus himself as a character, the widow traditions anchored in the Apocryphal Acts and reflected in the Pastorals represent a different sort of appeal to the patronage of the apostles, this time on behalf of the widows. This paradigm has been

employed with very striking and fruitful results by Davies, Kraemer, MacDonald, and Burrus.[36] I will not repeat the details of
their arguments here, except to note that Kraemer, MacDonald,
and Burrus are all attentive to the marks of oral tradition visible
in the stories even in their written form. Davies, MacDonald, and
Burrus all demonstrate the exclusive predominance of women's
concerns as well as the absence of men's.[37] MacDonald shows
there are just no good men in the Thecla legend except for the
Apostle Paul, and even he is shown to have cold feet.[38] We find a
striking parallel to the female viewpoint of the Apocryphal Acts
in the widow stories of the Elijah-Elisha cycle, a group of stories
emanating from an analogous milieu in which the dispossessed
pious, including widows, banded together around the glorified
memory of a popular prophet to gain what strength they could
against the encroachments of a religious institution which
exploited them and sought to co-opt the legends they cherished.[39] Rentería notes that "It is significant that the opposition
in the story [of the raising of the Shunammite's son] comes from
males—her husband, Gehazi, and even the prophet himself. The
story is constructed to appeal to a woman's point of view."[40]

    Burrus is not quite so confident of the origin of the stories in
the communities of celibate women:

> It is intriguing to speculate—though difficult to
> prove— that the women who told the chastity stories
> might have lived together in communities which
> embraced women of all ages and classes and which
> may have been supported not by the institutions of the
> patriarchal church, as Davies suggests, but by the
> wealthy women among them.[41]

---

36. Davies, *Revolt*, 69, 73; Kraemer, "Conversion of Women," 299-302;
Burrus, *Chastity as Autonomy*, 72-77, 85, 103; MacDonald, *Legend*, 34-53.
37. Davies, *Revolt*, 86-87; MacDonald, *Legend*, 34-37; Burrus, *Chastity as
Autonomy* , 72-76.
38. MacDonald, *Legend*, 36.
39. Otto Eissfeldt, *The Old Testament: An Introduction*, trans. Peter Ackroyd (New York: Harper & Row, Publishers, 1965), 295; John Gray, *I & II
Kings: A Commentary*, 2nd ed. Old Testament Library. gen. eds. Peter Ackroyd, James Barr, John Bright, G. Ernest Wright (Philadelphia: Fortress
Press, 1970), 371-372, 375, 466-467, 470; Rentería, "Elijah," 99-100.
40. Rentería, "Elijah," 107.
41. Burrus, *Chastity as Autonomy*, 103.

The reason for her hesitance to go all the way with the reconstruction of Kraemer, Davies, and MacDonald may be that she is not convinced that the women who told the stories were willing to put their money where their mouths were. Perhaps such stories, told by women who remained in their domestic situation, functioned as an escapist steam valve. "Wouldn't it be nice . . .?" "Y'know, sometimes I think I'd like to chuck it all and go preach the gospel where there are no men to badger me with 'Woman, what shall I eat? What shall I drink? What shall I wear?' Oh well, that camel dip's probably ready by now. Guess I better go check it. See you girls tomorrow."

In other words, "The crossing of boundaries does not necessarily represent the historical experiences of the tellers; it may instead reflect their fantasies."[42]

Peter Brown rejects the notion of female authorship, apparently whether of the Acts as wholes or of the individual stories. Instead, he argues, the male authors of the Acts were just "using women to think with."[43]

A similar theory is propounded by Kate Cooper, who suggests that the women of the Apocryphal Acts perform much the same sort of role as in classical Roman rhetoric, as a symbolic index of the virtue of a public man and his single-minded commitment to the civic good. If such a man were married to a virtuous wife and heeded her modest moral encouragement, he was by that token not ruining himself with sensual indulgence with dangerous women (as Mark Antony was led astray from his commitment to the good of Rome by the wiles of a woman, Cleopatra). Cooper ably shows ("Insinuations of Womanly Influence: An Aspect of the Christianization of the Roman Aristocracy") that Augustine adapted this traditional rhetorical topos in order to convince Roman husbands of Christian women to convert to Christianity or to asceticism, seeking to persuade them that they ought to be led by the virtue of their wives, as were the great civic men of the past, to commitment to the polis, however, not of men, but of God.[44]

In the radical tales of the Apocryphal Acts, Cooper ventures ("Apostles, Ascetic Women, and Questions of Audience: New

---

42. Ibid., 90.
43. Brown, *Body and Society*, 153.
44. Kate Cooper, "Insinuations of Womanly Influence: An Aspect of the Christianization of the Roman Aristocracy," *Journal of Roman Studies* 82 (1992): passim.

Reflections on the Rhetoric of Gender in the *Apocryphal Acts*"), we have much the same urging of men to transfer their loyalty to the heavenly commonwealth from the earthly. The heroine of the story merely functions as the voice of conscience indicating the proper choice between two male exemplars: the Christian apostle on the one hand, and the husband attached to the pagan world-system on the other.[45] Both the authors and the audience of such tales, Cooper contends, are male.

The theory that stories of women influenced men to convert to ascetical Christianity in the days of the newly Christian Empire makes sense because Cooper can be sure that, precisely as a Christian who is a respectable Roman citizen, someone like Augustine can credibly invoke the traditional topos of civic rhetoric, since he shares it with Roman civic men whose Christian faith is more tenuous (or yet absent). But how applicable is this fundamentally important presupposition when we come to the Apocryphal Acts? There Christianity of any kind is still clearly a sectarian phenomenon, perceived as a dangerous extra- and anti-Roman force, hence the persecutions narrated in the tales. I do not think Cooper's paradigm, which is plausible for the age of Augustine, works so well for the chastity stories of the Apocryphal Acts.

Burrus wonders if the exploits of the ascetical women disciples may represent day-dreaming, while Cooper makes them rhetorical pointers to male virtues and allegiences. Cooper seems to think we have no evidence for the historical verisimilitude of the chastity stories, in the absence of which her theory of the stories' purely rhetorical character seems to gain strength. But this is far from true.

First, as Judith Perkins points out, we have more than one real-life analogue to the heroic celibate women of the Apocryphal Acts. Vibia Perpetua's autobiographical memoir reads almost like one of the Acts' chastity stories. A recent convert of the nobility, she either has abandoned her husband[46] or is a widow, in either case closely matching our heroines, and she resists with steely resolve the blandishments and tears of her father to aban-

45. Kate Cooper, "Apostles, Ascetic Women, and Questions of Audience: New Reflections on the Rhetoric of Gender in the *Apocryphal Acts*," in *Society of Biblical Literature 1992 Seminar Papers*, ed. Eugene H. Lovering, Society of Biblical Literature Seminar Papers Series, ed. Eugene H. Lovering, 31 (Atlanta: Scholars Press, 1992).
46. Kraemer, "Monastic," 351.

don the doomed course of Christian fanaticism.[47]

Kraemer notes that "many of [the Christian women monastics and ascetics] clearly left their husbands to take up the religious life, e.g., Maximilla in the Acts of Andrew."[48]

Justin Martyr relates in his *Second Apology* that the martyr Ptolemaeus, a Christian teacher, was handed over to the authorities by an irate husband whose wife, having just converted to Christianity under Ptolemaeus' instruction, served him a bill of divorce, refusing to indulge in sensual pleasure any longer.[49] Again, we might be reading the *Acts of Andrew*.

The letters of Pelagius to Celanthia and of Augustine to Ecdicia, as Cooper herself notes,[50] both seek to mediate the marital strife which resulted from Christian women declaring to their astonished husbands a unilateral decision for continence. In fact, Cooper's own discussion of Augustine's letter to Ecdicia shows just how similar to those in the chastity stories Ecdicia's situation was. The newly celibate Ecdicia had gone so far as to declare herself a widow by donning the symbolic widow's weeds. Her husband was willing to put up with even this much, out of regard for her piety, but it was just too much when she started disbursing the family wealth, giving it to itinerant monks, in utter disregard for the future needs of her children. Here we see in living color both the anti-familial ethos of the widow movement as MacDonald describes it[51] and the eagerness of widow patronesses to support charismatic itinerants, against the opposition of the church establishment, here represented by Augustine, the bishop, who takes Ecdicia to task for what he deems her misguided generosity.

The criticism of Ecdicia by Augustine is quite revealing. If the role of ascetical women in the Apocryphal Acts is to be judged as sharing the rhetorical agenda of Augustine in his effort to convert Roman civic men, it is extremely odd that Augustine's letter to Ecdicia attempts to dissuade her from exactly the sort of female radicalism the Acts' chastity stories depict! Augustine chides his correspondent with the reminder that the worthy women of old were far more modest in the exercise and display

47. Judith Perkins, "The Apocryphal Acts of the Apostles and the Early Christian Martyrdom," *Arethusa* 18 (1985): 220.
48. Kraemer, "Monastic," 351.
49. Perkins, "Apocryphal," 219, 220.
50. Cooper, "Insinuations," 156.
51. MacDonald, *Legend*, 46-47.

of their virtue and were thus able to influence their husbands subtly but surely toward the good, whereas her recent course of action must have, as indeed it has, the very opposite effect, as the husband is goaded by reaction into greater vice.[52] Here we might think of Maximilla's rude departure from her husband Aegeates' bed. Aegeates' reaction begins as that of a sensitive husband who cannot understand the rebuff but rapidly moves to rage and threats; his gentle reminders of their past life together turn into threats of imprisonment and persecution.[53]

Augustine's complaint against Ecdicia is that she has abandoned the traditional role of the moderate wife who could function as both her husband's conscience and as a public index for his virtue. I see the rhetorical function of the stories in the Apocryphal Acts as diametrically opposed to that employed by Augustine.

Cooper wrongly states that MacDonald's attribution of the stories in question to women story-tellers was based solely on the jibe of the Pastor to the effect that Timothy should no longer give heed to "old women's tales" (1 Timothy 4:7).[54] And, Cooper points out, this phrase had become a cliché for wild tales unworthy of credence, whatever their origin. MacDonald readily admitted this.[55] His point was rather that in the case of the stories in question, there were other factors suggesting that it was no mere figure of speech, that the stories had in fact originated among women.

Chief among these factors was the unremitting hostility toward males, none of whom was presented in a postive light (even Paul has his bad moments in the *Acts of Paul and Thecla*).[56] It seems to me that MacDonald's argument, far from being oblivious of the functions of rhetoric in the Thecla episodes, is in large measure based on a shrewd and sharp-eyed reading of that rhetoric. By contrast, Cooper makes no reference to the good woman/bad man slant of the stories. It appears that, if we are to

52. Cooper, "Insinuations," 158-159.
53. Codex Vaticanus Fragment of the *Acts of Andrew*, 4, in Edgar Hennecke, *New Testament Apocrypha, Volume Two: Writings Relating to the Apostles, Apocalypses and Related Subjects*, ed. Wilhelm Schneemelcher. English trans. ed. Robert McL. Wilson (Philadelphia: Westminster Press, 1965), 409-410.
54. Cooper, "Apostles," 152.
55. MacDonald, *Legend*, 14, 56-58.
56. Ibid., 34-37.

bring into the discussion the traditional Roman civic rhetoric of a woman as an index of the virtue of a man, we might rather see in the chastity stories a turning of the traditional topos on its head: the ascetical heroism of Thecla and her sisters serves to call the bluff of male virtue *in toto.* Deny them their precious genital adventures and, one and all, they reveal themselves as a pack of snarling wolves, even the most respectable and apparently upstanding of them!

Cooper questions the verisimilitude of the chastity stories,[57] but many Christian women in Late Antiquity saw in the stories enough verisimilitude to the actual option of female conversion that they emulated the stories in real life. Ruether notes that the celibate women of the fourth century took Thecla as their model,[58] proclaiming themselves "new Theclas." If reader response indicates any sort of kindred-spiritedness with the tellers and transmitters of the tale, then I would call the phenomenon of the New Theclas a good argument that these stories arose precisely in the circles, the communities, of Theclas, so to speak.

Thus I feel it is safe to suppose that the matrix of the stories of celibate women emanated from actual communities of such women in the early church.

In subsequent chapters I will be trying to show the close similarity between the widow traditions of the Apocryphal Acts and those contained in Luke-Acts. My inference will be that Luke, too, drew his widow traditions from communities of widows with whom he was in contact. Let me now simply note some previous suggestions for the sources of Luke's widow traditions which point in the same direction.

Leonard Swidler suggested that either the L source seen as a written "proto-Gospel," or perhaps more likely, the oral traditions embedded in such a proto-gospel, came through the channel of female tradents which he identifies with the women followers of Jesus (Luke 8:3)[59] and with members of the order of widows, which he deems the immediate post-Easter reorganization of Jesus' female companions.

> It is not likely that in a very male-oriented society men would have been particularly aware of the vital signif-

---

57. Cooper, "Apostles," 148.
58. Ruether, "Mothers of the Church," 74.
59. Leonard Swidler, *Biblical Affirmations of Women* (Philadelphia: Westmister Press, 1979), 262.

icance of many of the things Jesus said and did relating to women, whereas to sensitive women they
would have seemed as loud as thunderclaps. These
women, then, having experienced or noticed these
things, would have been the ones to remember them
and pass them on and would have been the ultimate
source for the women material in the . . . uniquely
Lucan women passages.[60]

Much the same thesis had been proposed earlier by Vincent Taylor[61] and, earlier still, though in a slightly different form, by Harnack, who thought Luke owed all the women traditions not to the
ministering women, but rather to the daughters of Philip.[62] E.
Jane Via seconds Swidler's theory.[63]

The historicizing bias of Swidler and Via is shared by Jo Ann
McNamara, who traces some of the Lukan traditions straight
back to Mary of Nazareth:

In her middle years, Mary was joined by other women
who shared the conviction that her son had a unique
and important message for them. These women are
among the sources behind the sources for the life of
Jesus: they were among the original witnesses from
whose testimony the gospels were drawn. . . . They
represent an active tradition, therefore, which must
have been known to the evangelists and surely found
its place in the construction of the literary Jesus, the
permanent form of the man passed down to poster-
ity.[64]

In my view, the sandal is on the wrong foot here. I believe
the female characters invoked as eyewitnesses by Swidler, Via,
and McNamara are themselves literary figures, and that they are
in turn the fictive counterparts of the widows who first told the
stories. McNamara comes closer to this way of seeing it when
she mentions the "many . . . women mentioned in the *Acts of the*

60. Ibid., 304-305.
61. Taylor, *Behind*, 214, 248, 260.
62. Adolf Harnack, *Luke the Physician: The Author of the Third Gospel and
the Acts of the Apostles*, trans. J. R. Wilkinson, Crown Theological Library
20 (London: Williams & Norgate, 1911), 153-156.
63. E. J. Via, "Women in the Gospel of Luke," 50.
64. McNamara, *New Song*, 15.

Apostles and the Pauline letters [who were] active evangelists" passing on traditions of Jesus' friendly and liberated dealings with women.[65] Neal M. Flanagan ascribes "the frequent mention of widows in Luke's Gospel . . . and the appearances of them in the early Church" to Luke's personal contact with groups of widows who were evolving into a quasi-office within the Church."[66] Flanagan, too, envisions the New Testament characters as historical individuals, making Luke an actual companion of Paul.[67] When Luke has Peter quote Joel concerning "your daughters" prophesying, he must have been thinking of Philip's daughters,[68] whom he knew personally.[69]

Despite the simplistic historicizing involved, I believe these scholars are right to locate Luke's special widow traditions in a stream of early Christian female story-telling— just like the Apocryphal Acts' stories.

The Apocryphal Apostles

If the widows of these stories stand for the communities of celibate women who told the tales, for whom should we look hiding behind the masks of the apostles (and Jesus)? Davies and MacDonald,[70] followed by McNamara and Schüssler Fiorenza,[71] see as the bearers of the apostolic names of Peter, John, Andrew, Thomas, and Paul the wandering charismatic apostles and prophets of the late first through third centuries. We read of them in 1 John 2:19; 4:1-5; 2 John 7, 10-11; 3 John 3, 5-10; *Didache* 11-13.

Once again, the situation behind the popular traditions of Elijah and Elisha offer a striking parallel. Rentería says,

> These tales emerged under extreme conditions of change, probably originating as first-person stories told by people whose lives had been touched by their

---

65. Ibid.

66. Flanagan, "Position of Women," 300.

67. Neal M. Flanagan, *The Acts of the Apostles, Introduction and Commentary,* 2nd ed., New Testament Reading Guide 5 (Collegeville, MN: Liturgical Oress, 1964), 4.

68. Flanagan, "Position of Women," 300.

69. Again, so Harnack, *Luke,* 157.

70. Davies, *Revolt,* 29-32; MacDonald, *Legend,* 47.

71. McNamara, *New Song,* 78-79; Schüssler Fiorenza, *In Memory of Her,* 313.

interactions with some prophetic figure. They were
then probably passed on by family-members and
friends, some eventually becoming adopted into a particular clan's promotion of a prophetic figure in a bid
for political power.[72]

Even so, Tertullian is keenly aware that women press their case
for being entitled to teach and to baptize by appealing to the
story of Paul and Thecla.

I would say the two scenarios described by MacDonald and
Davies on the one hand and Rentería on the other are quite analogous, and this correspondence is all the more impressive for
being the issuance of two apparently independent lines of
research.

What Davies and MacDonald suggest with regard to the historical counterparts of the apostles of the Apocryphal Acts Gerd
Theissen had already suggested for the figure of Jesus in the Gospels. In fact, Davies notes that Theissen's research really provides the natural grounding for his own, though he formulated
his theory in ignorance of Theissen's.[73]   Elizabeth A. Clark also
sees Theissen as strategic reinforcement for Davies.[74]   I agree,
but, again, it seems to me that the very ignorance of Theissen's
parallel case strengthens Davies's by virtue of the fact that they
independently came to exactly parallel conclusions, even as Rentería did.

In several articles, including "Itinerant Radicalism: The Tra-
dition of Jesus' Sayings from the Perspective of the Sociology of
Literature," as well as those collected in *Sociology of Early Palestin-
ian Christianity*,[75] Theissen developed the thesis that behind
many of the most radical discipleship demands of the Synoptic
Jesus stood a chain of tradents who had adopted as their own the
Spartan, vagabond manner of life mandated in those sayings.
They had left behind all family, property, and secular livelihood

---

72. Rentería, "Elijah," 99-100.

73. Davies, *Revolt*, 49.

74. Elizabeth A. Clark, review of *The Revolt of the Widows: The Social World
of the Apocryphal Acts*, by Stevan L. Davies, in *Church History* 51 (1982):
336.

75. Gerd Theissen, *Sociology of Early Palestinian Christianity*, trans. John
Bowden (Philadelphia: Fortress Press, 1978); see also the articles collected in Theissen, *Social Reality and the Early Christians: Theology, Ethics,
and the World of the Earliest Christians*, trans. Margaret Kohl (Minneapolis:
Fortress Press, 1992).

(Mark 10:29). They wandered from town to town, their only guide the stipulations of the Mission Charge (Matthew 10:5-23; Luke 9:1-5; 10:1-12; Mark 6:7-11). They wasted not a minute in worrying what they should eat or drink or what they should wear on the morrow, seeking the Reign of God instead (Matthew 6:25, 31-33; Luke 12:29-31). Their heavenly Father would see to their needs as he did those of the ravens and the lilies, both of whom God had assigned more important duties than spinning or farming (Matthew 6:26-30; Luke 12:24, 27-28). The Father would provide daily bread (Matthew 6:11; Luke 11:3) through the agency of those in a receptive house or town who reckoned the laborer worthy of his hire (Luke 10:7; Matthew 10:10). As for those who did not? It would go easier on the rankest sinners of Sodom and Tyre on the day of judgment (Matthew 10:15; Luke 10:13). These sayings, Theissen reasoned, could have no possible *Sitz-im-Leben* except among those who actually lived such lives, much as the Cynic apostles did. Who could take such sayings seriously for a moment if the teacher of them did not himself live by them, at least as far as the audience could see? These sayings have occasioned anxiety among Christian householders and burghers for nigh onto two thousand years; who would not rather have let them lapse into oblivion? Surely no one would have troubled continuing to quote such logia who did not relish being able thus to call attention to one's own heroic obedience to the most radical demands of discipleship.

But then, by the same token, how could such unblinking, bolt-upright disciples ever have gained and retained a hearing among the townspeople whose very largesse they implicitly condemned? If all were to heed the commands of the Cynic Christ, who would be left to offer his brethren their providential food and shelter? Theissen envisioned a situation much like that of early Buddhism. The monks wandered and begged, teaching the *dharma* that there was Nirvana for none but those who left off all craving, abandoned home and family, pursuing the only "right livelihood," mendicancy and meditation. Granted, the common pious of the countryside, on whose donations the brethren survived, were too much of this world of Samsara to attain Nirvana, though here and there one might heed the call. However, by their very acts of charity and almsgiving, they might win a place in a lower heaven.

So with the preaching of the itinerants of the Jesus movement: there was an "easy path" for the laity. Their alms would not go for naught. No, he that assisted a prophet would receive the same reward as the prophet he aided (Matthew 10:41-42), which was only fair once you thought of it, since the giver makes the prophet's work possible. In just the same way, the Philippians were assured that their friendly donations were really nothing so mundane, but in fact a vicarious sharing in Paul's mighty gospel work (1:5; 4:15). Again, this is why the Elder warns Kuria not even to give so much as a greeting, much less an open door, to those false prophets who deny the incarnation: she would be inviting a share of their well-deserved damnation (2 John 11)!

On the day when the Son of Man comes and divides the sheep of salvation from the goats of Gehenna, one's lot will be determined, not by one's confession of Christ!, but rather—by how one has treated those poverellos of the gospel, the wandering brethren of the Son of Man (Matthew 25:31-46).

Brethren they were—and more. They were the vicarious presence of the Son of Man himself, speaking with his voice like the sound of many waters. Had not Christ himself so mandated it? "He who hears you hears me" (Matthew 10:40; Luke 10:16). Here is the charter for an early Christian deluge of prophecy in the name of the Risen One that might have attributed to him a hundred times as many sayings as Bultmann had thought! Here Theissen had mapped the natural *Sitz-im-Leben* of the prophetic "sentences of holy law" isolated as a separate gospel tradition-form by Käsemann.[76] The charismatics exulted to speak with the authority of the Son of Man, because in the mantic state the line between the Son of Man and the least of these his brethren became thin to the vanishing point.

Many sayings attributed to Jesus receive new meaning under Theissen's model. Had the historical Jesus really predicted the apocalyptic coming of the Son of Man as an entity different from himself? Among other factors Bultmann was led to think so by the otherwise odd fact that in the dominical sayings the Son of Man is always "he," practically never "I."[77] Yet once Vielhauer pointed out that Jesus' preaching of the Reign of God, i.e., the eternal state of bliss, was at odds with the notion of the Son of Man coming to rule an earthly interregnum, and that in no saying does the Jesus tradition associate the two;[78] once Maurice Casey

---

76. Ernst Käsemann, "Sentences of Holy Law," in *New Testament Questions of Today*, trans. W. J. Montague (Philadelphia: Fortress Press, 1979), 66-81; cf. Perrin, *Rediscovering*, 22-23.

showed that the Danielic text depicting one like a son of man had never given rise to either a messianic figure or a messianic title in Judaism;[79] once Norman Perrin showed how all the gospel Son of Man sayings seemed to presuppose a *Christian* exegetical tradition identifying Jesus as the fulfillment of Daniel 7:13; Psalm 110:1; Zechariah 12:10ff[80]—what remained of the Bultmann hypothesis?

If Jesus had not actually spoken of the apocalyptic Son of Man, and all those texts were Christian compositions, why did they preserve or create a distinction between the "I" of the speaker and the "he" of the Son of Man? Theissen found the answer. "I" stood for the wandering charismatic himself, whose word of judgment would be made good by his heavenly proto- type- counterpart Jesus the returning Son of Man. The latter was "he." So at first the "he" was Jesus, not the "I."[81] The "I" only flipped over to refer to Jesus once the whole saying was later attributed to him, and only once this had happened could the question of "he/the Son of Man" being anyone other than Jesus arise.

Let us picture the scene: The faithful stand in a circle about the visiting prophet, whose all-white eyes and ecstatic utterances signal that he is now the mouthpiece of Higher Powers. Like the shamans of a thousand cultures, he speaks forth a word of privileged, penetrating knowledge that cuts to the heart and convicts of sin, of righteousness, of judgment (John 16:8). Some, convicted,

---

77. Rudolf Bultmann, *Theology of the New Testament,* vol. 1, trans. Kendrick Groebel (New York: Charles Scribner's Sons, 1951), 29-31; Ferdinand Hahn, *The Titles of Jesus in Christology: Their History in Early Christianity,* trans. Harold Knight and George Ogg (New York: World Publishing Company, 1969), 33-34; H. E. Tödt, *The Son of Man in the Synoptic Tradition,* trans. Dorothea M. Barton, New Testament Library, eds. Alan Richardson, C. F. D. Moule, and Floyd V. Filson (Philadelphia: Westminster Press, 1965), 294-296.

78. Philipp Vielhauer, "Gottesreich und Menschensohn in der Verkündigung Jesu," in *Festschrift für Günther Dehn,* ed. Wilhelm Schneemelcher (Neukirchen: Verlag der Buchhandlung des Erziehungsvereins Neukirchen, 1957), 57-79; the same point had been made earlier by Henry Burton Sharman, *Son of Man and Kingdom of God: A Critical Study* (New York: Harper & Brothers, Publishers, 1943), 89-90.

79. Maurice Casey, *The Son of Man: The Interpretation and Influence of Daniel 7* (London: SPCK, 1979), 137-139.

80. Perrin, *Rediscovering,* 173-185.

81. Theissen, *Sociology,* 27.

but less than eager to repent, nervously laugh off this peculiar fellow as filled with new wine (Acts 2:13) or mad (1 Corinthians 14:23), but to such a one the word thunders forth, we may be sure, with stabbing finger, "He that is ashamed of me and my words in this generation of adulterers, of him, I warn you, will the Son of Man be ashamed, when he comes with his avenging angels!"

Driven from town with jeers and peltings, he might turn back and signal doom with eyes ablaze like a flame of fire: "And you, Chorazin, will you ascend into heaven? Ha! I tell you, you shall be cast down to hell!"[82] Theissen's reconstruction of the role of the "wandering radicals" or "itinerant charismatics" has provoked various rejoinders from scholars who reject this or that aspect of it. Some might quibble with the application of a particular Synoptic saying. I myself think Bultmann's explanation of the blasphemy against the Son of Man saying is better than Theissen's.[83] But others lodge more serious objections against the theory as a whole.

Schottroff and Horsley are uncomfortable with Theissen's restriction of the poverty references and the exhortations to trust the providence of the heavenly Father to the rootless asceticism of the radicals. These critics would prefer to see the sayings in the context of a broader social concern with the involuntarily poor of a peasant society. They see Jesus' sayings as addressed to the dispossessed masses, exploited by the Temple State that sucked its own people dry in collaboration with Rome. Theissen, they object, restricts too narrowly the intention of Jesus' sayings as inculcating voluntary, ascetic poverty, "gospel poverty."[84]

But Theissen has not ignored the larger dimension. The situation he is envisioning is one wherein a wandering holy man, like Elijah, has the prophetic *hutzpah* to requisition a poor widow's last meal cake in a starving land (1 Kings 17:11-13),[85] where a common poor man may invest himself with heroic dignity, so hard to come by any other way in the situation, by renouncing his possessions for the sake of the Reign of God—even should it be that his possessions equaled no more than a crust of bread, a scrawny cow, a threadbare cloak, and a pile of debts. "We have left everything to follow you"—and good riddance, too! It wouldn't have been either the first or the last time someone had made virtue of necessity.[86]

Larger questions of the relation of the Jesus movement to other religious and political movements of the day, or whether the radicals represented a force for apolitical quietism, or whether the movement of wandering radicalism even represented the historical Jesus and his disciples do not concern us here. Schüssler Fiorenza rightly takes exception to the self-fulfilling prophecy invoked by Theissen that an egalitarian radicalism had of necessity, in the real world, to give way to patriarchal-

---

82. The *Sitz-im-Leben* imaginatively reconstructed by Theissen finds a fleshed-out parallel in the *Jetsün-Kahbum*, the hagiography of the Tibetan sorcerer-saint (hardly an improbable combination in Tibetan Buddhism of the Vajrayana) Jetsün-Milarepa. The saint recounts a return visit to his home village, where, while making his mendicant rounds, he tactfully sought to avoid meeting his villainous uncle who had earlier cheated him of his inheritance. He managed to run into trouble nevertheless:

> some of the youths of the place began to pelt me with stones. I, on my part, was afraid that I might fall a victim to their wrath and vengeance as a retribution for having employed black magic against them. So intending to intimidate them with my black-magical power, I cried out loudly: "O my Father, and ye Gurus of the Kargyütpa Sect! O ye myriads of blood-drinking and faith-guarding Deities! I, a devotee, am pursued by enemies. Help me and avenge me. Although I may die, ye Deities are immortal." Thereupon, all of them were terror-stricken; and they caught hold of my uncle, some who sympathized with me intervening and acting as mediators, while those who had stoned me asked my forgiveness. Mine uncle alone would not consent to give me any alms, but the rest gave me each a handsome amount, with which I returned to the cave. I thought that if I remained there any longer I should only be stirring the anger of the people; so I resolved to go elsewhere. (W. Y. Evans-Wentz, ed., *Tibet's Great Yogi Milarepa: A Biography from the Tibetan*, trans. Kazi Dawa-Samdup, with an Introduction and Annotations by W. Y. Evans-Wentz, 2nd ed. London: Oxford University Press, 1951: rept. 1974), 184-185.

Note here that the itinerant charismatic runs afoul of the villagers because of family connections, just as in the ideal scene in Nazareth in Luke 4, which I will argue in Chapter 3 has been built up in part from the traditions of itinerant prophets. His previous miracles come into play as well, "what he did in Capernaum."

Not only so, but just as the wandering radicals would warn that any indignity perpetrated on them would be answerable to the divine Son of Man, here the mendicant saint invokes his own heavenly patrons as a threat against persecutors. These divine patrons even include deified teachers of the sects past, just as the wandering radicals invoked the glorifed Jesus.

ism.[87] To say this, she protests, is to affirm that a society in which women share equality with men is foredoomed to failure, and this is a prophecy no one can be justified in making. Theissen's judgment is really more of a value judgment, another case of a supposedly descriptive statement being in fact a prescriptive one. But this apparent vestige of chauvinism does not follow even from Theissen's own analysis.[88] Thus we have every right to adopt his analysis without fearing that it will lead to androcentric conclusions.

Schottroff says that Theissen's radicalism comes mainly from the Q source.[89] Stegemann says the Cynic Jesus-persona is more the product of Luke's special material, a literary ideal created to prod the consciences of rich readers.[90]

It makes no difference to my thesis whether Jesus taught the radicalism described so well by Theissen, or whether he would have rent his garments at the very idea.[91] I hold only that Theissen has delineated the *Sitz-im-Leben* of an important group of Synoptic sayings, ascribing their transmission, even their creation, to the group of itinerant charismatic apostles attested outside the gospels in the Johaninne Epistles and the *Didache*.

So again we have good reason to see a close parallel to the scenario envisioned by Davies: the apostolic heroes of the Apoc-

---

83. Rudolf Bultmann, *History of the Synoptic Tradition*, trans. John Marsh (New York: Harper & Row, Publishers, 1972), 131; Theissen, *Sociology*, 28.
84. Luise Schottroff, "Sheep Among Wolves: The Wandering Prophets of the Sayings-Source," in *Jesus of Nazareth and the Hope of the Poor*, 49; Richard A. Horsley, *Sociology and the Jesus Movement* (New York: Crossroad Publishing Company, 1989), 105-128.
85. Rentería, "Elijah," 115.
86. Theissen, *Sociology*, 33-37.
87. Gerd Theissen, *The Social Setting of Pauline Christianity: Essays on Corinth*, ed. and trans. with an Introduction by John H. Schutz (Philadelphia: Fortress Press, 1988), 109-110.
88. Schüssler Fiorenza, *In Memory of Her*, 79-84.
89. Schottroff, "Sheep Among Wolves," 48-51.
90. Stegemann, "Following of Christ," 82-83; Wolfgang Stegemann, "Wanderradikalismus im Urchristentum? Historische und Theologische Auseinandersetzung mit einer interessanten These," in *Der Gott den kleinen Leute: Sozialgeschichtliche Bibelauslegungen, Vol. 2: Neues Testament*, eds. Luise Schottroff and Wolfgang Stegemann, 74.
91. Theissen seems willing to admit the same distinction. Even if he has correctly described the wandering Jesus-prophets, these may conceivably have been a mutant strain of the Jesus tradition, not reflecting the practice of Jesus himself. *Sociology*, 3-4.

ryphal Acts, like Jesus the Son of Man in parts of the gospels, are
literary masks for many now-nameless local charismatics who
once had their own followings.

If Davies is correct, then we have an important clue to the
origin of the whole Acts genre. I suggest that the extravagant
wonder-laden Apostolic Acts began as inflated aretalogies,
résumés if you will, produced by the wandering charismatics on
their own behalf.

In his classic work *The Opponents of Paul in Second Corinthians*, Dieter Georgi comes very near to saying just that. He is
concerned to distance Paul from the triumphalism of his rivals.

> Paul did not put much emphasis on apostolic signs.
> Nevertheless those signs had served as a recommen-
> dation of the superapostles. It appears that Paul's
> adversaries asked that those recommendations be
> written up for them. Their conduct revealed that it
> was far from them to let any of their achievements be
> forgotten. The letters of recommendation thus were
> something like chronicles of the deeds of pneumatic
> power performed by the adversaries of Paul.[92]

Walter Schmithals describes the same phenomenon in
broader terms: "It is one of the characteristics of the missionary
aretalogies of antiquity to string a number of individual stories
on to the thread of an apostle's wanderings."[93]

Eventually the letters of recommendation, already essentially chronicles, series of brief anecdotes (detailed accounts
might not pass scrutiny), growing more streamlined the more
new ones were added, would at some point lose their vestigial
letter form and turn into outright narrative aretalogies, first perhaps by assuming the shape of encyclicals addressed to whom it
may concern, or being edited together by the charismatics themselves and presented to every church.

I suggest that the very sense it would make of the origin of
the Acts genre reflects the glow of plausibility back on Davies's

92. Dieter Georgi, *The Opponents of Paul in Second Corinthians* (Philadelphia: Fortress Press, 1986), 244.
93. Walter Schmithals, *Paul and James*, trans. Dorothea M. Barton, Studies
in Biblical Theology, eds. C. F. D. Moule, James Barr, Peter Ackroyd,
Floyd V. Filson, G. Ernest Wright, no. 46 (Naperville, IL: Alec R. Allenson, 1965), 86.

theory.

Earlier I ventured the judgment that the origin of the chastity stories in circles of celibate widows and virgins is implied by the readiness with which later readers took up these texts and sought to mold their lives in accord with them. If they functioned as effective conversion propaganda[94] it is likely that they were composed for just that purpose by people seeking conversions into their own ranks. If this is a plausible argument, allow me to apply it again on behalf of Davies.

Peter Brown draws attention to the third-century Manichean Elect as intentionally emulating the heroes of the Apocryphal Acts.

> The heroes and heroines of the *Apocryphal Acts* were the heroes and heroines also of the Manichean church. But the Manichees were real men and women: throughout the late third and fourth centuries, Paul and Thecla walked the roads of Syria together, in the form of the little groups of Elect men and women, moving from city to city.[95]

If the Manichees saw in the texts of the Apocryphal Acts such a living, breathing persona that they felt compelled to emulate it and then found it practicable to do so, it seems reasonable to infer from this that the persona they glimpsed reflected reality equally on the other side: the Acts stories called into being circles of ascetics like those from which they had first emerged.

Widows, Itinerants, and Bishops

I hope we may now take as sufficiently established that in the early church, even in the period of Luke-Acts, there were both groups of consecrated widows/virgins and numbers of wandering charismatic apostles. Next I will treat the claim of Davies and MacDonald that the two had an important mutual relationship.

Brown and Davies refer to the walking men of whom such a dim view is taken in the *Clementine Epistles on Virginity*.[96] These itinerant charismatics, much given to exorcisms and spiritual chants, would wander from town to town in second- or third-century Syria. They would make calls on women or men

---

94. Kraemer, "Conversion of Women," 299.
95. Brown, *Body and Society*, 202.
96. Ibid., 196-197; Davies, *Revolt*, 90-94.

pledged to virginity, to whom they would teach some doctrines repugnant to Pseudo-Clement. He found it shocking that these men would claim to emulate the apostles of the Lord and yet dare to dwell with virgin women. Davies takes this to mean that they took up temporary residence in the houses of consecrated women. Though it is possible that what is under criticism here is the ostensibly chaste travels of holy men with the *virgines subintroductae*,[97] the jibe that, once comfortably ensconced, they are idle and refuse any work implies the sort of residence Davies describes.

I suspect that these arrangements were modelled on, or at least justified with reference to, the stories of Elijah and Elisha who stayed regularly, and apparently for some length of time, with certain pious widows.

Lucian's account of the Christian-turned-Cynic itinerant Proteus Peregrinus provides another glimpse into the shared world of widows and itinerants. When Peregrinus the Christian wanderer arrived in one Christian community he was welcomed with open arms. All heeded his pronouncements and seemed even to regard him as a second founder, next to Christ, an echo, I suspect, of the fact that he would have prophesied in the person of Christ: "Whoever hears you hears me."

At any rate, when the authorities jailed him, he was daily visited by his greatest devotees, the widows, with their charges the orphans in tow. Here are the widows, closely resembling those in 1 Timothy, attendant upon the wandering charismatics.

And, if we look closely enough, we can see that even 1 Timothy assumes the widows to have been in a special way attendant upon itinerant teachers. To earn a place (in truth, to retain one) in the official order of widows a woman must have "washed the saints' feet" (5:10), i.e., accommodated the travelling "saints" in a befitting manner (note the same pairing of saints and widows in Acts 9:41).

These visiting dignitaries must have retained the esteem of the Pastor, but it is equally obvious that some such visitors did not meet with his approval. Their appearance of godliness was pure sham (2 Timothy 3:5). They "creep into houses and lead

---

97. H. Achelis, "Agapetae," in *Encyclopaedia of Religion and Ethics*, 1980; Clark, *Ascetic Piety*, 265-289; Rosemary Rader, *Breaking Boundaries: Male/Female Friendship in Early Christian Communities*, Theological Inquiries: Studies in Contemporary Biblical and Theological Problems. ed. Lawrence Boadt (New York: Paulist Press, 1983), 62-71.

captive silly women laden with sins, led away with divers lusts"
(v. 6). The intellectual curiosity of their women audiences is
scoffed at in v. 7: "who will listen to anybody and can never
arrive at a knowledge of the truth." We catch here the same ridi-
cule Juvenal aims at erudite women in his *Sixth Satire:*

> So avoid a dinner-partner with an argumentative
> style, who hurls well-rounded syllogisms like sling-
> shots, who has all history pat: Choose someone rather
> who doesn't understand *all* she reads. I hate these
> authority-citers, the sort who are always thumbing
> some standard grammatical treatise, whose every
> utterance observes all the laws of syntax, who with
> antiquarian zeal quotes poets I've never heard of. Such
> matters are men's concerns. If she wants to correct
> someone's language she can always start with her
> unlettered girl-friends. A husband should be allowed
> his solecisms in peace.

Note the same annoyance with women presuming to teach their
male betters, the jocose dismissal of female interest in intellectual
questions.

Next the heretical itinerants are compared with Jannes and
Jambres, the Egyptian foes of Moses, runners up in the contest of
magic arts. This implies that these false teachers were miracle-
working (or miracle-claiming) superapostles like the walking
men and the opponents of Paul in Corinth, and like the itinerants
of the Apocryphal Acts.

I suggest that these apostles found in the consecrated widows their most receptive audience, since these latter, to a far
greater extent than the conventional householders of the
churches or their bishops, actually shared much of their radical,
ascetic ethos. In turn, the widows found in these charismatics
their most important champions against the encroachments of
the patriarchal church on their rights of support, autonomy, and
ministry. I suspect that a scribal addition to the text, Matthew
23:14, preserves something like the original form of a doom oracle first pronounced by one of these prophets against the ecclesiastical authorities encroaching on the widows of the church:
"Woe to you hypocrites, for you devour widows houses and for a
pretense make long prayers!"

"The social situation in the Acts appears to have been triangular, composed of charismatic apostles, communities of conti-

nent women, and Christian men whose authority stemmed from the legitimacy of office."[98]   "The women in such a community would have probably been financially dependent on men like Pseudo-Clement and emotionally drawn to itinerant apostles."[99]

The triangular relationship Davies describes recurs through the socio-religious history of the Mediterranean basin. Scott D. Hill's essay, "The Local Hero in Palestine in Comparative Perspective," illustrates how from Elijah to Jesus to medieval Muslim *welys*, or saints, to modern Shi'ite *imams*, the dynamics are much the same: the holy man occupies a marginal position with respect to the society and its structures. He has either come on the scene from somewhere else, or has distanced himself from the standard centers and structures of power, or has separated himself from the community behaviorally by celibacy, hermetic wandering, fasting, or trances.   Precisely as a marginal figure he wields power that the establishment cannot hope to match.

He strikes fire from the imagination of the people. The holy man aligns himself with an oppressed element within society or with a disadvantaged village against a larger state structure. In doing so he becomes a projection, almost an incarnation, of the group he champions.   His unique marginalized perspective enables him to detect fault-lines running through the power structures, as well as untapped sources of power lying unsuspected among a weary people. These forces and tensions he is able to manipulate to the advantage of his constituency and to gain concessions on their behalf. They in turn render him veneration, even worship.

Even after death his power continues, as his shrine, relics, and legends continue to be defended, rallied around, invoked on his partisans' behalf. If he is an occulted *imam* his intervention in the community may continue by the agency of a *bab*, or gate, to the hidden *imam*, who issues directives from the departed saint's adytum. Or, like the closely similar Mahayana *bodhisattvas*, who claim to be reincarnations of saints of the past, "Often living men are viewed as incarnations or representatives of a known local hero."[100]

John the Baptist would be a perfect example of the type. He

---

98. Davies, *Revolt,* 87.
99. Ibid., 93.
100. Scott D. Hill, "The Local Hero in Palestine in Comparative Perspective," in *Elijah and Elisha in Socioliterary Perspective,* 43.

comes from distinguished roots, a priestly line, yet he has become a desert-dwelling hermit. From the wilderness he emerges wearing a hair shirt and calling for repentance. He is imagined by some to be the living embodiment of another ancient local saint, Elijah the prophet. This distinctly unworldly man somehow gains political influence by invoking the ancient adultery laws against the reigning tetrarch, who, like the last Shah of Iran, had learned in his Westernizing sophistication to flout the ancient ways. So great does his influence become that Herod Antipas has him arrested, an attempt to capture his chess opponent's king and win the game. But even after death John's name is still enough to send a shudder through the religious establishment who had also opposed him (Mark 11:27-33), and the one who sends the shudder is himself popularly thought to be a living embodiment of the Baptist (Mark 6:14; 8:27-28), so the cycle begins again.

The Prophet Muhammad is another good illustration: after he is alienated from his illustrious kin group, the Quraiysh clan of Mecca, by his iconoclastic preaching, his aid is sought by one of the two factions vying for control of Yathrib, a city to the north. When things become too dangerous in Mecca, the Prophet accepts the timely invitation. As an outsider with neither roots nor interests in the conflict, he is able to tilt the balance of power, but unlike most holy men, he actually becomes a temporal ruler. Yathrib is renamed Madinah ("City" of the Prophet).

Rentería traces out precisely this triangular relation between, first, Elijah, Elisha, and the later prophets or sons of the prophets representing them; second, the poor of Israel, including dispossessed farmers and widows cheated out of their inheritance; and third, the omnivorous Omrid state which sucked the peasantry dry, its activities blessed by the collaborating hierocrats of Dan and Bethel.

I cannot help seeing an exact analogy between this situation and that described by Davies as obtaining between, first, the church establishment as represented by the Pastoral and Pseudo-Clementine Epistles; second, the enrolled widows, either helpless in their dependence on the church dole, or, as McKenna suggests,[101] impoverished by the church which demanded the gift of their money as a condition of joining the order and then penuriously doled it back out in widows' mites; and, third, the wild-card charismatics who were unafraid to take up the cause of their

---

101. McKenna, *Women of the Church*, 41.

kindred spiritual poor, the widows. They had such credibility as heeders of the call of the wandering Christ that their thunderings against the authorities could not simply be ignored. Hence the utility of the widows appealing to them in person, or to their stories after their deaths or departures, or to still others who later carried on their tradition in their name—or stories which placed upon their heads the haloes of the New Testament apostles.

It is not hard to see why, as Davies suggests, the exploits of the second-century itinerants would have been preserved under the names of the apostles. The former would have had as much or more right to place themselves under the aegis of "apostolic succession" than their stolid rivals the bishops. Like the *welys* and *imams*, they were in some ways reincarnations or representatives of their predecessors who had walked the same apostolic road before them, just as the itinerant prophets of the Synoptic logia were living mouthpieces of the ascended Son of Man.

Though the circulation of stories of pro-widow apostles would itself have continued to advocate the widows' interests even in the absence of any living apostolic counterparts, such flesh- and-blood counterparts still seem to have been on hand through the first three or four Christian centuries, as we have seen. Thus I suggest that the circulation of the stories, veiling contempoary charismatics under the names of the New Testament apostles, was an attempt to buttress these figures' advocacy of the widows by claiming for the itinerants the mantle of true apostolic succession, rivaling or even countering the claims of the bishops to be the true sons of the original apostles.

Apostles and Donor-Figures

At this point two hesitations of Virginia Burrus as to Davies's reconstruction may be taken up briefly. She is not sure that the presence of wandering apostles in the chastity stories of the Apocryphal Acts implies any flesh-and-blood counterpart amid the circles of ascetic women who first told the stories.

On the one hand, Burrus suggests that the invocation of the names of Paul, John, Peter and the rest may simply represent a claiming of ancient apostolic sanction for the style of life the women were undertaking.[102]

Interestingly, Pheme Perkins has just the opposite hesitation about Davies's scenario. While Burrus follows Kraemer in seeing

---

102. Burrus, *Chastity as Autonomy*, 107-108.

behind the Acts' celibate women historical counterparts but doubts whether they were associated with apostolic itinerants, Perkins does not question the reality of the itinerants but thinks that

> the radical continence stressed in the apocryphal acts . . . may have been an imaginative explanation of how the apostles could have been among the widows while ordinary mortals in the author's church had to adhere to [more conventional social] safeguards. . . . It need not be a direct reflection of social practice.[103]

The apostles were real enough, but the ascetic women may be a fiction.

Either alternative is of course possible, but in view of the considerations marshalled above it seems to me we may grant Davies's scenario a high degree of historical plausibility.

On the other hand, Burrus notes that the apostolic figures in the chastity stories have the function of "donor figures" in fairy tales. Like a fairy godmother making Cinderella eligible for the prince's attentions after all, Paul, Thomas, or Andrew is simply the catalyst whose presence vitalizes the heroine, Thecla, Mygdonia, Maximilla, to break with conventional drudgery and find new freedom in Christ the Heavenly Bridegroom.[104]

Her point here is to show that the stories, though narrating the exploits and even martyrdoms of the apostles, are really stories about the ascetic women. The stories were told by and about them to foster conversion to the same habit of life among the hearers. I think she proves her point: the stories are really about Mygdonia, not Thomas; Maximilla, not Andrew; Thecla, not Paul.

But I suspect there is another implicit point here. Burrus may mean to say that, again, the figures of the apostles are simply necessary ingredients of the narrative. The stories would read the same way whether or not there were ever itinerant charismatics making the rounds of the widows' houses. Thus to speculate as Davies does that the stories preserve traditions about the charismatic apostles is an unnecessary hypothesis.

---

103. Pheme Perkins, review of *The Revolt of the Widows: The Social World of the Apocryphal Acts,* by Stevan L. Davies, in *America* 144 (June 6, 1981): 470.

104. Burrus, *Chastity as Autonomy,* 75, 77.

To this implicit objection I think Rentería supplies an answer as she describes the function of the encounter between oppressed widows and miracle-working prophets:

> The relationships between the prophet and the men and women with whom he interacts in these stories is a clue to the prophet's role as a resistance figure. For both men and women who interact with him, the transaction empowers them as social actors. For women this empowerment is within the social arena of the family; for example, the poor widow is enabled to feed her son and save him from death, and thus saves her own family standing as well as her husband's (2 Kgs 4:8-36); and the guild prophet's widow saves her children from debt slavery (2 Kgs 4:1-7). In this way, in a time when their social lives are being torn apart by forces they cannot control—nature and a corrupt monarchy—the prophet restores the women to their roles as mothers; and in the case of the Shunammite and the poor widow, he gives them new roles as patronesses of a Yahwistic prophet.[105]

One immediately apparent difference between the stories Rentería discusses and the chastity stories Burrus is considering is that the former redeem women within the family structure while the latter redeem them precisely by lifting them out of the family structure. Yet the difference is only a variant produced by the presence or absence of encratite doctrine, which we would not expect to find in ancient Israel.

Bracketing this difference we can see a striking similarity in that both sets of stories utilize the holy man as a vehicle for the empowerment of women. Not only that, but both groups of tales feature women as giving shelter and aid to the holy man in return. Rentería admits that the stories continued to have this enabling function for the hearers of the stories long after the passing of the prophets (cf. Hill's study of local heroes, above, in this connection). But she argues, as we have seen, that the most probable *Sitz-im-Leben* for such stories is one in which a real, live local hero or holy man actually brought people hope of standing against oppressors with a chance of success or at least with the renewed dignity of self-reliance.

---

105. Rentería, "Elijah," 116.

Since the evidence for the occurrence of such figures is abundant, as Hill (and Brown, see below) has shown, it would seem arbitrary to insist that the literary function of the donor figure could not have arisen from a historical prototype. Indeed one might even suggest that such a story is effective just insofar as it keeps alive the memory of a prophet's enabling power.

(I must pause to note that nothing in the proposed scenario implies that communities of celibate women were somehow dependant on the spiritual power of male itinerant teachers. The point is rather that the "enabling" function of the itinerant apostles as envisioned here consisted of their employment as a defensive buffer against the encroachments of another powerful group of Christian men, the ecclesiastical hierarchs. What I am suggesting, in dependance on Davies, is a symbiotic relationship of mutual advantage between two charismatic groups of powerful persons, the itinerants and the widows. Each group, however, had certain vulnerabilities that the other might aid in protecting.)

Peter Brown traces the role of the local hero into the church of Late Antiquity. He describes how the saints and martyrs of the Western church remained (exactly in the manner described by Hill) powerful after their deaths by dint of the catalytic power of their relics as making the "heavenly friends"[106] available at the site of their tombs and in the reading of their martyrologies. Even as the living dead they walked the delicate tightrope between social interest groups. The people of the country churches did not much care for the pedantic blusterings of the urban bishops if they could plug directly into divine power at the local rustic shrine of the saint. Hence the efforts of the bishops to relocate the relics within the cities and to co-opt these zones of coveted sacred space for their own precincts.

These developments were for the most part in the West; but in the East similar events centered about the tensions between settled bishops and wandering or eremitic holy men. These continued to function as uniquely objective, disinterested mediators and courts of appeal for village disputes, even as shamans had done the world over since time immemorial. Pairs and parties would trudge out to the pillar of Symeon the Stylite, as once they had taken their disputes before Moses (Exodus 18:13-16) or Jesus (Luke 12:14).

---

106. Peter Brown, *The Cult of the Saints: Its Rise and Function in Latin Christianity* (Chicago: University of Chicago Press, 1981), 69-84, 125.

Abraham the hermit—to take one example of many—
came to a pagan village. It was a village of many owners, a village, that is, of independent farmers without a
landlord who could act as their patron. When the tax
collector arrived, Abraham was able through his
friend in Apamea to arrange a loan for the village.
From then on he was declared patron of the village . . .
it has been usual to treat the rise of the holy man in
Syria as the rise of an indigenous figure, linked to the
villagers and drawing his power from an ability to
express the grievances and values of the native Syriac-
speaking population in contrast to, and often in opposition to that of the Greek towns. If, however, the holy
man exercises his power on the model of the rural
patron, the logic of this particular institution excludes
such a simplistic view. The patron was a go-between.
He stood between town and village.[107]

The holy man was a patron of a specific type. His role
was made effective through being strictly delimited.
For he was the ideal patron. Relations with him were
shorn of the abrasive qualities of normal patron-client
relations. He was a non-participant in society. Socio-
logically he was not human: he lived the life of an
angel. . . . This meant, in fact, that any obligation
incurred towards him was not like the normal, crip-
pling and humiliating obligations that linked the villager to his fellow human beings.[108]

Brown also notes that, as in the case of the rivalry between
living bishops and dead saints, the wandering holy men were not
much appreciated by church hierarchs, whose routinized charisma just could not compete with the real thing and had to be
very careful in challenging it.[109]

Marginality and Patronage

I believe that the triangular relationship among the Pastor
and his ilk, the widows, and the itinerant charismatics exactly
reflects the dynamics described by Brown for a slightly later

---

107. Peter Brown, *Society and the Holy in Late Antiquity* (Berkeley: University of California Press, 1989), 158-159.
108. Ibid., 161.
109. Ibid., 140, 232.

period. I will seek briefly to demonstrate this by applying to the Davies scenario the concepts of marginality and patronage.

Schottroff points out, in critique of Theissen's picture of the ethos of the wandering radicals, that "To the nonwandering radicals, the wandering radicals have nothing to say that is connected with their own kind of life; at any rate their preaching to sympathizers is not concerned with the radical ethos."[110] Davies sees the same problem:

> However asocial, the apostle is moral in the sense of disapproving of such deeds as theft, murder, adultery, and revenge. He does not oppose moral order but social structure. Implicitly, the more continent, enduring, and free from social obligations an individual is, the more moral he will be. The apostle exists and functions to convert others to Christianity, not merely to advocate social dissolution. Here lies a problem. In some fashion those he converts must band together, for Christianity as a religion is focused on a community of believers. . . . There is a tension here, a conflict between the asocial ideal embodied in the apostle himself and the Christian end the apostle functions to attain. The Christian social structure that emerges at least partially because of the activity of the apostles will have to be one which to some extent rejects the asocial virtues of apostles and, therefore, disowns the apostles themselves. The Didache . . . shows evidence of this process. There, apostles are implicitly disvalued in that their presence in the church community is required to be as brief as possible.[111]

Yet there is a branch of the community where they find a welcome, and that is among the widows.[112]

We have here a situation readily amenable to analysis in the "grid/group" categories of Mary Douglas as adapted by Bruce J. Malina.[113] According to Malina, a social entity may be said to have a "high grid" quotient when the world seems to them to live

---

110. Schottroff, "Sheep Among Wolves," 49.

111. Davies, *Revolt*, 36.

112. Ibid., 92-93.

113. Bruce J. Malina, *Christian Origins and Cultural Anthropology: Practical Models for Biblical Interpretation* (Atlanta: John Knox Press, 1986), iv. "This work is not an interpretation of her thought, nor is it concerned with reproducing her ideas properly and adequately." Grist for his mill.

up to their hopes and values.[114] For them "God's in his heaven, and all's well here below." By contrast, a "low grid" quotient would mean a group lives alienated from the norms and conditions of what it views as a fallen age, as strangers in a strange land, "sojourners and pilgrims" (cf. 1 Peter 1:17). (Malina is using the notion of high and low grid rather differently than Mary Douglas, for whom a society might be characterized as "high grid" if its inhabitants are governed by a high degree of social definition, role specification and duty, etc. Low grid societies are marked by less definition and lower expectations of its inhabitants. For her, "low grid" would not denote, as it does for Malina, an index of social disaffection.)[115]

A social entity may be called "weak group" if the members have little sense of belonging to a group at all. As individualists, they feel aloof or alienated even from others with whom they might share much in common. One goes one's own way, ever in parallel to others. "Strong group," on the other hand, denotes a strong sense of belonging, perhaps reinforced by a tension or even hostility over against other groups.[116]

The second-century churches represented by the Pastoral Epistles and Luke-Acts have lost the apocalyptic fervor characteristic of early Christianity. These Christians are coming to feel at home in the world and to seek respectability within it. But here and there various forms of Christian radicalism try to fan into flame the dying embers of what once was. Montanist and Gnostic movements, like the Desert Fathers of a somewhat later period, are living protests against the accommodation to this age. Among these expressions of discontent we may place both the itinerant charismatics and the widows.

Of these parties we may readily class the churches of the Pastorals and Luke-Acts as at least tending towards the "high grid/strong group" end of the spectrum. For them there is less tension than there once seemed between Christian discipleship and "what is right in the sight of all men" (Romans 12:17—part of the late Pastoral stratum). Yet the contrast between Christian faith and the pagan faiths is sharp (sharper in fact, I suspect, than it was earlier on, when Christianity was largely the product of

114. Ibid., 17-18.
115. Mary Douglas, *Natural Symbols: Explorations in Cosmology*(New York: Pantheon Books, 1982), 58-61.
116. Ibid., 54-64.

syncretism as new converts brought insights and beliefs from
their old faiths to graft onto their new one).[117]

The itinerant charismatics were on the opposite end of the
spectrum. They still preached doom and gloom: "Come out of
her, my people, lest you take part in her sins, lest you share in her
plagues!" (Revelation 18:4). The world was not their home. "The
Son of Man has not where to lay his head" (Matthew 8:20). So
they were "low grid." The world could not suit them less.

Yet they were also clearly "weak group." As Davies says,
"The apostles themselves could not have been the role models for
members of a community; by their itineracy they are external to
any permanent community."[118] Though we do later hear of
groups of "walking men" in Syria, I suspect that at most the charismatics traveled by twos as the Synoptic Mission Charge mandated. Between larger groupings than this there must often have
been rancor and rivalry, just as we see depicted between Paul and
his Corinthian competitors.[119] Both sought the same bases of
support in the open market of prophecy and miracle. Note how
the writer of 1 John, apparently the master of a troop of circuit-
riding prophets, takes the trouble to undermine the success of a
new split-off from the franchise by writing negative letters of recommendation against them to every place where they might pass
(1 John 2:18-19; 4:1-6; 2 John 7-11).

If the established churches were "high grid/strong group"
and the itinerants were "low grid/weak group," where do the
widows fit in? They were "low grid/strong group." By accepting asceticism they had certainly rejected the mores of the world
about them. As Mary Douglas says, the bodily orifice restrictions
of a social group tend to mirror the limits of their permissible
contacts with larger society. Categories of unclean foods tend to
mirror categories of outsiders with whom fraternization and
intermarriage are impossible. Douglas herself points to early
Christian female asceticism as a prime example.[120] The sexual
inviolability of each individual woman mirrored the sealing off

117. Richard Reitzenstein, *Hellenistic Mystery Religions: Their Basic Ideas
and Significance*, trans. John Steely, Pittsburgh Theological Monograph
Series, ed. Dikran Y. Hadidian, 15 (Pittsburgh: Pickwick Press, 1978), 149.
118. Davies, *Revolt*, 52.
119. Theissen, *Social Setting*, 40-53.
120. Mary Douglas, *Purity and Danger: An Analysis of Concepts of Pollution
and Taboo* (London: Routledge & Kegan Paul, 1966; Baltimore: Pelican
Books, a division of Penguin Books, 1970), 186-187.

of the group as a whole from the wider society, like the thick walls of the later convents. With such a high wall for a group boundary, the widows and virgins would surely count as "strong group," as well.

The rigid boundaries erected by ascetical women's communities do not mean that the groups were in fact hermetically sealed off from the sinful society around them. The very erection of the barriers presupposes that traffic between the camp of the saints and the sinners without was a genuine danger—else why build the walls? In our day, the Amish insulate their children from the outside world all the more carefully since the attraction to it is great. "How ya gonna keep 'em down on the farm after they've seen Paree?"

> Like the social body, so too the individual body is plagued by boundary problems. Strong group/low grid is as formal and precise as strong group/high grid in the use of titles, in interpersonal interactions, and in the maintenance of all semblance of order, regularity, and self-control. However, in the low grid situation social control, like self-control, is under attack and can break down quite easily. Bodily boundaries, like social boundaries, are all too porous; invaders penetrate all too readily, whether evil spirits, wicked thoughts, perverse ideas, or uncontrollable urges.[121]

We see this boundary anxiety, activated by physical and social boundary transgressions, as consecrated virgins left their pledge behind and married their hitherto-celibate partners (1 Corinthians 7:8-9, 27-28, 36-38; 1 Timothy 5:11-12).

How could our three groups have related to each other? Insofar as "group" issues were concerned, the widow houses had more in common with the churches, especially since many widows needed the alms or stipend of the church. But when it came to questions of grid, the itinerants were kindred spirits with the widows, since both had opted out of the world system. So contra Schottroff, the wandering radicals did have something to say to the sedentary radicals. By contrast they had almost nothing to say to or to hear from the bishops, and vice versa.

As just anticipated, high walls may yet be porous, and there was bleeding from one group to another along the margins. Just

---

121. Malina, *Christian Origins*, 39.

as some itinerants sought to stay for a longer or shorter time in a community, so did some women pull up stakes and become the chaste companions of the itinerants along the roads. I will have more to say of the reflections of such women in the Gospel of Luke later on.

As Brown and Hill show, it is, ironically, the very marginality of the wanderers that made possible their effective role as mediators, even as patrons of a sort. I would suggest that in the triangular relationship between the churches, the widows, and the itinerants, we can detect a tension between two different types of patronage, both well described by Halvor Moxnes. Between the churches and the widows there existed a simple patron-client, superior-inferior relationship.[122]

The church patron traded the tangible goods of food, clothing, and money for the intangible good of honor, of being considered a benefactor. Officially the intangible good tendered by the widow in return was her ceaseless prayer. Actually she traded some measure of self-respect, being willing to occupy the position of charity recipient, for the material goods needed.

But between the widows and the itinerants there held good a "patron-broker-client" relationship.[123] That is, the itinerant was a broker between God and human beings, and he offered revelations and healing miracles from his own heavenly patron. The widows received these gratefully and in return provided temporary food and shelter. Here there was more of an equal footing, and the widows themselves earned the honor of being patronesses of the wandering prophets. It was a mutual exchange of goods, and the widows made back the honor as benefactresses that they lost as the recipients of church charity.

Scholars have already discerned some of these various elements here and there in Luke-Acts. For example, Schaberg notes how Luke describes women in both the roles of clients of the church and providers of hospitality for male apostles.[124] Moxnes sees Jesus and his disciples as exercising the role of brokers in the broker-patron-client model.[125] Stegemann, Esler, and Karris all

---

122. Halvor Moxnes, "Patron-Client Relations and the New Community in Luke-Acts," in *The Social World of Luke-Acts: Models for Interpretation*, ed. Jerome H. Neyrey (Peabody, MA: Hendrickson Publishers, 1991), 265; cf. Rader, *Breaking Boundaries*, 12-13.
123. Moxnes, "Patron-Client," 265.
124. Schaberg, "Luke," 280.
125. Moxnes, "Patron-Client," 265.

describe Luke's concern for the poor in terms of simple benevolence toward them from above, a stance clearly in accord with the Pastorals (1 Timothy 6:17-19).[126] Dillon and Koenig have seen the figures of Theissen's wandering charismatics behind many of the stories in Luke's Gospel about the travels and reception of Jesus and his disciples.[127] On all this I will build, but I believe that thus far no one has sought to use the scenarios reconstructed by Kraemer, Davies, MacDonald, and Burrus as the key to the widow traditions. I propose that, once we see these several stories and sayings as having taken form against the socio-religious dynamics described in this chapter, they will be seen to make an altogether new and surprising sense.

---

126. Stegemann, "Following of Christ," 110-112; Philip Francis Esler, *Community and Gospel in Luke-Acts: The Social and Political Motivations of Lucan Theology,* Society for New Testament Studies Monograph Series, ed. G. N. Stanton, 57 (New York: Cambridge University Press, 1989), 184-185; Robert J. Karris, *What Are They Saying About Luke-Acts? A Theology of the Faithful God* (New York: Paulist Press, 1979), 97; Moxnes, "Patron-Client," 267.

127. Richard J. Dillon, *From Eye-Witnesses to Ministers of the Word,* Analecta Biblica 82 (Rome: Biblical Institute Press, 1978), 239-249; John Koenig, *New Testament Hospitality: Partnership With Strangers as Promise and Mission,* Overtures to Biblical Theology, eds. Walter Brueggemann and John R. Donahue, no. 17 (Philadelphia: Fortress Press, 1985), 85-86, 91-94.

Chapter Two

Female Prophecy:
Anna and the Daughters of Philip

Literary Detection

In 1955 Frank Moore Cross and David Noel Freedman suggested that the great victory song hymning the destruction of Pharaoh's host in Exodus 12:1-18 originally stood in the text attributed to Miriam, but has subsequently been transferred to Moses.[1] Forty-four years later[2] Phyllis Trible suggested that this alteration was just part of a larger and systematic program of extirpating what was once an important complex of Miriam traditions in which she was seen as both leader and prophetess, if not actually a goddess.

If one looks carefully at the text of Exodus 21, one notices the lingering telltale hint that the Song originally belonged to Miriam, before she fell under chauvinistic suspicion: she seems to begin the song, as she did in the pre-history of the text, only to be silenced. Only the first two lines escape her mouth before she falls wordless (v. 21) forever, or at least until her Song was restored unto her through the careful scholarly labors of those mentioned here.

What we have here is an example of the scholarly detective work of imaginative reconstruction at the scene of the crime that Schüssler Fiorenza applies to the New Testament. And it is occasioned by a foul deed, a crime, so to speak, done to Miriam at some stage of the tradition. In this chapter I ask if there is reason to believe that Luke has similarly omitted the prophecies of women that once stood in his sources. And if so, is there a chance we may recover what was lost? It all depends on whether he has left behind any clues at the scene of the crime. I make bold to say that he has. At any rate, the game is afoot!

Anna's Silent Song

The first thing we read about Anna is that she was a proph-

---

1. Frank Moore Cross and David Noel Freedman, "The Song of Miriam," *Journal of Near Eastern Studies* 14 (1955): 237.
2. Phyllis Trible, "Bringing Miriam out of the Shadows," *Bible Review* 5 (February 1989): 19.

etess (Luke 2:36), yet the last thing we will hear is any prophecy attributed to her. What else can we surmise about her? It is virtually impossible to miss the similarity of the thumbnail sketch of Anna to the portrait of devout widows in 1 Timothy chapter 5. Commentator after commentator remarks on it. The character of Anna bears a striking resemblance to the Christian widows of the late first century (Tetlow).[3] "She is represented as a devoted widow like the faithful widows of the Church (1 Tim, v. 9.)" (Creed).[4] "The most detailed description of Christian widows found in 1 Tim 5:3-16 contains many features which match Luke's description of Anna" (Nolland).[5]

Even more interesting is the observation of a few scholars that in writing the description of Anna, Luke was thinking of widows in his own church community. Goulder speaks of "Anna, the very pattern of Lucan church widows."[6] Tetlow infers from the similarity to 1 Timothy 5:3-16 that "in his composition of the character of Anna, Luke may actually have been writing about Christian widows who were active in the Church in his own time."[7]

I think this is almost right, save that perhaps we should say the silent Anna now met with in the text reflects Christian widows the way Luke would *like* them to be: silent (1 Timothy 2:11). As we will see, Anna, as first scripted, may have once reflected those widows by speaking forth as they, too, once had.

Certain striking statistics of Anna's life are provided, as if to serve as credentials. We are told that "she was of a great age, having lived with her husband seven years from her virginity, and as a widow till she was eighty-four" (Luke 3:36b, RSV). As many scholars now note, the RSV translation is probably wrong, underestimating her great age. More likely Luke means us to

---

3. Tetlow, *Women and Ministry*, 102.

4. John Martin Creed, *The Gospel according to St. Luke* (London: Macmillan & Co., 1950), 43.

5. John Nolland, *Luke 1-9:20*, Word Biblical Commentary, ed. David A. Hubbard and Glenn W. Barker, vol. 35A (Dallas: Word Books, Publishers, 1989), 122; cf. Herman Hendrickx, *The Infancy Narratives*, Studies in the Synoptic Gospels (San Francisco: Harper & Row, Publishers, 1984), 111; Schaberg, *Luke*, 283; Simpson, *Pastoral Epistles*, 73; Hanson, *Pastoral Epistles*, 97.

6. Goulder, *New Paradigm*, 260.

7. Tetlow, *Women and Ministry*, 102; Celeste J. Rossmiller, "Prophets and Disciples in Luke's Infancy Narrative," *The Bible Today* 22 (June 1984): 364.

understand that she is 105 or 106 years old, like the Old Testament Judith, another epic widow.

As Godet pointed out, the precision of the language implies Luke is carefully differentiating three periods; thus we should take the figure eighty-four to denote the duration of the third period, not her current age.[8] In the same vein, Plummer draws attention to the probable force of the word *heos* as meaning not "until she was as old as," but rather "up to as much as" eighty-four years of widowhood.[9] That Luke means to prepare the reader for an exceedingly great age for Anna is implied by the pleonasm *probebkuia en hemerais pollais* in v. 36.[10] J. K. Elliott adds an argument from Luke's style: "When he gives an age or duration of time Luke applies the figure *directly* to the nearest verb (e.g. Luke 13:11, 16). This would encourage our attaching the 'eighty-four years' to her period of widowhood rather than our reading it as an amplification of [*probebekuia*] in the previous verse."[11]

Alternatively, though it seems less likely to me, Anna's age may be a numerical cipher. Varela suggests that the figure eighty-four represents the multiplication of the twelve of the tribes and the patriarchs by the seven of perfection. The implication: "She was an old woman who had lived a perfect married life, and an even more perfect widowhood."[12]

Yet another possibility, raised by Thurston in her study of the widows, is that the text means to tell us that Anna had lived in a celibate marriage, presumably like that of the *virgines subintroductae*.[13] It is interesting to note the witness of Tatian's *Diatessaron* on this point, though Thurston does not invoke it. William L. Peterson says that of the various versions of the *Diatessaron*, the Persian Harmony says that Anna "remained seven years a virgin with her husband," while the Stuttgart and Zürich Harmo-

8. F. Godet, *A Commentary on the Gospel of Luke* (New York: I. K. Funk & Co., 1881), 89.
9. Plummer quoted in M. P. John, "Luke 2. 36-37: How Old Was Anna?," *Bible Translator* 26 (February 1975): 247.
10. John, ibid.
11. J. K. Elliott, "Anna's Age (Luke 2:36-50)," *Novum Testamentum* 30 (February 1988): 101.
12. A. T. Varela, "Luke 2. 36-37: Is Anna's Age What Is Really in Focus?," *Bible Translator* 27 (April 1976): 446; cf. Goulder, *New Paradigm*, 260-261; Wayne Vohn Whitney, "Women in Luke: An Application of a Reader-Response Hermeneutic" (Ph.D. diss.: Southern Baptist Theological Seminary, 1990), 156-157.
13. Thurston, *Widows*, 24.

nies recount that Anna "remained with her husband seven years in her virginity." These variants, from opposite ends of the Roman world, are so similar that "one is forced to conclude that this reading stood in Tatian's *Diatessaron*."[14] Can it be that we see here the original reading of Luke's own text? As Peterson notes, Tatian himself was an Encratite, and so the reading may simply represent a tendentious alteration. But then Tatian was reading earlier copies of Luke than ours, and I am not inclined to brush off such evidence too quickly.

But why are we supplied with such data? "No other place in the gospel will make it clear why we have to be told her exact age" (Jan Wojcik).[15] I suggest the narrative falls in with a pattern observable in the encomia on pious widows in the early church, whereby their feats of long continent endurance are held up for admiration and emulation. Castelli provides a summary which will give the idea nicely:

> The evidence for the ages of women devoting their chastity to God varies, though many appear to have done so early in life. Palladius tells of Talis, a woman who followed the ascetic life for eighty years, of Taor, who was a virgin for sixty years, and another virgin, unnamed, who was ascetic for sixty years as well. Macrina was twelve when she decided to remain a virgin; Olympias was widowed at nineteen and refused to remarry; Blesilla, Paula's daughter and Eustochium's older sister, began her ascetic life at her widowhood at twenty; Melania the Elder, widowed at twenty-two, pursued asceticism, and her granddaughter, Melania the Younger, renounced the world at twenty, after seven years of marriage.[16]

I believe that Anna's statistics reflect just such a context of women's asceticism, even if she is an ideal character.

It is interesting to survey the various reactions of critics to the fact that whereas Simeon and Anna seem to be paired off in the story, Simeon breaks forth in one of the canticles while Anna's

14. William L. Peterson, "Tatian's Diatessaron," in *Ancient Christian Gospels* by Helmut Koester (London: SCM Press, Philadelphia: Fortress Press, 1990), 423.
15. Jan Wojcik, *The Road to Emmaus: Reading Luke's Gospel* (West Lafayette, IN: Purdue University Press, 1989), 113.
16. Castelli, "Virginity," 81.

words are vaguely summarized. William Manson represents the phallocentric perspective of his generation which saw nothing at all odd in the disparity: "The mention of the aged Hannah the prophetess forms a suitable pendant to the recognition by Simeon."[17]

Tannehill remains blithely oblivious:

> Simeon's inspired words, to be sure, are quoted, while we receive only a summary of Anna's (2:38). Nevertheless, the summary suggests that they were similar in content to the joyful words of Mary, Zechariah, and Simeon. . . . In any case, women as well as men can be inspired speakers of God's revelation in Luke-Acts.[18]

This is a strange conclusion from the text before us! One wonders just *when* Anna's oracles "were" similar to Simeon's. Does Tannehill imagine that the scene is a transcript of historical reality? I feel sure he does not. The only option left is that originally a pre-Lukan oral tradition or written source supplied Anna's words, and they were much like Simeon's, but Luke has suppressed them. As we will see, some scholars long ago suggested just this possibility.

I suggest this is a case of Paul de Man's paradox of blindness and insight, whereby we can only understand some elements of a text as long as we remain blind to others.[19] In this case, scholars friendly to the idea of women's full participation in the ministry are free to see elements of the text that seem to point in this direction, but it simply does not occur to them that Luke's redaction might be pointing in the opposite direction. Jane Kopas can actually write, seeing nothing amiss, that "Anna's testimony is valued no less than Simeon's because she is a woman."[20]

Except, apparently, that Luke deems it not worth quoting![21] Thurston does notice the strange silence of Anna, yet she homes

17. William Manson, *The Gospel of Luke*, Moffatt New Testament Commentary, ed. James Moffatt (New York: Richard R. Smith, 1930), 22.

18. Robert C. Tannehill, *The Narrative Unity of Luke-Acts: A Literary Interpretation, Volume 1: The Gospel according to Luke* (Philadelphia: Fortress Press, 1986), 134-135.

19. Paul de Man, *Blindness and Insight, Essays in the Rhetoric of Contemporary Criticism*, 2nd ed. revised. Theory and History of Literature, vol. 7 (Minneapolis: University of Minnesota Press, 1983), 106.

20. Jane Kopas, "Jesus and Women: Luke's Gospel, *Theology Today* 43 (February 1986): 194-195.

in on exactly the wrong conclusion. If Anna were simply a Lukan creation, he might have made her the vehicle for another canticle. But he does not. We might conclude from this fact that he cannot have been the women's partisan many would like to think him. But in fact Thurston infers that Anna must be a historical figure whom Luke could not omit, faithful recorder that he was, even though her history served no purpose of his.[22]

Is this the Luke known to critical scholarship? Is Luke not rather in the habit of creating speeches he thinks suitable for his characters, historical or not? Thurston owes her suggestion to Schleiermacher, who was a great historicizer, at least when it came to his favorite evangelists Luke and John. We will see that

---

21. Whitney notes that Simeon "actually had speech narrated, while Anna did not. Since this element went unchallenged within the text it is a valid stumbling block [in the way of a pro-feminist reading of Luke], but not a major one" (Whitney, "Women in Luke," 314). Whitney's is an analysis of Luke using the feminist reader-response methodology of Patrocinio P. Schweikart. He disclaims any attempt to recover the author's or redactor's intent and is content merely with reporting on how the text strikes him, noting and seeking to resolve the aporias in the text, tensions between what he calls "Continuity/Legitimation" elements, where Luke's text seems to enshrine sexist oppression of women, and "Discontinuity/Revolutionary" elements, which seem to challenge a more traditionalist understanding.

Why are both sets of phenomena present in the text? Whitney once suggests that the traditionalist elements stem from the original Palestinian Jewish milieu of the traditions, while the subsequent redaction of these in a Hellenistic milieu accounts for the more forward-looking elements (66).

Elsewhere he guesses, somewhat inconsistently, that the androcentric bias evident in the text likely stems from the milieu of the redactor as well as from his male biases (205).

In either case, he does not much care what Luke may have intended. He freely admits what I suspect to be the case with Tannehill and others discussed here: his agenda is that of a liberal Christian who regards the text as the scripture of his church and as an instrument of good news announcing liberation to women as well as other oppressed people. Thus, as long as the discontinuous items in the text seem to him to outweigh their opposite numbers, then the liberal Christian reader may continue to read the text as scripture with a clean conscience (37, 94-95, 122, 323).

I am not sure Whitney's reading of the text has any more value than as a kind of autobiographical or confessional piece, but at least he is clear about what he is doing, while Tannehill often seems to be doing the same thing and gratuitously identifying the result with Luke's intention.

F. F. Bruce, another thoroughgoing harmonizer and historicizer, makes almost the identical wrongheaded argument in the analogous case of the silent prophetesses in the house of Philip.

It has begun to dawn on Raymond E. Brown that something is just not right:

> the joining of the Anna episode to the Simeon scene may seem artificial in the sense that not even a word of hers is recorded. . . . In one way this is peculiar: for of the four OT women who are called prophetesses two have canticles associated with them. The canticle of Deborah in Judg 5 is well-known, and a short canticle is attributed to Miriam in Exod 15:21. Miriam was probably the original singer of the canticle that begins in Exod 15:1, although later tradition attributed it to Moses.[23]

What is peculiar is that what Brown recognizes in the case of Miriam seems not to occur to him for a moment when it comes to Anna. Blindness and insight.

Tetlow is beginning to get things in focus, but she can only see men (and women) as trees walking:

> Simeon is the dominant figure. He is mentioned first and the text of his two prophetic utterances is given. The character and actions of Anna are described in the third person, but she herself does not speak according to the Lukan narrative.[24]

But instead of drawing what might seem the obvious lesson from these observations she imposes Conzelmann's dispensationalism on the text, placing Simeon and Anna in the period of Israel, when women can proclaim God's word alongside men (never mind that Anna *doesn't*). Tetlow is prepared to recognize the silencing of women thereafter as she moves into "die Mitte der Zeit."[25]

Schaberg realizes that Anna's silence is pregnant with

---

22. Thurston, *Widows*, 23-24.
23. Raymond E. Brown, *The Birth of the Messiah: A Commentary on the Infancy Narratives of Matthew and Luke* (Garden City, NY: Doubleday & Co., 1977), 466.
24. Tetlow, *Women and Ministry*, 102.
25. Ibid., 103.

Lukan meaning: "Anna the prophet . . . is given no speech."
"Unlike Simeon . . . Anna is given no canticle and the Spirit is not
said to be with her, though it is three times said to empower Simeon . . ., who has two canticles."[26] This is because "Luke thinks of
a woman's proper attitude as that of a listener, pondering what is
not understood, learning in silence."[27]

All true enough, but if Luke were creating freely here, why
would he almost make Anna speak, but not quite? Why not total
silence? To repeat Schleiermacher's question, though not his
answer, what is she doing here at all? Why does Luke prepare us
to hear her break into inspired song, and then withhold it? It
would make sense if he were working from a source. Then the
odd items just noticed would fall into place as telltale marks of
redaction. They did lead up to Anna's canticle in the source, but
Luke has excised it, transferred it elsewhere.

Sahlin, followed by Leaney, suggested just this, though the
question of Luke and women never entered his head. What troubled him was the oddity that in a hymn now sung by Zechariah
in welcome of his new son John the Baptist, we find references to
the boy as the newly erected horn of salvation from the dynasty
of David (Luke 2:69) who will expel the heathen and make possible true divine service without fear from pagan oppressors. Of
whom speaketh the prophet this? of his own son, or of some
other man's?, ask Sahlin and Leaney. Certainly not of John the
Baptist! Rather, obviously the messianic child, his embryonic
cousin.

> If the Benedictus is a Messianic hymn, a place for it
> must be found in connection with the birth of Jesus.
> Sahlin suggests plausibly that it originally stood as the
> song of Anna, the substance of her words to those who
> watched for the redemption of Jerusalem (ii. 38): i. 68
> harmonizes excellently with this introduction of Anna
> and the direct address to the child in verse 76 agrees
> perfectly with the situation. Again, for Anna to utter a
> song of praise balances Symeon's song (ii. 29), and
> [otherwise] there is a sense of anticlimax in the mere
> "she spoke about him" after the elaborate description
> of Anna in verses 36-37.[28]

26. Schaberg, "Luke," 281, 283.
27. Ibid., 281.

Farris's objection to Sahlin's theory is interesting: "no adequate explanation has been given to account for the transposition of the hymn to its new location."[29] True, Leaney speculates that Luke might have felt he needed something for Zechariah to say now that the cat no longer had his tongue. But this is pretty weak. It is a case of phallocentric blindness at its densest that none of these critics can see the real issue: Luke wanted to silence the woman prophet bequeathed him by his source.

Farris also objects against Sahlin and Leaney: "the description of the prophet of v. 76 is so heavily influenced by the synoptic description of John that the most reasonable interpretation must surely be that John himself is the 'child' to whom v. 76 is addressed."[30] But Leaney had already noted that it is perfectly conceivable for Luke to have characters call Jesus a prophet. And Farris begs the question by having v. 76 "influenced" by the Synoptic Baptist tradition. "Reminiscent" might be a more objective term, and then it would be evident that, while the Davidic savior might also be said to go before Adonai, the wording, commonly applied by Christians to John after "the Lord" had come to mean for them the Kurios Jesus, gave Luke an apparently Johannine peg on which to hang his actually rather clumsy transfer of the canticle to Zechariah.

Luke's Source

What suppositions are made necessary by the Sahlin-Leaney theory? It obviously implies that Luke is working with a source that already had essentially the same narrative, with the canticles assigned to various characters. Is this a viable view of the passage given recent scholarship? I venture to say it is.

Richard A. Horsley is mainly concerned with the canticles themselves, not so much with the narratives with which they are surrounded. Nonetheless he says that "the language in these songs is more highly Semiticized than that in the surrounding narrative—which is already noticeably more Semiticized by comparison with the rest of Luke's writing"[31]—a conclusion consis-

---

28. A. R. C. Leaney, *A Commentary on the Gospel According to St. Luke,* Harper's New Testament Commentaries, ed. Henry Chadwick (New York: Harper & Brothers, Publishers, 1958), 24-25.
29. Stephen Farris, *The Hymns of Luke's Infancy Narratives: Their Origin, Meaning, and Significance,* Journal for the Study of the New Testament Supplement Series 9 (Sheffield: JSOT Press, 1985), 56.
30. Ibid.

tent with the supposition that the canticles already stood in the narrative as Luke first read it, though not necessarily attributed in every case to those now shown singing them.[32]

Similarly, Farris argues at great length for a Hebrew substratum for the whole infancy section, canticles and narrative frame alike. By Raymond Martin's criteria for detecting translation Greek based on a Semitic original, "Luke 1-2 as a whole and also in its various parts consistently displays translation Greek frequencies."[33] Farris admits that "One cannot tell [simply from the linguistic factors] . . . whether there is one source behind Luke 1-2 or several, nor whether the source or sources were oral or written."[34] I would argue that the marks and motives of Lukan redaction are so apparent that this consideration itself implies there was a single, probably written, source to be thus redacted.

Raymond Brown, a proponent of the theory that the canticles are original Greek compositions,[35] appeals to Fitzmyer against Farris: "Fitzmyer, a world-acknowledged expert on the Aramaic of Jesus' time, is blunt (*Gospel* 1. 309): 'There is no evidence that the magnificat ever existed in Semitic'."[36] This is no refutation at all, but rather a blatant case of the "appeal to authority" fallacy. And it is interesting that in the second edition of Fitzmyer's commentary, the words quoted by Brown no longer appear, though Fitzmyer maintains his judgment that the apparent Semiticisms are just elements of Septuagintal stylistic pastiche.[37]

Against this we may pose Farris' contention that the "Septuagintalisms" argument seems circular. Why are they all concentrated here in the infancy narratives? Because the scene is more

---

31. Richard A. Horsley, *The Liberation of Christmas: The Infancy Narratives in Social Context* (New York: Crossroad Publishing Company, 1989), 108.

32. John Shelby Spong (*Born of a Woman: A Bishop Rethinks the Birth of Jesus* [San Francisco: HarperSanFrancisco, a division of HarperCollins Publishers, 1992], 108-109) speculates that Luke's source contained narratives but no canticles. It was a mystery play, a pageant performed in a Jewish-Christian community—in pantomime! Luke added the dialogue. If anyone can credit the idea of a script with no words, plus the anachronism of a Christmas pageant four centuries before the invention of Christmas, I welcome such a one to accept the bishop's theory.

33. Farris, *Hymns*, 56.

34. Ibid., 62.

35. Brown, *Birth of the Messiah*, 252.

36. Raymond E. Brown, "Gospel Infancy Narrative Research from 1976 to 1986: Part II (Luke)," *Catholic Biblical Quarterly* 48 (1986): 666.

"biblical"? Yet it is the "biblical," i.e. Hebrew or Aramaic, flavor of the language that creates this impression to begin with! Surely the rest of the gospel is filled with Old Testament allusions, yet in terms of Semitisms or "Septuagintalisms," we find nothing like these canticles or even their narrative frame. Why not? Unless they represent a distinct source.[38]

Another argument for Luke's use of a pre-existent Aramaic source containing the canticles is suggested by the words of the angelic annunciation in Luke 1:32-33, 35. They mirror quite closely the words of a similar Messianic oracle contained in one of the recently published Dead Sea Scrolls, 4Q246, *The Son of God*. This is a piece of an Aramaic pseudo-Danielic apocalypse. The relevant text reads as follows: "He will be called [son of the Gr]eat [God;] by His Name he shall be designated. He will be called the son of God; they will call him son of the Most High."[39] When a close parallel to Luke's text stands before us nowhere else but in an Aramaic document, it seems most natural to suggest that Luke derived it from a similar Aramaic text.

I believe the Sahlin-Leaney theory of Lukan redactional transfer of the Benedictus from Anna to Zechariah is entirely plausible, a strong reading (or rather "misreading") of the narrative. But I want to go further and argue that the source redacted by Luke stemmed from the consecrated Christian widow communities. As it happens, several previous theories about the origin of the canticles fit my hypothesis quite well.

I begin with the theory, championed by Raymond E. Brown and derived from Albert Gelin and others, that the canticles come from members of a closely or loosely organized group of so-called *Anawim*, the devout "poor" of Israel.[40] These were the humble of the land who lived on the margin of survival and agonized over the subjugated status of their homeland. Their piety was shaped by a long tradition of psalmody and prophecy in the Old Testament. "This poor man cried and Yahweh heard him,

---

37. Joseph A. Fitzmyer, *The Gospel According to Luke I-IX: A New Translation with Introduction and Commentary*, Anchor Bible, eds. William Foxwell Albright and David Noel Freedman, vol. 28A (New York: Doubleday, a division of Bantam Doubleday Dell Publishing Group, 1981), 312.

38. Farris, *Hymns*, 36-37.

39. Robert Eisenman and Michael Wise, trans. and eds., *The Dead Sea Scrolls Uncovered* (Rockport, MA: Element, 1992), 70.

40. Browm, *Birth of the Messiah*, 350-352.

and saved him out of all his troubles" (Psalm 34:6). As implied in this Psalm and many others like it, Gelin said, the poor were in a special way "clients of Yahweh."[41] Their help was going to come from him or from nowhere. One might just curse one's poverty and God for making one poor (Psalm 73 tells of a man who almost went this route, vv. 11, 15; cf. Job 2:9), but if one didn't, the alternative was to learn patient and abject absolute dependence on the Almighty. And it is thus that

> the vocabulary of poverty has been enriched with religious value. Its terms are transposed to a spiritual plane. Words that once denoted a [simple] sociological reality came to mean an attitude of soul. [And so] the words 'anawim, 'aniyyim, dallim, 'ebyonim, took their place in the vocabulary of the theology of grace.[42]

At first this God-receptive poverty was occasioned by plain economic poverty. One thinks again of Rentería's analysis of Elijah and Elisha and their legends as the cherished property of the destitute of the Omrid state, holding onto a piety counter to that of the fat and sleek of Bethel and Dan. But the experience of the Exile (Gelin was thinking mainly of the Babylonian Exile, but surely we may include the Assyrian as well) imparted new dimensions to the piety of poverty. The aristocrats and their priestly lackeys were hauled off to foreign empires, leaving the peasantry to fend for themselves. "And I will leave in the midst of you a poor and needy people; and they shall hope in the name of Yahweh" (Zephaniah 3:11-13).

Trito-Isaiah prophesied to the community which returned from the Exile, humbled by the experience, to a Jerusalem by no means as glorious as in its heyday. "He has sent me to bring good tidings to the anawim, he has sent me to bind up the brokenhearted, to proclaim liberty to the captives and the opening of the prison to those who are bound" (Isaiah 61:1b-2). Here was, supposedly, a chastened remnant Israel that would never grow proud and rebellious like the stiff-necked people before the Exile. One can scarcely boast "My own hand has gotten me this" if one has nothing.

I should think Paul Hanson's brilliant reconstruction of the

---

41. Albert Gelin, *The Poor of Yahweh,* trans. Kathryn Sullivan (Collegeville, MN: Liturgical Press, 1964). 50.
42. Ibid., 26.

Sitz-im-Leben of Trito-Isaiah and Deutero-Zechariah,[43] as well as Mowinckel's delineation of the relative deprivation of the Psalm-writing Korah-guild Levites[44] both go a long way toward securing the general notion of an *Anawim* piety in these literatures. Gelin's sketch of the *Anawim* as a self-conscious religious party has come under severe attack, e.g., by Norbert Lohfink, D. P. Seccombe, and Richard A. Horsley, who rejects the whole notion of "some socially disembodied Jewish spirituality."[45]

But this seems to me an unperceptive and unhelpful caricature. Gelin ties the evolution of the poverty language of spirituality to concrete social conditions at every step.

Horsley wants to make the canticles of Luke 1-2 evidence for Jewish peasant revolutionism, and he wants to put Brown's and Gelin's reading of the canticles to rest. But he seems to be guilty of perpetuating the very same "spiritual versus political" dichotomy he bemoans. After all, the texts in question are hymns, implying some kind of piety! Recalling Schüssler Fiorenza's hermeneutical dictum that "it is necessary to acknowledge the 'hermeneutical privilege of the oppressed' and to develop a hermeneutics 'from below,'"[46] I would suggest as a possible analogy with the canticles the Spirituals of the enslaved Africans in the Antebellum South. Can anyone here drive a wedge between true economic poverty and a spiritual poverty reminiscent of Matthew 5:3?

43. Paul D. Hanson, *The Dawn of Apocalyptic: The Historical and Sociological Roots of Jewish Apocalyptic Eschatology* (Philadelphia: Fortress Press, 1975), 263-287.
44. Sigmund Mowinckel, *The Psalms in Israel's Worship*, trans. D. R. ap-Thomas (Nashville: Abingdon Press, 1962), II 82; Hanson, *Dawn*, 267; Martin Noth, *A History of Pentateuchal Traditions* (Englewood Cliffs, NJ: Prentice-Hall, 1972), 196.
45. Horsley, *Liberation*, 64; cf. Norbert Lohfink, "'Von der 'Anawim-partei' zur Kirche der Armen: Die bibelwis senschaftliche Ahnentafel eines Hauptbegriffs der 'Theologie der Befreiung,'" *Biblica* 67 (1986): 153-176; David Peter Seccombe, *Possessions and the Poor in Luke-Acts*, Studien zum Neuen Testament und seiner Umwelt, ed. Albert Fuchs, series B, Band 6 (Linz: Studien zum Neuen Testament und seiner Umwelt, 1982), 24-28. Seccombe wants to argue that Luke has adopted Second Isaiah's use of "the poor" to refer to Israel as opposed to the great pagan nations who oppress her, but he is eventually unable to maintain his case, finally admitting that Luke applies the epithet to the disciples of Jesus in a figurative fashion.
46. Schüssler Fiorenza, *Bread Not Stone*, 50.

Gelin traced the evolution of poverty-spirituality as far as the gathering of the Dead Sea Scrolls sect.

> Eventually it was realized that these spiritual values could be preserved only if the material conditions of poverty were reinvented; this is the meaning of the vow [i.e., the covenant] that took shape in the desert of Judah. True spiritual poverty can never exist without material poverty. Is this not the lesson that the Qumranites teach at the threshold of the New Testament?[47]

Indeed, the existence of the Dead Sea Scrolls sect, who sang, "For thou wilt deliver into the hands of the poor the enemies from all the lands, to humble the mighty of the peoples by the hands of those bent to the dust" *(War Scroll* 11:13),[48] as well as the self-styled "Ebionites" would seem to be sufficient proof that in the days of the early church there were plenty of people who viewed themselves as the pious poor, not least the Jerusalem church (Galatians 2:10). And among the newly published Dead Sea Scrolls, see the numerous references to the pious *Anawim* in the text called *Hymns of the Poor,* 4Q434, 436.[49]

If we find ourselves looking for a group of Christian *Anawim* from whom the canticles of Luke's infancy source might have stemmed, is there any better candidate than the widows,[50] whose embodiment appears in the source as Anna the prophetess? In the pre-Lukan version she and her canticle formed the very climax. This is precisely what we would expect in a widow tradition.

Whether William Ramsey was in any position to recognize it if he saw it, I will not venture to say, but it is interesting to note that he thought to detect "a womanly spirit in the whole [infancy] narrative, which seems inconsistent with the transmission from man to man."[51]   Ramsey, absurdly, to my way of thinking, inferred from this that the narrative embodied the recollections of

---

47. Gelin, *Poor,* 74.
48. Cf. Thurston, *Widows,* 24, on the possibility of an order of widows attached to the Dead Sea Scrolls sect.
49. Eisenman and Wise, *Dead Sea Scrolls,* 233-241.
50. Cf. Robert Murray, *Symbols of Church and Kingdom: A Study in Early Syriac Tradition* (New York: Cambridge University Press, 1975), 28-29.
51. William Ramsey, *Was Christ Born in Bethlehem?* (London: Hodder & Stoughton, 1898), 88; quoted in Charles Caldwell Ryrie, *The Role of Women in the Church* (Chicago: Moody Press, 1978), 25.

the Virgin Mary. But if he is judged correct about the female perspective of the material, I think we can account for it by positing the origin and transmission of the story and the canticles among the widow communities.

Here one cannot help but think of the story in 1 Samuel, where another Hannah prays, yet her voice is silent.

> Hannah was speaking in her heart; only her lips moved, and her voice was not heard; therefore Eli took her to be a drunken woman. And Eli said "How long will you be drunken? Put away your wine from you." But Hannah answered, "No, my lord. . . . I have drunk neither wine nor strong drink, but I have been pouring out my soul before the Lord" (1:11-15).

Eli's brusque words to Hannah strikingly recall the jeers of the crowd on the day of Pentecost, and in both cases the reader is to discount the objection. The New Testament Anna speaks without words because Luke no more than Eli trusts the utterances of women which he fears will be as drunken gibberish.

Philip's Daughters Who Do Not Prophesy

I believe we have another, very similar, case of the Lukan silencing of women in what remains of the story of the four daughters of Philip (Acts 21:8-14). Again, Tannehill sees nothing amiss here, nothing that might make us think twice about the cherished notion that Luke promotes women's ministry:

> Before the prophet Agabus is introduced in 21:10, the narrator mentions that Philip had "four virgin daughters who were prophesying" (21:9). We hear nothing further about them. Apparently the narrator simply wanted to mention that there were female prophets in the early church. . . . In any case, women as well as men can be inspired speakers of Gods revelations in Luke-Acts.[52]

Even though they don't.

Luke Timothy Johnson tries valiantly to avoid recognizing the subtext of the passage, protesting that it cannot mean what it seems to mean:

---

52. Tannehill, *Narrative Unity: Luke*, 134-135.

> There may be no special point attached to the reference to Philip's daughters as "virgins" (*parthenoi*), although prophetesses in Hellenistic religion . . . were often *parthenoi*. . . . In later apocryphal Acts of the Apostles, we begin to see the formation of distinct groups of Christian "virgins" (see *Acts of Paul and Thecla 7*). The anarthrous present participle *propheteuousai* should be taken as a means of identifying them rather than to something they did on this occasion.[53]

He as much as admits that what we seem to see here is a community of prophetic, celibate women of a type well known in the second century, who would naturally be expected to prophesy in the story before us, but who for some reason do not. Why does Luke describe them in terms of their characteristic function of prophecy if that function is to prove utterly irrelevant to the story?

F. F. Bruce, ever the harmonist, takes the odd silence of women who, after all, are introduced as prophetesses, as evidence, as if he needed any, for the sterling historicity of the account. "Had the writer of Acts been a romancer, he would certainly not have missed the opportunity of putting some specific prophecies into the young ladies' mouths."[54] Here Bruce parallels Schleiermacher's argument that Anna must be a historical figure, since Luke did not grace her with a song to sing when he was passing out the music to the other characters.

But my response here is the same as in the former case: the very artifice of the narrative is what leads us to expect the female characters to say something in the first place, and the surprising fact that they do not should prompt us to ask whether we have not the remnants of a disfigured literary source.

Wellhausen found it puzzling that the four women "are indeed expressly introduced as [*propheteuousai*], but afterwards make no use at all of their talents, no matter how much the occasion calls for it."[55] Similarly Conzelmann: "There appears to be no reason for the mention of the four prophetic daughters,

---

53. Luke Timothy Johnson, *The Acts of the Apostles*. Sacra Pagina Series, ed. Daniel Harrington, vol. 5 (Collegeville, MN: Liturgical Press, 1992), 369-370.
54. F. F. Bruce, *Commentary on the Book of Acts* (Grand Rapids: William B. Eerdmans Publishing Company, 1960), 424.
55. Julius Wellhausen, quoted in Haenchen, *Acts*, 603.

because in this instance they do not prophesy; but the comment does contribute to the mood for the following episode. Does this comment come from the source . . .?"[56] Indeed, I think, it does, originally accompanied by a prophecy, which was rudely displaced by Luke's redaction.

Haenchen's own solution, that there was no prophecy, either by the women or by Agabus, in the itinerary source Luke used, seems to me the most miserable of all options: it envisions Luke using, for some reason, a terse, barren source that amounted to a set of bones minus any meat. At any rate, it only pushes the problem back one step: if Luke was going to supply a prophecy of doom, why did he not attribute it to the women, who were already mentioned in the source as being on the scene? Why bring in Agabus from off stage, unless the point was to keep the women conspicuous precisely in their silence?

This, of course, is also why Luke does not remove them altogether from the account. They must be shown being silent, in the spirit of Origen's later rationalization (*Fragment on 1 Corinthians* 74) that they used to prophesy, all right, but only behind the closed doors of their father's house![57]

Rackham and Bauernfeind had so vigorously followed the trajectory set by the introduction of the four prophesying virgins that they leaped the gap even after the bridge had been washed out, reading what was not in the text: "the following verses suggest that they too uttered warnings to S.Paul."[58] "Dass in den prophetischen Reden der vier Jungfrauen auch die Ereignisse der nächsten Zukunft berührt worden sind, darf man im Sinne der Erzählung wohl annehmen."[59] Loisy's eye, as usual, was keen:

> In the account of the halt at Caesarea, in the house of
> Philip, the mention of his four prophetically-gifted

56. Hans Conzelmann, *Acts of the Apostles,* trans. James Limburg, A. Thomas Kraabel and Donald H. Juel, Hermeneia Series, ed. Helmut Koester (Philadelphia: Fortress Press, 1987), 178.

57. Claude Jenkins, "Origen on 1 Corinthians," *Journal of Theological Studies* 10 (1908-1909): 41-42; MacDonald, *Legend,* 35; Schüssler Fiorenza, *In Memory of Her,* 301.

58. Richard Belevard Rackham, *The Acts of the Apostles: An Exposition,* Westminster Commentaries, ed. Walter Lock (London: Methuen & Co., 1901; rpt. 1951), 400.

59. Otto Bauernfeind, *Kommenatar und Studien zur Apostelgeschichte,* Wissenschaftliche Untersuchungen zum Neuen Testament 22 (Tübingen: J. C. B. Mohr [Paul Siebeck], 1980), 241.

> daughters would naturally be followed by some pre-
> diction on their part, but none is forthcoming. Instead
> of it the compiler has substituted a prediction by Aga-
> bus (10-11). . . . But the conclusion of the incident (12-
> 14), which comes from the source, seems to indicate
> that Paul's answer followed a prediction given by
> Philip's prophetic daughters.[60]

What became of the missing oracle? Loisy and Wendt sur-
mised that Luke did not so much substitute another prophecy as
substitute another speaker for the same prophecy: the surprised
Agabus, whom one may imagine rudely whisked away by authorial fiat, like poor Habakkuk who, right in the middle of dinner,
was carried by the angel to the side of Daniel, a fellow prophet
who needed a hand (Bel and the Dragon vv. 33-39). Wendt:
"something has been omitted from the report in the source,
namely the fact that it was these daughters of Philip who tear-
fully spoke of Paul's fate."[61]

Jüngst even thought that it was originally one of the women
who performed the prophetic charade of the girdle-binding.[62]
Loisy, however, could not imagine that such peculiar gymnastics
were any more than Lukan embellishing, since he could envision
neither the prophetesses nor Agabus as being sufficiently spry to
master the requisite contortions.[63] Yet perhaps the truth lies
somewhere between Jüngst and Loisy.

Your Daughters Shall (Not) Prophesy

The mention of binding oneself with a girdle in the course of
a mantic trance reminds me of the closing sequence of the *Testament of Job*, in which Job, having bequeathed all his worldly
goods to his sons, is petitioned by his three daughters for an
inheritance of their own. Has he quite forgotten them? No,
indeed not. From a strongbox Job produces

60. Alfred Loisy, *The Origins of the New Testament*, trans. L. P. Jacks (London: George Allen & Unwin, 1950), 215.
61. Hans Heinrich Wendt, *Die Apostelgeschichte*, Kritisch-exegetischer
Kommentar über des Neue Testament, ed. H. A. W. Meyer, part 3, 9th
ed. (Göttingen: Vandehoeck & Ruprecht, 1913), 298n, quoted in
Haenchen, *Acts*, 603.
62. Johannes Jüngst, *Die Quellen der Apostelgeschichte* (Gotha: Perthes,
1895), 177, quoted in Haenchen, *Acts*, 603.
63. Alfred Loisy, *Les Actes des Apôtres* (Paris: Emile Nourry, 1920), 785,
quoted in Haenchen, *Acts*, 603.

three cords of many colours, such as no man could
possibly describe; for they were not of earth but of
heaven, flashing with sparks of fire like the rays of the
sun. And he gave one cord each to his daughters, saying, Take them and gird them around you, that they
may keep you safe all the days of your life and fill you
with every good thing (46:7-9).

It seems that when in the canonical Book of Job God told Job to
"Arise, gird yourself like a man, and I will speak with you," he
gave Job the wherewithal to do it! The mystic cords, one infers,
were necessary to enable Job to hear the voice from the cyclone
and make sense of it. Having no further need, one must suppose,
to hear from the Almighty (he will be seeing him face to face soon
enough!), he passes them on to his daughters. Donning them, the
virgins break forth into glossolalic ecstasies!

Hemera got up and wound her rope about her . . . and
she assumed another heart, no longer minding earthly
things [cf. 1 Corinthians 7:34]. And she gave utterance
in the speech of angels, sending up a hymn to God
after the pattern of the angels hymnody; and the Spirit
let the hymns she uttered be recorded on her robe.
And then Cassia girded herself, and she too experienced a change of heart, so that she no longer gave
thought to worldly things. And her mouth took up
the speech of the heavenly powers, and she lauded the
worship of the heavenly sanctuary. So if anyone
wants to know about the worship that goes on in
heaven, he can find it in the hymns of Cassia. And the
remaining one, the one called Amaltheias-Keras [=
"Cornucopia"], put on her girdle; and she likewise
gave utterance with her mouth in the speech of those
on high. Her heart too was changed and withdrawn
from worldly things; and she spoke in the language of
the cherubim, extolling the Lord of Virtues, and proclaiming their glory. Anyone who would pursue the
Father's glory any further will find it set out in the
prayers of Amaltheias-Keras. (48:1-3; 49:1-3; 50:1-3)[64]

---

64. I am using R. Thornhill's translation of the *Testament of Job* in H. F. D.
Sparks, *The Apocryphal Old Testament* (Oxford: Clarendon Press, 1984),
645-646.

Pieter W. van der Horst suggests that the *Testament of Job* stems from a charismatic community of women, including widows,[65] who are actually depicted as a singing group in the book:

> "I had six harps and a six-stringed lyre. And every day, after the widows had been fed, I would get up and take the lyre and play it for them, and they would sing. And with the harp I would remind them of God, so that they might glorify the Lord" (14:1-3).

Spittler has suggested, plausibly to my mind, that since the only *Sitz-im-Leben* known to us combining glossolalia with interpretation of the Bible is not Judaism but the early church, we ought to locate the *Testament of Job* in a Montanist milieu.[66] Certainly women prophets were prominent among them, and they were not much later than Luke by my reckoning. In either case, we have reason to believe that the techniques of prophetic ecstasy displayed in the scene just quoted from the *Testament of Job* represent those actually used by prophetic virgins, either Jewish or Christian. And if that is the case, I suspect it is equally the case with Philip's daughters.

That is, my guess is that the source or tradition Luke used originally had Philip's daughters don oracular girdles (cf. the old Ephod breastplate) to foretell, Cassandra-like, the doom of Paul. In turn, this version of the story reflected the actual practice of early Christian prophetic women. These women would have been found in the communities of widows, just as van der Horst suggests in the case of the *Testament of Job*. Indeed the similarities between the three virgin daughters of Job and the four virgin daughters of Philip are numerous and striking, pointing to more than a coincidence.

Both groups of women are presented as daughters, i.e., dependents, of a famous pious man. In the lore of the Dionysiac

---

65. Pieter van der Horst, "Images of Women in the Testament of Job," in *Studies on the Testament of Job*, eds., Michael A. Knibb and Pieter van der Horst, Society for New Testament Studies Monograph Series, ed. G. N. Stanton, 66 (New York: Cambridge University Press, 1989), 114.
66. Russell P. Spittler, "Introduction to *Testament of Job*," in *The Old Testament Pseudepigrapha Vol. 1, Apocalyptic Literature and Testaments*, ed. James H. Charlesworth (New York: Doubleday & Co., 1983), 834; Russell P. Spittler, "The Testament of Job: A History of Research," in *Studies on the Testament of Job*, 58-69.

religion, a movement of prophetic women, we hear of several sets of three sisters inspired by Dionysus, all designated as daughters of a named father, the daughters of Minyas at Orchomenos, of Proteus at Argos, of Eleuther at Eleutherae, of Cadmus at Thebes.[67] It bears mention that the groups of inspired Maenads were understood to play the symbolic role of the nurses of the infant Dionysus, hence the nursing of woodland animals at the breast of the Bacchantes in Euripides' *Bacchae*. Legend had it that baby Dionysus was also suckled by the goat Amaltheias (Capricorn).[68] Is it coincidence that one of Jobs Maenad-like daughters is named Amaltheias-Keras, "Amaltheias' Horn"? Conceivably the occurrence of the name in the *Testament of Job* may denote a now-untraceable connection, perhaps some syncretism issuing in a kind of Jewish Maenadism.

In view of all this, we might wonder if the Job text dimly attests the existence of a group of consecrated women under the patronage of a pious benefactor of widows. They would have been his spiritual daughters, not necessarily his biological offspring. They may have included both younger virgins and aged widows, both, as we have seen, mentioned as spiritual singers in the *Testament of Job*. Philip's daughters, too, may have been spiritual daughters of their benefactor, not necessarily natural ones.

Indeed, in view of the claim of Papias to have met and conversed with the daughters of Philip, I wonder if their presence in a story about Paul should not be recognized as an anachronism. Can these women already have been renowned prophetesses in the mid-50s and yet still available as informants in the era of Papias nearly a century later? I suspect it is the failure to understand the figurative connection between a household of consecrated charismatic virgins and their patron saint Philip that led somewhere along the line to this apparent anachronism. If "Daughters of Philip" was the name of a long-lived prophetic sisterhood, cherishing the pro-widow traditions of the itinerant Philip, rather than referring to members of an actual nuclear family, there is no reason both Paul and Papias might not have encountered different members of the group many decades

67. E. R. Dodds, ed., *Euripides, Bacchae*, with Introduction and Commentary by E. R. Dodds, 2nd ed. (Oxford: Clarendon Press, 1960), xxvi; Walter F. Otto, *Dionysus: Myth and Cult*, trans. with an Introduction by Robert B. Palmer (Bloomington: Indiana University Press, 1965), 172-173.
68. R. F. Willetts, *Cretan Cults and Festivals* (London: Routledge & Kegan Paul, 1962), 215.

apart.

H. E. Coker admits that "In the four 'virgins' or 'unmarried daughters' there is a temptation to see implied here a kind of order of 'virgins.'" But he concludes his senses must be deceiving him: "It is to be doubted though that such an order existed this early in the life of the Church." Infected with the epidemic historicizing bias he must relegate the women to the status of mere "precursors," a harmonizing euphemism meaning that they just do not fit where they should in his time line.[69]

Philip, of course, is one of the Seven chosen to see to it that the Hellenistic widows were no longer neglected in the table service (Acts 6:1-6). Job, on the other hand, is said to have seen to the widows' food needs as well: "My slaves who cooked the widows' food grew weary. . . . And I would put an end to their fault-finding and complaining" (13:4; 14:5; cf. the murmuring of or on behalf of the widows, to which the appointment of Philip was the solution in 6:1). This is perhaps a development of the exchange between Job and his accuser Eliphaz of Teman in the canonical Book of Job. Eliphaz assumes that Job must have merited his miseries by, say, refusing to aid widows (22:9), Job indignantly replying that he did no such thing (31:16).

To Job's daughters are ascribed certain glossolalic hymns cherished by the *Testament*'s community, as we have seen. Interestingly, Rackham, innocent of these matters, hypothesized that "The daughters of Philip may have exercised their gift in the utterance of such hymns as that of the Blessed Virgin."[70]

Recall what I suggested above as to the widow origin of the infancy source with its canticles. In this connection it is interesting to note the words of Gregory of Nyssa as he waxes rhapsodic anent the glories of consecrated virginity: "The power of virginity . . . is such that it abides in the heavens with the Father of Spirits; it is in the chorus of the celestial powers."[71] In Methodius's *Symposium* he promises consecrated virgins that they will be enthroned near Christ, their Heavenly Bridegroom, one with his choir, and dispensing his rewards to the sanctified.[72] In the fifth-

---

69. H. E. Coker, "Women and the Gospel in Luke-Acts" (Th.D. diss.: Southern Baptist Theological Seminary, 1954), 138, 139.
70. Rackham, *Acts*, 400.
71. Clark, *Women in the Early Church*, 119.
72. Rosamund M. Nugent, *Portrait of the Consecrated Woman in Greek Christian Literature of the First Four Centuries* (Washington, DC: Catholic University of America Press, 1941), 16.

century *Discourse of St. John the Divine Concerning the Falling Asleep of the Holy Mother of God* we read that once the body of Mary arrived in Paradise all worshipped it to the strains of heavenly music: ". . . and a melody . . . praised him that was born of her: and unto virgins only is it given to hear that sweet melody wherewith no man can be sated." It would not be surprising if already in Luke's time the community of virgins/widows were the composers of inspired hymns, like the celibate Therapeutridae of Philo.[73]

As if the mere fact of their prophetic gift were not enough to parallel Philip's daughters with Jobs, we ought to remember that Philip himself is probably to be associated with the practice of glossolalia, as this was in all likelihood what Luke intended that Simon Magus saw and wanted to buy in Acts 8:18-19. And for Luke there is but a thin line separating prophecy from tongues (Acts 2:11; 10:46; 19:6). Both groups of women, then, seem closely associated with glossolalia. And when each group appears in a single narrative in which girdles, of all things, are associated with prophecy, surely it is no mere coincidence.

Lastly, it is interesting that neither text actually contains the content of the women's prophecies. The narrator of the *Testament of Job* recounts:

> After the three had finished singing their hymns, I, Nereos, Job's brother, sat down . . . and I listened to my brother's three daughters as they discussed together the great things. And I wrote down this book, except for the hymns and the signs of the word, for these are the mysteries of God. (51:1-4)

Luke, on Loisy's and Wendt's theory, which I accept, omitted to include, not the revelation, but the identity of its author, a rather significant difference. Loisy and Wendt hazarded no guess as to Luke's reason for the rather cumbersome change. Tetlow and D'Angelo both correctly see the way the redaction of the passage is leaning, though without seeing the full extent of Luke's surgery.[74]

We know that in the late second century Philip's daughters were an exegetical battleground in the debate over women's min-

---

73. Kraemer, "Monastic," 344.
74. Tetlow, *Women and Ministry*, 108; D'Angelo, "Women in Luke-Acts," 453.

istry. Even in their silence they spoke volumes, as if by a potent glance that needs no words. The Montanists appealed to them, and Origen sought to rebut such proof-texting, special-pleading that the daughters only proclaimed the word of the Lord behind closed doors, not in public (*Fragment on 1 Corinthians* 74). Here is the trajectory along which Acts 21:8-9 may be placed at an earlier stage: in its original form as a widow tradition it provided a stronger precedent for the Montanist position; in redacting it as he did, Luke was already trying to silence the text as Origen later did for the same reason.

It is interesting here just to note the theory of Benjamin W. Bacon that the Apocalypse of John is not, as is often said, the only member of the apocalypse genre that is not pseudonymous.[75] Perhaps its true author employed "John" as a pen name much as others used "Enoch" or "Baruch." But why?

Does not the very genre of apocalypse flourish when prophecy is on the wane, or officially frowned on? And are apocalypses not usually attributed to faith heroes of a previous generation who were not prophets but scribes or patriarchs? Suppose the Johannine apocalyptist were someone living in one of the seven cities in Asia Minor to whom the Revelation was addressed, say Ephesus, and suppose the apocalyptist chose the name of John in veneration for his martyrdom along with his brother James (as Papias reports, and as scholars still debate). Suppose that martyrdom were hinted at in the text by masking John and James as the two witnesses killed in Jerusalem after calling down fire on their enemies as the Sons of Thunder once proposed (Luke 9:54)?

Bacon chose as the author one of Philip's daughters whom Polycrates of Ephesus says moved there (Eusebius, *Ecclesiastical History* 3.31.3). Here is a prophetic figure with a definite reason to use a pseudonym as the century wore out, and with it the church's patience with female prophecy. Whether Bacon is correct or not (and I am not inclined to dismiss his theory out of hand) the daughters of Philip do seem to have received the same treatment at Luke's hands: their prophecy survived through history attributed to a male prophet instead. And they, like Anna, were showcased as embodiments of the tame Christian woman who sits in silence while men speak the word of God.

---

75. Benjamin W. Bacon, "The Authoress of Revelation—A Conjecture," *Harvard Theological Review* 23 (July 1930): 247-249.

CHAPTER THREE

Not in Nazareth:
The Widow of Zarephath and Naaman the Leper

A Composite Passage

Luke's story of the rejection of Jesus at Nazareth (Luke 4:16-30) has occasioned a very large number of studies, a sign that the passage so treated is a trouble spot. About all that exegetes seem able to agree on is that Jesus enters the synagogue, where he is remembered, then manages to goad the congregation into forming a lynch mob, which, thanks to providential authorial fiat, he effortlessly escapes. After a review of critical opinion on the passage and its problems I will venture that the reference to the widow of Zarephath provides a clue to trace the origins of the special Lukan material in the passage. It will be seen to have originated among the circles of Hellenistic, charismatic widows and to have served originally to advance their own interests against their rivals among the Hebrew widows, mirroring the situation of Acts 6:1. While Luke betrays knowledge of a crisis situation for women in Acts 6 (though even there he employs the tradition, as we will see in Chapter 10, as a springboard for introducing his preferred male heroes), in Luke 4 the original association of the material has been eclipsed.

Exegetes divide over how to account for the puzzling aspects of the story. Some, like Bultmann, suggest that Luke has composed most of the material in the scene that does not come from Mark. Others try to salvage as much as they can of the story as traditional material knit together with minimal transitional material by the evangelist. C. M. Tuckett would be a good representative of this view. He sees Luke as drawing most of the non-Markan material from Q.

But even Bultmann and his camp do not deny that Luke used some traditional items in composing the scene. In this chapter I want to focus on two of these items. The first is the unit comprised by vv. 25-27, the recollection of Elijah's mission to the widow of Zarephath and Elisha's cure of the Syrian leper Naaman.

Many scholars, notably Evans, Marshall, Fitzmyer, and Schürmann,[1] note that vv. 25-27 just do not seem to fit the adjacent verses. Bultmann says they

> clearly came to Luke from the tradition. . . . There is no
> proper connection between vv. 25-27 and what pre-
> cedes; even if v. 24 is a gloss, there is no connection
> with v. 23. . . . In order to fit vv. 25-27 in, Luke has, as I
> suppose, constructed a scene on the pattern of Mk. 6:1-
> 6, and at the same time in v. 23 used the [*parabole*]
> which had been handed down in another context.[2]

Others hold that it does fit its context reasonably well but admit
nonetheless that it is a piece of independent tradition grafted in
here by Luke.[3]

The reason 25-27 cannot follow from 23 even with the omission of 24 is succinctly stated by Schürmann:

> Die zweite Pointe VV 25ff mit ihrem Ausblick auf die
> spätere Heidenmission ist in der Vaterstadtszene an
> sich nicht grundgelegt. Sie gibt der Perikope eine
> neue universalistische Dimension. V 23 heisst der
> Gegensatz Nazareth—Kapharnaum, in VV 25ff
> Israel—Völkerwelt.   Dass ausserdem V 25 mit der
> (ursprünglich) gleichen [*amen*-] Formel beginnt wie V
> 24, macht eine Naht sichtbar.[4]

Tannehill reiterates: "the sharp change in point of view, with
no attempt to relate the two aspects, is here a reflection of the sep-

---

1. C. F. Evans, *Saint Luke,* TPI New Testament Commentaries, gen. eds.
Howard Clark Kee and Dennis Nineham (London: SCM Press; Philadelphia: Trinity Press International, 1990), 275; I. Howard Marshall, *Commentary on Luke,* New International Greek Testament Commentaries, eds.
I. Howard Marshall and W. Ward Gasque (Grand Rapids: William B. Eerdmans Publishing Company, 1978), 180, 188-189; Fitzmyer, *Luke I-IX,*
526; H. Schürmann, *Das Lukasevangelium, Erster Teil, Kommentar zu Kap. 1,
1-9, 50,* Herders Theologischer Kommentar zum NT. (Freiburg: Herder,
1969), 241-244.
2. Bultmann, *History,* 32.
3. W. R. F. Browning, *The Gospel According to Saint Luke: A Commentary,* A
Torch Biblical Commentary, gen. eds. John Marsh and Alan Richardson
(New York: Collier Books, 1962), 61; Larrimore C. Crockett, "Luke 4:25-
27 and Jewish-Gentile Relations in Luke-Acts," *Journal of Biblical Literature* 88 (1969): 178; Robert Hausman, "The Function of Elijah as a Model
in Luke-Acts" (Ph.D. diss.: University of Chicago, 1975), 94.
4. Schürmann, *Lukasevangelium,* 243.

arate origin of these sayings."[5]

Tannehill goes on to reject Masson's proposed harmonization that what Luke/Jesus means is to argue from the greater (God's prophets didn't ever heal fellow countrymen) to the lesser (his prophet cannot be expected to heal his fellow townspeople). Precisely what is missing in the text, Tannehill notes, is any indication of such a connection. Even more contrived are the attempts, along somewhat the same lines, of Koet,[6] Combrinck,[7]-Hill,[8] and Nolland.[9]

It all reduces to the question of

> whether these verses were originally meant to be understood in light of that limited historical situation [i.e., why no miracles in Nazareth?]. When we relate these verses to Luke-Acts as a whole, we discover a different explanation of the position and function of these verses: they were inserted here by Luke in order to suggest the connection between the rejection of Jesus and his turning to others which occurs at Nazareth and the rejection of the gospel by the Jews and the turning of the missionaries to the Gentiles which Luke will trace in Acts. (Tannehill)[10]

As for vv. 25-27 themselves, prior to Luke's redactional interest in them, "these verses provide an argument from the Old Testament for a mission to the Gentiles and are most naturally explained as arising from the early church's argument over a mission to the Gentiles."[11]

Bultmann sees in the verses a slightly different nuance. They presuppose the Gentile mission, to be sure, but the focus is rather

---

5. Robert C. Tannehill, "The Mission of Jesus According to Luke iv 16-30," in *Jesus in Nazareth,* ed. W. Eltester (Berlin: de Gruyter, 1972), 59.

6. B. J. Koet, "'Today this Scripture has been fulfilled in your ears,' Jesus' explanation of Scripture in Luke 4:16-30," *Bijdragen* 47 (1986): 383, 392.

7. H. J. B. Combrinck, "The Structure and Significance of Luke 4:16-30," *Neotestamentica* 7 (1973): 38.

8. David Hill, "The Rejection of Jesus at Nazareth (Luke 4:16-30)," *Novum Testamentum* 13 (1971): 169.

9. Nolland, *Luke,* 201.

10. Tannehill, "Mission," 59.

11. Ibid., 60; cf. Stephen G. Wilson, *The Gentiles and the Gentile Mission in Luke-Acts,* Society for New Testament Studies Monograph Series, ed. Matthew Black, 23 (New York: Cambridge University Press, 1973), 40-41.

on the bypassing of the unresponsive Jews. "It may well be a secondary community construction, introduced into the anti-Jewish polemic of the Gentile Christian Church."[12]

The verses would then be an expression of the Gentile triumphalism rejected in Romans 11:17-19. This, of course, would have to be a very late sentiment. How early could it have become clear that the Jews, virtually *in toto*, had rejected the Christian gospel? Luke 4:25-27 are looking back from some time in the early second century at the earliest (as are Romans 11:17ff, by my reckoning, part of a late section added to the body of the epistle).[13] Schmeichel suggests that "Luke wanted to make the statement of rejection so absolute that there was no single instance of acceptance to be found in all of Israel."[14] Lukan redactional intent aside, the passage itself can be taken to imply something very much like the totalism Schmeichel describes. And thus it is revealed as a parallel to a well-known Q saying, "not even in Israel have I found such faith" (Luke 7:9b).

Yet at the same time, Nolland is exactly wrong when he says,

> nor is there a stress on what outsiders received (two people aided is hardly an impressive achievement): the emphasis falls rather on the many needy widows and lepers in Israel who remained without help, despite the fact that there was a prophet in Israel (2 Kgs 5:8).[15]

Rather, the point is surely to contrast the many left unaided with the chosen few who were helped: "There were plenty of widows

---

12. Bultmann, *History*, 116.

13. On the late date of Romans 9-11 see the summaries of the opinions of Bruno Bauer, Daniel Völter, Friedrich Spitta, W. C. van Manen, Robert Martyr Hawkins, and J. C. O'Neill in Albert Schweitzer, *Paul and His Interpreters: A Critical History*, trans. W. Montgomery (London: Adam & Charles Black, 1912), 143, 149, and in J. C. O'Neill, *Paul's Letter to the Romans* (Baltimore: Penguin Books, 1975), 286-287, 295, 301, 307; W. C. van Manen, "Romans (Epistle)," *Encyclopaedia Biblica*, 1914, 4134-4136. Other discussions of the theory provide little except outraged fulminations against it.

14. Waldemar Schmeichel, "Christian Prophecy in Lukan Thought: Luke 4: 16-30 as a Point of Departure," in *Society of Biblical Literature 1976 Seminar Papers*, ed. G. MacRae (Missoula: Scholars Press, 1976), 295.

15. Nolland, *Luke*, 201.

in Israel to choose from had he wanted to help an Israelite, but he chose a Gentile widow instead." The former were rejected all right, but the point of highlighting that fact is to underscore the preference for the few helped. They were perhaps worth more than the rest put together! Or such was the inference.

The Gentile Widow

I would like to suggest that we take the reference to the widow of Zarephath as a pointer to the origin of vv. 25-27 in the *Sitz-im-Leben* of the widows. Specifically I think we have here the widows' own side of the dispute recorded in Acts 6:1-6, which is told there from a rather different viewpoint. Let me hasten to point out that I hardly imagine Acts 6:1-6 to represent events so early in the Christian community as Luke makes them seem.

The rejection by most scholars of Henry Cadbury's theory that the Hellenists of Acts 6 are Greeks[16] depended on a naive historicizing tendency, as if the one thing we could not question in the story is the placement of the scene in the early days of the Jerusalem church. Actually, in view of Luke's redactional habits, I should say that finding the incident in its actual historical position is the last thing we ought to expect! Would it not make more sense to envision the dispute over distribution among Hebrews and Hellenists as occurring in some place like Antioch? And, as Georgi points out, it would be more natural for Jews to be called "Hebrews" outside their homeland.[17]

I suspect the tendency to anchor the story in Jerusalem comes from the connection of the story to the primitive communism of the Jerusalem church. But scholars have long known that the Jerusalem communism is another Lukan invention, an attempt to portray the earliest church as the primordial community of friends who share all their possessions, the ideal attested in several Greek writers from Plato onward.[18]

The story clearly depends on some kind of food distribution, but we have that aspect covered in the simple fact that the prob-

16. Henry J. Cadbury, "The Hellenists," in *The Beginnings of Christianity, Part I: The Acts of the Apostles*, eds. F.J. Foakes Jackson and Kirsopp Lake, Vol. V, Additional Notes to the Commentary, ed. Kirsopp Lake and Henry Cadbury (London: Macmillan & Co., 1933), 59-74.
17. Georgi, *Opponents*, 41-46.
18. Martin Dibelius, "The First Christian Historian," in *Studies in the Acts of the Apostles*, ed. Heinrich Greeven (London: SCM Press, 1973), 128; Kirsopp Lake, "The Communism of Acts", in *Beginnings* V, 140-151.

lem is with the neglect of one category of widows to the advantage of another. Distribution of alms or the church stipend to
widows was well known to Luke, or at least was current in his
general time-frame, as we can see from 1 Timothy chapter 5.

Joseph B. Tyson views the Hellenist widows as Gentiles pure
and simple.[19] So does Larrimore C. Crockett.[20] Crockett thinks
the point of Luke's inclusion of 4:25-27 in his gospel is to anticipate and facilitate Jewish-Gentile table fellowship, perhaps a
problem among the community for which he writes. He cites
Acts 6:1-6 among other passages where the issue seems to be
implicit.[21] I am attempting to tie the two passages more closely
together. I say they are two sides of the same coin.

Tyson perceptively suggests that the problem with distribution to Hellenist and Hebrew widows stemmed from the same
cause as the dissention in Antioch that led to the split between
Cephas and Paul (Galatians 2:11-14). The problem was whether
Gentile widows had to keep kosher to get anything to eat.
Hebrew members of the congregation simply could not bring
themselves to handle the food the Gentile widows were accustomed to, so the latter went without, like the bleeding man in the
roadside ditch, whom ceremonial purity regulations required the
passing priest and Levite to leave where he was (Luke 10:29-32f).
But just as a Samaritan who gave not a thought for the purity
laws was religiously able to help the man in need (vv. 33-35), so
the selection of fellow Hellenists (Gentiles) made it possible for
the Gentile widows to receive their rations again with ceremonial
compromise on no one's part.

But where comes Luke 4:25-27 in all this? I suspect it arose
amid the bitter acrimony over food. Hence the recollection of the
starving widow, not an Israelite, whom God and his prophet
(also not a Jew, by the way, but a "Samaritan," i.e., an Israelite of
the North!) did not abandon. Here, incidentally, is the answer to
Esler's question,

> If . . . scholars are correct in seeing in the references to
> the widow of Zarephath and to Naaman the Syrian in
> Lk 4.25-7 a prediction and authorization by Jesus of a
> future Gentile mission what are we to make of the

---

19. Joseph B. Tyson, "Acts 6:1-7 and Dietary Regulations in Early Christianity," *Perspectives in Religious Studies* 10 (1983): 157-158.
20. Crockett, "Jewish-Gentile Relations," 183.
21. Ibid., 182-183.

> widow's being numbered among the poor who were
> on the brink of death by starvation (1 Kgs 17.12)?[22]

The pericope came from widows whose rations were endangered because of a dispute against Hebrew Christians over dietary laws.

As Rentería shows quite clearly, the Old Testament traditions of Elijah and Elisha and their widow clients must have functioned as enabling stories for exactly such people as were portrayed in the stories. They never lost that function. In Luke 4:25-27 (the precedent of) Elijah's patronage is claimed for the Gentile widows with a sidelong sneer at the Hebrews, at whom the Almighty must look askance as he did in Elijah's day.

Naaman the Syrian

If the interest of the Christian widows in the figure of Elijah and that of the widow of Zarephath is natural enough, we must still account for the presence of Naaman in the pericope. Can he be made to fit into a widow *Sitz-im-Leben*? Indeed he can.

Crockett shows how natural it is to suppose that Luke understood the Naaman story as a prefiguration both of the healing of the Centurion's slave (Luke 7:1-10) and of the conversion of Cornelius and those like him who enriched the church both spiritually and monetarily when they joined. The uncleanness of Naaman equals the uncleanness of the Gentile *per se*. The Centurion's concern for his servant recalls the concern of Naaman's servant girl for him. In both cases the servant is the cause of the Gentile military man approaching the man of God. And the uncleanness is taken away by baptism/dipping. Naaman's loaded saddlebags prefigure Cornelius' liberal alms as well as the liberality of the Centurion (as painted by Luke's redaction of the Q tradition) bankrolling the erection of a new synagogue.[23]

The Centurion story is pre-Lukan in most of its essentials, though Luke may well have created Cornelius from whole cloth. But the similarity of Naaman and the Centurion must have been obvious to others beside Luke, as must have been the parallel between Naaman and the wealthy Gentile patrons of the church.

I suggest that such patrons would have been especially important to Christian widows who received individual benefac-

---

22. Esler, *Community and Gospel*, 164.
23. Crockett, "Jewish-Gentile Relations," 182-183.

tions from the wealthy (1 Timothy 6:17-19) or whose patronage by wealthy individuals saved them from dependence on the church. One such independent patron would be the Roman senator Marcellus in the *Acts of Peter*, a patron of widows who lived in his home.

I think what would have caught the eye of widows in the Naaman story was the instrumentality of Naaman's slave girl, who put him on the trail of the man of God, playing the role of the angel in Luke's Cornelius story.[24] The maiden/virgin is in effect the conduit of Naaman's healing/baptism just as truly as the prophet! We have seen that widows taught, and as late as the *Didascalia* they were still teaching the faith to outsiders, though the author thought they ought to stop since they could not help but make the faith a laughingstock. Naaman, led to baptism and cleansing by the agency of a maiden worshipper of the true God, stands for Gentile patrons converted to the faith by widow evangelism.

What You Did in Capernaum

Verse 23 seems to be another piece of pre-Lukan tradition.[25]

---

24. Laffey notes the glossing over of the important role the servant girl played in the original story (Alice L. Laffey, *An Introduction to the Old Testament: A Feminist Perspective* [Philadelphia: Fortress Press, 1988], 136-137). I wonder if that story in its canonical form represents a curtailment of an original, fuller version of the story formed on the lines of the stories of Joseph, Daniel, and Esther, in which a Jew living as a captive in a foreign land does some favor for his or her Gentile master and rises to high prestige as a result. These were all, of course, paradigms for young Jews of the Diaspora. I suspect that, before being toned down by the Deuteronomic redactor, the Naaman story made the role of the servant girl even more important. One surviving vestige of the earlier version is the panic of the Israelite king when he receives the letter: if Elisha did not heal Naaman was there the danger of Syro-Israelite war? The suspense over whether Naaman will overcome his outrage at the humiliating anticlimax of Elisha's prescription assumes a new dramatic importance. War and peace hang in the balance. All hinges on the success of the servant who pleads with Naaman to try the immersion anyway. I suspect that in the original, this servant was the same one who had suggested Naaman visit Elisha in the first place. It is dramatically most natural for her to finish what she started, urging her master to take the final step as she had urged him to take the first.

25. Godet, *Luke*, 238; Walter Grundmann, *Das Evangelium nach Lukas*, Theologischer Handcommentar zum Neuen Testament III (Berlin: Evangelische Verlagsanstalt, 1966), 122; Fitzmyer, *Luke I-IX*, 526, 535.

One major reason to think so is the apparent reference to miraculous deeds already done at Capernaum. According to Luke's
chronology there can as yet have been no such deeds! Conzelmann tells us we must take the "you will say" to mean that the
synagogue audience is not at that moment prepared to make
such a demand but that at some time in the future they *will*[26]—an
incredible harmonization, if I may presume to say so, since the
issuance of the present scene clearly rules out any possibility that
Jesus will ever return to town to hear such a demand! Miracles at
Capernaum he will do; return to Nazareth, where his picture is
on the post office wall, he will not.

Grundmann seems to agree with Conzelmann that Luke
intends a prediction, but he admits it represents a refashioning of
an older version of the pericope in which the reference to deeds
wrought in Capernaum was an allusion to the recent past, not the
future: "So ist in der Gestaltung des Lukas aus einem Hinweis
auf geschehene Ereignisse in der älteren Fassung der Nazareth-
perikope eine Vorhersage kommender Ereignisse geworden."[27]

Evans thinks that the phrase "What we have heard you did
at Capernaum, do here also in your own country" did not form
part of the proverb Jesus says is sure to be cast at him.[28] Yet I suspect that just this, or most of it at any rate, is what constituted the
proverb. It looks to me as if "Physician heal thyself," a well-
known proverb, has been inserted by Luke, just as he loves to
insert popular bits of Aratus or Diodorus here and there throughout his narrative (Luke 23:42; Acts 4:19; 17:28; 20:35; 26:14). Perhaps Luke, like Mark, knew the second half of the proverb as it
appears in Thomas 31, ". . . neither does a physician cure those
who know him." I suppose that neither evangelist quotes it
because each feels that strictly speaking it was not correct: Jesus
had in fact cured some people with whom he was acquainted,
like Peter's mother-in-law, Mary Magdalene, etc. So, as Bultmann
suggested, Mark narratized it into the inabilityof Jesus to heal the
Nazarenes because of their lack of faith, while Luke substituted a
similar proverb for it (just as he substituted a more upbeat Psalm
quote, 31:5, for the easily misunderstood Psalm 22:1, in Mark).

I think, too, that Luke added "in your own country" to the

---

26. Hans Conzelmann, *The Theology of St. Luke*, trans. Geoffrey Buswell
(New York: Harper & Row, Publishers, 1961), 31-38.
27. Grundmann, *Lukas*, 122.
28. Evans, *Saint Luke*, 273.

end of v. 23, modelling it on "in his own country" in v. 24, from Mark, in order to make the traditional piece in v. 23 fit the Markan saying better.

What we are left with as the traditional core of v. 23 is this: "And he said to them, 'Doubtless [or, some translate "perhaps"] you will quote me this proverb, "What we have heard you did at Capernaum, do here also."'"

The introductory phrase, "Perhaps you will say to me," may sound like a clumsy piece of Lukan transitional tape, but I think rather of the Stoic-Cynic diatribe form so often used in Romans (1:13; 2:1, 3; 3:1, 3; 4:2; 6:3; 7:13; 9:19; 11:2, 19; 14:4, 13, 15, 19, 20, 22), whereby the soap-box preacher anticipates objections from possible hecklers in the crowd. There are numerous uses of the same device in the *Qur'an* as well (e.g., 41:25; 46:7; 81:22, 25, "No, your compatriot is not mad . . . nor is this the utterance of an accursed devil."). And here is the clue that this proverb that the speaker expects to be twitted with is a stock jibe he knows is coming at a certain point in his presentation. "I know just what you're thinking, my friends!"

Schürmann thinks that this verse comes from Q,[29] a collection of traditions from the wandering radicals of the Jesus movement.[30] Another possibility is that it came from the special Lukan source, rightly linked by Dillon with the itinerant charismatics.[31] In either case this saying originated with the itinerants. They were prepared for some skepticism once they had unfurled

29. H. Schürmann, "Zur Traditionsgeschichte der Nazareth-Perikope Lk 4, 16-30," in *Mélanges bibliques en homage au R. P. Beda Rigeaux*, eds. A. Descamps and A. de Halleuxi (Gembloux: Duculot, 1970), 187-205, cited in C. M. Tuckett, "Luke 4, 16-30, Isaiah and Q," in *Logia: Les paroles de Jesus—The Sayings of Jesus. Memorials Joseph Coppens*, ed. Joel Delobel, Bibliotheca Ephemeridum Theologicarum Lovaniensium 59 (Leuven: Leuven University Press, 1982), 344.

30. It seems to me that the case for the occurence of the Isaiah 61:1-2 citation in Q is strengthened by the use of the same text in an explicitly Messianic context in the newly published Qumran text 4Q521 *The Messiah of Heaven and Earth:* "[The Hea]vens and the earth will obey His Messiah, [and all th]at is in them. . . . He shall release the captives, make the blind see, raise up the do[wntrodden.] . . . then He will heal the sick, resurrect the dead, and to the Meek announce glad tidings" (1, 8, 12; Eisenman and Wise, *Dead Sea Scrolls*, 23). When we find the same citation in the Hebrew *Messiah of Heaven and Earth*, it is no surprise for it to occur in the Palestinian Aramaic Q.

31. Dillon, *Eye-Witnesses*, 238-242.

their aretalogies of mighty deeds done in Capernaum, Bethsaida, and Chorazin (Luke 10:13-15/Matthew 11:21-24). Now they beat the skeptic to the punch, rather in the fashion of the story-teller of the miracles of Jesus who anticipated the audience's doubts right in the middle of the tale by having the disciples or bystanders voice the same incredulity (Mark 5:30, 40; 6:37; 8:4; 9:22-23).

Marshall takes v. 23 to mean that Jesus should provide signs to attest the verbal claims that he has made.[32] Similarly O'Fearghail: "Jesus suggests to his listeners that they may ask him to attest his claims."[33] That's the point, right enough. But the historicizing bias shows itself when scholars do not ask after the *Sitz-im-Leben* for the transmission of such a saying. Again, I think Theissen has implicitly provided it.

Short of healing anyone, what would the itinerant, every eye on him, follow up with? Surely here was the utility of the saying, "Only an evil and adulterous generation seeketh after a sign. No sign will be given it save the sign of Jonah, for as Jonah was himself a sign to the Ninevites, so shall the Son of Man [—again that identification with the least of these his earthly brethren!] be unto this generation" (my paraphrase of what I take to be the Q original behind Luke 11:29-30). Luke has changed the initial phrase, which at first cleverly warned the crowd before they implicated themselves by asking for a sign. He has added the wooden "This generation is an evil generation" to implicate the generation in which Jesus was crucified.

One must wonder if Bethsaida (Luke 10:13) had declined to repent because actually they had seen no miracles, only heard of those alleged to have been performed at Capernaum (Luke 10:15). And Capernaum in turn hadn't repented because they didn't believe the tales about the itinerant's feats in Chorazin and saw none for themselves. And so on. One recalls the restraint of the rabbis of Constantinople during the visit there of the seventeenth-century messiah Sabbatai Sevi: "So far we have not beheld a single miracle or sign but only the noise of rumors and testimonies at second hand."[34]

As to the likelihood of a street-corner prophet repeatedly using such a device, we may compare many instances in the

32. Marshall, *Luke,* 187.
33. Fearghus O'Fearghail, "Rejection at Nazareth: Lk 4 22," *Zeitschrift für die Neutestamentlische Wissenschaft* 75 (1984): 72.
34. Gershom Scholem, *Sabbatai Sevi: The Mystical Messiah 1626-1676,* Bollingen Series 93 (Princeton: Princeton University Press, 1973), 612.

Qur'an, where the inspired speech of the Prophet anticipates the crowd's jeering demands for an attesting miracle, for the lack of which he has plenteous excuses at the ready (e.g., 3:183-184; 20:133).

In this chapter I have been less concerned with the redactional intentions of Luke than with the leftover clues and hints as to the origin of three pieces of the tradition he used in building the scene as we read it. He seems to have used fragments of oral tradition stemming from various quarters of the scenario traced out by Davies. The reference to the widow of Zarephath in vv. 25-26 reflects the contentions between Hebrew and Hellenist widow communities, a tension also glimpsed in Acts 6:1. The recollection of Naaman in Luke 4:27 was at first a testimonial to the faith of wealthy Gentile patrons of the consecrated widows. The Stoic-style diatribe anticipating the response of a skeptical audience (v. 23) comes from the rhetorical arsenal of the wandering charismatics who championed their fellow-ascetics, the widows.

CHAPTER FOUR

Women Received Back Their Dead:
The Widow of Nain and Dorcas

Pre-Lukan Traditions

Our next pair of candidates for widow-tradition pericopes are the stories of the resurrections of the son of the widow of Nain (Luke 7:7-17) and of Dorcas of Joppa (Acts 9:36-42).

The traditional character of the story of the widow of Nain is apparent from its kinship to a whole cycle of Hellenistic tales in which a wise man or master physician narrowly saves from premature burial someone who has lapsed into a deep coma or been poisoned but still just barely lives. The closest of these to Luke's version is one found in Philostratus' *Life of Apollonius of Tyana:*

> Here too is a miracle which Apollonius worked: A girl had died just in the hour of her marriage, and the bridegroom was following her bier lamenting as was natural, his marriage left unfulfilled, and the whole of Rome was mourning with him, for the maiden belonged to a consular family. Apollonius then witnessing their grief, said: "Put down the bier, for I will stay the tears that you are shedding for this maiden." And withal he asked what was her name. The crowd accordingly thought that he was about to deliver such an oration as is commonly delivered as much to grace the funeral as to stir up lamentation; but he did nothing of the kind, but merely touching her and whispering in secret some spell over her, at once woke up the maiden from her seeming death; and the girl spoke out loud, and returned to her father's house, just as Alcestis did when she was brought back to life by Hercules. And the relations of the maiden wanted to present him with the sum of 150,000 sesterces, but he said that he would freely present the money to the young lady by way of a dowry. (IV: XLV)

It seems to me that Fuller, Klostermann, and Bultmann are right: Luke 7:11-17 is just the Jesus version of the story applied elsewhere to Asclepiades, Apollonius, and several others.[1] As we now read it, it has taken on a superficial biblical patina

— 83 —

derived from the stories of Elijah reviving the widow's son (1 Kings 17:17ff) and of the raising of the Shunammite's son by the ministrations of Elisha (2 Kings 4:18ff). Brodie and Goulder make the Nain story a Lukan creation, modelled on the Elijah and Elisha stories,[2] while Helms sees it as the creation of "Either Luke or some Greek-speaking Christian behind Luke,"[3] but this is entirely unnecessary.

A comparison with the Apollonius version above reveals that even the two most pronounced of the apparent borrowings from Elijah's adventure, the meeting of the procession at the city gate and the tender reunion, "he gave him to his mother," are both traditional features of the story, or just as well might be. Apollonius, too, meets the funeral cortege at the city gates. Fuller notes that the story "took place at the gates of the city of Rome,"[4] as suggested by the detail that the mourners are on their way out of the city to bury the woman in the countryside, while the whole city looks on, implying they have reached the city limits.

The reunion, too, occurs in the Apollonius version, when it is noted that "she returned to her father's house." Granted, these features might come from 1 Kings, but there is no particular reason to think so. If Philostratus derived them from floating oral tradition, Luke could just as well have done the same.

Even Robert A. Hausman, whose aim is to demonstrate Luke's redactional interest in Elijah as a model for Jesus, must admit

> The story is probably not a Lukan composition, since there are many semiticisms in the text. It comes from a source that had probably already been shaped by the Old Testament stories of the raising of a widow's son by Elijah (1 Kg. 17:17-24) and Elisha (2 Kg. 4:32-37).[5]

Fuller admits the story has been Christianized by the addition of Elijah-Elisha coloring. In what did this coloring consist? Of course, in the wording at the beginning and end of the Nain

1. Reginald H. Fuller, *Interpreting the Miracles* (London: SCM Press, 1974), 64; Bultmann, *History*, 215.
2. Thomas Louis Brodie, "Luke-Acts as an Imitation and Emulation of the Elijah-Elisha Narrative," in *New Views of Luke-Acts*, 81. Goulder, 382.
3. Randel Helms, *Gospel Fictions* (Buffalo: Prometheus Books, 1989), 64.
4. Fuller, *Miracles*, 64.
5. Hausman, "Function of Elijah," 70.

story, where v. 12's "gate of the city" (*te pyle te poleos*) seems to have been copied directly from 1 Kings 17:10's "gate of the city" (*ton pylona tes poleos* in the LXX). This by itself would be pretty slender evidence, a rather nondescript phrase given the implied location in the tradition anyway. But it assumes a bit more weight when we remind ourselves that, if archaeologists have rightly pegged Luke's Nain, the town had no gate. But then perhaps it is the name, not the gate, of the city that is the added feature, since Nain is near Shunem, from the Elisha story.

A more definite Lukan echo of the LXX of 1 Kings is the wording in Luke 7:15: "And he gave him to his mother" (*kai edoken auton te metri autou*), verbatim the same as the corresponding phrase in the LXX of 1 Kings 17:23. Nolland notes these tips of the turban to the Greek text of 1 Kings, but he suggests that the feature of the dead man being the *only* son of the widow must survive from the Hebrew original, since it is omitted in the LXX. The LXX influence, what there is of it, comes, then, at a secondary stage, not just of the tradition, but of the assimilation of it to the Elijah tale. And as Nolland says, there is no particular reason to assume it was Luke who Septuagintalized the story. Perhaps it reached him this way.[6]

Widow Patronage Stories

The single clear allusion to 1 Kings, then, is the phrase "he gave him back to his mother." What is the significance of this fact? I suggest it represents no mere Septuagintal window dressing but rather signals the key element of the story, namely that the miracle is not done in the first instance for the dead man, but for the widow herself, as several commentators note. Swidler, for instance: "When Jesus raises the young man, he *gives him back to his mother;* she is clearly the center of concern."[7] This story depicts Jesus as the benefactor and patron of widows, just as the Old Tes-

---

6. Nolland, *Luke*, 321.
7. Swidler, *Biblical Affirmations,* 215; Thurston, *Widows,* 25; Barbara J. MacHaffie, *Her Story: Women in Christian Tradition* (Philadelphia: Fortress Press, 1988), 17; Marla J. Selvidge, *Daughters of Jerusalem* (Scottdale, PA: Herald Press, 1987), 102-103; Ben Witherington, *Women in the Ministry of Jesus,* Society for New Testament Studies Monograph Series, ed. G. N. Stanton, 51 (New York: Cambridge University Press, 1987), 77; E. J. Via, "Women in the Gospel of Luke," 42; John J. Pilch, "Sickness and Healing in Luke-Acts," in *Social World of Luke-Acts,* 195; Xavier Harris, "Ministering Women in the Gospels," *The Bible Today* 29 (March 1991): 111.

tament cast Yahweh in the role of the defender of widows (Exodus 22:22-24), even if no man would trouble to defend them.

According to Rentería, such was precisely the point of the Elisha resurrection (as well as of its twin in 1 Kings 17) many hundreds of years before:

> The story . . . does not resolve itself the moment the son revives, but rather when Elisha returns him to his mother [in 2 Kings 4:36: "Take up your son." Cf. 1 Kings 17:23], thus confirming to her and the audience that the prophet can be counted on to keep his obligations to his followers.[8]

Remember, Rentería argues that the stories of Elijah and Elisha ministering to poor widows must have been the property of such women associated, exactly as in the stories themselves, with the sons of the prophets, the conventicles that passed down the stories. This is a precise analogy to what I am urging for the origin and transmission of the Lukan special widow traditions.

Jane Kopas senses the presence of widows behind the telling of the Nain story: "She represents another example of a group of those in need, widows who are among the most oppressed or neglected of society."[9] Nolland catches the resemblance (I would say analogous identity) between the woman of Nain and the "true" widow of 1 Timothy 5:5, "left all alone."[10] I suggest that the point of the Nain story is to encourage the "counter-hegemonic" resistance of Christian widows against the patriarchal hierarchy represented by the Pastor. Jesus, as often in Luke's special material, as well as the Q material, stands for his earthly vicars, the itinerant charismatics.[11] Recall the triangular relationship between the bishops, the widows, and the itinerant apostles. As the bishops encroached on the liberty and ministry of the widows, the widows could resort to the charismatic, volatile authority of the itinerants, which none gainsaid with impunity, though soon enough the church hierarchy would grow strong enough to silence their voice.

But "routinized charisma" had not yet quenched the real thing, and so their association with the itinerant apostles pro-

---

8. Rentería, "Elijah," 108.
9. Kopas, "Jesus and Women," 195.
10. Nolland, *Luke*, 324.
11. Dillon, *Eye-Witnesses*, 265-266.

vided the widows leverage, a counterweight to the hegemony of
the patriarchal church. It had been the same in Omrid Israel,
when the widows sided with the sons of the prophets against the
Temple State, or better, the State Temple.

The irony is that, by trying to co-opt these "counter-hegemonic" stories by canonizing them in the Deuteronomic History,[12] the established religious hegemony ultimately guaranteed
the survival of the stories, the implications of which continued to
be clear despite their confining canonical contexts.[13] Even so,
though Luke represents the patriarchal establishment, he has preserved, and tried to co-opt, several stories of the widows and
their patrons the itinerants. I am attempting to let those long-
smothered stories speak for themselves on women's behalf.

I am arguing that the Nain story is to be located in a long
line of socio-literary continuity reaching back to Omrid Israel and
forward to the second- and third-century patriarchal church. I
have compared the widow-empowering function of the Nain
story with that of similar Elijah and Elisha stories. It remains to
close a gap by showing how such stories continued to be told on
behalf of widows in the next couple of centuries, the period in
which Davies locates the triangular relationship I have borrowed
to illuminate two earlier, biblical, periods. It happens that we
actually have three close parallels to the Nain story in the Apocryphal Acts of succeeding centuries. The *Acts of Peter* recounts
how

> one of the widows who were nourished in Marcellus'
> house, standing behind the multitude, cried out: O
> Peter, servant of God, my son is dead, the only one
> that I had. And the people made place for her and led
> her unto Peter: and she cast herself down at his feet,
> saying: I had only one son, which with his hands fur-
> nished me with nourishment: he raised me up, he car-
> ried me: now that he is dead, who shall reach me a
> hand? Unto whom Peter said: Go, with these for wit-
> ness, and bring hither thy son, that they may see and
> be able to believe that by the power of God he is
> raised. . . . Now the young men which were come
> examined the lad's nostrils to see whether he were

---

12. Scott D. Hill, "Local Hero," 57; cf. John Dominic Crossan, *The Historical Jesus: The Life of a Mediterranean Jewish Peasant* (New York: HarperCollins, Publishers, 1991), 142-156.
13. Rentería, "Elijah," 122-123.

indeed dead; and seeing that he was dead of a truth,
they had compassion on the old woman and said: . . .
we will take him up and carry him thither that he may
raise him up and restore him unto thee. . . . [The] widow's son also was brought upon a bed by the young
men, and the people made way for them and brought
them unto Peter. And Peter lifted up his eyes and
stretched forth his hands and said: O holy father of thy
Son Jesus Christ, . . . raise up the son of this aged
widow, which cannot help herself without her son.
And I, repeating the word of Christ my Lord, say unto
thee: Young man, arise and walk with thy mother so
long as thou canst do her good; and thereafter shalt
thou serve me after a higher sort, ministering in the lot
of a deacon of the bishop. And immediately the dead
man rose up, and the multitudes saw it and marvelled,
and the people cried out: Thou art God the Saviour,
thou the God of Peter, the invisible God, the Saviour.
(XXV, XXVII)

This story has been embedded in a larger narrative treating
of the contest between Peter and Simon Magus. I have sought to
abstract what remains of what was most likely a self-contained
pericope. At that, however, I would guess that Peter did not
originally say he was merely quoting Jesus, but that "I say to you,
arise" was a genuine parallel or else a sign of the Nain story having been retold of Peter in the course of oral transmission. This is
the only clear allusion to the Nain story that I can see. The
woman having lost her only son is just part of the plot: she must
be left destitute for the death to be a dire enough emergency.[14]

Even if the whole story were built up in dependence on the
Nain story, we would still have the continuation of the story-type
of a resurrection on a widow's behalf, not the dead man's. Note,
however, the attempt of the redactor to obscure the widow-focus
by adding the peculiar business about the future ecclesiastical
career of the revived son as a deacon of the bishop: here is the
hand of the patriarchal hegemony trying to usurp the patronage
of Peter: now Peter is raising the son for the benefit of the episco-

---

14. Similarly, I feel sure that originally the acclamation simply praised
Peter as the God and Saviour. Elsewhere in the *Acts* Peter is actually
worshipped by those he heals, but he reins in their enthusiasm with a
quick lesson in monotheism. Here the redactor has built the correction,
clumsily, into the acclamation itself.

pate, "a higher sort" of service.

And that the widow in this story is a member of the Christian community of widows is explicit: she is one of the widow group attached to the house of the patron Marcellus. Would they have been called daughters of Marcellus? I wonder. At any rate, I believe that what is explicit in her case is implicit in that of the widow of Nain: she is a church widow (or stands for them in the mind of the original teller and audience).

Another tale of the same type appears in the *Apostolic History of Abdias* (sixth century by M. R. James's reckoning, who also thinks the text may preserve otherwise lost episodes from the earlier *Acts of John*):

> While the apostle was thus speaking, behold there was brought to him by his mother, who was a widow, a young man who thirty days before had just married a wife. And the people which were waiting upon the burial came with the widowed mother and cast themselves at the apostles' feet all together with groans, weeping, and mourning, and besought him that in the name of his God, as he had done with Drusianna [hence the link with the *Acts of John*], so would he raise up this young man also. And there was so great weeping of them all that the apostle himself could hardly refrain from crying and tears. He cast himself down, therefore, in prayer, and wept a long time: and rising from prayer spread out his hands to heaven, and for a long space prayed with himself. And when he had done so he commanded the body which was swathed to be loosed. . . . Then Stacteus arose and worshipped the apostle.[15]

Certain elements of this story remind us both of the story of the widow of Nain's son and of the raising of Lazarus, but that it has its own integrity as a piece of floating oral tradition (and that, I am supposing, among the consecrated widows) is evident from the inclusion of an item attested in the Apollonius version, namely that the son's death was especially poignant because of his brand new marriage: he had died practically while on his

---

15. M. R. James, *The Apocryphal New Testament: Being the Apocryphal Gospels, Acts, Epistles, and Apocalypses, with Other Narratives and Fragments Newly Translated by Montague Rhodes James* (Oxford: Clarendon Press, 1924, rpt. 1972), 260-261.

honeymoon.

Still another story from the same stock appears in the *Acts of Philip*.

> When he was come out of Galilee, a widow was carry-
> ing out her only son to burial. Philip asked her about
> her grief: I have spent in vain much money on the
> gods, Ares, Apollo, Hermes, Artemis, Zeus, Athena,
> the Sun and Moon, and I think they are asleep as far as
> I am concerned [cf. 1 Kings 18:27]. And I consulted a
> diviner to no purpose. The apostle said: Thou hast
> suffered nothing strange, mother, for thus doth the
> devil deceive men. Assuage thy grief and I will raise
> thy son in the name of Jesus. She said: It seems it were
> better for me not to marry, and to eat nothing but
> bread and water. Philip [replied]: You are right. Chas-
> tity is especially dear to God. She said, I believe in
> Jesus whom thou preachest. He raised her son, who
> sat up and said: Whence is this light? and how comes
> it that an angel came and opened the prison of judg-
> ment where I was shut up? where I saw such torments
> as the tongue of man cannot describe. So all were bap-
> tized. And the youth followed the apostle. (I:1-5)

It is always possible that this story was copied from the Nain story, but it would be circular to argue that it must have been. And in any case, it is a new telling, much changed, hence a new tale. Note the independent use of another Elijah motif: this time, not one of the resurrection stories, but rather the contest of gods atop Mount Carmel. Here we see again the continuity with the old Israelite Elijah-Elisha traditions of the sons of the prophets and their sometime patronesses, sometime clients, the widows.

And the connections of this story with the circles of ascetic women cannot be mistaken, as the miracle is practically made conditional on the widow's embracing perpetual celibacy, vege-tarianism, and abstinence from wine.

Note the parallel with the story of the woman with the issue of blood, where (Mark 5:26) it is remarked that the woman had wasted much money on the ineffective ministrations of doctors. But here it is the sacrifices to the deaf idols of the heathens on which the woman has squandered her money. She henceforth turns from them, converting to Christ. I suspect that many such women brought cherished notions with them from paganism

where these did not seem incompatible with the new religion.[16]
In Chapters 6 and 12 we will see how certain familiar mythemes
did seem to color the piety of widows at important points.

The similarity both to the counter-hegemonic Elijah/Elisha
tales, and to the tales of the Apocryphal Acts in which widows
are aided by wandering prophets and apostles, strongly implies
that the story of the widow of Nain and her son arose in the same
sort of circles and served the same purposes. In all these stories
God looks after his widows through the agency of his wandering
servants, especially insofar as the widows need a defender
against the official patriarchy.

But I think we can be a bit more specific still, in light of a
clue from 1 Timothy, the charter of a new order restricting and
encroaching on the traditional models of Christian widowhood.
The loss of a widow's only son is especially acute because he is
understood to be her only means of support. That is clear in all
these stories. But in the face of the encroachment witnessed in 1
Timothy, I submit that the larger issue valorizing the Nain story
was that, by recalling her son to life, Jesus saves the widow from
the condition that would force the tellers and hearers of the tale
to compromise their autonomy by going on the church dole with
all the restrictions this had lately come to imply. For one thing,
there would be no more repeating of old women's tales like this
one.[17]

Growth in the Telling

Before I move on to consider the story of Dorcas of Joppa, let
me make three more observations on the tradition history of the
Nain story.

First, let us suppose that the original Hellenistic recussita-
tion tale, before it received the leavening of Elijah and Elisha
motifs, was very close to the Apollonius version. We can readily
explain the choice of a Galilean locale and of Jesus as the identity
of the miracle worker, but why the change-over from a woman
having died on the eve of her wedding to the death of an only
son? If the story as we read it in Luke were simply a "Christianization" of the tale, as Fuller says,[18] this particular change would
be totally superfluous.

---

16. Reitzenstein, *Hellenistic Mystery Religions*, 149.
17. MacDonald, *Legend*, 73.
18. Fuller, *Miracles*, 64.

The story has not been so much Christianized as it has been "widowized" by conforming it to the Elijah and Elisha traditions, already current in widow circles. And, recalling the Philip story, the story could not very well countenance having Jesus rescue a virgin from death to hand her over to the degradation of the marriage bed! Better dead than bed! Thecla would have preferred it that way. So the lost child must be a widow's son whose loss is tragic for other reasons entirely.

Second, one might hypothesize that any group of religious widows might have taken a special interest, not only in the Elijah and Elisha stories, but also in the story of Ruth,[19] where widowed women learn to depend on one another's resourcefulness.[20] Is there any sign of Ruth's influence on the widow traditions of Luke-Acts? No and yes.

As it happens, the Nain story continued to grow in the telling. Razi (d. 1210), an Islamic commentator on the *Qur'an*, tells us that Jesus "passed by the dead son of an old woman so he petitioned God and the [man] came down from the bier, returned to his family and continued to live and a child was subsequently begotten by him."[21] The same tradition was known to Tabarsi (d. 1153), who describes the resurrections wrought by Jesus, including

> the son of the old woman whom he passed by when
> he was dead and on his bier. Jesus invoked God and
> he sat up on his bier and came down from the necks of
> the men [who were carrying him], put his clothes on
> and returned to his folk. He continued to live and a
> child was begotten by him.[22]

Here, I speculate, is the widow redaction of the story of Ruth. In its canonical form the Ruth story seems to tilt more toward her than to Naomi, though both are important. At the conclusion of the Book of Ruth it is Naomi to whom the new baby

---

19. Science fiction historian Sam Moskowitz raised this question during a discussion of my thesis: mustn't the story of Ruth and Naomi have been of considerable interest to the hypothetical widow communities?

20. Laffey, *Old Testament*, 208-209; Phyllis Trible, *God and the Rhetoric of Sexuality*, Overtures to Biblical Theology, eds. Walter Brueggemann and John R. Donahue (Philadelphia: Fortress Press, 1978), 195.

21. Neal Robinson, *Christ in Islam and Christianity* (Albany: State University of New York Press, 1991), 146.

22. Ibid., 174.

is presented. "And the women of the neighborhood [said] . . . 'A child has been born to Naomi,'" ending her long bitterness at being bereft and alone with no male progeny to carry on the line (Ruth 4:17). The widow of Nain corresponds to Naomi, but Ruth has dropped out of the picture, replaced by a son. Why?

The ascetical ethos of the widows could no longer view Ruth as a heroine because she could not function as a role model: she was a woman who first pledged faithfulness to a fellow widow (Ruth 1:16-17) and then finished by marrying another husband! She had "broken her first pledge" (1 Timothy 5:11-12)!

Yet, as we have seen, it was deemed right and proper for a widow to have living relatives to support her, especially to keep her off the church roll with its attached strings. So not only is her son restored to her, but in a subsequent telling he becomes a male Ruth, providing the Naomi-analogue with a grandson as well!

Third, in other subsequent versions of the story, attested in the *Book of the Resurrection of Christ by Bartholomew*, the Nain widow is named Leah and is numbered among the holy women who travelled about with Jesus through Galilee. The "sinful woman" of Luke 7:36-50 has become a member of the group as well. I wonder if here we do not have a hint that this latter Lukan story was also a piece of the widow tradition, as I think is abundantly clear on other grounds, and as will be seen in the next chapter.

It is interesting to note that Schürmann associates the same three pericopes as following immediately upon one another in Luke's source: "the pre-redactional sequence was Lk 7,11-17,36-50; 8, 2-3."[23] Swidler thinks these passages belong in a woman-written special source used by Luke. Obviously I agree with the general idea here. We do have a vestige of an oral or written Gospel of the Widows, but, as we will see, there was rather more to it.

Tabitha Cumi

Having laid the groundwork for widow stories of the same type, I can treat of the story of Dorcas of Joppa and her return to life (Acts 9:36-42) in somewhat shorter compass. As far back as Eduard Zeller, the great Tübingen critic, it has been observed that this story, despite its notable similarity to the Jairus story (Luke 8:41-42, 49-56) seems not to be a Lukan creation on the basis of

---

23. Schürmann, *Lukasevangelium*, 440-441, 448, cited in Dillon, *Eye-Witnesses*, 242.

that story for the simple reason that the Dorcas story is closer to the Markan version of Jairus (Mark 5:22-23, 35-43) than to the Lukan (Luke 8:41-42a, 49-56).

Had Luke created it himself in order to provide an example of Peter following in the footsteps of his master, would he not have stuck as close as possible to the prototype?[24] The difference is that Peter empties the room of mourners, as Jesus does in Mark but not in Luke. The implication of these facts is that the Dorcas story is an independent tradition descended from a common prototype, perhaps even from the Jairus story, but at an earlier stage. Someone else derived it from Jairus, not Luke.

However, Lake and Cadbury suggested an alternative explanation for the difference, an explanation that would be compatible with Lukan composition of the Dorcas story (suggested recently by Roloff and Lüdemann).[25] Lake and Cadbury marked the intriguing phenomenon whereby, as Luke carries over Markan stories into his own gospel, he seemingly omits details from Mark, holding them in reserve to use later in stories or transition pieces in Acts. In this manner Luke seems to have omitted Jesus' healing hem (Mark 6:56) from the story of the woman with the issue of blood in order to transform it into Peter's salvific shadow in Acts 5:15-16. Mark 13:32's warning that the eschatological itinerary remains unknown to prying mortal eyes has gone over (along with the disciples' thick-headedness, it would seem) to Ascension Day (Acts 1:7). The charges of bomb-throwing anarchism made at Jesus' trial (Mark 14:56-64) have fallen silent there to be redirected at Stephen in Acts 6:11-14. The contemplated arrest of Jesus among the people at Passovertide (Mark 14:2) has

---

24. Eduard Zeller, *The Contents and Origin of the Acts of the Apostles, Critically Investigated. To Which is Prefixed, Dr. F. Overbeck's Introduction to the Acts, from DeWette's Handbook.* Vols. I and II. trans. Joseph Dare (London: Williams & Norgate, 1876), I, 271; II, 310-311; G. W. H. Lampe, "Miracles in the Acts of the Apostles," in *Miracles: Cambridge Studies in their Philosophy and History,* ed. C. F. D. Moule (London: A. R. Mowbray & Co., 1965), 176; Franz Neirynck, "The Miracle Stories in the Acts of the Apostles," in *Les Actes des Apotres: Traditions, redaction, theologie,* ed. J. Kremer, Bibliotheca Ephemeridum Theologicarum Lovaniensium 48 (Gembloux: Leuven University Press, 1979), 198; Hausman, "Function of Elijah," 108-109.

25. Jürgen Roloff, *Die Apostelgeschichte,* Die Neue Testament Deutsch, eds. Gerhard Friedrich and Peter Stuhlmacher, 5 (Göttingen: Vandenhoeck & Ruprecht, 1981), 190; Gerd Lüdemann, *Early Christianity According to the Traditions in Acts: A Commentary* (Minneapolis: Fortress Press, 1989), 122.

been reserved for the arrest of Peter and James in Acts 12:4, because this time popular favor has run out and the coast is clear.[26]

Thus perhaps in Acts 9 Luke has also brought over from the Jairus story the command to clear the room. The reason would not be far to seek. As the scene with Peter shows, Luke must have taken Mark's notice of the room-clearing to denote that Jesus wanted to pray in private over the corpse, since this is what he has Peter do in Acts, once everyone else is gone. But Jesus, in Luke's view, did not need to pray. He was a divine being himself and could simply command life to return. Hence Luke translates the linguistic fossil "*talitha cumi*" as "Child, arise"; it had been retained in the Hellenistic church as an incantation in a barbaric tongue, and Luke's Jesus hardly had need of such tricks as exorcists used in Luke's day.

Plausible as this reasoning is, there remain problems. For one, Luke is hardly ashamed to have his Jesus seen praying. As is well known, he introduces the theme in several places where it was absent in his sources (Luke 3:21; 6:12; 9:18; 9:29; 11:1; 22:32; 23:46). And for another, what is *talitha* doing over in Acts made into a proper name?

As Cadbury notes, Luke tends to omit snatches of foreign speech wherever he can.[27] So perhaps he has made it into a name in Acts 9 (as Baur long ago suggested).[28] But then we must ask why he did not adopt the simpler expedient of making Jairus' anonymous daughter bear the name Tabitha. The Lukan Jesus could have said to *her*, "Tabitha, I say to you, arise." Presto: no indelicate Aramaic.

The only way to account for Tabitha as a substitute for *talitha* in so similar a setting in Acts is to posit a pre-Lukan transformation of the Jairus story into the Dorcas story. We must assume that the Aramaic original of the healing command had been preserved as a magic formula, as it appears in Mark, remembered for the sake of efficacy. Origen tells us that the

---

26. Henry Cadbury and Kirsopp Lake, "English Translation and Commentary," in *Beginnings of Christianity*, vol. IV, 8, 54-55, 69, 111, 134.
27. Cadbury, *Making*, 123-126.
28. Ferdinand Christian Baur cited in Heinrich August Wilhelm Meyer, *Critical and Exegetical Handbook to the Acts of the Apostles*, trans. Paton J. Gloag, trans. rev. William P. Dickson, with preface and notes to the American ed. by William Ormiston (New York: Funk & Wagnalls, Publishers, 1883), 195.

effective use of the divine names depends on their being chanted in the original language:

> If we were to translate the name . . . into Greek or another language we would effect nothing. . . . We would say the same also of the word Sabaoth, which is frequently used in spells, because if we translate the name into "Lord of the Powers" or "Lord of hosts" or "almighty" (for its interpreters explain it differently) we would effect nothing; whereas if we keep it with its own sounds, we will cause something to happen, according to the opinion of experts in these matters. (*Contra Celsum* 5.45)

Somewhere in the Hellenistic world, among readers who no longer used the story as an exorcistic charm,[29] the meaning of the strange, virtually glossolalic, syllables was lost. The closest anyone could come to making sense of it was as a similar-sounding Jewish name, Tabitha. But since Greek-speakers were reading it, they felt more comfortable with a Greek equivalent of this Aramaic name. Hence Dorcas. Haenchen: "This detail derives from his source, which had already translated the Aramaic words into Greek. It will also have supplied the translation of Tabitha by Dorcas."[30]

Another possibility is the suggestion of Kreyenbuhl of an original Aramaic Peter story, translated into Greek, which then descended along two lines, in the process begetting the Jairus story as its variant. Luke would have known the Dorcas and Jairus stories as two different units of tradition.[31] At any rate, I conclude with Conzelmann that "This account of the raising of a dead person originally circulated independently, as the beginning of the story indicates."[32]

In line with this observation, note that among the motifs inventoried by Tannehill[33] as occurring both in these stories and

29. Davies, *Revolt,* 24-28; cf. Raphael Patai, *The Hebrew Goddess* (New York: Discus Books, a division of Avon Books, 1978), 188-190 on the similar use of entire Elijah stories as exorcism formulae in the Middle Ages.
30. Haenchen, *Acts,* 339.
31. In Neirynck, "Miracle Stories," 186.
32. Conzelmann, *Acts,* 77.
33. Tannehill, *The Narrative Unity of Luke-Acts: A Literary Interpretation, Volume 2: The Acts of the Apostles* (Minneapolis: Fortress Press, 1990), 126-127.

in the Elijah and Elisha resurrections, the Dorcas story shares
with Elisha, but not with any version of Jairus, the detail of the
woman's eyes opening. It shares only with Elijah the detail of the
dead body lying in state in an "upper room." This sounds to me
not so much like direct literary dependence, but rather like the
spontaneous embellishment of oral transmission, mixing elements from similar stories which one can no longer quite keep
distinct in one's mind.

Further, the presence of details from the stories of Elijah's
and Elisha's miracles would certainly be consistent with the story's transmission through widow-community channels. In fact I
would suggest that if, contra Kreyenbuhl, the Jairus story was the
prototype for the Dorcas story somewhere along the line, before
either reached Luke, then the Jairus story was transformed at the
hands of the widows into a story centering about one of their
own, Dorcas. From early times Dorcas was held up as an example
of the pious church widow.[34] Thurston thinks "she may provide
an example of the unenrolled widow"[35] as shown in 1 Timothy 5.
Rackham had already said, "Tabitha is the type of the Christian
woman devoted to practical good works, as distinct from the
more contemplative virgin or [enrolled] 'widow' devoted to
prayer."[36]

To delineate things further, McKenna points out that

> Tabitha (Dorcas) was no doubt one of the widows, but
> she was in a different position from the others. She
> was a dispenser of charity, they were receivers. This
> does not mean there were two separate categories of
> widows. Receiving and giving were both part of the
> state of widowhood. Tabitha and the other widows
> represented two aspects of the same state.[37]

In other words, Dorcas is one of the women who have widows in
1 Timothy 5:16. She was not on the church roll herself, since she
was self-sufficient and wealthy enough, like the later mistresses
of widow houses, to support others not so fortunate.

The widows mentioned in the passage are understood as a
special religious category, contra Conzelmann,[38] as they are dif-

---

34. Clark, *Women in the Early Church*, 183-184.
35. Thurston, *Widows*, 42.
36. Rackham, *Acts*, 145.
37. McKenna, *Women of the Church*, 43.

ferentiated from the rest of the believers: saints and widows (v. 41). Thurston and McKenna understand this,[39] while Bruce can only imagine that Luke means to line up Christians over here, and pagan and Jewish widows, recipients of Dorcas' ecumenical charity, over there.[40] So far from there being a class of church widows, too late a phenomenon (Bruce realizes with the apologist's tactical instincts) for the days of Simeon Kepha, he demotes them to ancillary unbelievers! Women as special disciples (Dorcas is the only one of whom *mathetria*, the feminine of "disciple," is used [9:36] in the whole New Testament) once again become invisible, thanks to the phallogocentric bias that the Bible as the word of God must fit the one genre, history, that male theologians deem compatible with truth.

What of the purpose of the story that accounted for its creation and transmission in the early church? Harnack thought it had none, which was all the better, since with any *Tendenz* eliminated, we might take it to be unsullied, albeit useless, history, always the important thing for Western scientific phallogocentrism. "It is . . . favourable to the hypothesis of a primary tradition that the story, in spite of its crudity, is fixed in form and ministers to no special tendency."[41] By contrast, Willimon has some insight into the text:

> We are reading a discontinuous story of the marginalized, a story lovingly recounted by widows and people like them, a story which echoes II Kings 4:32-35 suggesting that, like the prophets of old, apostles bring power to bear on behalf of the poor.[42]

This is precisely the understanding of Rentería as to the function, as we have seen, of the Old Testament tales to which Willimon refers, and he is right on target in his understanding of the Dorcas episode.

Let me note that, again, just as in the story of the widow of Nain, the resurrection is performed for the sake of what might first seem to be sideline characters, in this case not so much for

---

38. Conzelmann, *Acts*, 77.
39. Thurston, *Widows*, 34; McKenna, *Women of the Church*, 42.
40. Bruce, *Acts*, 212.
41. Adolf Harnack, *The Acts of the Apostles*, trans. J. R. Wilkinson, Crown Theological Library 27 (New York: G. P. Putnam's Sons, 1909), 102.
42. Willimon, *Acts*, 85.

Dorcas, whom we may suppose to have gone on to her reward, but rather for the sake of her clients (Acts 9:39) who cannot get along without her. "My desire is to depart and be with Christ, for that is far better. But to remain in the flesh is more necessary on your account" (Philippians 1:23b-24).

In the *Acts of Peter* we read of yet another resurrection of a woman's son by Peter, but before he speaks the word, he wins a promise from the wealthy mother to share the price of the rich funerary tokens with the poor men who are acting as pall bearers. And what is left over must be distributed among the widows (chapter XXVIII). Here, too, a resurrection miracle is made to benefit the widows.

But this is not all the Dorcas story has in common with traditions preserved in the *Acts of Peter*. As Zeller pointed out long ago, the very notion of an apostle as one who may be sent for to raise the corpse of one who has inconveniently died, as if he were a professional necromancer, "is quite in the manner of legendary fiction."[43] Lampe thinks it odd that Peter does not heal Dorcas by reference to God, Jesus, or the name, as elsewhere in Acts.[44] This is because, as Neirynck observes, the apostle is here depicted not as a mere servant of Christ, but as himself something of a second Christ: "as a divine-man in continuity with Jesus"[45]—just as in the Apocryphal Acts.

C. K. Barrett wisely warned

> This conjunction of the historical (or quasi-historical) and the theological in the person of the apostles is less striking and central than the same conjunction in the person of Jesus of Nazareth, but no one who is concerned about the history and theology of the earliest church can afford to neglect this aspect of its life.[46]

The danger is the blindness typified by Harnack in the quote given just above, or by Dibelius when he decrees that "The examples intended for preaching one seeks in Acts . . . in vain, for so far there has not been any preaching about the apostles in the

---

43. Zeller, *Acts*, I, 271.
44. Lampe, "Miracles," 176.
45. Neirynck, "Miracle Stories," 202.
46. C. K. Barrett, *The Signs of an Apostle*, Cato Lecture 1969, Introduction to American ed. by John Reumann (Philadelphia: Fortress Press, 1972), 11.

early Church."[47]

The Dorcas story Dibelius classifies as a legend because of the edifying tone and the apparent hagiographical doting on Peter and Dorcas.[48] But just here he misses the point. The point of the story is as Willimon describes it and as Rentería describes that of the Old Testament prototypes on which it is based: God vindicates and protects his widows through his itinerant holy men. Thus the double focus of the story: there is one of each, a widow and a holy man, highlighted in it. It is a lesson aimed at the fast-consolidating patriarchal church for whom the apostles are no more God's wandering angels but rather a list of names to be used as pedigrees, credentials for the "nascent catholic" church. Can we be still more specific? How would the widows have heard this story? For them, as no doubt for the teller, Peter has saved the group of widows from having to go on the church dole (1 Timothy 5:16), bereft as they would otherwise be of the care of their patroness and fellow widow. (That the Peter character could be depicted as something of a free lance over against a grumpy church hierarchy is still evident in Luke's own Cornelius story and its aftermath [Acts 11:1-3].)

Going on the church dole would have meant a significant loss in autonomy and freedom in ministry. One would have to hold one's tongue while all the Pastors and Tertullians and Ignatiuses and Lukes pontificated. But, thank God!, he has sent his apostle to safeguard the freedom of the widows, as sometimes he still did when an itinerant would arrive and, speaking by the Spirit of Jesus, utter some oracle such as "Mary has chosen the better part, and it shall not be taken from her!"

---

47. Martin Dibelius, "Zur Formsgeschichte des Neuen Testaments," *Theologische Rundschau* New Series 3 (1931), quoted in Haenchen, *Acts*, 35.
48. Martin Dibelius, "Style Criticism of the Book of Acts," in *Studies in the Acts of the Apostles*, 12-13.

CHAPTER FIVE

Do You See This Woman?
The Sinner in Simon's House

Many Problems, Many Solutions

Luke's story of the anointing of Jesus (Luke 7:36-50) has been a hothouse for critical reconstructions. There are two reasons for this. First, the passage is so similar to the anointings of Mark 14:3-9, Matthew 26:6-13, and John 12:1-8, and yet so different, that one inevitably wonders whether we have two separate stories or one, based on two original events or one. And if there is only one single event or original tradition, then the complexities of transmission history must be faced, and this itself is a stumbling block to many because of the free play it implies for the tradition stream.

Second, the text by itself seems to be criss-crossed with seams and fissures. Or, to change the metaphor, the story conveys the impression of an old house once built according to an architectural pattern, but since added onto many times, spoiling the symmetry, no matter how useful the new wings may be.[1] Since my own reconstruction depends on a particular estimate of those phenomena of the text, I must briefly survey the apparent inconsistencies in the text and evaluate previous interpretations.

A Pharisee, whose name, oddly, we do not learn until much later on (v. 40), invites Jesus to dinner in his home. Nothing is said, in the setting of the scene, of other guests or hangers on. Jesus seems to have been reclining at table for some time, long enough, at any rate, for rumor of his whereabouts to circulate through the town! After some interval, the news comes to the ears of a certain woman of ill-repute. She takes the time to locate a jar of precious ointment and to make her way to Simon the Pharisee's house. Though much time must have passed by this point, we later hear (v. 45) that she has been with Jesus since he entered!

In light of the woman's reputation, how are we to imagine her to have gained access to the house? Luke's Pharisees are not

---

1. This image was suggested by a narrative description of such a house in August W. Derleth, "The Peabody Heritage," in *The Survivor and Others* (New York: Ballantine Books, 1962), 46-47.

in the habit of entertaining riff-raff like this woman. We may picture her to have crashed the party, flinging the door open and making a beeline for the reclining savior, but how would she have had time and liberty to perform the rather elaborate ritual Luke describes, standing behind him weeping, then stooping to place her face against Jesus' feet long enough for copious amounts of tears to bathe them, then drying them with her hair, then kissing them (repeatedly according to v. 45!), and finally smearing his feet with ointment? Did both Jesus and Simon wait till this process was complete to say anything?

Wherein lies the need for prophecy for Jesus to know of the woman's reputation if Simon and everyone else in town knew it? If the point is rather that Jesus must already know what sort of woman she is and therefore should have recoiled from her touch promptly, why does Luke not say this clearly? And if this is what Luke has in mind, why would the Pharisee not himself immediately have ejected her polluting presence from the house? Or is Simon's silence a trap, giving Jesus enough rope to hang himself by proving he is no prophet? But if this is the case, then the Pharisee has already made up his mind that Jesus is a false prophet, and surely he would have been committing the very sin he condemns in Jesus by having a false prophet to dinner in the first place!

Similarly, how can Simon have neglected to show his guest the most common amenities, as Jesus charges in vv. 44-45? If he had no definite opinion of Jesus, the bare possibility of his being a prophet, to say nothing of common courtesy, surely would have moved Simon to demonstrate simple civility. On the other hand, if Simon treats him rudely because he is already convinced that Jesus is a false teacher, what on earth is he doing inviting him over?

Jesus defends the woman with an analogy, the point of which seems to be that one will have more love the more one is forgiven. Yet this does not seem to fit the case of the woman before him, since we have no indication that Jesus had already forgiven her sins, while vv. 47-48 plainly have Jesus forgive her sins after her display of love. Was her love the result of prior forgiveness, or was she forgiven because she loved much? And in this case, why did she love much? And finally, it is only after Jesus has told Simon that she has been forgiven, a saying that the hearers (who suddenly materialize out of nowhere in v. 49!) take as a performative utterance enacting her forgiveness, that Jesus pronounces the woman forgiven (v. 50)—and this on the basis, not of her love, but of her faith, of which we have heard nothing hitherto.

This story is contradictory almost to the point of incoherence, a circumstance to which popular Bible readers remain oblivious simply because they never look closely enough at the vase to see the cracks. But scholars have looked closely and for a long time. What have they come up with?

Strauss argued with his typical ingenuity and eagle eye that Luke 7:36-50 is a tradition-blended hybrid of (1) the anointing in the version substantially identical between Matthew and Mark which features a *woman defended by Jesus* for *anointing* his head, and (2) the story of the *woman defended by Jesus* as she lies *at his feet* accused of adultery (John 7:53-8:11) or of many sins (*Gospel according to the Hebrews*). The result is the tale of a woman anointing Jesus' feet and being accused of many sins, then being defended by Jesus. Thus Strauss sees it in his *Life of Jesus Critically Examined*,[2] but in his *New Life of Jesus* (or *Life of Jesus for the German People*), Strauss makes it a purposeful redactional combination by Luke, who wanted to demonstrate the self-motivation of the sinful woman, seeking out Jesus even as the Prodigal Son resolved to return home with his tail between his legs.[3] In either case, Strauss implies that it is Luke who has inserted the parable.

I think C. H. Dodd offers pretty much the same account of things as in Strauss's *The Life of Jesus Critically Examined*, though with less detail, when he says that

> the variations [between the three versions of the anointing] arose in the course of oral transmission, and . . . the cross-combinations of different features and details are incidental to the process of shaping individual units of narrative out of the primitive, unformed, tradition. On this hypothesis, each evangelist used independently a separate strand of tradition, and the strands overlapped. In the process of embodying the unit of tradition in a written composition each evangelist has, no doubt, contributed something of his own, but the substance of the *pericope* in each of its three forms is traditional.[4]

---

2. Strauss, *Life of Jesus Critically Examined*, 409-412.
3. Strauss, *The Life of Jesus for the People*, Vol. II, 2nd ed. (London: Williams & Norgate, 1879), 300-302.

The basic core was the anointing of feet or head, someone's complaint, and Jesus' defense. From there some tellers of the tale began to explain the act as an anointing for burial, others perhaps as a royal anointing, others as an act of loving devotion or repentance. Luke received this last version, then elaborated it with the addition of the omitted amenities and presumably with the parable.

Wellhausen judges that Luke had rewritten Mark's anointing story, incorporating the parable of the two debtors and adding the concluding application to the woman, plus Jesus' parting benediction (v. 48), as well as the shocked reaction in v. 49, and the reiteration, as if over the dismayed voices of the Pharisees, in v. 50.[5]

Bultmann thought Luke began with the parable and the concluding moral in v. 47, then added the narrative of the woman, his free rewriting of the Markan anointing story, to serve as a frame, just as many aphorisms later attracted an explanatory frame, making them into apophthegms. Verses 48-50 introduce the alien polemical theme of whether Jesus has the right to forgive sins (cf. Mark 2:6-7) and so must be judged a secondary accretion.[6]

While the hypotheses of the most excellent Strauss, Wellhausen, and Bultmann are never lightly to be set at naught, in the present case one cannot help but feel that they do not quite satisfy. In short, there is just too much else going on in the passage for which their reconstructions do not account. For example, if the story of the woman in Simon's house is a frame created by Luke, all in one piece, as it were, then why does it swarm with improbabilities as a story, and why does it fit the parable so badly? Of course, the problem here is that the parable appears to teach that great love is a result of great forgiveness, while the story read apart from the parable would certainly lead one to infer the moral that love covers a multitude of sins.

Burton Scott Easton saw an original story consisting of vv. 36-43, the rest being subsequent additions.[7]   William Manson

4. C. H. Dodd, *Historical Tradition in the Fourth Gospel* (New York: Cambridge University Press, 1963), 172.

5. Wellhausen, *Das Evangelium Lucae* (Berlin: G. Reimer, 1904), 31-33, cited in Marshall, *Luke,* 305.

6. Bultmann, *History,* 19-20.

7. Burton Scott Easton, *The Gospel According to St. Luke: A Critical and Exegetical Commentary* (New York: Charles Scribner's Sons, 1928), 106.

observed that the verses containing the application (vv. 44-46) introduce a new motif, and thus "it is not improbable that they represent an elaborative addition to the parable."[8] But against this theory I would invoke Fitzmyer's form-critical objection: as Easton and Manson picture the original pericope, it is already a hybrid of pronouncement story and parable. It cannot have begun thus.[9]

C. F. Evans posits that the pre-Lukan tradition amounted to vv. 36-39, 44-47, the parable being Luke's addition, vv. 48-50 his compilation from traditional materials.[10] But this leaves him stuck with the incongruity of the churlishness of the host, as Evans himself calls it, as an alien piece introduced later, either as an afterthought or (more probably) as a reinterpretation of the beginning of the story by a later redactor.

Luke Timothy Johnson's view is that between Luke's anointing and Mark's there is an unbridgeable gap like that separating Lazarus and Dives. "There are . . . so few points of specific contact that it is difficult to defend even the hypothesis that a shared tradition is being used."[11] This strikes me as a retreat to the source-critical safety-zone of T. W. Manson and other scholars who seemed sometimes reluctant to appreciate the implications of form-criticism and the dynamics of oral transmission: they wanted to minimize the flexibility of the tradition and the redactional freedom of the evangelists by chalking up every difference in wording or event to the use of a different tradition or source, behind which they were singularly loathe to inquire. This vagueness seemed to allow them to hint at the "two events" harmonization without explicitly saying so.[12]

---

8. W. Manson, *Luke*, 85.

9. Fitzmyer, *Luke I-IX*, 684; cf. Vincent Taylor, *The Formation of the Gospel Tradition* (London: Macmillan & Co., 1957), 70; Martin Dibelius, *From Tradition to Gospel*, trans. Bertram Lee Woolf (New York: Charles Scribner's Sons, n.d.), 144.

10. Evans, *Saint Luke*, 361.

11. Luke Timothy Johnson, *The Gospel of Luke*, Sacra Pagina Series, ed. Daniel Harrington, vol. 3 (Collegeville, MN: Liturgical Press, 1991), 128.

12. Burnett Hillman Streeter, *The Four Gospels, A Study of Origins* (London: Macmillan & Co., 1951), 210; T. W. Manson, *The Sayings of Jesus* (London: SCM Press, 1937 as Part II of *The Mission and Message of Jesus*: issued as a separate volume, 1949; study ed., 1975), 74, 149, 176-177, 200, 224, 313, 323, 327; E. Earl Ellis, *The Gospel of Luke*, New Century Bible Commentary, gen. eds. Ronald Clements and Matthew Black (Grand Rapids: William B. Eerdmans, 1987), 121.

Marshall, in a similar vein, makes light of the entangling alliance between the two very different Markan and Lukan anointings by appeal to Dodd's suggestion that secondary features of the two stories rubbed off on each other in transmission.[13] Yet it is precisely the secondary features which are different and problematical!

Thomas L. Brodie's fascinating theory has Luke producing our pericope by the process of "imitation" by "internalization." Beginning with the suggestion that the Nain story is a Lukan creation on the basis of the story of Elijah's resurrection of the widow's son, Brodie goes on to make Luke's anointing, too, an imitation of an Old Testament prototype, this time the stories of Elisha in 2 Kings 4:1-37, featuring the widow with the vessels of oil and the Shunammite woman.

Brodie bases his case on certain similarities or parallels between the stories in question, one set of which, he suggests, has been broken up and redistributed into basic narrative or thematic building blocks for the other.

The character Simon the Pharisee, Brodie thinks, was developed by Luke from both the initially distant Shunammite, suspicious of Elisha at first, and Gehazi who fails to carry out the mission assigned him by the prophet. The sinful woman comes from the Shunammite woman and the widow of the guild prophet who pours the self-replenishing oil. The parable's two creditors were suggested by the widow's creditor who wants to take her two children as debt slaves.

Simon's dinner invitation to Jesus is derived from the Shunammite's invitation to Elisha to stay with her. Her conception of a son inspired Simon the Pharisee's implied change of heart at the end of the Lukan story. The sinful woman's debt is a moral one, while the guild prophet's widow's debt is a financial one, but both debt crises are mediated by the prophet, Jesus in the one case and Elisha in the other, and the former was derived from the latter.

Several of the similarities are indeed striking, and, while a Structuralist exegesis might disclose highly illuminating results from these data, to argue direct literary dependence as Brodie does seems far-fetched.

Brodie argues that

---

13. Marshall, *Luke*, 306.

it does not . . . seem reasonable to say that the link
between the texts is due to oral tradition. There is no
known process of oral transmission which is capable
of transforming a text in a way that is so complex and
coherent. It is the literary explanation, and the literary
explanation alone, which is capable of accounting for
the data.[14]

But I question whether the result is not rather too complex
and insufficiently coherent. It seems odd that if Luke were to
exercise such radical freedom in remixing the elements of his Eli-
jah/Elisha sources, that he would not have come up with a
smoother result, free of the infelicities that have given both critics
and apologists headaches. Why wouldn't he have ironed out the
glaring inconsistency between the parable and its frame, for
instance? Why the jarring nonsense about Simon neglecting the
most basic social amenities for a guest he himself has invited?
The story is not coherent enough for an artist working with the
creative freedom Brodie allows Luke.

And is there, as Brodie claims, really no process of oral tradition that could result in the kind of thing we see in Luke 7:36-50?
C. H. Dodd's discussion of the relation of the several anointing
stories sketches a scenario that would seem to account for Brodie's connections between the Elisha story and Luke 7:36-50:

the materials out of which [the gospel pericopes] were
formed were already in existence, as an unarticulated
wealth of recollections and reminiscences of the words
and deeds of Jesus—mixed, it may be, with the reflections and interpretations of his followers. [Dodd's
footnote at this point: "Especially reflections and interpretations prompted by the study of Old Testament
scriptures in their bearing upon the career of Jesus and
his Passion in particular."] It was out of this unformed
or fluid tradition that the units of narrative and teaching crystallized into the forms we know.[15]

As far back as Strauss it ought to have been obvious that
people must have had an especially hard time keeping separate

---

14. Thomas Louis Brodie, "Luke 7, 36-50 as an Internalization of 2 Kings
4, 1-37: A Study in Luke's Use of Rhetorical Imitation," *Biblica* 64 (April
1983): 482.
15. Dodd, *Historical Tradition*, 171-172.

in their minds what tradition said about Jesus and what memory said about the biblical tales of Elijah and Elisha.[16] Insofar as we find Old Testament motifs in Luke's stories of the Centurion, the widow of Nain, and the woman in Simon's house, I think they entered the picture well before these stories came into Luke's hands.

Robert Holst proposes a more orthodox form-critical account of the origin and development of the pericope under discussion. Here is a nutshell version in Holst's own words:

> Luke knew and used a more primitive version of the anointing story [than Mark's]. Luke's sensitivity on ethical issues led him to modify the story in several ways. He deemphasised the value of the myrrh. The original wisdom saying [which later grew, in the tradition stream used by Mark, into "The poor you always have with you, but you do not always have me"] is replaced with dialogue teaching the blessings of love and repentance. To heighten the irony of the dramatic situation, the woman is characterized as an outcast and Simon is portrayed as a critical, unloving Pharisee.[17]

The original, in Holst's reconstruction, read:

> Jesus came to Bethany to the house of Simon the leper. And there they made a supper for him. And a woman bringing an alabaster jar of myrrh, valuable nard, anointed the feet of Jesus with the myrrh and with her tears and wiped them with her hair. Certain men reclining there said, "Why was this myrrh not sold for three hundred denarii and (the money) given to the poor?" Jesus said "Leave her alone. You always have the poor with you; love (?) you do not always have."[18]

Holst dismisses vv. 39-50 as being Luke's work, while the change from the feet to the head ("=" royal anointing) he ascribes to a heightening of the Christology in a different channel of transmission.

16. Strauss, *Life of Jesus Critically Examined*, 1972, 83-84.
17. Robert Holst, "The One Anointing of Jesus: Another Application of the Form-Critical Method," *Journal of Biblical Literature* 95 (1976): 446.
18. Ibid., 443-445.

Holst's reconstruction, while generally on the right track, suffers from two fatal flaws in its specific analysis. First, Holst leaves largely unaddressed the standard problems of narrative incoherence and lack of verisimilitude. His explanation does not explain enough.

Second, he has sketched out a pronouncement story without a viable pronouncement! "I suggest that the apophthegm originally ended with a wisdom saying. One can only guess what the original saying was. . . . Perhaps the statement spoken was, 'The poor you always have with you; love you do not have.'" Or: "The poor you always have with you because God's will you do not always do." Or: "The poor you always have with you. The commandments of the Torah you do not always have." Or: "The sons of the poor you always have with you; the son of man you do not always have."[19]

But none of these will do. As Rudolf Otto once commented in another connection, none of these candidates would be "an ancient Wisdom saying but, if I may be permitted to say so, a silly saying."[20] Gerd Theissen's alternative, to be explored below, is surely to be preferred.

Stage One: Prophetic Privilege

I come the long way round to my own reconstruction, contributing the latest in a series of ducks to be shot down by the next scholar to enter the exegetical arcade. I propose that there was originally a story of the anointing of Jesus' head by an unnamed woman disciple in the house of Simon Peter. As to this last point, I think it makes the best sense of an oddity noticed by several scholars. "This is the only instance where Christ addresses a critic by name."[21] It is "one of the few occasions in which a partner in dialogue is addressed by name."[22] Schweizer notes that "The name Simon [is] not introduced until surprisingly late in Luke 7:40."[23] My guess is that this is because the name

---

19. Ibid., 445.
20. Rudolf Otto, *The Kingdom of God and the Son of Man: A Study in the History of Religion*, rev. ed., trans. Floyd V. Filson and Bertram Lee Woolf (Boston: Starr King Press, 1957), 235.
21. Easton, *Luke*, 106.
22. Frederick W. Danker, *Jesus and the New Age: A Commentary on St. Luke's Gospel*, rev. ed. (Philadelphia: Fortress Press, 1988), 170.
23. Eduard Schweizer, *The Good News according to Luke*, trans. David E. Green (Atlanta: John Knox Press, 1984), 138.

was *not* at first that of an opponent or outsider. Its occurrence is a vestige of the original identity of the complainer as Simon Peter.

Dammers ventures that the parable came originally from the story of the resurrection appearance to Peter, now tranferred, in part, to Luke 5:1-11. There the parable was a reply to Peter's ashamed cry, "Depart from me, O Lord, for I am a sinful man." This last, unmotivated in its present Lukan context, would make much better sense as a reference to Peter's cowardly denials, as Harnack saw long ago.[24] That this connection is far from arbitrary is clear from the fact that the miraculous catch of fish with which the saying "depart from me" is connected in Luke, is a resurrection miracle in John 21:1-14, and in the same Johannine context (21:15-19) Jesus also seems to reassure Peter about the matter of his denials, eliciting an affirmation of love for each of the previous denials.[25]

To Simon's protestation of unworthiness, Jesus would have addressed the parable of the debtors: if Simon loved his Master more than these, it was because he was forgiven more, namely his denials. The bigger the apostle is, the harder he falls, and the better off he is for having done so, being in line for a fatter share of forgiveness.

If Dammers is correct, then we have a clue as to how the forgiveness parable came to be transferred to its present location: it had to do with Simon Peter originally and was at some later stage redirected to him as a rebuke occasioned by his self-righteous carping at someone else's apparent sin. This was one time that what he bound on earth wasn't going to stick in heaven! Though not at first a part of this story, the subsequent transfer of the parable here shows that this "Simon" was originally understood to be Peter.

Luke, the final redactor, had perhaps intended to expunge Simon Peter from the story entirely, replacing him with an unnamed Pharisee. However, absent-mindedly leaving in a later occurrence of the name, he created Simon the Pharisee.

Peter is often enough cast in the role of the blundering straight-man in the gospel tradition. Why not here? It would not even be the only time criticism of Peter had been subsequently transferred to some other convenient whipping-boy; Jesus'

---

24. Harnack, *Luke,* 227.
25. A. H. Dammers, "Studies in Texts: A Note on Luke vii, 36-50," *Theology* 49 (1946): 80.

rebuke to Peter as Satan (Mark 8:33) is redirected to Judas in John 6:70-71.

If Simon and the woman were both members of Jesus' entourage, this would obviate the notorious difficulty of the woman getting into a Pharisee's house and then not being promptly chased out. "Certainly an ordinary public sinner would not have been admitted, or if she had entered, she would have been unceremoniously ejected."[26]

The multitude of attempts by harmonists to cover up this outrage against verisimilitude are as variegated as they are implausible. The apologist Witherington envisions a general policy whereby such trick-or-treating by the socially dubious would have occasioned nary the raising of an eyebrow.[27] Caird, too, throwing sober judgment to the winds, assures us that the practice of holding open house for notorious riff-raff was "not uncommon."[28]

W. Manson, equally desperate to save face for the passage, follows Klostermann in an unwittingly revealing choice of "historical" precedent for the scene presented here; the *Arabian Nights*, he reminds us, pictures people entering the dwellings of the rich at random when they hear festive music.[29] Festive music? At the house of so sour-pussed a host as Luke depicts? Not likely. Talbert joins him in this exegetical expedient.[30] But Luke himself casts doubt on the possibility of such an explanation: he assumes it would be of the most extraordinary for the poor and despised to be welcome at a feast (14:12-14, 21).

Plummer suggested that "The woman very likely entered *with* Christ and His disciples in order to escape expulsion. Fear of it would make her begin to execute her errand directly the guests were placed."[31] But this reconstruction runs afoul of the detail, quite significant as I will argue, that "*from the time I came in* she has not ceased to kiss my feet" (v. 45), implying a state of affairs beginning more than a moment previously and somehow

---

26. A. Legault, "An Application of the Form-Critique Method to the Anointings in Galilee (Lk 7, 36-50) and Bethany (Mt 26, 6-13; Mk 14, 3-9; Jn 12, 1-8)," *Catholic Biblical Quarterly* 16 (1954): 140.

27. Witherington, *Women in the Ministry*, 55.

28. G. B. Caird, *The Gospel of St. Luke*, Pelican New Testament Commentaries (Baltimore: Penguin Books, 1972), 114.

29. W. Manson, *Luke*, 84.

30. Talbert, *Reading Luke*, 86.

31. Plummer, *Luke*, 203; cf. Jeremias, 126.

tolerated up to this point; indeed the scene only erupts into con-
frontation once Jesus addresses the host's unspoken concern. We
must rule out Plummer's hit-and-run anointing in the Pharisee's
house.

So originally the story portrayed Simon Peter and a woman
disciple known to him. What was the nature of his complaint?
We may imagine him to have griped at the waste of ointment, a
detail retained in Mark, where Simon has become Simon the
leper. At first the nucleus of the Lukan version read this way:

> Simon Peter muttered "Why was this ointment thus
> wasted? It could have been sold for three hundred
> denarii, and the proceeds distributed among the
> poor!" Jesus, answering, said to him, "Simon, I have
> something to say to you." And he said to him, "Say
> on, teacher." Jesus said, "The poor you always have
> with you, and whenever you wish you can help them,
> but you do not always have me."

This form of the story, I am convinced, stems from the ministry of the itinerant charismatics. The pronouncement "The poor
you always have with you, and whenever you wish you can help
them, but you do not always have me" is, as Theissen brilliantly
suggests,[32] certainly to be explained as the utterance of one of the
wandering prophets and represents precisely the sort of thing
condemned in the *Didache* 11:12, "But whoever shall say in the
Spirit, 'Give me money, or something else,' do not listen to him;
on the other hand, should he tell you to give on behalf of others
in need, let no one judge him."

Here we are lucky to be able to hear two sides of a dispute.
Some in the congregation seem to think of such extravagance
showered upon a prophet as untoward, especially when there are
the local poor to be fed. The reply: "But surely this is different!
We are to receive Brother Proteus as Christ himself! What we do
to him we do to Christ! He said so himself, last time he was
here!" How was this dispute resolved? For the moment, by a
convenient oracle from the mouth of the prophet himself: "The
poor ye have always with you, and whenever ye will ye can do
good unto them, but ye have not always me! So snap to it!"

We find another parallel in a similarly self-serving revelation conveniently vouchsafed the Prophet Muhammad by his

---

32. Theissen, *Sociology*, 39.

Lord:

> Prophet, We have made lawful to you the wives to
> whom you have granted dowries and the slave-girls
> whom Allah has given you as booty; the daughters of
> your . . . uncles and . . . aunts. . . ; and the other women
> who gave themselves to you and whom you wished to
> take in marriage. This privilege is yours alone, being
> granted to no other believer. . . . We grant you this
> privilege so that none may blame you. (*Qur'an* 33:49-
> 50)

Brother Proteus won the battle but lost the war: such
unseemly conduct led in the long run to regulations such as that
in the *Didache* passage just quoted. And the church, as it consoli-
dated its structure and routinized its charisma, grew more reluctant to put out the welcome mat for the itinerants, Diotrephes (3
John 9-10) being a famous example. But the widows' houses
would welcome them, in return for the support they lent the widows' interests, for as long as their intimidating prophetic words
retained some clout.

Eventually they faded away, but the itinerants in their "holy
arrogance" (Jerome) had managed to bequeath a saying to the
gospel tradition, albeit one that many readers would rather not
have found there, if the truth be known.

By the way, I should imagine that Theissen's explanation
meets Dodd's objection that the anointing story cannot rightly be
counted a pronouncement story, since the punchline is not of
general applicability, applying only to Jesus himself.[33] As it turns
out, it *is* of wider applicability: it was used as a general defense of
all the wandering prophets who came in Jesus' name and were
"received as the Lord" (*Didache* 11:4).

Stage Two: Scandalous Fellowship

Next the original cause of complaint, the extravagant treatment of the prophet (who was after all supposed to be an
ascetic!), was replaced with another cause of outrage from the
same motif-field: his association with women who scandalously
fawned over him in public, devotees of the Lord whom he represented in the flesh.

It is from such devotion, rampant in the Apocryphal Acts

---

33. Dodd, *Historical Tradition*, 162.

and reflecting the relations between the itinerants and the widows/virgins (as Davies argues), that we get all the suggestions of the derivation of the Apocryphal Acts genre from the Hellenistic Romance genre. The "love at first sight" motif in the novels is repeated in the Acts when, e.g., Thecla is so taken with Paul's preaching of continent Christianity that she is moonstruck for days, precisely as when Charikleia and Anthea first see their destined beaus. Just as in the Apocryphal Acts, Lucian's *The Death of Peregrinus* shows a round-the-clock vigil at Peregrinus' prison cell by his ardent followers, the widows. Like the heroines of the Acts, they did not hesitate to bribe the guards if they might thus see or pass the night with their beloved apostle (12).

Davies suggests that the emotional devotion shown the apostles in the Acts has more than a fortuitous connection with the fact that in every one of the major Acts, Jesus himself at some point appears to his followers in the physical likeness of the eponymous apostle. If Thecla and Mygdonia loved Jesus Christ, how were they liable to feel toward his only visible representative? "Without having seen him you love him" (1 Peter 1:8a). "He who does not love his brother whom he has seen, cannot love God whom he has not seen" (1 John 4:20b). Thecla and her sisters loved Christ the more, if we are to believe the testimony of the Acts, for loving his earthly vicars.

In the Acts we receive abundant notices that the devotion of the converts to celibate Christianity, showering such chaste attentions on their new gurus, did not pass unnoticed by their husbands—especially since the women had ceased having sexual intercourse with their heathen mates, saving themselves for the Heavenly Bridegroom. Often the jealousy kindled by the homewrecking apostles of the Acts led to their martyrdoms. I will have more to say on this feature of the chastity stories in the next chapter, but now suffice it to say that the apostles were suspected as seducers and cuckolders.[34] In the same vein, and demonstrating the verisimilitude of these legends, Peter Brown notes how wandering ascetics in Late Antique Syria were frequently blamed for suspicious village pregnancies and were viewed dimly by landed church people generally.[35]

Indeed, I do not think we can rule out there having been some truth behind these suspicions. I wonder what we are to

---

34. Davies, *Revolt*, 82; Kraemer, "Conversion of Women," 303.
35. Brown, *Society and the Holy*, 114.

make of passages like this one in the *Acts of Andrew*, where the apostle says to Mygdonia: "I rightly see in you Eve repenting and in myself Adam being converted; for what she suffered in ignorance you are now bringing to a happy conclusion." If the apostles did see themselves as the earthly vehicles of the Heavenly Bridegroom to whom they had betrothed their female converts, who can say that they did not on occasion enact a bit of "realized eschatology"?

Apart from the Acts we have abundant evidence during the same general period of the scandal occasioned by the *suneisaktoi*, or *virgines subintroductae*, or *agapetae*, women who lived and/or travelled with holy men, in a relationship of Platonic chastity. While Tertullian advocated the arrangement, Chrysostom denounced it in no uncertain terms: it brought reproach on the church and provided a sooner-or-later irresistible trap of Satan, even for the most pious.[36]

We even have a case of this concern for Christian seemliness specifically applied to the situation of alms at mealtime, the occasion for the trouble in Luke 7:36-50. In Hippolytus' *Apostolic Tradition* we read the instructions governing invitations to widows and the precautions clergymen must take:

> If at any time any one wishes to invite those widows who are advanced in years, let him feed them and send them away before sunset. But if he cannot [have them under his own roof] because of his clerical office, let him give them food and wine and send them away, and they shall partake of it at home as they please.[37]

What Hippolytus wishes to restrict, first, is the entertaining of the young widows by Christian men, and especially at night, when not even elderly ladies may remain. But for clergy especially any sort of hospitality is out of the question, presumably either because of the possibility of scandal-mongering, or because of the possible temptations.

I maintain that the second transitional stage of the story behind Luke 7:36-50 aimed at defending the itinerants against these charges of unbecoming behavior with devoted women. "If this man were a prophet, surely he would see what such dis-

---

36. Achelis, "Agapetae," 177; Rader, *Breaking Boundaries*, 62-71; Clark, *Ascetic Piety*, 265-282.
37. Quoted in Gryson, *Women*, 23.

graceful behavior means!" At this stage, the mean-spirited host, willing to believe the worst, was presumably still Simon Peter. It wouldn't be the first time he was depicted as minding the things of men and not of God. The story at this stage:

> And he went into Simon's house. And behold a woman brought an alabaster flask of ointment and standing behind him at his feet, weeping, she began to wet his feet with her tears, and wiped them with the hair of her head, and kissed his feet, and anointed them with the ointment. Now when Simon saw it he said to himself, "If this man were a prophet, he would have known who and what sort of woman this is who is touching him, for she is a sinner." And Jesus answering, said to him, "Simon, I have something to say to you." And he answered and said to him, "Say on, teacher." Jesus said, "I tell you, her sins are forgiven for she loved much."

She is guilty, if anything, of an excess of loving devotion: her behavior is excessive, but surely excusable. If love covers a multitude of sins it certainly mitigates this pecadillo.

Note here the contrast with Acts 16:14-15, where Lydia says to the itinerant Paul and his colleagues, "If you have judged me faithful to the Lord, come to my house and stay." As Moxnes says, Paul has given her the gift of the gospel, and she means to reciprocate with the gift of hospitality. "Paul's acceptance of her insistent invitation means a recognition of her loyalty and a granting of honor."[38] In this case we can see the same elements present in the Lukan story of the woman in Simon's house. It also involves the question of what is proper in the case of an itinerant preacher receiving hospitality from a patroness. Only Simon does not regard the woman in his home to be a faithful disciple, because of her excessive behavior. Thus he does not think the visiting preacher should accept her attentions.

Between the three characters in the story we can pick out the actors in the triangular relationship described so well by Davies. Peter is the suspicious church patriarch, somebody like the Pastor or Pseudo-Clement. That an apostle could be cast in such a role is apparent from documents like the *Pistis Sophia*, the *Gospel of Mary*, and the *Gospel of Thomas* (saying 13) where the evangelist

---

38. Moxnes, "Patron-Client," 262.

does not hesitate to have both Peter and Matthew stand for the mainstream church with its defective knowledge of the mysteries of Christ, while Thomas stands for the writer's own marginalized conventicle of esoteric illuminati.

Even so here, why not grant the presumptuous claim of the ecclesiarchs to represent Peter and the apostles—if one is going to cast oneself and one's congeners in the role of Jesus Christ! And such a role the itinerants thought was theirs by right as those whom he had told "he who hears you hears me." If the dull-witted *psuchikoi* and hypocrites of the churches wanted to criticize their innocent relations with their female disciples and hostesses, let them. The Lord looketh upon the heart.

And the woman in Simon's house? Of course she stands for the widows, increasingly suspicious in the eyes of the church hierocrats, and taking refuge with the itinerant charismatics, whose advocacy they cherished and rewarded with hospitality as they washed the feet and anointed the weary brows of these walkers in the way of Christ. It is to the woman that the focus of the evolving pericope will turn in the third stage of its growth.

But I must first pause to pay due homage to the suggestion of Gilbert Bouwman which anticipates my discussion here. As his reconstruction bears half on the itinerants and half on their patronesses, this seems the place to mention it. Bouwman had the acuity of insight to surmise that the *Sitz-im-Leben* of the pericope had to be located in such a framework.

What lay behind the reproach suffered by both Jesus and the woman he defended? Bouwman underscored the important role of women assisting the missioners to the Gentiles, grateful converts turned from the error of their ways by the apostles whom they henceforth spared no pains to assist. Lydia comes to mind. But often such women had unsavory pasts, albeit now washed away in baptism. But not everyone could so easily dismiss their suspicions. Had such women really repented?

Or might these women's past habits not in some measure still cling to them? And should the missioner risk scandal and defilement by accepting such hospitality?

> Es liegt fast auf der Hand, dass irgendeine dieser Frauen bei ihrer Bekehrung nicht nur ihren fremden Göttern den Rücken kehrte, sondern noch viel mehr. Die Herzlichkeit der Sünderin, die in diesem Bericht so breit geschildert wird, ist das Kennzeichen vieler

Frauen, die auf die gleiche Bahn geraten sind. Aber die neuen Pharisäer missbilligen es, dass der Missionar seinen Einzug bei diesen Bekehrten nimmt, weil ihre Vergangenheit nicht ganz sauber war. Das scheint mir der Hintergrund des Berichtes zu sein.[39]

In a similar fashion Jack T. Sanders also proposes that lurking behind the Pharisaic opponents of Jesus in Luke, notably Simon, we should recognize Christian proponents of ideas rejected by the evangelist, only Sanders sees the issue involved as primarily that of Torah observance.[40] Stegemann argues a similar case, only for him the Pharisees stand for the rich and respectable of the Christian community over against their poor coreligionists whom they are inclined to despise.[41]

Unlike Bouwman I do not attribute to women converts shady pasts. To do so seems to me an arbitrary reading of anti-women bias into the text. As I read it, the pericope in its second stage was a rejoinder to those who criticized the great devotion shown by women patrons to their Christomorphic guests. This might have seemed shameful and shocking to the staid, but there is no reason to take the side of the critic of women in reconstructing the *Sitz-im-Leben* by assuming that they had a checkered past.

Stage Three: Merry Widows

In the third stage of development the focus has shifted to the woman. I suggest we see her as one of the "younger widows" at whom the Pastor takes aim. In his fevered imagination, these women are "voluptuaries" (1 Timothy 5:6), oversexed, growing "wanton against Christ" (v. 11), idlers, gadabouts, busybodies (v. 13). Easton[42] and Guthrie[43] tender the shocking suggestion, no doubt correctly, that the Pastor envisions the younger widows as supplementing their church dole by resorting to prostitution! Men have never believed women could seriously undertake the

39. Gilbert Bouwman, *Das Dritte Evangelium* (Düsseldorf: Patmos Verlag, 1968), 154.

40. Jack T. Sanders, *The Jews in Luke-Acts* (Philadelphia: Fortress Press, 1987), 106, 176.

41. Stegemann, "Following of Christ," 88-89.

42. Burton Scott Easton, *The Pastoral Epistles: Introduction, Translation, Commentary and Word Studies* (New York: Charles Scribner's Sons, 1947), 152.

43. Guthrie, *Pastoral Epistles*, 101.

chaste life. In the same way the overactive imagination of the Pastor just cannot believe in the sincere chastity of younger women, hence they must be turning tricks! Better, apparently, to burn than to marry!

Malina explains this cultural prejudice:

> women not under the tutelage of a male—notably widows and divorced women—are viewed as stripped of female honor [and, one might add, of the male moral "protection" that would otherwise keep them out of trouble!], hence more like males than females, therefore sexually predatory, aggressive, hot to trot, hence dangerous. . . . This cultural attitude towards widows is clearly articulated in 1 Tim. 5:3-16.[44]

No less in Luke 7:36-50.

That the younger widows or virgins were the focus of outrage on the part of male ecclesiarchs is clear also from the grumpy admonitions of the Carthaginian fathers Tertullian (*On the Apparel of Women* 2.2) and Cyprian (*De habitu virginum* 5.15-19).[45] Consecrated women, having renounced sexual intercourse, insisted on the right to adorn themselves for the sheer beauty of it (in the spirit of Matthew 6:16-18, one might add). If they happened to arouse the lusts of brutish men, too bad. That was the men's problem to deal with.

As McNamara summarizes it, the North African widows "continued to give lavish parties and even to attend weddings, where they were regularly seen participating in the bawdy jokes and horseplay that normally accompanied those events."[46] Of course these must have been well-to-do women who could pay their own way. Hence Tertullian and Cyprian had to rest content with apparently ineffective exhortations, since there was no church stipend for them to threaten to cut off.

Can such women be envisioned in Luke 7:36-50, where the woman, after all, has gotten very expensive ointment from *some-*

---

44. Bruce J. Malina, *The New Testament World: Insights from Cultural Anthropology* (Atlanta: John Knox Press, 1981), 44; cf. Bruce J. Malina and Jerome H. Neyrey, "Honor and Shame in Luke-Acts: Pivotal Values of the Mediterranean World," in *Social World of Luke-Acts*, 44.
45. McNamara, *New Song*, 116-117.
46. Ibid., 117.

where? Her ability to afford such perfume might suggest that she was a prostitute, but then why descend to such an explanation, which, on my reading, is the very thing this version of the story meant to rebut? Perhaps she is simply wealthy and willing to shower her gratitude on her favorite holy man, sparing no expense.

Here we have the source and meaning of the characterization of the woman in Simon's house, the characterization, of course, that the story raises only to refute. The woman is "that sort of woman," and what has she done? She is making trouble precisely in the course of "gadding about from house to house."

Just as the average miracle story introduces the skepticism of the bystanders in order to knock it down, so the suspicions against the young widow are set up for Jesus to disarm. How does he do this? By simple reference to the humble service rendered him (actually to the itinerants for whom he stands). Simply put, in the very terms used elsewhere by her detractors, she "is well attested for her good deeds, as one who has . . . shown hospitality, [and] washed the feet of the saints" (1 Timothy 5:10).

It is at this point that we can place the insertion into the story of the retrojected neglect of social amenities by Jesus' host which serves to underscore the hospitality of the widow above and beyond the call of duty (vv. 44-46). The secondary nature of these verses is widely recognized.[47]

In this version it is assumed that the woman, not yet a gatecrasher, is supposed to be where she is, at her station, doing just what she is doing. Otherwise why did the host raise no objection to the woman's actions which she has been performing since the point of Jesus entering the house? She gave him the treatment any guest might expect to receive upon entering.

And Jesus did receive it on entering, only not from the host. Rather it was the young widow who went far beyond what was required in making the travelling saint feel welcome and honored. Simon is not actually said to have neglected the attention that decorum required be paid to the guest. It wasn't his job. Nonetheless, the widow, whose job it was (predictably, reduced to the tasks of slavery by male ecclesiarchs), did her job and more. She went the second mile by showing genuine devotion, not perfunctory duty. And in making herself a servant she

---

47. W. Manson, *Luke,* 85; Evans, *Saint Luke,* 363; Dillon, *Eye-Witnesses,* 241.

showed herself greater than he that remained sitting at table (cf. Luke 22:27). That is the point of the otherwise bizarre vv. 44-46.

Again, this way of reconstructing the story makes sense of what is otherwise utter nonsense. If the woman were simply a whore who burst in on the scene, why would she not have been given the bum's rush at once? How could she have lingered long enough to caress Jesus from the moment he entered? Easton tries to escape the difficulty: "'Since the time I came in' is hyperbolic; the narrative really thinks of the kiss that Simon omitted."[48] What omission? I am arguing that it is assumed that Simon was letting the woman do what she as a widow was supposed to be doing, washing the feet of the saints, albeit pouring it on a bit thickly. If this is not the case, then Simon's behavior is just inexplicable.

If Simon is a Pharisee (which on my reading he will only become in Luke's redaction), how can it be that he omits to show common courtesy to a man who he thinks may actually be a prophet of God?[49] And if he doesn't seriously entertain the possibility, why did he invite him in the first place? Jesus consorting with a prostitute could hardly compare to the evil of inviting to be ones' guest a known deceiver of Israel! Wouldn't a Pharisee have recoiled with loathing at the thought of sharing a table with Jesus Pandera? Talk about eating with sinners (Mark 2:16)!

Yet this incredible scenario is swallowed without a burp by traditional exegetes. Rayner Winterbotham bemoans that the host "could not bring himself to be polite, not even to be commonly civil, to his invited guest."[50]

In its present Lukan form, to be sure, the story teems with these difficulties because Luke has left the sedimentary layers of the story exposed, so that it is now "lacking in verisimilitude."[51] Dammers is right: "The host's action in refusing ordinary hospitality is incomprehensible. . . . That Jesus should call attention to it is also unnatural."[52]

At this stage, however, the story still circulated as an apologetic on behalf of the young widows against the aspersions cast their way in 1 Timothy 5:6, 10-13. It must have sounded some-

---

48. Easton, *Luke,* 108.
49. Johnson, *Luke,* 128.
50. R. Winterbotham, "Simon and the Sinner: St. Luke vii. 36-50," *Expositor* 1 (1877): 224-225.
51. Creed, *Luke,* 109.
52. Dammers, "A Note on Luke," 78.

thing like this:

> He reclined at table in Simon Peter's house. And
> behold, a woman brought an alabaster flask of oint-
> ment, and standing behind him at his feet, weeping,
> she began to wet his feet with her tears and wiped
> them with the hair of her head, and kissed his feet and
> anointed them with the ointment. Now when Simon
> saw it, he said to himself, "If this man were a prophet,
> he would have known who this is and what sort of
> woman this is who is touching him, for she is a sin-
> ner." And Jesus said to him, "Simon, I have something
> to say to you." And he answered, "Say on, teacher."
> Then turning to the woman, he said, "Do you see this
> woman? I entered your house, you gave me no water
> for my feet, but she has wet my feet with her tears and
> dried them with her hair. You gave me no kiss, but
> from the time I came in she has not ceased to kiss my
> feet. You did not anoint my head with oil, but she has
> anointed my feet with ointment."

Thus I differ from Dillon, who is nonetheless not far from
the kingdom of God since he does at least see that the passage,
àla Bouwman, must be connected in some way with the tradition
of the itinerants. But whereas Dillon thinks Luke has made an
originally simple lesson of repentance into a story of how the itinerants often received a warmer reception from marginal, sinful
folk than from the high and mighty,[53] I think, rather, that the
story reveals a polemical edge on behalf of the widows, which
the widows added once they heard the story from the itinerants
in its previous form.

The itinerants had circulated the tale as a defense of themselves for receiving the extravagant attentions of their patronesses. As the itinerants told it, it was the genuineness of their
prophethood that was at stake. As remoulded by the widows,
their own reputations became the central concern. The story only
becomes a bland lesson of repentance in its latest, Lukan form.

Stage Four: Luke's Version

Luke has harmonized the last two versions, both of which he
could easily have heard. He could not brook the criticism of the

---

53. Dillon, *Eye-Witnesses*, 240-242.

Prince of Apostles, so Simon Peter became Simon the Pharisee. He added the phrase "who was a sinner" to v. 37, to make the narrative voice confirm the suspicion of Simon, which up till now had been confuted by what followed. To reapply the story, he shoved down its throat the alien parable of the two debtors. (Or should we call it a phallocentric rape of the widow text, forcibly inserting his male-vindicating interpolation into the textual zone of women's self-affirmation?)

He conflated the two replies to Simon, adding to the first the phrase "which are many," in order to make her sin something more than the extravagance shown the visitor. Further, he tacked on "but he who is forgiven little loves little" in order to harmonize the preceding saying with the parable. Verses 48-50 seem to be derived from Mark 2:5-7 and are intended as a hasty reminder that forgiveness is the prerogative of Jesus, twitting the Jews with the fact.

The square peg of the parable, teaching as it does that gratitude follows on forgiveness, just does not fit the round hole of the story which teaches that forgiveness is a reward for love. The indefatigable apologists, who think some benefit would accrue if we could save the story from critical dissection, have wasted great efforts in the salvage operation, all, ironically, to demonstrate the hopelessness of their cause.

Many scholars take refuge in the tactic of trying to read v. 47, "Therefore I tell you her sins . . . are forgiven for she loved much," as if it meant "And I can tell she must at some point previously have been forgiven; otherwise she wouldn't love so much." In other words, she has that look that Jesus has come to associate with the peaceful, forgiven soul. Rank psychologizing, I call it. But that does not bother Browning,[54] Morris,[55] the translators of the Jerusalem Bible, Danker ("'Love' here means to demonstrate affection"—it *has* to!),[56] Johnson,[57] and Tannehill,[58] who as much as admits it is a harmonization, but he is sticking with it anyway! And of course Ben Witherington accepts it without so

54. Browning, *Luke*, 80.
55. Leon Morris, *Luke: An Introduction and Commentary*, rev. ed., Tyndale New Testament Commentaries, ed. Leon Morris (Leicester: Inter-Varsity Press; Grand Rapids: William B. Eerdmans Publishing Company, 1989), 163.
56. Danker, *New Age*, 170.
57. Johnson, *Luke*, 128.
58. Tannehill, *Narrative Unity: Luke*, 117.

much as blinking.[59]

Marshall's effort at reconciling Luke with himself is the greatest failure because the most extensive attempt. Since Luke himself saw no contradiction, Marshall reasons, we ought not to see one either, as if Luke were somehow in a better position to notice it than we. This is no more than to say, "If we could talk to Luke, I bet *he'd* be able to iron it out for us!" And he has: Marshall concludes Luke must have held the "her love attests her having been forgiven" view, since this is the best sense anyone seems to be able to make of it—as if this were not to beg the question.[60]

Similarly, he invokes Wilckens's puzzling verdict that since the parable of the debtors must originally have addressed some such situation as described in the passage we need not seek to pry the two apart.[61] Again, completely circular.

In order to save the parable as part of the original story Marshall must, following Zahn and in company with a number of the others cited above, make the supposition that Jesus had already forgiven the woman on some previous occasion unreported by Luke. He knows that some might question such an expedient, but again Marshall settles the issue by a fallacious appeal to authority: Schürmann, surely no axe-grinding inerrantist (like Marshall himself, he implicitly admits), agrees as to a previous contact between Jesus and the woman.[62]

Kilgallen tries to obviate the difficulty here by positing the moment of prior forgiveness as being given in the text after all, if not in the pericope itself, then in the neighboring text, in the previous story where Luke contrasts the people who submitted to John's baptism and the Pharisees who did not. The woman is one of the former, Simon one of the latter. He reasons that this connection would also explain why Simon regards the woman as still a sinner (but so does Luke! Cf. v. 37): Simon considers that John's baptism was merely "from men." It was in vain, and she is still in her sins. Equally the theory seems to explain why Simon has been "forgiven little": he was not baptized unto repentance.[63]

This line of reasoning seems to contradict itself, implying that Simon thought John's baptism both to be genuine ("I just

---

59. Witherington, *Women in the Ministry*, 56.

60. Marshall, *Luke*, 306.

61. Ibid., 307.

62. Ibid.

63. J. J. Kilgallen, "John the Baptist, the Sinful Woman, and the Pharisee," *Journal of Biblical Literature* 104 (1985): 678.

don't happen to need it, is all.") and to be spurious ("She's kidding herself, poor fool!"). And why would the woman, one of John's converts, show such gratitude to Jesus? Kilgallen seems to be saying that the two would have been pretty much interchangeable in view of Jesus' linking of himself and John as common children of Wisdom in his eulogy for John (7:35). Or does Kilgallen mean that the woman's gratitude is for the kind words anent John, her personal savior? Or does she perhaps imagine that Jesus is John raised from the dead?

Also Kilgallen seems to see more of a link between the two passages than in fact there is, thinking of the Matthean parallel to Luke 7:29-30, Matthew 12:32, where the prostitutes have repented at John's preaching, and the sinful woman of Luke 7 would seem to be one of these. But it is fatal to this linkage that Luke has nothing about prostitutes in either his version of the eulogy of the Baptist, or, explicitly, in the story of the woman in Simon's house.

But even if we accept Kilgallen's view it leaves unaddressed the question of the viability of Luke 7:36-50 as a self-contained unit of tradition. Did it ever travel down the tradition stream in its present form unconnected with the adjacent text? In fact we may accept most of Kilgallen's suggestions and still be no further along in explaining the internal fault lines and sediment-layers in the pericope. Hence the need for more than a flat literary analysis criss-crossing the text synchronically.

D. A. S. Ravens tries to build on Kilgallen's work by showing that Luke 7:50-8:1 is based on Isaiah 52:7. The Lukan passages contain several words and cognates in common with the LXX of the Isaiah passage, especially the words for evangelizing, peace, salvation, and *feet*. "How beautiful are the feet of one preaching glad tidings of peace, as one preaching good news; for I will publish thy salvation, saying, O Sion, thy God shall reign." This might explain why Luke has the woman anoint Jesus' feet instead of his head, since she would be beautifying the feet of the one bringing the evangel of God's reign.[64] But since we do not know that Luke created the other parallels to the Isaiah text, we may only be dealing with his juxtaposition of pre-Lukan units.

John J. Donahue is no more successful in his wrenching of the text: "In paraphrase, Christ's argument runs this way: 'You,

---

64. D. A. S. Ravens, "The Setting of Luke's Account of the Anointing: Luke 7.2 - 8.3," *New Testament Studies* 34 (1988): 286.

Simon, say that love flows from forgiveness, and because you think yourself just and with little to be forgiven, you love little. But I say to you that forgiveness flows from love—from love of me whom you are so quick to reject.'"[65]

If it comes to the point where we have to rewrite the text to make it bear our interpretation, then we might think twice about the latter. Also, this view again cannot explain why a Pharisee should have sought the company of a seducer of Israel.

All in all, I deem it more probable that the seams in the text are like growth rings in an old tree, and that the story has grown from one defending itinerants who require special privilege at the expense of poor relief, to one defending them for accepting the scandalous devotion of grateful patronesses, to one told on behalf of those patronesses, the widows. Rather than the sensualists and sinners they are suspected of being, they prove themselves more devout than their detractors by the loving quality of the menial service they render to those who come in the name of Christ. Only subsequently did the redactor Luke give the story its present, most difficult, form.

Several of the previous form- and redaction-critical treatments reviewed here suffered, it seems to me, from not having available to them as a likely option for the pericope's *Sitz-im-Leben* the triangular relationship between the widows, church officialdom, and the itinerant charismatics. The adoption of this scenario enables us to make good sense of the tale in various stages of its evolution. We can distribute the various contradictory features in the present conflated version among several hypothetical previous oral versions, much as Pentateuchal critics succeeded in restoring the four great sources of the Pentateuch by disentangling the redundancies and contradictions of the canonical whole. Not only so, but the triangular relationship itself provides a clearer map than form critics usually have for tracing the transmission route of the tale between its successive shapers.

---

65. J. J. Donahue, "The Penitent Woman and the Pharisee: Luke 7:36-50," *American Ecclesiastical Review* 142 (1960): 420.

CHAPTER SIX

Chaste Passion:
The Chastity Story of Joanna

The Ministering Women

Luke 8:2-3 seems to be a note added as an afterthought: Jesus and his disciples are on a tour of Galilee, as we expect them to be. And suddenly, as if to whet our curiosity, Luke adds the news that the men he has named were accompanied on their journeys by a group of very colorful-sounding women. As Derrida might say, each clause of the two verses seems to be a reading head for a text that Luke does not supply us.[1] Each of these women has a story, or rather, is a story.

Of Mary Magdalene we are casually told that she had been haunted by seven demons! Perhaps they were the notorious gang of seven that lived in the waste places, who returned with a friend to occupy the exorcised man (Matthew 12:43-45). Surely there was a story told about Mary's torments and deliverance, and there must be a reason we do not hear it.

Joanna appears only in Luke. Of her we are told intriguing details, details that cannot have ended here: she was the wife of one Chuza, Herod's steward and/or boyhood chum. Susanna is named for the chaste heroine of the Greek Daniel. Didn't this New Testament Susanna have a story as colorful as that of her prototype? She must have.

Many traditions of the women of the early church are, no doubt, irretrievably lost. And yet I think we have not entirely lost the story of Joanna. Indeed I make the audacious claim that we can more or less fully recover her story, and in this chapter I will make the attempt to do so.

Scholars have by no means ignored the brief mention of Mary, Joanna, Susanna and the rest. Most of the discussion of the women has focused on the question of their precise role in the entourage of Jesus. Luke says they "provided for them (or him) out of their means." In what did this provision consist? What did they do? There have been four answers to this question.

Some suggest the women did domestic chores for the men.

---

1. Jacques Derrida, "Living On. Border Lines," in *Deconstruction and Criticism,* no ed. (New York: Continuum Publishing Corporation, 1979), 107.

Oh, to be sure, they weren't sent to the kitchen when the teaching began, but they were mainly there to—what? Roll up the sleeping bags? How many domestic chores can there have been for a wandering group of mendicant preachers? At any rate, Witherington piously coos:

> Being Jesus' disciples did not lead these women to abandon their traditional roles in regard to preparing food, serving, etc. Rather, it gave these roles new significance and importance, for now they could be used to serve the Master and the family. The transformation of these women involved not only assuming new discipleship roles [for Witherington this means "continu[ing] in the Master's presence and learn[ing] from him"], but also resuming their traditional roles for a new purpose.[2]

Witherington does grant that there were women among the Seventy, so that these women may even have preached the gospel. He thus tries to distance himself from Hengel, who makes the women domestics pure and simple.[3] But since the Seventy are clearly a figment of Lukan redaction meant to anticipate the Gentile Mission, a barely narrative peg on which to hang more mission instructions, I do not see how it can even be meaningful to posit the inclusion of the women, or any other particular character for that matter, among the fictitious missioners. We have no right to assume that Luke would have worked out such fine connections. He certainly gives no hint of it.

Tannehill and Via seem to subscribe to the same view of the women's essentially domestic role.[4] Sim soundly refutes Witherington, and implicitly Tannehill and Via as well, pointing out that while the ministering women are not actually said, like Peter's mother-in-law (Luke 4:38-39), to serve meals, the male disciples,

---

2. Ben Witherington, "On the Road with Mary Magdalene, Joanna, Susanna, and Other Disciples—Luke 8 1-3," *Zeitschrift für die Neutestamentlische Wissenschaft* 70 (1979): 244-245; Witherington, *Women in the Ministry*, 118.

3. Martin Hengel, "Maria Magdalena und die Frauen als Keugen," in *Abraham Unser Vater: Juden und Christen im Gesprach über bie Bibel, Festschrift für Otto Michel, zum 60. Geburtstag,* eds. Otto Betz, Martin Hengel, Peter Schmidt (Leiden: E. J. Brill, 1963), 247-248.

4. Tannehill, *Narrative Unity, Luke,* 138; E. J. Via, "Women, Service, Meal," 38; see also Danker, *New Age,* 225; Whitney, "Women in Luke," 223-224.

in other passages in the gospels, are.[5] However, I would not be as sure as Sim that the role of the male disciples in serving the food at the miraculous multiplication of loaves and fishes counts as evidence for the historical Jesus and the practice of his entourage, for these stories are obviously legends.

One might reply that even legends might preserve the memory that the men prepared the food. But I am afraid not. The stories are probably eucharistic in their symbolism, and then the role of the men serving is a reflection of the exclusion of women from the eucharistic ministry.

The case of John 4:7-42, where the men go into the village to shop, is of no more help, since it implies the complete exclusion of any women from the entourage of Jesus: once the men are gone Jesus is alone. Others, including Schuyler Brown and Quentin Quesnell, see the women in Luke 8:3 as implied preachers of the gospel, deriving this opinion from what they perceive to be the general Lukan job description of disciples, among whom they number the women.[6]

Still others understand the women more on the order of patronesses who paid the bills for Jesus and his disciples, out of their own means. Sim thinks that few of them could have been wealthy, Joanna an apparent exception, and that all pooled their resources.[7] Luise Schottroff says that the women of Galilee are indeed pictured as patronesses, but that this is anachronistic, retrojected into the gospel from the situation of the early church: "The wealthy women walk with them on this journey. (Are we to imagine that they carry large money-bags behind the disciples?)."[8] Schottroff and Jervell both recognize the historical prototype of these patronesses in the upper-class ladies who support the apostles in Philippi and Thessalonica.[9] But it was not these

---

5. D. C. Sim, "The Women Followers of Jesus: The Implications of Luke 8:1-3," *Heythrup Journal* 30 (1989): 56-59.

6. Schuyler Brown, *Apostasy and Perseverence in the Theology of Luke,* Analecta Biblica 36 (Rome: Pontifical Biblical Institute, 1969), 88; Quentin Quesnell, "The Women at Luke's Supper," in *Political Issues in Luke-Acts,* eds. Richard J. Cassidy and Philip J. Sharper (Maryknoll, NY: Orbis Books, 1983), 68; Selvidge, *Daughters,* 113.

7. Sim, "Women Followers," 57; Selvidge, *Daughters,* 114; McKenna, *Women of the Church,* 37.

8. Luise Schottroff, "Women as Followers of Jesus in New Testament Times: An Exercise in Social-Historical Exegesis of the Bible," in *The Bible and Liberation, Political and Social Hermeneutics,* ed. Norman K. Gottwald (Maryknoll, NY: Orbis Books, 1989), 420.

ladies who travelled from place to place. To put them, too, "on the road," as Witherington would have it, is like the Priestly writer inventing the Tabernacle so as to have the Temple of a later era accompany the Israelites in their wanderings.[10] The last alternative is that suggested by Dillon, who sees correctly, I think, that the women are neither the retrojection of the later patronesses, nor historical figures associated with Jesus, but rather a retrojection of the travelling *suneisaktoi* or celibate partners or sister-wives of the itinerants of the early church.[11] Such arrangements were more common in a residential situation, but that there were travelling couples of the same kind is clear enough.

With Crossan, I suspect this arrangement is in view already in 1 Corinthians 9:5.[12] But we might also look to the first of the two pseudo-Clementine epistles on virginity which denounce "shameless men, who, under pretext of the fear of God, have their dwelling with maidens, and so expose themselves to danger, and walk with them along the road and in solitary places alone—a course which is full of dangers" (X).

A puzzling reference in the *Didache* 11:11 may well refer to the chaste missionary couples when it warns of some strange prophetic behavior which is to be tolerated but not emulated, with the hint that it may be damnable by God, but not subject to human judgment, since after all, who knows? The itinerant was

---

9. Ibid.; Jacob Jervell, "The Daughters of Abraham: Women in Acts," in *The Unknown Paul, Essays on Luke-Acts and Early Christian History* (Minneapolis: Augsburg Publishing House, 1984), 147, 153.

10. Gryson has a point: the Markan parallel (15:40-41) makes it unlikely that Luke hatched the idea himself (Gryson, *Women*, 2), but Luke may have inherited and embellished an anachronism. Note that Mark does not specify the financial nature of the support implied by Luke. It is this feature which makes the women look like prototypes of the later patronesses.

Also, it is just possible that the mention of the women in Mark, which suddenly intrudes without any preparation, unlike in Luke, is a later harmonizing gloss. A few manuscripts (C, D, and some others) omit at least the phrase "and ministered to him". See Coker, "Women and the Gospel," 61 and the sources cited there.

B. W. Bacon thought that the mention of the women formed part of the true Markan text, but that it represents a Markan borrowing from the Lukan special source (*The Gospel of Mark: Its Composition and Date* [New Haven: Yale University Press; London: Humphrey Milford/Oxford University Press, 1925], 196).

11. Dillon, *Eye-Witnesses*, 245; Brown, *Body and Society*, 43.

12. Crossan, *Historical*, 335.

to be allowed a measure of "prophetic blasphemy," as was the messiah Sabbatai Sevi,[13] as one who had been caught up beyond mortal standards of conventional good and evil. "No prophet who has been tried and is genuine [on other grounds], though he enact a worldly mystery of the Church, if he teach not others to do what he does himself, shall be judged by you: for he has his judgment with God" (*Didache* 11:11).

Here I return to my speculation that the suspicions of sexual intercourse between the wandering saint and his female disciple may not have been always or altogether unfounded. The language of the *Didache* passage reflects that of the contemporary Epistle to the Ephesians, in which Paul is made to quote Genesis 2:24, "For this reason a man shall leave his father and mother and be joined to his wife, and the two shall become one." He goes on to say, "This is a great mystery, and I take it to mean Christ and the church, however, [as a secondary application,] let each one of you love his wife as himself" (v. 33). Was the "mystery" regarding the church, a mystery that could be called "worldly" (*musterion kosmikon ekklesias*), that of the *hieros gamos* performed by the itinerant prophet and his female partner to bespeak the union of Christ and the church?

The *Didache* seems to suspect the propriety of such prophetic enormities, yet not to dare to reject them. As we have just seen, the pseudo-Clementine epistles come from a time when such behavior was no longer tolerated. But the *Didache* had at least decided that such risky behavior was off limits for ordinary mortals; so much so that if a prophet went over the line and taught such libertinage, he was automatically to be written off as a false prophet.

Is there any evidence that any of them did so teach the laity? As it happens, there is. We find it in a fragment, preserved in Epiphanius' *Panarion*, of the Gnostic text *The Great Questions of Mary* (i.e., the longer of two similar texts with the same title): the Risen Christ

> gave [Mary Magdalene] a revelation, taking her aside to the mountain and praying; and he brought forth from his side a woman [cf. the words of Andrew to Maximilla: "I rightly see in you Eve repenting and in myself Adam being converted."] and began to unite with her, and so, forsooth, taking his effluent, he

13. Scholem, *Sabbatai Sevi*, 242.

showed that "we must so do, that we may live"; and
. . . when Mary fell to the ground abashed, he raised
her up again and said to her: "Why didst thou doubt,
O thou of little faith?" (*Panarion* 26.8.2-3)

It is the fear of such teaching, as Jesus does in the story, of Tantric discipleship that led to some of the suspicions held against the itinerants and the women who were so devoted to them. I imagine it worked the other way round as well: that there were women apostles, such as I picture Mary Magdalene to have been,[14] who had male companions, and in her case these arrangements may have caused her to receive the epithet "the Harlot." But typically, it was mostly the evidence concerning males and their female companions that trickled down the centuries.

Not Likely

Now we have to ask whether the picture of Jesus and his men wandering through Galilee with a group of unattached women in their train can possibly reflect historical memory of the life of Jesus.

Scholars do not fail to note the drastic clash with contemporary Jewish mores entailed by such a procedure on Jesus' part. From this fact they proceed in several directions. We are told, first, that it was not unusual for women to support religious scholars out of their own means. I am by no means persuaded that the evidence usually cited even bears on the point, much less proves it.[15] But supposing that Jewish women might support rabbis, do we have a true parallel with Luke 8:3? Not for a moment. For all their differences, Witherington and Sim agree that the very idea of a rabbi followed about by a band of women would have been infamous and unthinkable.[16] If Jesus and his disciples thus flouted Jewish decorum what are the implications?

A whole legion of Christian feminist apologists has pointed to the gender-mixed group of travellers as evidence for the radi-

---

14. Robert M. Price, "Mary Magdalene: Gnostic Apostle?," *Grail: An Ecumenical Journal* 6 (June 1990): 54-76. For female itinerant pairs see Mary Rose D'Angelo, "Women Partners in the New Testament," *Journal of Feminist Studies in Religion* 6 (1990): 65-86.
15. I defy anyone to draw Witherington's conclusions from the material he cites from C. G. Montefiore and H. Lowe, eds., *A Rabbinic Anthology* (New York: Schocken Books, 1974), 423-424, 415-416, 23-25.
16. Witherington, "On the Road," 245; Sim, "Women Followers," 54.

cal departure of Jesus from the restrictions of Jewish society.[17] Here we have an example of what might be called "dissimilarity apologetics," a device whereby apologists for the Christian religion in general or Christian feminism in particular seem to apply Perrin's "criterion of dissimilarity" to the vexing question of the cultural forms of revelation. There is a desire to claim the freedom to reapply "acculturated" New Testament values in new ways appropriate to one's own culture, yet to want to isolate some of them as the truly revealed values (e.g., male-female equality) by showing how they could *not* be accommodated to the cultures of biblical times. If some Christian stance seems to mark a "radical departure" from (or, better yet, a "radical reversal" of) current practice, we may be sure we can spot the revelation, not a mere accommodation to the culture of the time. So scholars have cheerfully pointed to the fact of Jesus allowing women to accompany him in his travels as evidence for his transcendance of his androcentric culture.

Leaving aside the implicit anti-Judaism in all this, let me just note the methodological flaw. It seems to me that if one begins by superimposing a particular paradigm on the data and then finds data that do not fit, one either concludes one is applying the wrong paradigm or that one has misread the data. The one thing one cannot do is to use the paradigm against itself. One cannot coherently show how the phenomena transcend the appropriate paradigm! To be consistent one must interpret the data in accord with the paradigm or else find a new one. One cannot begin with the proposition that the Jesus movement is to be interpreted in Jewish categories and then proceed to argue that aberrant aspects of the Movement show it to have been a nonconformist movement. It may have been, but the method cannot show us this. It is limited by what Berger, dependent on Kahn and Wiener, calls the "surprise-free" nature of the method.[18]

The contributors to the volume *The Social World of Luke-Acts* make abundant use of models derived from Mediterranean peasant anthropology, dealing with factors like dyadic identity con-

17. Robin Scroggs, "Paul and the Eschatological Woman: Revisited," *Journal of the American Academy of Religion* 42 (1974): 535; Tetlow, *Women and Ministry*, 93; E. J. Via, "Women in the Gospel of Luke," 46; Swidler, *Biblical Affirmations*, 194.
18. Peter L. Berger, *A Rumor of Angels: Modern Society and the Recovery of the Sacred* (Garden City, NY: Anchor Books, a division of Doubleday & Company, 1970), 16, 19.

cepts, limited good, male and female shame and honor, grid and group, patronage, etc. Items from the gospels are cited in abundance to show how well the paradigm fits the data. But sooner or later we come to a stubborn item in the gospels which does not seem to fit, and we are back to dissimilarity apologetics. Jesus "radically transcended" this or that ancient norm or value,[19] and here is where we can behold the gospel in its fullness. One suspects that lurking here is a surviving shadow of the belief that Jesus was a god entering the world from without, with a divine knowledge of a better way, which he taught in dribs and drabs as dull mortals could assimilate it. Or he was Schleiermacher's religious genius and hero who saw far ahead of his time. None of this has anything to do with anthropology or history. It must be banished, left in church, when one dons one's scholarly cap.

So I agree with Schüssler Fiorenza: if it isn't possible in Judaism it must be ruled out for the *Sitz-im-Leben Jesu* as well. "The reconstruction of the Jesus movement as the discipleship of equals is historically plausible only insofar as such critical elements are thinkable within the context of Jewish life and faith."[20] If Jesus seems to be leaping out of his cultural skin, surely this means we are misreading the text, that we are applying the wrong paradigm to construe the data, or that we are dealing with an anachronism. For instance, some aspect of the Hellenistic church is being retrojected by the evangelists into the "middle of time" when the Son of God walked the earth for the purpose of authorizing the practices of the later church.

Is the Gospel picture of the wandering band of men and single women possible in first-century Judaism? We may gauge its likelihood by the amount of controversy the arrangement is said to have generated. If historically authentic, the travelling arrangements of Jesus' entourage may be expected to have invited comments akin to those which made of him a glutton and a drunkard on the strength of his associations with tax collectors and sinners. Surely Jesus' travelling with single women would have been at least as much a subject for attack and defense as Jesus' ministry to the outcasts which scholars see as having generated several parables.[21] And how much might that be? Schab-

19. Neyrey, ed., *Social World of Luke-Acts*, 27, 75, 145, 259, 264, 265, 267, 380.

20. Schüssler Fiorenza, *In Memory of Her*, 107.

21. Jeremias, *Parables*, 124-126; Perrin, *Rediscovering*, 90-93.

erg notices the deafening silence here:

> Scholars often remark that the practice of including
> women in such a ministry was scandalous. If this is
> true, why did that scandal leave no mark on the tradi-
> tions, and why was the practice never explicitly
> defended? Unfortunately, these questions cannot be
> answered on the basis of present knowledge of the
> activities and life-styles possible for Jewish women in
> the time of Jesus.[22]

Schaberg's best guess is that perhaps the radius of Jesus' travels
was not great and that the women came out from their homes to
meet him each day, rather, I should imagine, like well-wishers
stationed with cups of lemonade for the runners in a marathon.

In an earlier day, Oscar Holtzmann noticed the lack of controversy, but he made apologetical hay out of it:

> there could hardly be a more beautiful testimony to
> the deep impression produced by the earnest, holy
> bearing of this body of people, disowned by their own
> nation, than the fact that no offence was taken, so far
> as we know, by anyone of their many contemporary
> enemies at the consorting together of these men and
> women in a band that was now ceaselessly moving
> about from place to place.[23]

Crossan counters that there is indeed evidence that Jesus'
contemporaries were scandalized by these living arrangements.
Did they not call him a friend of prostitutes?[24] In fact, as far as
we know, they did not. Perhaps Crossan is thinking of Matthew
21:28-32, where Jesus is made to note that prostitutes repented,
not, however, at his preaching, but rather at that of John!
Besides, the ladies of the night are absent from the Lukan parallel
(7:29-30). Jesus does say that the prostitutes and publicans will
enter God's kingdom before the Pharisees (Matthew 21:31), but
this saying need mean no more than that the Pharisees are lower
than the lowest, not to give any comfort to the harlots.[25]

So we know of no circumstances in which the roving male-

---

22. Schaberg, "Luke," 287.
23. Oscar Holtzmann, *The Life of Jesus*, trans. J. T. Bealby and Maurice A.
Canney (London: Adam & Charles Black, 1904), 307.
24. Crossan, *Historical*, 335.

female band of itinerants could have flourished in Judaism. And we also hear of no controversy being attached to the supposed practice of Jesus in this regard. And we know that precisely such arrangements did exist in the early church, where we have seen the evidence of the controversy they occasioned. Everything that is missing in the *Sitz-im-Leben Jesu* is in place in the *Sitz-im-Leben Kirche*. Clearly it is in the latter that we should place the story of Jesus' Galilean women.

Chastity Stories

It is striking that when we thus locate it we find that there is a whole class of stories into which the report of Joanna and the women fits quite nicely. They are the chastity stories discussed by Ross Kraemer and Virginia Burrus. In what follows I hope to make clear that fragments of such a chastity story involving Joanna and Jesus are embedded here and there in the Gospel of Luke. But first I must briefly review the basic, common outline of the chastity story.

Kraemer, who first isolated the form, synthesizes the plot:

> Each [story] relates the conversion of a woman whose husband, fiancé, lord, or father is of relatively high social status in a community which an apostle has recently entered. Persuaded by the apostle's teachings to accept Jesus, the woman adopts a sexually continent way of life, which is the principal feature of her conversion. If already married, she withdraws from her husband; if unmarried, she vows to remain a virgin. . . . The principal male in the woman's life invariably opposes her newfound asceticism, and frequently threatens the woman, the apostle or both. Such threats are never successful: the woman continues her association with the apostle and her practice of chastity. As a result, both apostle and woman are imprisoned, scourged, or otherwise punished. Frequently, as in the martyrdoms of Thomas, Andrew, and Peter, the angered husband is the direct cause of the apostle's death; only rarely does the husband convert. The woman does not renounce asceticism in any of the accounts; rather she lives chastely outside of her hus-

---

25. Richard A. Horsley, *Jesus and the Spiral of Violence: Popular Jewish Resistance in Roman Palestine* (San Francisco: Harper & Row, Publishers, 1987; Minneapolis: Fortress Press, 1993), 213-214.

band's home, and in some cases, such as those of Thecla and Charitine, she even joins a band of wandering
Christian apostles.[26]

Here is Burrus's slightly different summary, in outline form:

1. Apostle arrives in town.
2. Woman goes to hear apostle preach.
3. Woman vows chastity.
4. Husband attempts to violate vow.
5. Apostle encourages woman.
6. Woman resists husband.
7. Husband/governor imprisons apostle.
8. Woman visits apostle in prison (encouragement; baptism).
9. Husband/governor attempts to kill apostle.
10. Apostle dies or is rescued (leaves the scene).
11. Husband/governor persecutes woman.
12. Woman is rescued.
13. Woman defeats husband/governor (who may be converted or punished, and never succeeds in persuading the woman).
14. Woman is freed (allowed to remain chaste).[27]

Kaestli challenges the viability of Burrus's delineation of the form, pedantically pointing out what she admitted to start with, that not every single element is necessarily present in every one of the stories.[28] The same thing could be said about any "form" in the gospel tradition. Admittedly we do not find the element of the bystanders' skepticism in every single miracle story, but we do find it often enough that we are justified in speaking of a definite form of the miracle story which includes it. Kaestli seems to misunderstand the notion of an ideal type. It is just that: ideal. The reality does not always fit it but can be meaningfully measured against it.

As will become clear shortly, comparison of the two form-summaries shows both how in broad outline the story of Joanna is unmistakably such a chastity story, and how only fragments of it (though, fortunately, the most important ones) remain after Luke's rude handling.

---

26. Kraemer, "Conversion of Women," 300.
27. Burrus, *Chastity as Autonomy*, 34-35.
28. Jean-Daniel Kaestli, "Response," *Semeia* 38 (1986): 121-122.

Also note that Burrus in two respects corrects and modifies Kraemer's outline: first, the woman is not always imprisoned, though the apostle is. Second, even where the particular heroine's conversion is not the immediate cause of the apostle's death, it may still be the apostle's continence-preaching that is the cause of his death, and, as Burrus notes, there are no chastity stories that do not issue in apostle martyrdoms, or at least imprisonments, though she speculates that such may once have existed.[29]

One more thing I would add is that when the apostle does not escape he may yet rise from the dead, as do Thomas and Paul, and implicitly, John. In this as so many other aspects they are only following in the footsteps of their Lord, and I will argue that would make very good sense if all the stories were imitations of the chastity story of Joanna, which issued in the Passion of Christ and his resurrection.

The Chastity Story of Joanna

First we may remind ourselves that Joanna is not mentioned in any of the other gospels. We will see that the same is true of various other features of Luke which fit rather neatly into the basic outline of the chastity story. This fact already predisposes one to be on the lookout for a special source of Luke that would have contained them all. Obviously many scholars have tried to isolate and characterize special Lukan sources. Some of their efforts will help us here.

First, the most obvious respect in which the Joanna material resembles the chastity stories: she is the wife of a high-born official, placed close to Herod Antipas, yet here she is, moving about in public with Jesus of Nazareth! How on earth has she come to be doing this? Luke preserves no comment on an irresistibly noteworthy item. Surely one never raises such a point except to comment upon it! It is by itself a question, not an answer, and the teller of the tale in which it was raised must also have answered it. Luke does not answer it; hence he did not raise it. Someone else, who first raised it, also answered it. But Luke, in taking over the pre-existing story, whether in oral or written form, has suppressed the answer. Why he has done this will become apparent; but basically, since the point of these stories was to assert the apostolic liberation of women, through celibacy, from the control of powerful men, this is hardly a message that Luke, as we have

29. Burrus, *Chastity as Autonomy*, 99-100.

come to know him, would want to pass along to the women in his audience!

Also, no doubt Richard Pervo is correct when he notes the absence from Acts of any of what Burrus calls chastity stories: "The canonical author did not wish to portray Christianity as a destabilizing factor in social life. Had he known of such tales as may decorate the Apoc[ryphal] Acts, he would have kept his silence."[30] Here again we think of the social apologetic of the Pastorals. But Luke did not keep complete silence.

Then we must ask why he retained any reference to Joanna at all. Here is where Jervell and Schöttroff are right on target: Luke wants to use Joanna as a precedent for wealthy women patrons for the missionary movement. He retrojects this arrangement into the sacred time of apostolic authorization. Hence he retains Joanna's link with Chuza so as to make clear that Joanna was a wealthy patroness. But back to our story.

Commentators have occasionally wondered about the strange fact of Joanna's absence from her husband's side. Godet, with the ingenuity of the precritical exegete who had to be all the more nimble for having so narrow a space in which to maneuver, fancifully suggested that Chuza was the *basilikos* mentioned in John 4:46-53, whose son Jesus healed! He was so grateful to Jesus that he lent him his wife as a follower.[31] Plummer and Ryrie, as might be expected, follow Godet here as faithfully as they pictured the holy women following at Jesus' heels.[32]

Closer to the mark are those who, like Wojcik, see that "Perhaps it hints that Jesus has divided a household."[33] Sim: "There were . . . some who braved public condemnation by leavingtheir husbands to follow Jesus."[34] But these are mere hints. Why would she have done it? What does it mean that she did it? Surely there is a story to this: not just facts behind it, but a *story* behind it. A chastity story. (Luke may have read a written account, but then again it may have been a fairly detailed oral telling that he heard.)

In that story we would have read or heard of a day when Joanna, perhaps in her sedan chair, happened to pass a place where she heard Jesus preaching "about righteousness and

---

30. Pervo, *Profit with Delight*, 128.
31. Godet, *Luke*, 233.
32. Plummer, *Luke*, 216; Ryrie, *Role of Women*, 36.
33. Wojcik, *Road*, 134.
34. Sim, "Women Followers," 55.

encrateia and future judgment" (cf. Acts 24:25, where a similar wealthy wife of an official hears such a speech from Paul). Telling her bearers to stop, she listens awhile as peasants on the edge of the crowd note her presence with slack-jawed amazement. As the Nazarene preacher finishes his simple but powerful words, Joanna pulls open the ring-hung satin drapes of her palanquin and steps forth from the shelter of royalty. Not noticing the smelly raggedness of the humble crowd, at which only an hour before she would have flinched in disgust and fear, she strides through the crowd, flustered guards scurrying after her. They listen as she asks the preacher, "Sir, what must I do to be saved?"

Jesus, showing neither surprise nor any sign that he is impressed at her rank, answers that she must give away what she owns and follow him, leaving board and bed alike. She vows to do so, as her guards look knowingly at each other: "What will Chuza have to say about *that*, eh?"

Some weeks later, after long, unexplained absences of his wife, Chuza summons her and confronts her with the information his men have reported. Has she gone out of her mind? We may imagine him speaking much as Charisius demands of Mygdonia in the *Acts of Thomas,* "Why didst thou not have regard to thy position as a free woman and remain in thy house but go out and listen to vain words and look upon magic works?"

In the Apocryphal Acts Xanthippe is married to a highly placed friend of Caesar, while Maximilla and Artemilla are married to governors, with Tertia the king's wife and Mygdonia the wife of a friend of the king.[35] Joanna fits the pattern perfectly as the wife of the steward of Herod Antipas. And just as in all the other cases, we must surmise that Chuza sought his royal friend's help in bringing his wife back into line, as well as settling the score with the troublemaker who took her away from him.[36] Thus it is more than coincidence that in Luke's gospel we hear that Herod is seeking to kill Jesus (13:31). Now, I think, we can see what supplied his motive.

---

35. Burrus, *Chastity as Autonomy*, 99.
36. Antoinette Clark Wire, "The Social Function of Women's Asceticism in the Roman East," in *Images of the Feminine in Gnosticism*, ed. Karen L. King, Studies in Antiquity and Christianity, gen. ed. James M. Robinson (Philadelphia: Fortress Press, 1988), 323.

Herod versus Jesus

Where did Luke derive the information that Herod wanted Jesus dead? Not from Mark, since there Herod is simply frightened by one whom he thinks to be the ghost of John the Baptist (Mark 6:16). Luke changes this notice in Mark to "John I beheaded, but who is this about whom I hear such things?" (Luke 9:9). Why this change? I agree with Joseph Tyson that Luke means to show Herod resolving to kill Jesus as he had John.[37] If so, he had to change Mark's note, since Herod can hardly have intended to kill a dead man a second time! Thus in Luke he does not think Jesus is the shade of John. And where has he heard these things about Jesus? From an old friend named Chuza. That Luke did not derive Herod's murderous designs on Jesus from Mark 3:6, where the Herodians, presumably Antipas' spies, conspire with the Pharisees to put Jesus to death, is apparent from the fact that Luke omits this note. He must have preferred a different account.

Only in Luke's gospel does Jesus stand trial before Herod Antipas. There have been several attempts to account for this difference from the other gospels. What have scholars made of the trial? Some account must be given of the fact of its uncanny similarity in some respects to the trial before Pilate in Matthew and Mark, transferring to Herod's trial the mockery of the soldiers and the accusations of the priests.

Some scholars of an older generation sought to vindicate the historical veracity of the trial. In general, I think we can safely rule out this option. As Goulder succinctly puts it: "It is remotely unlikely that it is historical, since it is not in Mark."[38]

A. W. Verrall, to defend the narrative against the charge of being a mere doublet of the Pilate trial, had to reinterpret the text, against its manifest intent, as follows:

> Herod, when he saw the celebrated Jesus, was delighted above measure. For he had been wishing to see him a long while, because he had been hearing much about him. He was hoping too to see some feat performed by him. And he persisted in questioning him at some length, though the Master made him no answer. And there stood the chief priests and the

---

37. Joseph B. Tyson, *The Death of Jesus in Luke-Acts* (Columbia: University of South Carolina Press, 1986), 134.
38. Goulder, *New Paradigm*, 757.

> scribes, accusing him with all their might. But Herod
> with his forces [i.e., in view of his great military
> might,] thought him not important [i.e., as a threat],
> and jested thereupon [i.e., at Pilate's expense, the latter
> apparently thinking he was a threat], and, having
> clothed him with fine apparel [as a sign of respect to
> Jesus], sent him back to Pilate. And that very day
> Pilate and Herod were made friends, having before
> been at enmity with one another.[39]

Very clever, but on this reading, whence the new alliance of
Herod and Pilate, whom the event, understood this way, must
have driven still farther apart?

Streeter, Sherwin-White, and Hoehner think that Pilate
might indeed have remanded the prisoner to Herod as a way of
smoothing the tetrarch's feathers which Pilate had ruffled in that
little incident reported in Luke 13:1, when he butchered some
Galilean tourists while they were busy offering sacrifice in the
Temple.[40] Since he had exceeded his jurisdiction in that case, by
executing Herod's subjects (did they have diplomatic immunity
away from home?), he took especial pains to let Herod have the
privilege of trying a fellow Galilean. But, as Walaskay remarks, it
is more than a little difficult picturing Pilate showing such concern, even as a matter of political expediency: what would he
have cared what Antipas thought? What did he have to fear from
him? And besides, here Luke has surely just garbled the massa-
cre of three thousand sacrificing Galileans by Archelaus. This is
building an apologetical edifice on some pretty sandy soil.

Dibelius made the proposal that the whole trial is a Lukan
redactional creation on the basis of Psalm 2:2b, which Luke was
already looking forward to using in Acts 4:26. He needed to have
more than one heathen king to do the prophesied conspiring.[41] If
Matthew could make two donkeys out of one for prophecy's

---

39. A. W. Verrall, "Christ before Herod, Luke XXIII 1-16," *Journal of Theological Studies* 10 (April 1909): 345.

40. B[urnett] H[illman] Streeter, "On the Trial of Our Lord before Herod:
A Suggestion," in *Studies in the Synoptic Problem By Members of the Univer-
sity of Oxford*, ed. William Sanday (Oxford: Clarendon Press, 1911), 229-
231; A. N. Sherwin-White, *Roman Society and Roman Law in the New Testa-
ment* (New York: Oxford University Press, 1963; Grand Rapids: Baker
Book House, 1978), 31; Harold W. Hoehner, *Herod Antipas*, Society for
New Testament Studies Monograph Series, ed. Matthew Black, 7 (New
York: Cambridge University Press, 1972), 239.

sake, why couldn't Luke perform the same redactional mitosis with kings?

Loisy had already rejected this theory before Dibelius proposed it: "This text from the *Psalms* may have had some influence in shaping the Gospel-narrative, but it has not affected it very much and certainly cannot have created it."[42] Loisy is right: Luke simply cannot have taken a proof-text that makes two kings conspire to kill the anointed, and then, to fulfill it, have written up a story where one of these men pronounces Jesus not guilty!

Marion Soards salvages an important insight from the ruins of Dibelius's crashed theory: he surmises that the very fact of the early church's use of Psalm 2:2b as a proof-text implies a tradition (he would say a historical memory, but I look elsewhere for its origin) according to which Herod Antipas was indeed involved in the condemnation of Jesus.[43]

Walaskay offers a new variant on Dibelius' theme: suppose the trial of Jesus before Herod was instead a Lukan creation based on the trial of Paul before Herod Agrippa II in Acts? "Luke would not allow Jesus to be treated less fairly than his apostle; so he is also made to appear before a Herodian."[44] But who knows which way the dependence goes? Maybe the trial before Herod Agrippa II (as well, perchance, as Peter's before Herod Agrippa I, implied) is modelled on that of Jesus. Walaskay's theory will only seem attractive if we cannot find something better. And surely we can.

Another group of students of the trial problem suggest, somewhat vaguely, that Luke is using independent tradition (i.e., not derived from Mark or Q) somehow connected with Joanna and the story concerning her. Here we may include Fitzmyer, Hendrickx, Grundmann, Rengstorff, Moffatt, and Vincent Taylor.[45]

Caird, captive to the historicizing bias, suggests that the trial material stems, along with the rest of the Lukan Herod gossip,

41. Martin Dibelius, "Herodes und Pilatus," *Zeitschrift für die Neutestamentliche Wissenschaft* 16 (1915): 113-126.

42. Alfred Loisy, *Les Evangiles Synoptiques*, 2 vols. (Haute-Marne: Pres Montier-en-Der, 1907-1908; rpt. 1924), ii, 638, quoted and trans. in A. W. Verrall, "Christ before Herod," 322.

43. Marion L. Soards, "Tradition, Composition, and Theology in Luke's Account of Jesus before Herod Antipas," *Biblica* 66 (1985), 350.

44. Paul W. Walaskay, "The Trial and Death of Jesus in the Gospel of Luke," *Journal of Biblical Literature* 94 (1975): 88-89.

from the evangelist's own contacts with the Herod family.[46] I must confess that this seems no more likely to me than the once-popular assumption that Luke derived his information on the Nativity from the Virgin Mary.

For my purposes it does not matter greatly whether Luke was employing an independent Passion tradition or an independent written Passion narrative. In either case, as reflected in the *Gospel of Peter,* this version would have ascribed the condemnation and crucifixion of Jesus to Herod instead of Pilate.

Renan proposed a written source of this type:

> It is probable that this is a first attempt at a 'Harmony of the Gospels.' Luke must have had before him a narrative in which the death of Jesus was erroneously attributed to Herod. In order not to sacrifice this version entirely he must have combined the two traditions.[47]

Loisy agreed:

> The document, upon which Luke has drawn for information about the attitude of Herod towards Jesus, cannot, so far at least as concerns his part in the Passion, be that which was used by Mark. It was a source resembling the *Gospel of Peter,* possibly a former edition of this Gospel, and parallel to Mark and to Matthew. In it, all the main points of the trial by Pilate were transferred to Herod, so as to let it appear that the tetrarch gave sentence and directed the execution.[48]

45. Joseph A. Fitzmyer, *The Gospel According to Luke X-XXIV: A New Translation with Introduction and Commentary,* Anchor Bible, gen. eds. William Foxwell Albright and David Noel Freedman, 28A (New York: Doubleday, a division of Bantam Doubleday Dell Publishing Group, 1981), 1479; Herman Hendrickx, *The Passion Narratives of the Synoptic Gospels,* rev. ed., Studies in the Synoptic Gospels (London: Geoffrey Chapman, 1984), 83-84; Grundmann, *Lukas,* 424; Karl Heinrich Rengstorf, *Das Evangelium nach Lukas,* Das Neue Testament Deutsch 3 (Göttingen: Vandenhoeck & Ruprecht, 1969), 263-265; James Moffatt, *An Introduction to the Literature of the New Testament,* 3rd ed., International Theological Library, eds. Charles A. Briggs and Stewart D. F. Salmond (New York: Charles Scribner's Sons, 1918), 274-275; Taylor, *Behind,* 70.
46. Caird, *Luke,* 247.
47. Ernest Renan, *The Life of Jesus* (New York: Modern Library, 1927), 356.

Loisy also saw that this version of the Passion must have given in continuous sequence all the uniquely Lukan notices of Herod and his interest in Jesus:

> the story of Luke has long prepared us for the inter-vention of Herod. We are informed first that the tet-rarch desired to see Jesus, and again later, that he designed to put him to death. . . . All this, in the con-ception of the evangelist, is connected with the inci-dent now before us. But the train of events he probably did not make; he found it ready-made in a document or documents, containing notes of the rela-tion between Jesus and Antipas.[49]

Actually, the relation of hostility between Jesus and Antipas begins one step earlier, with the attachment of Joanna to Jesus' retinue, a connection Loisy could not readily make, not having the advantage of comparing notes with Kraemer and Burrus. Of course I think Loisy was completely correct as far as he went. The Passion source (whether we make it oral or written) so sharply perceived by his critical second-sight was none other than the chastity story of Joanna.

Recently, Tyson has revived or recapitulated the theory of Loisy and Renan. He defends the notion that there was a sepa-rate pre-Lukan Passion narrative in which the trial and execution of Jesus were the work of Herod Antipas, acting without Pilate. Like Renan and Loisy before him, he says Luke harmonized it with the Markan version in which Pilate is the villain. Making explicit what was implicit in Loisy and Renan, Tyson explains that by analogy with Mark, the soldierly mocking must presage an execution, not a verdict of not guilty![50]

In any version of the story, had Herod acquitted Jesus, would he not have freed him? He does not, thus he did not acquit him. But according to the contrivance of the harmoniza-tion he has clumsily effected, Luke cannot allow Herod to con-demn Jesus, since then Herod should have to execute him, cutting off any further use of Mark. Nor can he allow Herod to

48. Loisy, *Evangiles,* ii. 638, in Verrall, "Christ before Herod," 322-323; Loisy, *Origins,* 192.
49. Loisy, *Evangiles,* ii. 638, in Verrall, "Christ before Herod," 322.
50. Tyson, "The Lukan Version of the Trial of Jesus," *Novum Testamentum* 17 (1975): 257.

let Jesus go, since Jesus has to wind up dead, and that at the hands of Pontius Pilate. So Luke wanted to have his cake and to eat it. But his redactional fumbling at least makes it clear that in one of his sources it was Herod who condemned and executed Jesus.

Koester is willing to admit that the *Gospel of Peter*, where Herod does condemn Jesus, preserves some Passion material that must be judged form-critically as more primitive than anything in the canonical gospels. The references to Psalm 68:22, sprinkled throughout Matthew's Passion account, stand in their pristine unity in Peter. The dating of the crucifixion as being on the day before Passover, as in John, seems more primitive. And the presence of Mary Magdalene alone at the tomb, again as in John, seems to be of early provenance.[51]

Koester thinks the involvement of Herod in the proceedings is obviously secondary.[52] But this does not really militate against Luke's use of a source with the same tendency as Peter, since Luke is not necessarily an early gospel.

Crossan argues that a tradition whereby Herod was the one responsible for Jesus' death was current very early, contra Koester. Crossan posits the use by all four canonical gospels as well as Peter of a primary Passion account which he calls the Cross Gospel. "The *Cross Gospel* had Herod in charge of the proceedings while the intracanonical tradition had Pilate in charge of the proceedings."[53]   And, quite interesting for my purposes, Crossan notes that the same tradition of the Herodian execution of Jesus appears again here and there in the Apocryphal Acts.[54]

I will not venture to defend the hypothesis of the Cross(an) Gospel. I invoke Crossan, however, as yet another scholar who has noticed the tell-tale signs of a counter-Passion in which Herod Antipas played the villain, not Pilate. And Crossan's work links up traditions in the canonical gospels, especially

---

51. Helmut Koester, *Introduction to the New Testament, Volume Two: History and Literature of Early Christianity*, Hermeneia Foundations and Facets, ed. Robert W. Funk (Philadelphia: Fortress Press, and New York: Walter de Gruyter, 1982), 162-163.
52. Helmut Koester, *Ancient Christian Gospels: Their History and Development* (London: SCM Press; Philadelphia: Trinity Press International, 1990), 217.
53. John Dominic Crossan, *The Cross That Spoke: The Origins of the Passion Narrative* (San Francisco: Harper & Row, Publishers, 1988), 103.
54. Ibid., 86, 89.

Luke, on just this matter, with the same traditions in the Apocryphal Acts. I, of course, am doing the same thing, only I am suggesting that the chastity story of Joanna, leading into the martyrdom of Jesus, as chastity stories customarily led into martyrologies, was the link between canonical and apocryphal traditions. (Even if we do not make the pre-Lukan Joanna story the mother of all the rest, at least we may recognize that it belongs safely within the same genre.)

He Leads Our Women Astray

But even if we can pull the Herod execution tradition back into the pre-Lukan period, can the same be said for the specific chastity story element? Is there not too wide a gulf yawning between canonical and apocryphal traditions? I am not convinced Luke is all that much earlier than the earliest of the Apocryphal Acts, but there is an additional item of evidence, hitherto neglected, that bears on the question. That is the peculiar note in *1 Clement* to the effect that

> Through jealousy and envy the greatest and most righteous pillars of the Church were persecuted and contended unto death. . . . Peter, who because of unrighteous jealousy suffered not one or two but many trials, and having thus given his testimony went to the glorious place which was his due. Through jealousy and strife Paul showed the way to the prize of endurance . . . and thus passed from the world (*1 Clement* 5:2, 4-5, 7c).

Now just whose jealousy is Clement referring to here? Cullmann, after rightly dismissing previous suggestions that mere hatred, or the envy of the world for the privileges of the church, or Zealot intrigues are meant in *1 Clement*, proposes that the jealousy in question was that of the rival factions of Petrine and Pauline Christians who bickered to such an extent that they finally sealed the doom of the apostles, each faction informing on the leader of the other party.[55] Cullmann seems to envision the Petrine and Pauline factions as first-century counterparts to Hizbullah and the Amal Militia! The improbability of the suggestion scarcely requires comment.

---

55. Oscar Cullmann, *Peter: Disciple, Apostle, Martyr*, trans. Floyd V. Filson (Philadelphia: Westminster Press, 1953), 102.

The remaining alternative is simply that Clement already knows the traditions behind the chastity stories. It was the jealousy of estranged husbands that hounded the apostles to their deaths. Clement can already presume his readers are familiar with these traditions. What date would this give us for their currency? *1 Clement* is usually dated in the 90s C.E., since the persecution it alludes to is supposed to be that of Domitian (provided there *was* one[56]). If this date is to be accepted, then we would have an attestation of the circulation of the chastity traditions contemporary with Luke (on the consensus dating of Luke) or previous to him (on my reckoning).

At the Lukan trial Herod, unlike Pilate in any of the gospels, wants to see Jesus perform some prodigy. In other words, exactly as in the chastity stories of the Apocryphal Acts, the hero is viewed, unflatteringly, as a mere sorcerer, the assumption being that he has won the woman to himself by enchantment. As Burrus synthesizes, "in the view of the husband and governor, the apostle is a 'magician' or 'sorcerer,' and his religion is not one with which a virtuous woman concerns herself."[57] For example, in the *Acts of Philip,* the chaste Mariamne is thus accused: "She travels about with these magicians and no doubt commits adultery with them."[58] Slightly later, we find Byzantine holy men similarly despised by the ecclesiastical establishment as sorcerers.[59]

I suspect that we ought to place in the original context of the Herod trial an exceedingly interesting textual variant to Luke 23:5. Among the accusations made about Jesus include: "He leadeth astray both the women and the children" or "He alienates our sons and wives from us." In view are the wives like Joanna and sons like Zebedee's, who have been carried away by Jesus' preaching and joined him. This reading is found in two Old Latin manuscripts (often a haven for intriguing textual refugees from what I imagine to have been a Constantinian purging and standardization of the text, analogous to that performed upon the *Qur'an* by Caliph Uthman), Colbertinus and Palatinus. We also find it in Epiphanius' *Panarion* 42. 11. 6. lxx, attributed to

---

56. Christopher Rowland, *The Open Heaven: A Study of Apocalyptic in Judaism and Early Christianity* (New York: Crossroad Publishing Company, 1982), 407-410.
57. Burrus, *Chastity as Autonomy,* 92.
58. Brown, *Body and Society,* 100.
59. Brown, *Society and the Holy,* 299.

Marcion's text of Luke.

I find it significant that, in apparent ignorance of the chastity stories, Leonard Swidler spontaneously fills in what I deem to be precisely the *Sitz-im-Leben* of this reading:

> To generate the remembrance of this tradition many women followers of Jesus must have had a . . . new attitude towards the purity, or impurity, of their own bodies. . . . This so infuriated the men that they publicly denounced Jesus to the Roman governor and demanded that he be executed. These extremely early traditions attached to Luke (were they 'suppressed' . . .?) reflect the notion that Jesus' feminism was perceived as a capital crime![60]

But this reading can be no mere floating tradition anchored to Luke's text as the pericope of the adulteress was to Luke and John. It is clearly a continuation of the charges delivered at the Lukan trial. The only alternatives would seem to be either that someone embellished the text of Luke at this point, or that this statement was original to the text and was later suppressed, as its resemblance to the Apocryphal Acts was noticed and worried over. I choose the latter possibility. And since text criticism gives preference to the earliest reading, not the most amply attested in later sources, I should judge that the attestation of Marcion's text is about the most powerful textual witness one could ask. There is certainly no other evidence for the state of Luke's text nearly as ancient. The attestation is certainly stronger than that which led the translators of the New English Bible, rightly, to include the Old Latin reading "Jesus Barabbas" in Matthew 27:16-17.

My next suggestion is that this accusation came to Luke from the chastity story of Joanna. Perhaps the other accusations were originally made before Herod there, too, as implied by the reference to Galilee in Luke 23:5.

If Luke's Passion narrative contained the accusation that Jesus led astray wives and children, then the parallel with the chastity story martyrologies is virtually exact. Chuza has lost Joanna to Jesus. He enlists Herod's help to get her back and to eliminate the wizard Jesus. Herod is glad to oblige. He himself taunts Jesus as a magician and hears the accusation that he had enchanted and seduced wives (and children).

---

60. Swidler, *Biblical Affirmations*, 277.

But why would Luke have included a vestige of a tradition so odious to him? Simply in order to refute it! He rejects it just as surely as he rejects the notion that Jesus fomented tax revolt among the people. In the original story or tradition of Joanna, as in the chastity stories of the Apocryphal Acts, there was a measure of truth in such accusations, but not for Luke. He is glad to present it as one of a set of utterly groundless slanders.

Remember that there survive but remnants of the chastity story of Joanna, so not every element that originally would have belonged to it is apparent. Yet how striking it is that the narrative logic is so clear even in the story's broken state that McNamara, with no reference to the chastity stories, is compelled to fill in one of the missing elements:

> At least one of [the Galilean women] had money and influence and . . . may have made a last minute effort to save Jesus from his fate. Joanna, wife of Chuza, may well have taken advantage of the presence of Herod and his wife Berenice [*sic:* wrong Herod!] at Pilate's house on that fateful day to do some socializing of her own. Is it possible that a word or two might have accounted for the abortive attempt of Pilate's wife to prevent the condemnation of Jesus on the grounds that she had had a bad dream about it?[61]

We may forgive McNamara her precritical exegesis and bless her for her imagination. I would, however, be more inclined to take the snippet of Pilate's wife as a vestige of yet another chastity story in which Pilate's wife had become a disciple and now sought to intervene at the last moment as the heroines of the Apocryphal Acts do.

Elisabeth Moltmann-Wendel also comes surprisingly close to reconstructing the chastity story of Joanna with no inkling that such stories ever existed. She imagines a jaded Joanna, tired of court life, sickened at the sight of the severed head of the Baptist, and at some point healed by Jesus. This miracle excited Antipas' curiosity, and he wanted to see Jesus for himself. Refreshed by the open egalitarianism of Jesus' entourage, Joanna abandoned hearth, home, and husband to follow the Nazarene. She brought her wealth with her and may have been the one to supply the seamless garment of Jesus, the upper room, and the funeral

---

61. McNamara, *New Song*, 20.

unguents. As she stands by Jesus in his trials she is taking a great
risk being identified as one of the aristocracy aligned with a state
criminal.[62]   "What material for romances!"[63]   The lines of the
original story will simply not be obscured, despite the attempt of
Luke to silence them.

62. Elisabeth Moltmann-Wendel, *The Women Around Jesus* (New York:
Crossroad Publishing Company, 1990), 133-139.
63. Ibid., 134.

CHAPTER SEVEN

Blessed is the Fruit of thy Tomb:
The Daughters of Jerusalem and Mary of Cleopas

Mourning Women and Easter Vigils

It is a familiar cameo: the faithful women gather to see Jesus through to the end of his life, not knowing what the aftermath will be. If we did not take this feature of the gospel texts for granted, we should immediately see another striking feature shared with the chastity stories, where women are the best and sometimes even the only faithful disciples of Jesus. From whence may we suppose the gospel accounts of failed and fleeing male disciples contrasted with faithful female disciples to have come?

Even Luke, who now has the male disciples on the scene, must have begun with a story of this kind, as Schaberg shows. The note that "The women saw these things" (Luke 23:49) seems to have been glossed with a cosmetic reference to the male disciples, retroactively restoring them to where they had no stomach to be.[1] I suspect Luke has here added to his non-Markan Passion source, which was the continuation of the chastity story of Joanna. She had joined the ascetic gospel band, and now they mourn the death of their spiritual father/lover, just as in the Apocryphal Acts.

As in all the gospels the mourning of the women extends to their pilgrimage to the tomb of the beloved. From a *Religionsgeschichtlicheschule* standpoint, I do not see that there is any room to deny (though there is plenty of theological motive for wanting to) the contention of Johannes Leipoldt that in these stories we have a Christian adaptation of the myth, as well as the ritual, of the cults of Attis, Osiris, Baal, Tammuz, Sabazius, and the rest. In all these religions the yearly reenactment of the death and resurrection of the god was the special province of the women, who would wail and mourn and search for the body of the deity, recapitulating the mourning and searching of the divine consort Isis or Anath or Cybele.[2]

Is this an example of the "parallelomania" of which Samuel Sandmel accused history-of-religions scholars? I think not. Sandmel called it parallelomania when scholars posited direct literary

---

1. Schaberg, "Luke," 290.

dependence between two texts on the basis of parallels that might have arisen in other ways, or when on the basis of known parallels at some points scholars went on to infer parallels at other, unattested, points.[3] Yet in the case of the stories of the mourning women, there is no claim for literary dependence, as if Luke were alleged to have copied from a particular Attis liturgy. And the parallels to the other religions of dead and resurrected gods are attested precisely at the relevant points. Apologists have too often invoked "parallelomania" when they have wanted to evade the force of genuine parallels too close for orthodox comfort.

It did not require the efforts of scholarly parallelomaniacs to produce the anxiety of a Greek peasant woman attending the yearly Passion Play in her rural village, who explained her patently genuine distress to a tourist: "Of course I am anxious; for if Christ does not rise to-morrow, we shall have no corn this year."[4]

Peter Brown tells us that the martyrologies of the saints were first read at the tombs of the saints on the anniversary of their martyrdoms.[5] Sacred time would cycle back on such occasions, and the power of the saint would be palpable among his devotees. I would now like to suggest just such a ritual *Sitz-im-Leben* for the stories of the women at the tomb of Jesus.

The Passion narratives, so different from the tradition of kerygmatic preaching of the cross in terse formulae and explicated testimonia from Scripture, originated among the yearly Passiontide observances of the Christian widows who populated the story with characters like themselves. I doubt very much that we can find historical individuals behind the women disciples of Jesus. Instead they are personifications of the mourning women of the early church, reading themselves back into the story.

---

2. Johannes Leipoldt, "Zu den Auferstehungsgeschichten," *Theologisches Literaturzeitung* 73 (1948): 739; W. K. C Guthrie, *The Greeks and Their Gods* (Boston: Beacon Press, 1955), 162; Leah Bronner, *The Stories of Elijah and Elisha as Polemics Against Baal Worship*, Pretoria Oriental Series, ed. A. Van Selms, vol. VI (Leiden: E. J. Brill, 1968), 113.

3. Samuel Sandmel, "Parallelomania," *Journal of Biblical Literature* 81 (1962): 1, 4.

4. John Cuthbert Lawson, *Modern Greek Folklore and Ancient Greek Religion: A Study in Survivals* (Cambridge: Cambridge University Press, 1910), 573.

5. Brown, *Cult of the Saints*, 42, 81, 82.

Often New Testament scholars muse over the absence of any mention of the women at the tomb in the list of appearances in 1 Corinthians 15:3-11 or in the sermons of Acts. It is often suggested that women's testimony was not included for reasons of effective apologetics. All someone like Celsus would need to hear was that it was a couple of hysterical women who supposedly saw the Risen Christ (Origen, *Contra Celsum* II. 55). In accommodation to current prejudices, then, we are told, the women's testimony was omitted in some channels, preserved in others.

I do not think this is quite right. I would suggest that the stories of the women at the cross and the tomb were first the stock in trade neither of apologetics nor of preaching. They played a different role altogether, as liturgical myths in the circles of ascetic Christian women. Finally both rivulets ran together and collected in the literary rain puddles of the gospels.

I will have occasion to pursue these questions a significant step farther just below, and in the final chapter. But for now I will register my suggestion that the Passion narrative arose in the circles of widows, who after all viewed themselves as faithful to a Bridegroom who had been taken away, and for whom they must mourn (Mark 2:20), but who, like Osiris to Isis, might yet return to them. How interesting that, as Jeremias once pointed out, the bridegroom image is not attested as being associated with the Messiah in New Testament-era Judaism.[6] On the other hand, it had long been absolutely central to the resurrection myths of the dying and rising deities.

Similarly, I cannot help but posit the same origin or *Sitz-im-Leben* for the various chastity stories beginning with the recruitment of holy women and ending with the death (and sometimes the resurrection) of the apostle, leaving the community of his female followers mourning him but continuing in the strength of their sisterhood. Such stories must have begun as martyrologies to be read yearly among the circles of celibate women on the supposed date of the martyrdom of their favorite apostle. Thus it is no accident that we have no chastity stories that do not blend imperceptibly into apostolic martyrdoms or persecutions.

Of course the Passion of Jesus Christ issues in a resurrection. Thus Joanna's story next would have portrayed a joyous resurrection reunion with the slain savior, now revived. I have already

---

6. Jeremias, *Parables*, 52.

said that all the empty tomb narratives stem ultimately from the Easter vigils of the holy women of the early church, but I think we can follow the thread of this specific version, the chastity story of Joanna, a few steps farther. But, again, it is a matter calling for detective work, of reassembling the shards of the original artifact, shattered and buried by Luke.

First, though, it behooves us to ask again, why would Luke operate in such a fashion, knocking apart the stonework of an old monument to make his own new structure? It seems that in the early church resurrection visions functioned as apostolic credentials (1 Corinthians 9:1).[7] And Luke, as we know by now, is the last man in the church who would feel comfortable with a narrative in which the Risen Lord appeared first, or for that matter, at all, to a group of women, as if to commission them.

Let me be clear: I do not think that the women used their traditions for such a purpose. The pre-canonical pericope preserved in John 20:11-18, in which Jesus vouchsafes his single appearance before his ascension to Mary Magdalene, is the only exception, since the point there is to exclude the claims of the male disciples to have seen the Risen Lord at all.[8] Also Mary is alone at the tomb, implying the story concerns her alone, like that of Paul on the road to Damascus, which has pretty much the same point. By contrast, the stories of the group of women represent the retrojection of the holy women's Easter vigil. Nonetheless, Luke feared they might be appealed to as commissioning stories, as indeed later they were, and so he hid the evidence.

Daughters of Jerusalem

The first relic of the Easter chapter of Joanna's tale is, strangely enough, the saying of Jesus to the lamenting women on the Via Dolorosa in Luke 23:27-31. Neyrey has argued that this passage ought to be understood as a prophetic judgment oracle on doomed Jerusalem.[9] Luke has certainly peppered the narrative with such dark forebodings up to this point, so Neyrey's theory seems not unreasonable, at least in terms of Luke's redactional aims.

---

7. Reginald H. Fuller, *The Formation of the Resurrection Narratives* (New York: Macmillan Company, 1971), 41.

8. Price, "Mary Magdalene," 67.

9. Jerome H. Neyrey, *The Passion According to Luke: A Redaction Study of Luke's Soteriology* (New York: Paulist Press, 1985), 108-128.

Marion Soards, however, finds room to differ. He notes that Neyrey's interpretation requires that the "Daughters of Jerusalem" be understood as Jerusalem itself personified. Despite the occurrence in judgment contexts in the Old Testament of similar phrases, like "Daughters of Zion," Soards thinks Neyrey's theory too contrived. For himself, he cannot escape the too-clear characterization of the women as heart-broken sympathizers for Jesus. Is this really the way Luke would choose to picture the very city that had become an harlot, casting away its chance for peace? I don't think so either. But then Luke was not freely composing here. He was trying to fit scavenged bricks into a new arrangement, and they didn't always fit. His narrative here has in some respects the look of a medieval church built from the fragments of a nearby Roman ruin, a strange grandeur over which hovers a mist of frustrating half-recognition.

Soards carefully traces out the marks of the mourning women of Jerusalem having been real literary characters, not just a collective cipher for a city.

> The women . . . demonstrate grief as they smite themselves and bewail Jesus. From other contexts in Luke-Acts, both of these activities, as indicated by the rare verbs *koptein* and *threnein*, are typical of mourning; and so, one can say that the women are those members of the crowd who are distinguished by their mourning for Jesus.[10]

But is that really all one can say? Soards scratches his head: "it seems these women are characters whose precise identity cannot be determined from the narrative in which the reader encounters them."[11] Soards approaches the ark more and more closely, but he dares not touch it:

> throughout Luke's Gospel women are depicted as being supportive of Jesus in a special way as he is also especially supportive of them; so . . . the portrait here of the women is consistent with what one knows of them from the rest of Luke's Gospel.[12]

10. Marion L. Soards, "Tradition, Composition, and Theology in Jesus' Speech to the 'Daughters of Jerusalem' (Luke 23, 26-32)," *Biblica* 68 (1987): 230.
11. Ibid., 299-230.
12. Ibid., 230.

O Lord, I pray thee, open his eyes that he may see! Of course, these are the Galilean women themselves. By his reshuffling of the deck Luke has obscured their identity so well as to fool even as sharp-eyed an exegete as Soards. Who else could they be?

As Luke read (or heard) these words in his source, the chastity story of Joanna, the women were bewailing their beloved at his tomb, or on the way to it. Again, scholars have stubbornly managed not to detect this. Soards recounts how "Interpreters have labored to identify the women mentioned in 27a, frequently suggesting some relation between this verse and Zech 12, 10-14."[13]

> And I will pour out on the house of David and the inhabitants of Jerusalem a spirit of compassion and supplication, so that, when they shall look on him whom they have pierced, they shall mourn for him, as one mourns for an only child, and weep bitterly over him, as one weeps over a first-born. On that day the mourning in Jerusalem will be as great as the mourning for Hadad-Rimmon in the plain of Megiddo. The land shall mourn. . . .

"M.-J. Lagrange and, more recently, D. J. Moo have shown the improbability of this suggestion, saying that to reflect Zechariah 12 the Lukan Passion would need to have women mourning after the crucifixion, not before."[14] Exactly! In Luke's source that's just the way it was: the women mourned the dead Jesus. The incongruity noted by Lagrange and Moo stems, like the absurdities of Luke 7:36-50, from the redactional juggling of his sources by the evangelist.

But the Zechariah 12 reference has yet other secrets to yield up. I have already called attention to the striking conformity of the whole mourning-women motif to the pattern of ritual mourning of women for the slain fertility gods Adonis, Tammuz, Baal, etc. Now I must note that the mourning unto which the predicted lamentation is likened by the prophet Zechariah is the ceremonial grief for Baal under one of his regional pseudonyms.

Deutero-Zechariah, writing against the Temple hierocrats

---

13. Ibid., 228; cf. Fitzmyer, *Luke X-XXIV*, 1497.
14. Douglas J. Moo, *The Old Testament in the Gospel Passion Narratives* (Sheffield: Almond Press, 1983), 221, quoted in Soards, "Daughters," 228.

who have taken exclusive control of the covenant community of Judea after the return from the Exile, knows that the disenfranchised peasantry of the Judean countryside will know, almost certainly from experience, how poignant is the yearly lamentation for the fertility god. The women of Jerusalem had known it well decades before, when Ezekiel damned them for it:

> Then he brought me to the entrance to the north gate of the House of Yahweh; and behold, there sat women weeping for Tammuz. Then he said to me, "Have you seen this, O son of man? You will see still greater abominations than these" (8:14-15, cf. also Isaiah 17:10).

They must have been chanting something like the words of one Baal text: "Will you also, O father, die like mortals, or your court pass over to weeping? The women will sing, O father, on the heights, or do gods die? They will weep for you, O father, on the Mountain of Baal."[15]

I cannot help but think that the women's devotion glimpsed in historicized form in Luke 23:27 represents the continuation of these elements of popular women's spirituality, never fully stamped out by the official Jerusalem hierocrats despite their attempts to banish any object of devotion besides the male Yahweh.[16] The worship of Baal in various forms continued on through Hellenistic times[17] and eventually found its champion in the Wildean emperor Heliogabalus. Elements of this religion would have continued to be available to early Christian women.

When Jesus turns to the women and tells them not to waste their tears on account of him, that they will need these and more at some future time of greater danger to themselves, presumably at the fall of Jerusalem,[18] I see more fragments of a narrative in which his words assumed a decidedly different significance.

The address "Daughters of Jerusalem" is quite striking. It certainly has a biblical resonance to it. Where did it come from? A similar phrase, but in the singular, is found in Isaiah 37:22 and

---

15. Bronner, *Elijah*, 103.

16. Patai, *Hebrew Goddess*, 16-41; Saul M. Olyan, *Asherah and the Cult of Yahweh in Israel*, Society of Biblical Literature Monograph Series, no. 34 (Atlanta: Scholars Press, 1988), 70-74.

17. Joseph A. Fitzmyer, *Luke the Theologian: Aspects of His Teaching* (New York: Paulist Press, 1989), 149.

Zechariah 9:9; the phrase "daughters of Zion" is found often. Usually these phrases denote Jerusalem as a whole and perhaps the neighboring towns. But the exact phrase "daughters of Jerusalem" occurs in only one Old Testament writing, the Song of Songs, and there several times (1:5; 2:7; 3:5, 10; 5:8, 16; 8:4).

This text has been the object of much exegetical ingenuity. Attempts to understand it as a single love poem, or as a drama featuring two characters or three, have resulted in utter chaos. But another model makes sense of some of its strangest passages. Since 1906 several scholars have proposed to understand the book as a set of paschal hymns stemming from the worship of Tammuz and Ishtar-Shalmith ("the Shulammite"). This theory was first set forth by Wilhelm Erbt and followed a few years later by O. Neuschotz de Jassy's theory that the text was concerned with the similar death-and-resurrection mythology of Isis and Osiris. T. J. Meek argued again for the Tammuz-Ishtar version of the theory in 1920, based on similarities between passages in the Song of Songs and Akkadian hymn titles which seemed to belong to the cult of Ishtar and Tammuz. The biblical material, Meek argued, had been worked over to sanitize it in the wake of Yah-

---

18. Whitney makes a suggestion that Bultmann would surely have labeled "comical": he makes Jesus' words to the mourning women a feminist attack against the cynical manipulation and simulation of women's grief in the socially demanded display of professional mourning! Whitney's Jesus is saying,

> "If they kill me when I am fully challenging their restrictive rules and they still don't listen, how terrible it will be for those in bondage when I'm gone;" [or] "If society keeps women in such bondage when I'm actively loosing them, what a dreadful situation that forebodes in my absence." (Whitney, "Women in Luke," 277-278)

> The wailing women represented the imprisonment experienced by women in a society which limits them to certain roles. Professional mourning necessitated a numbing of true emotion for the sake of public display. . . . By not accepting their rehearsed sympathy he proclaimed judgment on the restrictive roles of women which kept them under the feet of a male-dominated society. (Ibid., 307-308)

But where does Whitney see any evidence that these women were a paid chorus spouting crocodile tears? Who hired them? Joseph of Arimathea?

wistic domination. The hymns were kept at all, not just burnt as the unclean trappings of idolatry, said W. H. Schoff, because they had become part of the Temple liturgy, Tammuz being long worshipped there, probably since Solomon's day, and could not simply be junked.[19]

In 1926 Wittekindt issued a whole commentary on the book understood as a Tammuz-Ishtar text. N. H. Snaith (1933-34) divided the text into two ritual cycles of spring and fall, stemming from the North Syrian rites of Tammuz-Adonis.[20]

In general the theory went on from strength to strength, receiving much in the way of pious outrage, but little in the way of scholarly refutation. The only serious weakness that could be aimed at it was that discussed in my introduction: that short of full and total documentation (of a suppressed phenomenon!), the theory could be safely ignored. It seemed there was no real proof that at the time of the writing of the Song of Songs the myths of Tammuz included the notion of his resurrection. And the Tammuz interpretation of the Song of Songs extended to include Ishtar's rescue of her lover from the netherworld.

But then new textual discoveries secured the myth of the resurrection of Tammuz/Adonis as sufficiently ancient to satisfy the objections.[21] Similarly, the bringing to light of the Ras Shamra texts provided all the evidence one might ask as to the ancient prevalence of myths of the dying god, son of El, who rises from the dead, receives the title "Lord" (= Baal), and assumes the lordship of all in heaven and earth.

The conclusion of Samuel Noah Kramer was that:

> From Mesopotamia the theme of the dead Dumuzi [= Tammuz] and his resurrection spread to Palestine, and it is not surprising to find the women of Jerusalem bewailing Tammuz in one of the gates of the Jerusalem temple. Nor is it at all improbable that the myth of Dumuzi's death and resurrection left its mark on the Christ story, in spite of the profound spiritual gulf

---

19. I am dependent here on Marvin H. Pope's survey of the history of this interpretation, in Marvin H. Pope, *Song of Songs: A New Translation with Introduction and Commentary*, Anchor Bible, eds. William Foxwell Albright and David Noel Freedman, 7C (Garden City, NY: Doubleday & Co., 1977), 145-151.
20. Ibid., 151.
21. Ibid., 153.

between them. Several motifs in the Christ story may
go back to Sumerian prototypes.[22]

The Tammuz-Ishtar interpretation, to which there has never
been any satisfactory challenge, would certainly give striking
meaning to passages like Song of Songs 3:1-3, where we may see
Ishtar seeking for her dead consort. The joy of their resurrection
reunion runs throughout the book, as does the celebration of
their union which renews the life of the earth. 8:6-7, with its affirmation that "love is strong as death, jealousy is cruel as the
grave," comes into sharp focus as eulogizing the determination
of Ishtar not to let her lover be lost to the grave. And finally, the
peculiar words of endearment, "my sister, my bride," make a
great deal of sense addressed by Tammuz to his sister Ishtar who
was also his divine consort. What sense it could possibly have
made, in the context of the barb-wired Levitical marriage codes,
as a reference to human lovers, I cannot imagine.

The daughters of Jerusalem in the only Old Testament text in
which they occur, then, seem to stand for the female devotees of
Ishtar, joining with both her mourning at Tammuz's death and
her joy at his resurrection. Specifically, they must have been
identical with the Jerusalem mourners of Tammuz despised by
Ezekiel. Is it pure coincidence that the fragment preserved in
Luke 23:28 has Jesus address his wailing female devotees as
"Daughters of Jerusalem"? I am not apologetically inclined
enough to think so. (I cannot resist at this point noting that the
name "Dorcas," as L. T. Johnson points out,[23] is the same word
used in the LXX of the Song of Songs for Tammuz the beloved,
e.g., in 2:9, pictured as a gazelle.)

The religious significance of the epithet "daughters of Jerusalem" has been changed by Luke into a geographical one, hence
the bafflement of Soards over the identity of the women, who,
like Peter at the campfire, are recognizable as Galileans. I do not
dispute that in the Song of Songs the women devotees are actually pictured as in Jerusalem; but the use of the song in local popular worship around the countryside must have led to the
broader figurative application of the title to Tammuz devotees
wherever they happened to live, much as we sing "O Zion haste,

22. Samuel Noah Kramer, *The Sacred Marriage Rite: Aspects of Faith, Myth,
and Ritual in Ancient Sumer* (Bloomington: Indiana University Press,
1969), 133, quoted in Pope, *Song*, 153.
23. Johnson, *Acts*, 177.

thy mission high fulfilling," referring to the Christian church.

Why Do You Weep?

Jesus tells them "weep not for me." Soards judges that the phrase is Lukan redaction, since we also find the words "weep not" in the Nain story, as well as added to the story of Jairus' daughter, where they did not appear in the Markan original.[24] But in the Nain story, we have a close parallel in the Apollonius resurrection story, and in it we find the same element: "put down the bier, and I will stay the tears that you are shedding for this maiden." So I would not be too quick to conclude that this feature was not present in the pre-Lukan tradition, in whatever precise words, either in the Nain story or the Luke 23:28 saying. In the hypothesized context of the Joanna story Jesus' admonition "Weep not!" must have been his resurrection greeting. All cause for weeping is at an end, for he is risen! But what of "rather weep for yourselves"? (The remainder, "and for your children," is a historicizing gloss to bend it to Luke's agenda, predicting the fall of the city in the generation after Jesus.)

I think the saying of the resurrected Jesus to Joanna and her sisters was "Daughters of Jerusalem, weep not for me, but weep for yourselves. For behold, if they do these things when the wood is green, what will happen when it is sere?" (23:28, 31).

When he comes to verse 31 Soards takes a deep breath and admits he has his work cut out for him:

> These lines are the most enigmatic portion of this pericope. Interpreters have puzzled over the origin of the verse. . . . Fifty years ago Finegan remarked that the derivation of this verse remains uncertain, and he is still correct.[25]

Yet I am sure that forty-four years ago Leipoldt solved the mystery. He speaks of "Luk. 23, 31, wo man ein Tamuz-Motiv fand: 'Wenn man das am grünen Holze tut, was soll am dürren werden?'"[26]

Bultmann, Jeremias, and Taylor noted the primitive Aramaic character of the verse, and Soards agrees that here we are dealing with pre-Lukan material.

---

24. Soards, "Daughters," 232.
25. Ibid., 238-239.
26. Leipoldt, "Auferstehungsgeschichten," 738.

> The content and form of v. 31 do make it unlikely this
> is a Lukan composition, for Luke is not given to such
> terse remarks. More likely, it is a piece of traditional
> material Luke preserved in this seemingly appropriate
> context in his Passion narrative.[27]

Easton decided it must be an authentic saying of Jesus.[28]   One
might as well make it an authentic saying of Tammuz.

At any rate I think the verse does represent Christianized
Tammuz tradition and that Luke got it right out of the Joanna
story. But what was the nature of the motif? The symbolism is
that of the moisture and/or life-giving sap of plants personified
by the young god. Like John Barleycorn he is cut down in his
prime only to spring back up again to new life. Many gods
embodied the same system of fertility associations, being pretty
much interchangeable avatars of the same basic mythos.

Let me turn to the recorded lore of another equivalent god
whose influence is also plain on the gospels at certain points, particularly John.

> Dionysus is [*Dendrites*] or [*Endendros*], the Power of
> the tree; he is [*Anthios*] the blossom-bringer, [*Karpios*]
> the fruit-bringer, [*Phleus*] or [*Phleos*], the abundance of
> life [cf., of course, John 10:10]. His domain is, in Plu-
> tarch's words, the whole of the [*hugra phusis*]—not
> only the liquid fire in the grape, but the sap thrusting
> in a young tree . . . all the mysterious and uncontrolla-
> ble tides that ebb and flow in the life of nature.[29]

The living god of vegetation renews his youth ever again,
but his devotees must grow old and die, as must have been much
on their minds: elderly women were plentiful in their ranks, as
Euripides *The Bacchae* makes clear. And remember, we are talking about *widow* traditions in Luke. These words would have
been especially poignant for such readers or hearers.

So what does happen when the wood is sere? Another
Johannine passage with unmistakable Dionysian roots (fully as
unequivocal as the direct appropriation of the Dionysian water-

27. Soards, "Daughters," 239.
28. Easton, *Luke*, 347.
29. Dodds, *Euripides, Bacchae*, xii; Walter Otto, *Dionysus*, 164-165.

into-wine miracle of John 2:1-11) is the True Vine discourse. "Dionysisch mutet Joh. 15,1 an: 'Ich bin der wahre Weinstock.'"[30] And there we read, though we do not like to, "he is cast forth as a branch and withers; and the branches are gathered, thrown into the fire and burned" (v. 6). That is what they do when the wood is dry. And to avoid that fate one must seek initiation into the greater mysteries of the god who imparts to his flock eternal life as well as earthly life to the apple and the grape.

In the Joanna story underlying Luke's Via Dolorosa episode, we catch yet another echo of Johannine tradition. Joanna's story had the Risen Christ contrast his own glad resurrection with the dry doom certain to overtake all mortals some day. John, who shares so many obscure points with Luke, also has such a prediction in John 21:18, where Jesus makes an analogous contrast between Peter's present virility and his future infirmity: "when you were young, you girded yourself and walked where you pleased; but when you are old, you will stretch out your hands, and another will gird you [cf. "and men bind them" in John 15:6] and carry you where you do not wish to go."

The Fourth Evangelist or a subsequent redactor has pressed this gloomy saying into service to get himself out of the bind caused by the inconvenient death of the Beloved Disciple, which gave the lie to the will-o'-the-wisp of Mark 9:1.

But originally the saying must simply have contrasted, in the fatalistic manner of popular wisdom, one's health and vigor, so soon gone, with the nullity of death, when one becomes an unwieldy side of meat, to be laid out, wrapped up, and hauled off to the morgue. In Bergman's *The Seventh Seal* Jöns the squire sings: "One moment you're bright and lively, / The next you're crawling with worms. / Fate is a terrible villain / And you, my friend, its poor victim."[31] Both the Joanna and the Johannine resurrection accounts included a version of the sad maxim.

Rising Gods

Though biblical scholars often profess skepticism at the possibility of the mixture of pagan elements with Christian ones, it is not in the least surprising. An earlier generation of scholars

---

30. Leipoldt, "Auferstehungsgeschichten," 738.
31. Ingmar Bergman, *The Seventh Seal,* in *Four Screenplays of Ingmar Bergman,* trans. Lars Malmstrom and David Kushner (New York: Touchstone Books, a division of Simon & Schuster, 1960), 141.

allowed themselves to be misled by the ancient propaganda of the Priestly Writer and the Deuteronomist into the belief that Israel had been monotheistic since the day Yahweh tapped Abraham on the shoulder. It has taken much labor to come to see the obvious, that for most of its history Israelite religion was polytheistic, worshipping Yahweh, his seventy sons who ruled the nations, and his consort Asherah, not to mention associated and allied deities such as Shahar, Tammuz, and Nehushtan.

Even after the supposed watershed of monotheism, the Fall of Jerusalem, when events were to have exorcised once and for all the demons of polytheism, we find in Jeremiah that the worshippers of the Queen of Heaven stuck by their guns, blaming the Exile precisely on Deuteronomic theology (Jeremiah 44:15-19)! Nehemiah and Ezra were much vexed at the pagan admixtures in the Jewish religion that greeted them on their return.

Even in the second century B.C.E. there is ample evidence of the continuance of popular polytheism. The tyrant Antiochus IV Epiphanes sought to force-feed Hellenism to his Jewish subjects, making them join in the Dionysiac processions (2 Maccabees 6:7), but we ought to remember that in the Maccabean books, like the Deuteronomic, we are reading the retrospective account of the monotheistic *hasidim*. It is far from clear that all Jews rejected or even resisted Hellenization. Indeed it is clear that they did not. Who is to say that many of them did not rejoice to take part in the worship of Dionysus, who was after all so similar to fertility gods they or their ancestors had worshipped—or still worshipped! Even 2 Maccabees admits that many of the Jewish freedom fighters were found in their death to have carried into battle the protective talismans of Semitic gods (12:40). And when the apocalyptist of the Maccabean-era Book of Daniel, stalwart foe of the Little Horn, wants to depict the investiture of the heavenly archetype of the holy people—he borrows a scene that looks for all the world like the passing of the sceptre from El to the young god Baal, fresh from his resurrection (Daniel 7:13-14)! The continued availability of Dionysus and Baal motifs among Jews in the time of Jesus should hardly surprise us.

I have often referred to the work of Rentería on the socio-literary background of the stories of Elijah and Elisha, so similar to the widow traditions of Luke-Acts in both form and function. These tales played a counter-hegemonic role, inspiring and nourishing a popular religious expression resistant to that of the official temple system in Bethel and Dan. Though Rentería does not say so, it seems natural to infer that these same circles may have been the refuge of many of the popular religious traditions which the official cultus sought to stamp out.

Again, misled by the Deuteronomic rewriting of the tradition, scholars have been content to suppose that Elijah, at least, was a staunch monotheist or monolater, and indeed, he is pictured as an enemy of Jezebel's importation of the worship of Baal Melkart. But as Olyan has shown, the note of the presence of the priestesses of Asherah at Mount Carmel, and of their route along with that of the priests of Baal, is a Deuteronomic gloss trying to conceal the fact that the contest that day was really, in effect, one between divine suitors for Asherah's hand![32] Elijah probably only opposed foreign gods but may have been quite content with more than one Israelite divinity. And so may his followers.

We might also suspect as much from the wide dissemination of Baal myths throughout the body of the Elijah and Elisha stories. In her study of these stories, Leah Bronner details pointed similarities between the myths of Baal and the stories of the two miracle-working prophets. Misled by her apologetical agenda, she draws the opposite conclusion to that suggested by the data that she amasses: she says the biblical stories mean to co-opt and refute the Baal myths in the spirit, one supposes, of "Anything you can do I can do better."[33] All she really demonstrates is that the two faiths had the same motifs, and that only the names were different.

Neither can one ignore the evidence collected long ago by Ignaz Goldziher to the effect that Elijah himself is a solar deity, what with his being "a hairy man" (2 Kings 1:8), his tresses, like Samson's, representing the sun's rays, and with his ascent to the zenith aboard a fiery chariot like Apollo's.[34]One might also mention the Tammuz myth embedded in the story, which we have discussed before, of Elisha and the cleansing of the leper. The latter's name is Naaman, another form of Naman, one of the names of Tammuz. I cannot doubt that his deliverance from the scourge of leprosy by burial beneath the surface of the holy river was already (as Paul would later make immersion) a figure for the dying and rising of the savior deity.

I believe, then, that there is sufficient available background for us to see how themes and motifs from the religions of resur-

32. Olyan, *Asherah*, 8.
33. Bronner, *Elijah*, passim.

rected gods with their mourning widow devotees could have survived on into Christianity, having long survived in the very circles of the poor of the land who formed the fertile soil for the religion of Jesus. When we find resurrection traditions featuring holy mourning women and brimming with Tammuz and Dionysus motifs, this is what the history of religions, if not ortho- dox predisposition, would lead us to expect to find.

Some Women Amazed Us

I imagine the Joanna story to have continued with the report of the women to the male disciples. Their testimony is contemp- tuously dismissed, exactly as Celsus the enemy of Christianity later would, as the deluded ravings of hysterical women. "Now it was Mary Magdalene and Joanna and Mary of James and the other women with them who told this to the apostles; but these words seemed to them an idle tale, and they did not believe them." In other words, the resurrection tradition of the women seemed like one of the old women's tales rejected by the Pastor.

We must not pass this notice by too quickly. One often hears that in "the gospels" the women's testimony is rejected. But it is so only here. Matthew's and John's disciples are never said to disbelieve the women, and Mark's disciples do not receive the news, so we do not know what they would have thought of it.

---

34. Ignaz Goldziher, *Mythology Among the Hebrews and Its Historical Development,* trans. Russell Martineau (New York: Cooper Square Pub- lishers, 1967), 167-168. When Gunkel calls the approach of Goldziher "discredited" (Hermann Gunkel, *The Legends of Genesis: The Biblical Saga and History,* trans. W. H. Carruth, with an Introduction by William F. Albright [New York: Schocken Books, 1964], 121), this judgment rightly applies only to the totalistic application of Goldziher's astronomical par- adigm. The appearance of other, more likely derivations of several Patri- archal stories and characters (such as Gunkel's own "genealogical link" theory of the Patriarchs as eponymous ancestors, or Alt's theory of Abra- ham, Isaac, and Jacob as the patrons of private ancestral cults) hardly makes Goldziher's explanations untenable in other cases where no bet- ter explanation has surfaced.

There is certainly no reason to demand that all the stories have the same root. Gunkel teetered on the same brink that he saw Goldziher plunging over, it seems to me, when he insisted that all the stories must be explained within one paradigm. Goldziher's ingenious readings of Old Testament myths as allegories of celestial phenomena viewed by nocturnal shepherds often had much more basis than mere etymology, contra Gunkel.

The Markan Appendix has skeptical disciples, but it may be secondary to Luke.

If it is alone in the canonical gospels, this version of the response to the women is not unique outside the gospels. Mary Magdalene gets pretty much the same chilly reception in the *Gospel of Mary* when she shares with the men the revelations vouchsafed her by the Risen One. Peter cannot believe what he is hearing: "Did he really speak to a woman without our knowledge and not openly? [Note the same reaction of the disciples in John 4:27, where Jesus has also imparted revealed truth to a woman in their absence!] Are we to turn about and all listen to her? Did he prefer her to us?" Mary, taken aback, like a rookie professor stunned at the obtuseness of the first freshman question, stammers, "My brother Peter, what do you think? Do you think that I thought this up myself in my heart, or that I am lying about the Savior?" (17-18).

These are stories told by women who are all too accustomed, as they know their female listeners will be, to having men stare at them as if they are crazy, spurning their advice and then blaming them for the results of the stupid thing they did instead. We find here essentially the same female viewpoint we do in the Apocryphal Acts' chastity stories, where Thecla, having proven herself by tortures and resisted temptations, asks Paul to baptize her and commission her to preach—but he won't! He is still not sure she's quite ready. What an allegory of those churches which are not sure it is time to ordain women, even though women have been running them for generations.

Paul even denies knowing Thecla at one point when things get hot. Similarly, Thomas, having preached the necessity of celibacy, is prevailed upon to persuade one woman to marry after all. These episodes' disillusionment about the reliability and sympathy of males who run the church in the name of the apostles, comes through loud and clear in Luke 24:10-11. Jane Schaberg hits it right on the nose: "The reader, of course, knows that the women's report is true, and the disciples, as the risen Jesus will later say, are foolish and slow of heart."[35] I fear Schüssler Fiorenza misses the point when she says, "Luke's gospel already attempts to play down the role of women as proclaimers of the Easter kerygma, by stressing 'that the words of the women seemed to the eleven [sic] an idle tale and they did not believe

---

35. Schaberg, "Luke," 291.

them.'"[36] No, the original narrator's perspective is shared with
the women, not with the men: the joke's on them. Women have
the last laugh here. Luke would never have written such a story.
But Schüssler Fiorenza is right in the most basic sense: Luke has
obscured the original resurrection tradition of the women, the
story of Joanna, in which the women did actually see the Risen
Christ. It is just that a few vestiges of it, one betrayed by the
female perspective of this verse, have slipped through.

So only fragments survive of the chastity story of Joanna.
But there is more than enough of it to allow its pristine form to be
glimpsed. That Luke already had available such a piece of wom-
en's tradition may imply either that Luke wrote later than many
have thought, or that this sort of women's tradition goes back
earlier in the history of the church than we thought (and as the
mention of the key theme of husbandly jealousy causing the
death of the apostles in *1 Clement* also implies). In any event I
think there is a strong case to be made for identifying as one of
Luke's sources a Passion narrative that was part and parcel of the
chastity story of Joanna. All scholars agree that the martyrdoms
of the apostles in the Apocryphal Acts are modeled to some
extent on the Passion of Jesus. I hope that we may now add the
judgment that this is true even for the chastity stories leading up
to those martyrdoms. If not, we may at least locate the Joanna
tradition as belonging to the same type.

Surprises on the Emmaus Road

In conclusion I want briefly to suggest that there is reason to
think that Luke knew yet another resurrection account stemming
from the circles of consecrated women. This is the universally
beloved Emmaus story. This story has already attracted a modicum of interest from feminist critics because of the intriguing
suggestion of Quesnell[37] that the unnamed disciple may have
been the wife of Cleopas, or a woman at any rate, as Schaberg
offers more generally.[38] Whitney considers the suggestion only
within the realm of possibility.[39]

I have long been struck with the close similarity between the

36. Elisabeth Schüssler Fiorenza, "Word, Power, and Spirit: Women in
the Early Christian Communities," in *Women of Spirit*, 52.
37. Quesnell, "Women at Luke's Supper," 68.
38. Schaberg, "Luke," 287.
39. Whitney, "Women in Luke," 301.

Emmaus story and a tale told at the Epidaurus Asclepium. It
dates from the fourth century B.C.E. and is in the nature of an
advertisement, being an inscribed testimonial tablet affixed to the
wall of the shrine:

> Sostrata of Pherae had a false pregnancy. In fear and
> trembling she came in a litter to the sanctuary and
> slept here. But she had no clear dream [the usual
> means for the god to manifest himself and prescribe a
> treatment] and started for home again. Then, near
> Curni she dreamt that a man, comely in appearance,
> fell in with her and her companions; when he learned
> about their bad luck he bade them set down the litter
> on which they were carrying Sostrata; then he cut
> open her belly, removed an enormous quantity of
> worms—two full basins; then he stitched up her belly
> and made the woman well; then Asclepius revealed
> his presence and bade her send thank-offerings for the
> cure to Epidaurus.[40]

No one will doubt that this story is older than Luke, that it
had had plenty of time to circulate, that by its very nature it
would have circulated widely, and that it is strikingly similar to
the Emmaus story. Dillon does not even mention it, though he
reviews all the suggested parallels to the Emmaus story that he
knows of, finding none close enough to have suggested the
Emmaus episode.[41] I do not mean to challenge Dillon's ful-
somely demonstrated conclusion that the Emmaus story as it
now stands is a thoroughly Lukan piece, but, as often, we cannot
rule out a thorough Lukan reworking of a pre-Lukan original.

While one might shrink back and grant merely that Luke has
used the same mythic motif, I see no reason not to go the whole
way and speculate that the Emmaus story is a direct descendant
of the Aesclepius story, with perhaps one intermediate step,
which I will now venture to reconstruct.

I posit a Christian adaptation of the Sostrata story in which
Cleopas travels the road with his pregnant wife (let us call her
Mary, the name of the wife of Clopas in John 19:25, another of the
holy women, in case Cleopas and Clopas may have been one and

---

40. Mary R. Lefkowitz and Maureen B. Fant, *Women's Life in Greece and
Rome: A Source Book in Translation* (Baltimore: Johns Hopkins University
Press, 1987), 122.
41. Dillon, *Eye-Witnesses*, 73-74.

the same, as Goulder[42] has again argued recently). They have learned that Jesus of Nazareth has gone to Jerusalem. They could not go see him in Galilee because of Mary's condition, but Jerusalem is only seven miles distant, and she cannot seem to give birth. Alas, when they reach the holy city they learn that the prophet Jesus has been crucified. They turn away in despair, for he had been their only hope for deliverance. On their sorrowful way home, a stranger joins them, asking after the cause of their dismay. This is when the reader hears of it, and indeed, as in the present form of the story, the risen Jesus only feigns ignorance for the sake of informing the reader. Jesus then heals Mary as his prototype Asclepius had healed Sostrata (whether by the same method or not, who can say?), but, as before, it is a false pregnancy.

Here is the original pre-Lukan setting for the strange beatitude on the barren womb, now found in Luke 23:29, "Blessed are the barren wombs and the breasts that never gave suck," an early tradition also found in the *Gospel of Thomas*. The saying was a piece of encratite paraenesis, floating free at first, as we still find it in *Thomas* 79, but that such materials could find their way into Easter contexts, e.g., resurrection dialogues cherished by the continent, is evident from the appearance of the same sort of material in the *Gospel of the Egyptians* quoted by Clement of Alexandria, where we seem to have a post-resurrection interview like those in many Gnostic works.

> When Salome asked, "How long will death have power?" the Lord answered, "So long as ye women bear children." . . . [And] when she said, "I have then

---

42. True, Clopas is an Aramaic name, while Cleopas is a contraction of the Greek Cleopatrus, but it was not uncommon for a Jew to take a similar-sounding Greek name as well, as with Jesus/Jason, Simeon/Simon, Thoma/Thomas, Saul/Paul (Goulder, *New Paradigm*, 784). And remember that John 19:25 has Mary of Clopas present at the cross, so both Cleopas and Mary of Clopas are characters in the Passion story. And Luke 24:18 has someone accompanying Cleopas *home*. Who is more likely than his wife? The identification seems natural.

To apply again the hermeneutic of suspicion, may we not see the outright rejection of the identification by most scholars as another example of the elimination of women from the resurrection appearance narratives, continuing the trajectory of the New Testament redactors themselves? In fact, may we not suspect that Cleopas' wife was at first named, as in John's gospel, and that Luke has made her anonymous?

done well in not bearing children," . . . the Lord
answered and said, "Eat every plant, but that which
has bitterness, eat not." (*Stromateis* 3.6.45.3; 3.9.66.1-2)

The reference here seems to be to the carnal knowledge of the
Edenic Tree of Knowledge, the partaking of which led to death
for the human race through the introduction of sex and procre-
ation, as many Gnostics and encratites read the story.

Luke has rewritten the story, minimizing the role of Cleopas'
partner and supplying an altogether different cause for the distress of the pair. The beatitude he has transferred to the Via Dolorosa, where it has been pressed into service as part of the doom
oracle on Jerusalem. With Luke 21:23 it now serves as a second
parallel to Mark 13:17, which is no doubt where he got the idea
for the reapplication.

Again, Luke has appropriated a resurrection account from
the circles of celibate women. He has carefully purged it of anything that might not fit the doctrines and ethos of his own
"nascent catholic" Christianity. But its outlines can be restored
with enough historical imagination.

CHAPTER EIGHT

Bread of Life, a la Carte:
Martha and Mary

An Oft-Told Tale

The story of Martha and Mary (Luke 10:38-42) takes up a brief five verses, yet it is important, and controversial, out of proportion to its length. I will argue that there are at least as many discernible transitional stages behind the present text as there are verses in it. And once these sedimentary layers are distinguished, I believe we may have a greater chance of mediating the dispute currently raging over the text. It will become evident that the earlier versions of the story still speak to the attentive reader, and that the different positions taken on the meaning of the passage are based on one or another stratum of it. The arguments across the text reflect the fact that the composite text argues at cross-purposes with itself.

Stage One: Hospitality to Itinerants

In the earliest stage of the story we can trace, its point seems to have been advice on the proper treatment of the wandering missioners, as Erling Laland noted.[1] Martha (whose name means "Lady of the House" and therefore denotes an ideal figure, created to embody the lesson she is to teach, even if by contrast) is the patroness of a house church, which of course was the standard church organization for a long time. Jesus, as so often in the gospel tradition, is a literary incarnation of the itinerant charismatics who were to be received as the very Son of Man. Given that it might as well be Jesus Christ himself that you were having to dinner, you might well not spare any expense, insurance against that day when the Son of Man would separate the liberal sheep from the stingy goats in the Last Round-up.

This understandable concern, the inculcation of which was after all the express purpose of the scare-story of Matthew 25:31-45, could and did lead to abuses. For one thing, the prophet himself might find it hard not to take advantage of it. It is this danger the *Didache* has in mind: "no prophet who orders a meal in the

---

1. Erling Laland, "Die Martha-Maria Perikope, Lukas 10, 38-42," *Studia Theologica* 13 (1959): 82.

Spirit shall eat of it; otherwise he is a false prophet" (11:9).

For another, the host or hostess might just kill the prophet with kindness, going overboard, tempting him to compromise his ascetic regimen. This seems to be the point of the Cynic advice given in a similar situation by Pseudo-Lucian:

> Well, suppose that a man sharing this same table pays no heed to the great variety of dishes, but chooses one of those closest to him sufficient to his need, and eats of this in moderation, confining himself to this one dish, and not so much as looking at the others; don't you consider this man to be more temperate and a better man than the other? (*The Cynic* 7)

Similarly Gregory of Nazianzen, extolling continence and asceticism, contrasts his state with that of the comfortable householder: "Your table is laden with viands; frugality nourishes me."[2]

But the third danger was that to the hostess herself. Why was the prophet there for Sunday dinner in the first place? For the sake of the afternoon gospel symposium at which he would preside, and in the Spirit if one were lucky. But if the lady of the house were fretting over getting the feast ready all at the same time, trying to prevent the goat from burning while the porridge wasn't ready yet—Oh dear! She might miss some dominical oracle that would one day wind up printed in India ink on gold-edged pages, and all because she had to check that dratted meat thermometer!

> Die immer wiederkehrende Situation der Martha-Maria-Geschichte wurde den ältesten Christen lebendig, wenn ein reisender Glaubensbote in einem Haus gastliche Aufnahme gefunden hatte. Die Frauen des Hauses werden sofort durch aüssere Sorge fur den Gast dermassen in Anspruch genommen, dass es ihnen unmöglich ist, dem Wort des Herrn zu lauschen. In dieser Lage erhält unser Herrenwort erneute Aktualität: Wenig ist notwendig von allem, was der Herr dieser Welt den Menschen als notwendige irdische Genusse vorgaukelt. Deshalb: Genügsamkeit und kein Überfluss! Kein so rastloses Mühen und Schaffen um die vielen Dinge zum Besten des Gastes, so dass dadurch die Hausfrau an dem einen Notwendigen

---

2. Nugent, "Consecrated," 24.

gehindert wird, nämlich sich still hinzusetzen und
gesammelten Sinnes der Heilsbotschaft zu lauschen.
Der Feind darf nicht durch äussere Geschäftigkeit den
Sinn ablenken und dadurch hindern, das Wort Gottes
zu hören und es zu bewahren (Lk. 11, 27-28).[3]

My only qualm with Laland's otherwise compelling intu-
ition of the *Sitz-im-Leben* of the pericope is that it does not man-
age to account for everything in it, to my satisfaction at least. He
is following the urging of the passage a bit too closely, choosing
only one of the exegetical points on Martha's table. On his reading, how can we account for the contrast with sister Mary? Even
the mention of her? I would suggest that we follow certain subtle
internal clues and scale the pericope down to the shorter text that
in the beginning probably served the purpose Laland ascribes to
it.

I suspect that when it meant what Laland said it means it
read like this:

> He entered a village, and a woman named Martha
> received him into her home. But Martha was dis-
> tracted with much serving. But the Lord said to her,
> "Martha, Martha, you are anxious and troubled about
> many things; few things are needful, or only one."

Why is there, in the canonical form of the text, no mention of
Mary in v. 38 if she shares the house with Martha? This fact
implies she is a subsequent addition to the text. The "But" which
opens v. 40 contrasted originally not with the silent posture of
Mary, but rather with the implied, now frustrated, fellowship
with the Lord one was led to expect and to envy in v. 38b. Like
Zacchaeus, Martha was lucky enough to have the Lord as her
guest that day. But see how she squandered the opportunity!

D'Angelo would like to see the story as a reflection of a missionary team, a historical Martha and Mary, well known in the
early church. The activity of such a pair may be adequately
attested by the claim of Carpocrates to have learned their doctrine.[4] There may well have been such an apostolic partnership.
And it may have been under the influence of their fame that

---

3. Laland, "Martha-Maria," 82.
4. D Angelo, "Female Partners," 77-81; cf. Schüssler Fiorenza, *In Memory of Her*, 271.

when, as I think, another woman was added to the story she was given the name Mary.

The only historical basis for the story as it stood in the first stage was that it was probably at such a house-church meal that a considerate and insightful itinerant spoke dominically to the harried hostess. But her name was not Martha, nor was his Jesus. In the gospel tradition, it seems to me, Jesus is almost as much an ideal figure as Martha. Usually he stands for nameless individuals now lost to us save for their prophetically pseudonymous words.

Stage Two: Conversion Propaganda

In the second stage of transmission the pericope gains Mary's subplot and becomes a recruitment paradigm for the consecrated women. The emphasis will be on Mary's choice of the angelic life. "She has *chosen* the better part." (The verse ended right there as of this stage, the rest being added in the next one.)

It thus came to function as a call for women hearers to consider the same choice, much like the various discipleship paradigms of the gospels.[5] Kraemer[6] and Burrus[7] suggest that the chastity stories functioned as conversion propaganda: "Women, do what Thecla did!" "Jesus is looking for a few good women!" So here. "Sister, aren't you like Martha? Wouldn't you rather be like Mary? Jesus wants you to be. Join us." I have not the space to undertake a history of the exegesis of this passage, but I must confess I find myself largely in accord with Origen's application (*Scholia in Lucam* 353), which became common, of the text to the inculcation of the contemplative life. It seems to me that it is basically the point in stage two. The Protestant hatred for the monastic and preference for the secular has led Protestant exegetes to dismiss Origen's interpretation with disdain, but it is they who are reading the text anachronistically, usually devotionalizing or psychologizing it.[8] They simply cannot tolerate the implied dominical blessing of a religious *Sitz-im-Leben* despised by Martin Luther.

I must pause to make sure I distinguish my interpretation

---

5. Matura, *Gospel Radicalism*, 30-31, 73.
6. Kraemer, "Conversion of Women," 299.
7. Burrus, *Chastity as Autonomuy*, 99.
8. William Barclay, *The Gospel of Luke*, rev. ed., Daily Bible Study Series (Philadelphia: Westminster Press, 1975), 141-142.

from what Schüssler Fiorenza calls the feminist apologetic view.[9]
A good representative of this approach, which I consider anachronistic, would be Irene Brennan, though examples could be multiplied.

> When Jesus quietly chides Martha for her insistence
> that Mary take the traditional woman's role, he makes
> it clear that he himself admits Mary into full disciple-
> ship, regardless of her sex. In so doing Christ admits a
> woman to an equal place with men in that preparation
> which will enable her to be actively engaged in the
> establishment of the Kingdom.[10]

There is not one word of such matters in the text as far as I
can see. Where did Brennan and others derive the notion that
Jesus was initiating Mary into full religious participation? I suspect it has something to do with the contrast frequently drawn
between our pericope and the supposed attitude of the rabbis
toward the religious training of women. We have often been told
that the fanatically misogynist rabbis forbade women to study
Torah, which was taken as meaning they could not study for
admission to the rabbinate. This description made it appear that
Jesus was doing the opposite, so that for Mary to "sit at his feet"
(cf. Acts 22:3) is tantamount to his inducting her as an apprentice.

At any rate, whence the generalization about rabbinism?
Usually the passage quoted was the saying attributed to Rabbi
Eliezer: "If any man gives his daughter a knowledge of the Torah,
it is as though he taught her lechery" (*M. Sotah* iii:4). Strong
words, admittedly, but it would be interesting to know what
wrung them from the good rabbi's lips. In fact we know, though

---

9. Schüssler Fiorenza, "Theological Criteria," 6.
10. Irene Brennan, "Women in the Gospels," *New Black Friars* 52 (1971): 293; Scroggs, "Eschatological," 535; Parvey, "Theology and Leadership," 141; Sim, "Women Followers," 59; Whitney, "Women in Luke," 223-224; Richard J. Cassidy, *Jesus, Politics, and Society: A Study of Luke's Gospel* (Maryknoll, NY: Orbis Books, 1978), 36; Danker, *New Age,* 224-226. Gail Paterson Corrington adopts the essential elements of the feminist apologetic model, yet she agrees with Schüssler Fiorenza that in the last analysis the pericope is oppressive to women. Where she differs from Schüssler Fiorenza is in her estimate that equality of discipleship is possible for Mary only at the cost of assuming a male role, pointedly abandoning the kitchen for the posture of sitting at the feet of the master, as male disciples did. (*Her Image,* 32-33).

it is seldom quoted. Eliezer is responding to a statement by Rabbi ben Azzai: "A man ought to give his daughter a knowledge of the Torah so that if she must drink [the bitter water, the test of chastity], she may know that her merit [acquired in pious study] will hold her punishment in suspense." As a rejoinder to this superstitious use of Holy Scripture as an indulgence, Eliezer holds that if things really worked the way ben Azzai envisions, and one could thus insulate one's daughter against punishment for lewdness, then one would have given her carte blanche for immoral behavior; one would have used the Torah as a cloak for sin in the worst way.

Is anyone here discussing the question of women in the rabbinate? Not by a long shot. In fact the opportunistic use of this piece of Mishnaic text on behalf of Christian feminism is on the same reprehensible level with the use of Scripture proposed by ben Azzai.

If the Martha and Mary story does not guarantee equal discipleship to women (an issue of which it is entirely innocent), what is the point of it? I think we find the key in the many excellent studies of early Christian asceticism by Ross Kraemer, Elizabeth Castelli, Elizabeth A. Clark, Carolyn Osiek, Jo Ann McNamara, Rosemary Ruether and others. These scholars have shown that consecrated celibacy offered women almost their only opportunity to achieve significant freedom from the domestic captivity most women endured, with the constant chores, the husband treating her like a child, etc. This included the possibility, because it included the necessary leisure, for scholarly study.[11]

> An irony of early Christian history is that the ascetic movement, which had so many features denigrating of women and marriage, became *the* movement that, more than any other, provided "liberation" of a sort for Christian women. *If* they could surmount their identification with sexual and reproductive functioning, women were allowed freedoms and roles they otherwise would not have been granted.[12]

> As widows, . . . particularly self-designated "true widows," the individual unmarried woman achieved an

---

11. Castelli, "Virginity," 82; Clark, *Ascetic Piety*, 187.
12. Clark, *Ascetic Piety*, 42; cf. Ruether, "Mothers of the Church," 72-73; Schüssler Fiorenza, *In Memory of Her*, 90.

autonomous status within the Christian community
second only to that of the virgins who had never sub-
jected themselves to the authority of a husband and
may well have defied the authority of a father.[13]

(I must pause here to listen to the dissenting voice of Gail
Paterson Corrington, who interprets the supposed autonomy of
consecrated widows and virgins as one more means of oppression in that the relative independence was purchased (from men)
at the too-high cost of the renunciation of female sexuality,
"becoming male" as *Thomas* 114 has it.[14] Yet the work of Joyce
Salisbury warns us that we dare not assume automatically that
celibate women experienced their continence in the way pro-
jected on them by men, i.e., as repentance from the sin of sexuality. Salisbury demonstrates that many of the celibate women
whose accounts have reached us show them embracing their sexuality and physicality, renouncing sexual intercourse as a purely
tactical move, because of the entangling domestic alliances the
marriage bed entailed. According to Salisbury, these women sac-
rificed a lesser good for a greater, intercourse for independence.[15]
If this was the case for Mary of Egypt, Melania, Constantina, and
other ascetic women of a later period, we certainly cannot simply
assume it was different for the women of Luke's era.)

McNamara sees the Martha and Mary passage as making
precisely the point that the rejection of domesticity was the path
to autonomy.

> If women were defined by marriage, by its sexual and
> procreative roles and by the gender-based labor
> assigned to married women, then their refusal of mar-
> riage might move them into a category that tran-
> scended womanhood. Mary had once chosen the
> better part in preferring spiritual instruction to domes-
> tic duties.[16]

As we have seen, and as Bassler and MacDonald have previously argued,[17] we can see in 1 Timothy 5:3-16 a clear attempt to

13. Jo Ann McNamara, "Wives and Women in Early Christian Thought,"
International Journal of Women's Studies 2 (1979): 589.
14. Corrington, *Her Image*, 89.
15. Salisbury, *Independent Virgins*, 111-125.
16. McNamara, *New Song*, 104.
17. Bassler, "Widow's Tale," 31-34.

restrict both the eligible membership and the allowable activities of the group of widows who received a church stipend. Our third stage will see the Martha and Mary pericope responding to such encroachments, but in stage two it reflects the greater freedom allowed by the church subsidy before the restrictions. We are fortunate to have a glimpse of the freedom made possible and indeed encouraged by these arrangements in 1 Corinthians 7:32-35, part of the Pastoral stratum of the epistle.

Eduard Grafe argued, followed by H. Achelis, though with a modicum of hesitation,[18] that the practice of the *suneisaktoi* is reflected in 1 Corinthians 7:36-38. Among the questions discussed in this section is that of the virgin who is blissfully free to be "holy in body and spirit," because, like the glossolalic virgin daughters of Job, she mindeth not the things of this world, notably a husband (v. 34).

I think it is implicit that such a free spirit lives on a church stipend (else how is her freedom possible?), anachronistic for the era of Paul the Apostle, but not for the later era of 1 Corinthians 7 (which opens a series of pseudonymous addenda to the letter organized with the repeated topical heading "Now concerning," just like the chapters of the *Didache*, which probably dates from the same period).

Many exegetes have observed the close fit between the virgins of this passage and the thumbnail portrait of Mary in Luke 10:38-42. T. W. Manson notes that "Mary is more concerned to attend upon the Lord without distraction (I Cor. 7, 35)."[19] Creed, too, sees that "Mary fulfills the ideal of St. Paul, I Cor. vii. 35 *euparedron to kurio aperispastos*. Martha, like the married woman in St. Paul, *merimna ta tou kosmou* (ib. v. 34)."[20] Indeed, the similarity is so close that Goulder says Luke created the story on the basis of reading 1 Corinthians 7![21]

Stage Three: Defending Ascetic Privilege

The third stage in transmission saw only the addition of the phrase "which shall not be taken away from her" onto the end. It was a response to the encroachments visible in 1 Timothy 5:3-16, where the holy leisure of the consecrated virgins ("younger wid-

---

18. Achelis, "Agapetae," 179.
19. T. W. Manson, *Sayings,* 263.
20. Creed, *Luke,* 154.
21. Goulder, *New Paradigm,* 493-494.

ows" who should "marry," not "remarry") is sneeringly reduced to mere "idling." As MacDonald shows, the trouble came because the male hierarchy found disturbing the theological products of that leisure and sought to close up the think tank.[22] Such freedom would henceforth be possible only in the widows' houses where several women might be supported by a wealthy fellow-widow or other patron, or among the emerging "heretical" movements like Montanism and the Marcionite church.

Against these restrictions a glossator or tradent probably supplemented the story with a new prophetic saying from one of the pro-widow itinerants, who didn't like what he saw happening and didn't mind letting the Lord Jesus say so! "It shall not be taken away from her!" The phrase as we now find it appended to the text (". . . *which* shall not be taken away from her") surely reads like an afterthought or a footnote. I suggest that is what it is.

We will see that in the next stage it is Martha's role which comes into question, but not yet. In stage three Mary's cloistered privilege is in jeopardy. I think the polemical stress is nicely caught by some commentators: "The incident . . . has for its point the defence of Mary" (William Manson).[23] "This must not be taken away from her . . . by Martha or anybody else; it is her inalienable right and possession, guaranteed by Jesus" (Marshall).[24] "Jesus protects the right of Martha's sister Mary to be free from domestic duties" (Tannehill).[25]

Stage Four: Silencing Women

The fourth stage represents, so to speak, the passage of the pericope over into the hands of the enemy, those from whom the stage-three version sought to protect Mary. As we have seen throughout the present work, Luke coopts previous traditions, altering them either drastically, as in the case of Joanna's chastity story, or else subtly, as he does here. Indeed, it is the redactional *placement* of the story more than anything else which imparts a new meaning to it.

Here I am going to follow Schüssler Fiorenza's exegesis, so I intend simply to summarize it. But I dissent from Schüssler

---

22. MacDonald, *Legend*, 76-77.
23. W. Manson, *Luke*, 132.
24. Marshall, *Luke*, 454.
25. Tannehill, *Narrative Unity, Luke*, 137.

Fiorenza in one important respect. She, like Schmithals ("darum möchte Lukas selbst der erste Erzähler gewesen sein."),[26] regards the text as a Lukan composition pure and simple. This I cannot accept for the simple reason that there are too many signals sent in different directions by the text, and, as I have argued, this is best understood as evidence that the text has grown in different directions in the process of transmission, of use and reuse.

Basically, once we get a feel for Luke's vocabulary and his understanding of church ministries we can deduce what he must have made of the passage. Whitney feels that Schüssler Fiorenza misjudges the import of the passage, neglecting Luke's otherwise positive and liberating treatment of women throughout his gospel.[27] But Whitney has got it the wrong way round. It is precisely the patronizing and curtailing character of Luke's redaction throughout that makes Schüssler Fiorenza's reading inevitable. Whitney is right about one thing, though: we must now try to read the pericope as part of the Lukan text, no longer as a pretextual oral tradition or pre-Lukan text. We must inquire after the way Luke himself read the text (and, as de Man would remind us, how precisely in so reading it Luke *rewrote* the text, without needing to change a single word). It seems he read it as eliminating the "serving," i.e., diaconate or gospel ministry, of women and reducing them to silent passivity.

Martha is not to be read as engaging in secular domestic tasks. To think so is to ignore the simple fact, already pointed out by Laland, that the early churches were house churches. The patroness of such a church was a minister of the church. (What else can 1 Corinthians 12 mean by the "gifts of helps and administration"?) She would have served at table, true, but this might include eucharistic service. Indeed, according to Acts 2:46, it would have to. Might it not have included preaching the gospel?

Though, as Schüssler Fiorenza reads him, Luke tries mightily to seal off table *diakonia* from the *diakonia* of the word in Acts 6:2, this piece of Lukan redaction is too short a skirt: it cannot cover the plain fact that the traditions available to Luke already depicted the Seven Luke designated for food distribution as mighty preachers and evangelists, as witness the subsequent

---

26. Walter Schmithals, *Das Evangelium nach Lukas*, Zürcher Bibelkommentäre, eds. Georg Föhrer, Hans Heinrich Schmid, and Siegfried Schulz (Zürich: Theologischer Verlag, 1980), 129.
27. Whitney, "Women in Luke," 226.

pneumatic adventures of both Stephen and Philip. (The link between Luke 10:38-42 and Acts 6:1-6 had been previously pointed out by other scholars.)[28]

J. Bradley Chance puts a new spin on the strange juxtaposition of the Seven's apparent restriction to the grocery detail and their subsequent depiction as superapostles: on the basis of Luke 22:28-30 he infers that for Luke "serving at table" means being the greatest in the community and possessing apostolic authority, so there is no incompatibility.[29] Similarly, Johnson suggests that Luke uses the appointment of the Seven to serve tables as a symbol of their receiving the same authority as the Twelve, since the authority of the latter had been symbolized by the willingness of the community to submit its possessions to them for redistribution. Now that authority is passed on to or shared with the Seven.[30]

Both reconstructions seem to me to run aground on the same rock: both would seem to entail the renunciation by the Twelve of their authority, since they expressly say they are done with table service. If Chance and Johnson are right, the Twelve seem to be abdicating authority, not sharing it. (I will propose in Chapter 10 yet another possible harmonization, but for the present I am willing to pursue Schüssler Fiorenza's exegesis at least as one strong reading, or misreading, as Bloom and de Man would say, of the text.)

But if Luke does divide ministry into that of the table (whether this means eucharistic service or food distribution to

---

28. Bo Reicke, "Instruction and Discussion in the Travel Narrative," in *Studia Evangelica: Papers Presented to the International Congress on The Four Gospels in 1957, Held at Christ Church, Oxford, 1957*, eds. Kurt Aland, F. L. Cross, Jean Daniélou, Harald Riesenfeld, and W. C. van Unnick (Berlin: Akademie-Verlag, 1959), 212-213; Birger Gerhardsson, *Memory and Manuscript: Oral Transmission in Rabbinic Judaism and Early Christianity*, trans. Eric J. Sharpe (Uppsala: Almqvist & Wiksells, 1961), 239-241; Jerome H. Neyrey, "Ceremonies in Luke-Acts: The Case of Meals and Table Fellowship," in *Social World of Luke-Acts*, 379.
29. J. Bradley Chance, *Jerusalem, the Temple, and the New Age in Luke-Acts* (Macon, GA: Mercer University Press, 1988), 107.
30. Luke Timothy Johnson, *The Literary Function of Possessions in Luke-Acts*, Society of Biblical Literature Dissertation Series no. 39 (Missoula: Scholars Press, 1977), 212-213. I do not challenge Johnson's brilliant discernment that Luke uses possessions as a symbol for selfhood, allegience, and relationships. But I am not sure it would get us out of the particular difficulty in view here.

the poor, or both) on the one hand and that of the word on the other, he seems to bar women from both. Martha (who, we may infer from John 11:27, may have been widely known as a preacher) is busy with what the text itself describes as serving the Lord Jesus—and is told not to bother! This woman, quick to speak on her own behalf, is condescendingly told to learn a lesson from the silent Mary, who sits at Jesus' feet with the mute devotion of the dog in the RCA ad, listening uncritically to "her master's voice."

Schüssler Fiorenza notes that

> if one reads the story in reference to the Pastorals' restricting women's leadership, specifically, for example, widows' leadership, then Martha casts quite a different figure [than she does in my hypothetical earlier readings of the story—RMP]. Martha functions as a prescriptive example for women in ministerial leadership not to be worried so much about the *diakonein* or ministry. The figure of Mary also takes on a quite different function, and the story gives quite a different message.[31]

And what is that message? Simply put, it is this: "Let a woman learn in silence with all submissiveness. I do not permit a woman to teach . . . she is to keep silent" (1 Timothy 2:11-12).

Schaberg also picks up on the link between Martha's "serving" and *diakonia* as ministry. She sees the passage splitting the ministry of the word and that of the table between the two sisters.[32] For Via the passage means to deal with the relative importance of the two ministries and their place in the liturgy.[33] The assumption behind the text, though not the point being argued in it, is that "women [are] fully enfranchised in both the meal and the hearing of the word."

But Schaberg has not given full weight to the fact that, as Schüssler Fiorenza notes, Mary is not shown doing any ministry of any kind other than sitting on her posterior and keeping her mouth shut, not getting in the way of ministering males. She is lucky to benefit from the ministry as practiced by God's chosen gender: men.[34] Against Via one must ask with Schüssler

---

31. Schüssler Fiorenza in "Minutes of the Discussion," *Protocol*, 49.
32. Schaberg, "Luke," 288-289.
33. E. J. Via, "Women, Service, Meal," 56.

Fiorenza, if the roles of women are not the point of contention why do women appear as characters at all? Women never just happen to appear in androcentric texts unless they are the issue.[35]

Stage Five: Emendations as Amendments

The fifth stage of the evolution of the pericope is that of textual alteration. The textual uncertainties in this passage are notorious. It is not my quixotic task to try to determine the true text as Aelred Baker and Gordon Fee have each attempted in recent years (and they come to different conclusions, Fee opting for the originality of "few things are needful, or one,"[36] while Baker chooses "one thing is necessary"[37]). I have not the impertinence to intrude like Elihu into the debates of Eliphaz and Bildad, so I will comment from the sidelines.

What does it mean that the text has been subject to scribal alterations which have produced the readings "few things are necessary," "few things are necessary, or one," "one thing is necessary," and the omission of all the matter between "Martha, Martha" and "Mary has chosen . . ."?

I suspect that the text was altered as a way of amending it back and forth once it had come to be viewed as a charter for the widows on analogy with the Synoptic Mission Charge, where we find, between the different gospels, as well as between rival manuscripts of the same gospel, inconsistencies as to whether the missioner may take along a staff, no staff, any money, extra sandals, etc. Surely these changes reflect amendments of the regulations by means of emendation of the regulatory texts.

So with the variants of Luke 10:42. Could the widows own anything? Was all property church property on loan to them? What sort of gifts could they receive? We know such debates were going on somewhat later.[38] And we know the early Buddhist, Jain, and other ascetics hotly debated great issues such as

---

34. Schüssler Fiorenza, "Theological Criteria," 7.

35. Schlüsser Fiorenza, "Minutes," 47.

36. Gordon D. Fee, "'One Thing Is Needful'?: Luke 10:42," in *New Testament Textual Criticism, Its Significance for Exegesis: Essays in Honor of Bruce M. Metzger*, eds. Eldon J. Epp and Gordon D. Fee (Oxford: Clarendon Press, 1981), 75.

37. A. Baker, "One Thing Necessary," *Catholic Biblical Quarterly* 27 (1965): 137.

38. Gryson, *Women*, 57-58, 68.

whether a loincloth were permissible to the true ascetic, or if even such a compromise with possessions would soon have material-ism crowding back in like a flood.[39] There is the famous story of Diogenes of Sinope, that his sole possession was a bowl for drink-ing water until the day he noticed someone cupping his hands to dip water from the river, whereupon the naked sage cast the bowl aside. *No* things were necessary!

In the present hypothetical tracing of the evolution of the Martha and Mary pericope I have suggested that a few stages of transmission were necessary to posit, not only one, as Schüssler Fiorenza, Schmithals, and others have done. Too many sets of fingerprints, the traces of too many contrary arguments, seem to be visible in the brief tale for it to have originated as we now find it. In the earliest stage the focus was on the proper extent of the hospitality to be showered on the wandering representatives of Jesus. Next, attention shifted to their allies, the celibate women, calling women listeners to leave Martha's kitchen as decisively as Levi had once left his toll booth. Subsequently the focus shifted to the defense of the very discipleship option to which listeners in the previous stage had been summoned, as the freedom of conse-crated women came to be threatened by male hierarchs who saw no use in the arrangement. Then the story was coopted by those who were the polemical targets in the previous stage, as Luke took over the story and, by redactional placement, made it a par-adigm for the ideal silent woman. The textual variations to which the passage eventually became subject are best under-stood, I have suggested, as reflecting various local amendments to the rules governing the possessions of women in the celibate households.

One short passage, yet so many stages and forms! The fun-damental axiom of form criticism reminds us that for a pericope to be passed on in the first place it must have had some particular point of utility, and that all else in the pericope would tend to be eroded away in the flowing stream of oral transmission. Then what appear at first sight to be minor details are to be suspected of being much more. Each must have had its own utility some-where along the way, else we would not be reading it now. Hence when we find features in the text that make plausible sense as distinct polemical points, as form critics we are entitled to congratulate ourselves that we have discerned the accretions added to the story as it was reapplied to new situations. Just as we suspect Mark 2:1-12 of being a conflation of a miracle story and a pronouncement story because in its present form it points

---

39. Sri Ramakrishna used to tell a parable that perfectly illustrates the point:

All for a Single Piece of Loincloth

A sadhu under the instruction of his Guru built for himself a small shed, thatched with leaves at a distance from the haunts of men. He began his devotional exercises in this hut. Now, every morning after ablution he would hang his wet cloth and the kaupina (loin-cloth) on a tree close to the hut, to dry them. One day on his return from the neighboring village, which he would visit to beg for his daily food, he found that the rats had cut holes in his kaupina. So the next day he was obliged to go to the village for a fresh one. A few days later, the sadhu spread his loin-cloth on the roof of his hut to dry it and then went to the village to beg as usual. On his return he found that the rats had torn it into shreds. He felt much annoyed and thought within himself, "Where shall I go again to beg for a rag? Whom shall I ask for one?" All the same he saw the villagers the next day and represented to them the mischief done by the rats. Having heard all he had to say, the villagers said, "Who will keep you supplied with cloth every day? Just do one thing—keep a cat; it will keep away the rats." The sadhu forthwith secured a kitten in the village and carried it to his hut. From that day the rats ceased to trouble him and there was no end to his joy. The sadhu now began to tend the useful little creature with great care and feed it on the milk begged from the village. After some days, a villager said to him: "Sadhuji, you require milk every day; you can supply your want for a few days at most by begging; who will supply you with milk all the year round? Just do one thing—keep a cow. You can satisfy your own comforts by drinking its milk and you can also give some to your cat." In a few days the sadhu procured a milch cow and had no occasion to beg for milk any more. By and by, the sadhu found it necessary to beg for straw for his cow. He had to visit the neighboring villages for the purpose, but the villagers said, "There are lots of uncultivated lands close to your hut; just cultivate the land and you shall not have to beg for straw for your cow." Guided by their advice, the sadhu took to tilling the land. Gradually he had to engage some labourers and later on found it necessary to build barns to store the crop in. Thus he became, in course of time, a sort of landlord. And, at last he had to take a wife to look after his big household. He now passed his days just like a busy householder.

After some time, his Guru came to see him. Finding himself surrounded by goods and chattles, the Guru felt puzzled and inquired of a servant, "An ascetic used to live here in a hut; can you tell me where he has removed himself?" The servant did not know what to say in reply. So the Guru ventured to enter into the house, where he met his disciple. The Guru said to him, "My son, what is all this?" The disciple, in great shame fell at the feet of his Guru and said, "My Lord, all for a single piece of loin-cloth!" (*Tales and Parables of Sri Ramakrishna* [Madras: Sri Ramakrishna Math, 1947], 18-21.)

in both directions, we must suspect that the survival of the various significant details in our pericope denotes the accumulation of "tradition barnacles." Had they no purpose, they wouldn't be there.

CHAPTER NINE

Justice Blind and Black-Eyed:
The Persistent Widow

Patchwork Parable

Luke 18:1-8 is often called the parable of the Unjust Judge. Yet few[1] doubt that the point being made has more to do with the widow who seeks, nay, at length demands, the assistance of the cynical judge. I will argue that we might do well to differentiate in our discussions of the passage between the parable of the Unjust Judge and the story of the Persistent Widow, since the former represents a development from the latter.

Some have argued that the parable is a Lukan creation from start to finish. If this were the case, it would obviously be vain to seek behind its present form a substratum of tradition originating amid the consecrated widows. But is it the case that Luke freely composed the pericope? Those upholding this theory include Drury, Linnemann, Goulder, and Freed.[2] Freed makes the most detailed case. He argues, as do the others in less detail, that the concerns, themes, and vocabulary of the parable all mark it as Luke's work. Yet often he must admit that while this or that word is a favorite of Luke it does appear in another New Testament writer. And as Goulder admits, "Linguistic considerations . . . can hardly prove more than that Luke has . . . put the parable in his own words."[3]

Freed also calls attention to the role of the widow as reflect-

---

1. Dan Otto Via, "The Parable of the Unjust Judge: A Metaphor of the Unrealized Self," in *Semiology and the Parables,* ed. Daniel Patte (Pittsburgh: Pickwick Press, 1976), 4.

2. John Drury, *Tradition and Design in Luke's Gospel: A Study in Early Christian Historiography* (Atlanta: John Knox Press, 1977), 164; Eta Linnemann, *Jesus of the Parables,* with an Introduction by Ernst Fuchs (New York: Harper & Row, Publishers, 1966), 119-124; Goulder, *New Paradigm,* 660-662; E. D. Freed, "The Parable of the Judge and the Widow," *New Testament Studies* 33 (1987): 38-60.

3. Goulder, *New Paradigm,* 660; cf. Vincent Taylor, *The Life and Ministry of Jesus* (New York: Abingdon Press, n.d.), 27; M. Dennis Hamm, "The Freeing of the Bent Woman and the Restoration of Israel: Luke 13, 10-17 as Narrative Theology," *Journal for the Study of the New Testament* 31 (1987): 24.

ing Luke's special concern with widows. From this fact he infers
that Luke has created the parable using one of his favorite characters.   Of course I draw just the opposite inference: since, as I
believe, the gospel evidences the use of pre-Lukan widow traditions elsewhere, my working hypothesis would be that such is
the case here as well. Besides this general consideration, however, I believe I can detect the signs of Luke's use of a traditional
source and his incomplete assimilation of it.   And, as Evans
points out, if it were the case that the text is a Lukan creation
from whole cloth

> it is likely to have been composed more smoothly as a
> unit, and to have fitted more closely into the context
> Luke supplied for it. The awkwardness of vv. 6-8a,
> which show no clear evidence of Luke's style, suggest
> rather that he was incorporating, perhaps not wholly
> successfully, a unit of tradition which already bore
> marks of use and adaptation in the church.[4]

In fact the various "blips" interrupting the smooth flow of
the parable have resulted in a number of views as to the composition history of this piece of tradition. Some scholars hold a theory
that is the mirror image of that offered by Freed, Drury, Linnemann, and Goulder: Jeremias's defense of the original unity and
authentic dominical origin of the parable is the best known,[5]
though the case has been taken up again recently by Hicks.[6]

Similarly Kümmel, Montefiore, and Ellis regard almost the
whole piece as unitary, subtracting only 8b ("Nevertheless, when
the Son of Man comes, will he find faith on the earth?") as a subsequent addition.[7]

Another group of critics, including Bultmann, Easton, Perrin, Tolbert, and D. Via, separate off vv. 6-8 as additions to the

4. Evans, *Saint Luke*, 636.
5. Jeremias, *Parables*, 153-157.
6. John Mark Hicks, "The Parable of the Persistent Widow (Luke 18:1-8),"
Restoration Quarterly 33 (1991): 209.
7. Werner Georg Kümmel, *Promise and Fulfilment: The Eshatological Message of Jesus*, Studies in Biblical Theology, eds. Peter R. Ackroyd, James
Barr, C. F. Evans, Floyd V. Filson, C. F. D. Moule, First Series 23 (London:
SCM Press, 1957), 59; C. G. Montefiore, *The Synoptic Gospels*, Vol. II, 2nd
ed. (London: Macmillan & Co., 1927), 1018; Ellis, *Luke*, 212 (Verse 8b
"may be Luke's application of the episode to the despair caused by persecution.").

original pericope.[8] Ott hones his scalpel and leaves vv. 6b-7 as a pre-Lukan addition, with 6a and 8 Luke's own supplements.[9] Fitzmyer should be included among this group, save that he would retain v. 6 as part of the original parable: "From the beginning some comment seems to be called for about the judge."[10] But this is just why one ought, in my view, to send v. 6 packing along with its fellow hangers-on. If I may invoke the text-critical axiom that the more difficult reading is to be preferred, it is just because v. 5 leaves us with a hung jury re the judge that someone, a first- or second-century preincarnation of Fitzmyer, felt compelled to close his case!

I believe the original stock of the pericope to have consisted of vv. 2-5. Form-critically we simply cannot miss seeing v. 6a ("And the Lord said . . .") as a redactional seam, and a specifically Lukan one at that, as Hendrickx observes:

> The Greek expression *eipen de* (plural: *eipan de*) is found 59 times in Luke and fifteen times in Acts, but only twice elsewhere in the New Testament (Jn 8:11; 12:6). In the narrative parts of the gospels, the expression 'the Lord' is, outside Luke where it occurs sixteen times, used of Jesus only five more times, namely in the Fourth Gospel. Here in Lk 18:6 it marks the transition from the parable to the interpretation. The exalted Lord [*in other words, Luke—RMP*] applies the parable to the actual situation of the Church.[11]

With the determination of the apologist to call those things that are not as though they were, Hicks seeks to vindicate the whole parable and its interpretation(s) as stemming from the earthly Jesus. He admits that *eipen de ho kurios* "ought to be regarded as Luke's editorial notation in order to set the parable

---

8. Bultmann, *History*, 209; Easton, *Luke*, 268; Perrin, *Rediscovering*, 129; Mary Ann Tolbert, *Perspectives on the Parables: An Approach to Multiple Interpretations* (Philadelphia: Fortress Press, 1979), 15-31; Via, "Parable," 4.

9. W. Ott, *Gebet und Heil: Die Bedeutung der Gebetsparänese in der lukanischen Theologie*, Studien zum Alten und Neuen Testaments 12 (München: Kösel, 1965), 32-72.

10. Fitzmyer, *Luke X-XXIV*, 1176.

11. Herman Hendrickx, *The Parables of Jesus*, rev. ed., Studien in the Synoptic Gospels (London: Geoffrey Chapman; San Francisco: Harper & Row, Publishers, 1986), 222.

off from its application," but he denies "that this marks off what follows as secondary."[12] He gives other Lukan examples (7:13; 10:1, 39, 41; 11:39; 12:42; 13:15; 17:5, 6; 19:8a; 22:61) as showing that such connective phrases are just Lukan stylistic transitional pointers. But almost every one of these texts is manifestly a redactional seam holding together disparate bits of traditional material, or linking such with Lukan composition.

As Glasson said, "It would be in keeping with Jesus' usual practice to leave his hearers to find the message for themselves."[13] I am not sure that we are in a position to know what "Jesus' usual practice" about anything was. But to make the same point in terms of the observable trajectories of Synoptic transmission, Bultmann documents the "tendency of the tradition to add such applications . . . it is very clear that the applications we find in the gospels are very often secondary."[14]

An Exemplary Story

Scholars who peel away vv. 6-8 as an addition or series of additions go on to debate whether the original teaching of vv. 2-5, inculcating prayer and endurance in a time of eschatological testing, has been generalized as a lesson on perseverance in prayer regardless of the circumstance (Bultmann), or rather perhaps the parable first taught general perseverance in prayer and was only later eschatologized.[15]

But I question whether vv. 2-5 had a thing to do with prayer at all. I think it did not, but that the supplementary verses were added on the basis of Sirach 35:14-19 to *make* it a teaching on prayer. (The similarity to the Sirach passage is common knowledge.)[16] Originally the pericope was an exemplary story, not really a parable at all.

The hearer was simply to do what the depicted widow did,

---

12. Hicks, "Parable," 210.
13. Francis T. Glasson, *The Second Advent: The Origin of the New Testament Doctrine* (London: Epworth Press, 1947), 90.
14. Bultmann, *History*, 184.
15. B. T. D. Smith, *The Parables of the Synoptic Gospels: A Critical Study* (Cambridge: Cambridge University Press, 1937), 151-153; Glasson, *Second Advent*, 91; C. J. Cadoux, *The Historic Mission of Jesus, A Constructive Re-examination of the Eschatological Teaching in the Synoptic Gospels* (New York: Harper & Brothers, Publishers, n.d.), 303; Perrin, *Rediscovering*, 130.
16. Jeremias, *Parables*, 155; Glasson, *Second Advent*, 45, 90; Hendrickx, *Parables*, 224.

because it was assumed that the hearer was a widow herself. She had none to speak up for her against those who devoured widows' houses except charismatic Jesuses like the one who first issued the woe of Matthew 12:14 against the church hierarchs who demanded that widows, to be enrolled, turn over whatever inheritance they had to the church who then doled out a miserable pittance in return.[17] And these charismatics carried no legal clout anyway. The widows were well advised to get justice by using the only weapon available to the powerless in such a situation, the slow, incremental terrorism of nuisance.

My interpretation is the trace, the suggestive empty track (Derrida), of the objections of Fitzmyer and others: "If one were to regard the parable as consisting only of vv. 2-5, then the parable would not be so much one about a dishonest judge as about an importunate widow."[18] Exactly! Why not? "Why should it be thought incredible among you that" a story should have a woman as its central concern?

"It is important to continue the characterization of the judge in Luke 18:1-5 in order to make it clear that what is true for a lesser character like the judge, will certainly be true for a greater character like God" (D. C. Benjamin).[19] That is, without vv. 6ff, the point about God delaying but not finally denying justice would not be clear. Even so: it isn't! It simply is not required by what is in vv. 2-5. Why must we insist on seeing it there?

Yet again, Hicks: "the parable, if it stood alone, would be indeterminate, and thus meaningless. It is a parable which requires interpretation if it is to have specific meaning."[20] Hicks's problem is that the plain meaning of the story as a story is not good enough for him. He wants esotericism. One recalls Derrida's observation: "The supposed 'commentary' of the 'i.e.' or 'in other words' has furnished only a textual supplement that calls in turn for an overdetermining 'in other words.'"[21] The interpretation cannot leave well enough alone and winds up telling a new story in the name of the old. To read is to rewrite.

But in fact Hicks sees quite plainly what the meaning of the story by itself is:

---

17. McKenna, *Women of the Church*, 41.
18. Fitzmyer, *Luke X-XXIV*, 1176.
19. D. C. Benjamin, "The Persistent Widow," *The Bible Today* 28 (April 1990): 217.
20. Hicks, "Parable," 212.
21. Derrida, "Living On. Border Lines," 75.

> The parable, then, envisions a widow demanding jus-
> tice. She is persistent in her request. At first the judge
> refuses, but then after a while gives in because he is
> afraid he will be disgraced publicly. The parable, then,
> falls within the prophetic picture of the poor widow
> against the powerful unrighteous judge. This time the
> widow wins because she is persistent.[22]

Hicks is right: without all the verses after v. 5, this is what we
would have left. But why isn't it enough?

Virginia Mollenkott,[23] followed by Margaret G. Adams, recognizes that the woman is at center stage, even despite the red
herrings thrown astride the path by Luke's redaction. "This story
seems to be a prime example of a teaching . . . of a model of a
woman who uses assertiveness to teach [sic: to secure?] justice."[24]

Few discussions of this parable can resist quoting or citing a
striking parallel to the story of the persistent widow from the
waning days of the Ottoman Empire, recounted by Henry Baker
Tristam. I happily yield as well:

> It was in the ancient city of Nisibis, in Mesopotamia.
> Immediately on entering the gate of the city . . . [one
> saw] a large open hall, the court of justice of the place.
> On a slightly raised dais at the further end sat the
> *Kadi*, or judge, half buried in cushions. Round him
> squatted various secretaries and notables. The popu-
> lace crowded into the rest of the hall, a dozen voices
> clamoring at once, each claiming that his cause should
> be the first heard. [Others got quicker results with a
> well-directed bribe, the verdict going to the highest
> bidder.] But meantime a poor woman on the skirts of
> the crowd perpetually interrupted the proceedings
> with loud cries for justice. She was sternly bidden to
> be silent, and reproachfully told that she came there
> every day. "And so I will," she cried out, "till the *Kadi*
> hears me." At length, at the end of a suit, the judge

22. Hicks, "Parable," 218.
23. Virginia Ramey Mollenkott, *Women, Men, and the Bible* (Nashville:
Abingdon Press, 1977), 79-80, cited in Margaret G. Adams, "The Hidden
Disciples: Lukes Stories About Women in His Gospel and in Acts"
(D.Min. diss.: San Francisco Theological Seminary, 1980), 117.
24. Adams, "Hidden Disciples."

impatiently demanded, "What does that woman want?" Her story was soon told. Her only son had been taken for a soldier, and she was left alone, and could not till her piece of ground; yet the tax-gatherer had forced her to pay the impost, from which as a lone widow she should remain exempt. The judge asked her a few questions, and said, "Let her be exempt." Thus her perseverance was rewarded.[25]

This story should demonstrate three things seldom if ever pointed out in applications of it to Luke 18:1-8. First, it shows quite clearly that such a story could circulate free of Lukan idiom, so that Luke need not have created his version from whole cloth *à la* Goulder, Drury, Freed, and Linnemann. Second, it shows how such a story could circulate with no reference at all to prayer. And third, it shows that a story like this could circulate just fine with no application attached. Insofar as it is judged a true parallel to Luke's story, and it is by many scholars, then it seems to me to support my exegesis that the substance of Luke 18:2-5 did circulate by itself with neither subsequent interpretation nor any reference at all to prayer.

J. Duncan M. Derrett dismisses Tristam's proposed parallel on the grounds that he seems ignorant of the difference between canonical courts where rabbinic law would hold good and secular courts where judges habitually cared not a fig for God or man. The widow is the villain of the story, he insists, because she has obviously skipped seeking God's justice or didn't like the judgment she got there and wants a second opinion.[26] This very exegesis is an amazing instance of how the welfare of women is placed a distant second after the niceties of ecclesiastical power politics.

But I am not even sure he is right about the widow taking her case to a secular Roman court. For one thing, Derrett begins with the gratuitous assumption that Luke knew what he was talking about. In fact it may rather be Luke, not so much Tristam, who was ignorant of the difference Derrett thinks is so important. For another, can we be so sure this woman is not pleading her

25. Henry Baker Tristam, *Eastern Customs in Bible Lands* (London: Hodder & Stoughton, 1894), 228. Among those who refer to it or quote it in part or in full are Smith, *Parables*, 150 and Jeremias, *Parables*, 154.

26. J. Duncan M. Derrett, "Law in the New Testament: The Parable of the Unjust Judge," *New Testament Studies* 18 (1971-1972): 180-182.

case before *Christian* arbiters such as we find in Matthew's "manual of discipline" section, 18:15-20, and 1 Corinthians 6:1-6 (a late section as witnessed by the fact that the author no longer understands the encratite coloring of the motif of *celibate* believers judging the fallen angels who sinned by lusting after the daughters of the human race, as is still correctly understood in Paul's Iconium beatitudes in the *Acts of Paul*)?

The Unjust Judge Is the Pastor

I suspect that the pericope attests the bitterness of Christian widows who had received peremptory treatment from church officials who viewed them and their problems with the jaundiced eye of the Pastor, who is ready to view the widows in the worst light possible, as heretics and prostitutes. Just because a man is appointed to administer the law of God hardly guarantees he will either fear God or regard human esteem. It was to religious men that these words were addressed: "How can you believe, when you receive glory from one another and do not seek the glory that comes from the only God?" (John 5:44).

So I think that the original point of the story of the persistent widow was to inculcate the doggedness (bitchiness?) she showed. The story, like many of the widow traditions we have examined, had exactly the same function as the widow stories of Elijah and Elisha, as described by Tamis Rentería:

> Peasants tell stories about these events, shaping the narrative to celebrate their own ability to make a marvelous breakthrough in the struggle against oppressive restrictions on human life by juxtaposing an oppressive context and an extraordinary breaking out of it.[27]

This message of self-reliance for widows has managed to glimmer through the encompassing bands of Lukan redaction and the thick layer of clinging tradition-barnacles. Jane Kopas sees that "Despite her lowliness in society, she recognizes a deeper claim to recognition, her equality as a human being. Thus she is raised up as an example of what can happen when one speaks up for herself."[28]

---

27. Rentería, "Elijah," 98, referring to Antoinette Clark Wire, "The Structure of the Gospel Miracle Stories and Their Tellers," *Semeia* 11 (1978): 109.

Why has the original story of vv. 2-5 been thus supplemented with an interpretation that supplies a new meaning and supplants the old one? Perhaps Luke saw that it had the potential of teaching a good lesson about prayer, once altered to "clarify" this point. But then Luke already has a story that makes pretty much the same point about persistent prayer, the parable of the friend at midnight (11:5-8). Why did he need another? I suggest his redactional motive was scarcely as innocent as that.

We have seen that Luke shares the woman-minimizing prejudices of the Pastor (I suspect this is quite natural, as he *is* the Pastor). The last thing he wants to inculcate is the notion that women must learn to rely on themselves! He has added vv. 6-8 just in order to cut the nerve of such resolve and to place women once again under the numbing opiate of dependence upon the male God who might be so magnanimous as one day to lend an ear—but don't hold your breath!

Jane Via sees the widow as grovelling right where Luke wants her: "the woman represents the persistent, humble petitioner before the deity."[29] Or, more to the point, before the deity's self-appointed male representatives, like Luke.

In short, the behavior of the deity here described is much like the impassive condescension of the Pastor. Exegetes have hastened to suggest that the parable means to contrast the reprehensible behavior of the misanthropic/misogynic judge with God's. If even the scoundrel of a judge will eventually get around to your case, how much more will God! But are we sure this is Luke's point?

One wonders if the dreadfully obtuse wording of verse 7, so labored over by commentators, is not intentional throat-clearing on Luke's part; to promise that God will promptly grant one's prayer is a bit too definite a pledge, a bluff too easily called. So Luke leaves himself an escape clause: he retreats into verbal obfuscation, as when Bilbo Baggins seems to thank all of his party guests for coming:

> *I don't know half of you as well as I should like; and I like less than half of you half as well as you deserve.* This was unexpected and rather difficult. There was some scattered clapping, but most of them were trying to work it out and see if it came to a compliment.[30]

---

28. Kopas, "Jesus and Women," 200; cf. Selvidge, *Daughters*, 109.
29. E. J. Via, "Women in the Gospel of Luke," 48.

Has Luke said God may delay or that he will not? I am not sure he wanted to be understood. He needed the room to maneuver, as theologians always have when called to account. And this confusion makes it anything but clear that God is being contrasted with the judge. Indeed the implication seems to me that one must resign oneself to expect that, whatever his reasons (and they are his business, not ours), God will behave pretty much like the judge. And what this really amounts to is giving divine legitimation to the same apparent (no doubt real) indifference of church leaders to the concerns of widows.

Look, for example, at the attitude expressed by the Twelve, Luke's darlings, in a clearly redactional bit of the story of the appointment of the Seven (a story I will deal with at greater length in the next chapter). They can scarcely hide their annoyance at having to take time out from more important, more logocentric matters ("preaching the *logos* of God") to waste their valuable time on a bunch of nagging hags. This phallogocentric scorn of women as a mere distraction is the attitude of the God who will surely get around to giving justice to his widows *mañana*, when he can clear some time for it.

Such a God is the alter ego (divine altar = male ego) of the Pastor, and of Luke, a God who has fresh oracles for Agabus and Zechariah, but silence aplenty for Anna, Philip's nameless daughters and Martha's voiceless sister.

The Widow Is the Widow

Luke did his work well. We might ask of the persistent widow as Jesus did of the woman in Simon's house, "Do you see this woman?" By and large, exegetes follow Luke's direction. They look right past her; she is no longer visible. The widow has been sublimated into an abstraction; she has been neutered and diffused as a figure for the whole Christian church. Stählin assures us that "the widow was a collective type or character for the early Christian audience . . ., a personification of the church in its time of struggle."[31]   Eduard Schweizer says the parable "inculcated the certainty that God hears the prayers of the oppressed 'widow' i.e., the community."[32]   Constance Parvey: "If

---

30. J. R. R. Tolkien, *The Fellowship of the Ring: Being the First Part of The Lord of the Rings* (New York: Ballantine Books, 1965), 54-55.
31. Paraphrase of Gustav Stählin, "Das Bild der Witwe," *Jahrbuch für Antike und Christentum* 17 (1974): 20, in Thurston, *Widows*, 27.

it is possible for even the most unlikely candidate—an annoying and troublesome old woman—to gain access to the Kingdom, it is certainly possible for anyone."[33] Selvidge: "The writer uses a story about a widow to demonstrate to the community that they must persevere and they will also overcome."[34] A. J. Mattill: "The widow is a metaphor for the eschatological community. . . . Luke's community knows itself as the rejected widow."[35]

The strange thing is, there is a lost element of truth here. The widow in the story *did* stand for the community of hearers among whom and for whom the story originally circulated: the community of widows.

---

32. Schweizer, *Good News*, 280.
33. Parvey, "Theology and Leadership," 142.
34. Selvidge, *Daughters*, 105.
35. A. J. Mattill, Jr., *Luke and the Last Things: A Perspective for the Understanding of Lukan Thought* (Dillsboro, NC: Western North Carolina Press, 1979), 90.

CHAPTER TEN

Cautionary Tales:
The Hellenist Widows and Sapphira

Widows Retrojected

In this chapter I will consider the prehistory of two stories
from the Acts of the Apostles. I will, as hitherto, be seeking to
show what functions these stories served vis-a-vis the consecrated widows. As I urged in Chapter 3, the stories must be dis-
engaged from their Lukan setting where they appear as episodes
in the life of the earliest Jerusalem community. The story of the
Seven reads much more naturally as located in a mixed congregation, say, in Antioch, at a later period. N. Walter agrees: the story
has been retrojected.[1]

Luke has placed the story in the sacred time of Christian origins in order to gain for the arrangements therein described the
irreproachability of that holy zone of divine foundings and
authorizations. For Luke, the dawn period of the Jerusalem
church is really as much a part of the middle of time as the time
of Jesus,[2] a paradigm for future generations. But we must not be
taken in by this.

It is revealing how scholars have often discerned the identity of the ecclesiastical widows in the Acts 6 passage yet without
being able to believe their eyes. But it *couldn't* be! Too early!
"Evidence for the existence of an order of widows at this early
stage is conjectural at best" (Thurston).[3]

Foakes Jackson admits that it *sounds* like the ecclesiastical
widows: "it may be possible that Luke, in his desire to make what
happened intelligible to his readers, is describing the difficulties
in regard to these 'widows' in language which would be understood by people of a later time."[4] In other words, the scene is

---

1. N. Walter, "Apostelgeschichte 6.1 und die Anfänge der Urgemeinde in
Jerusalem," *New Testament Studies* 29 (1983): 370-393.
2. Robert L. Wilkin, *The Myth of Christian Beginnings: History's Impact on
Belief* (Garden City, NY: Anchor Books, a division of Doubleday & Company, 1972), 31-33.
3. Thurston, *Widows*, 30.
4. F. J. Foakes Jackson, *The Acts of the Apostles,* Moffatt New Testament
Commentary, ed. James Moffatt (New York: Harper & Row, Publishers,
1931), 51-52.

anachronistic for the period in which he has set it. Foakes Jackson
seeks merely to salvage some historical core, some tenuous link
to the early church, using much the same strategy, lampooned by
Strauss, of those rationalists, who, having evacuated a miracle
story of all purpose of its telling, sought to salvage some negligi-
ble historical husk to save appearances.[5] Similarly, witness the
back-peddling of Jackson and Lake: "The care of widows was
naturally one of the chief functions of philanthropy in the ancient
world, and there is no real reason here for going outside the ordinary meaning of the word." No reason, that is, except for that
which the commentators themselves will immediately supply!
"But it is obvious that this passage regards the widows as receiving regular support, and this implies some organization of their
members. The further development of this organization can be
traced to the Pastoral Epistles (especially 1 Tim. v. 9ff)."[6]

But 1 Timothy 5:3-16 merely provides a fuller account of the
same phenomenon (as Rackham admits),[7] not a later one. The
only reason for thinking otherwise is the arbitrary postulate of
the historical accuracy of the Acts 6 story in its redactional setting. Instead, we must say of that story what F. C. Baur said of
the Pastoral Epistles themselves:

> One of the most decisive proofs of their later origin is
> the ecclesiastical institution of widows. . . . the passage
> can never appear in a clear light so long as the expres-
> sion [*chera*] is not taken in the sense which I have
> shown to be the ecclesiastical one (cf. especially Ignat.
> Ep. ad Smyrn., c. 13). . . . And if it thus appears that the
> passage can be satisfactorily explained out of the
> ecclesiastical vocabulary of the second century, this is
> the clearest possible proof that the [story] cannot
> belong to the apostolic age, when the church had no
> special order of the kind.[8]

Widow Welfare Stories

In the second and following centuries we see many exam-

---

5. Strauss, *Life of Jesus Critically Examined*, 91.

6. Cadbury and Lake, "Commentary," *Beginnings* IV, 64.

7. Rackham, *Acts*, 82, 400.

8. Ferdinand Christian Baur, *Paul, the Apostle of Jesus Christ: His Life and
Work, His Epistles and Doctrine*, trans. A. Menzies (London & Edinburgh:
Williams & Norgate, 1875), vol. 2, 103.

ples of stories in which an apostle is pointedly shown urging that donations be made to the consecrated widows, often rebuking apathetic churches in the process. These stories appear in the Apocryphal Acts and represent just the sort of thing that led Stevan L. Davies to recognize that behind the masks of the apostles Paul, Andrew, John, Thomas, and Peter stand the nameless charismatics of the early church, champions of their fellow ascetics the widows, against the ecclesiastical establishment which looked askance at both.

My only difference from Davies would be to extend the approach of Kraemer and Burrus and to recognize such stories, like the chastity stories, as pre-existing oral traditions later worked into the literary wholes of the Apocryphal Acts. I have already dubbed a related cycle of tales "widow patronage stories" in Chapter 4. These stories, idealized and transferred to the names of the canonical apostles, were propaganda such as Rentería describes, discussing the very similar Elijah and Elisha stories told about and by the poor, including widows like those who appear in the tales as clients of the prophets: "such stories may have been used by families, clans, and other factions to foster their own political and social status."[9]

I have already argued that the widow patronage stories of the widow of Nain and of Dorcas of Joppa performed exactly such a function, portraying Jesus and Peter as the enabling champions and defenders of widows left to destitution or at the mercy of the church dole. It remains to survey what might be more specifically labeled "widow welfare stories" from the Apocryphal Acts before we look at two counter-traditions found in the canonical Acts.

> Then he commanded Verus, the brother who attended him, to bring the old women (that were) in the whole of Ephesus, and he and Cleopatra and Lycomedes made preparations to care for them. So Verus came and said to John, "Out of the old women over sixty that are here, I have found only four in good bodily health; of the others <some are...> and some paralytic and others sick." And John on hearing this kept silence for a long time; then he rubbed his face and said, "Oh, what slackness among the people of Ephesus! What a collapse, what weakness towards God! O

---

9. Rentería, "Elijah," 118.

devil, what a mockery you have made all this time of the faithful at Ephesus! Jesus, who gives me grace and the gift of confidence in him, says to me now in silence, 'Send for the old women who are sick, and be with them in the theatre and through me heal them; for some of them who come to see this sight I will convert through these healings, which may be to some useful purpose. . . .'" So . . . he commanded the old women to be brought into the theatre . . . some lying on beds and others in a deep sleep . . . and John healed all their diseases by the power of God. (*Acts of John* 30, 32, 37).[10]

"Believe us, brother Peter; no one was so wise among men as this Marcellus. All the widows who hoped in Christ found refuge with him; all the orphans were fed by him. And what more, brother? All the poor called Marcellus their patron, and his house was called (the house) of pilgrims and the poor. The emperor said to him, 'I am keeping you out of every office, or you will plunder the provinces to benefit the Christians.'" (*Acts of Peter* 8)[11]

But Eubula having recovered all her property gave it for the care of the poor; she believed in her Lord Jesus Christ and was strengthened (in the faith); and despising and renouncing this world she gave (alms) to the widows and orphans and clothed the poor. (*Acts of Peter* 17)[12]

Marcellus came in and said, "Peter, . . . I have told the widows and the aged to meet you in my house . . . that they may pray with us. And each of them shall be given a piece of gold on account of their service, so that they may truly be called Christ's servants." . . . So Peter went in and saw . . . a widow that was blind, and her daughter giving her a hand and leading her to Marcellus' house. And Peter said to her, "Mother, come here; from this day onward Jesus gives you his right hand, through whom we have light unapproachable which no darkness hides; and he says to you through me, 'Open your eyes and see, and walk on

---

10. Hennecke, *New Testament Apocrypha*, 221-224.
11. Ibid., 289.
12. Ibid., 300.

your own.'" And at once the widow saw Peter laying
his hand on her. (*Acts of Peter* 19-20)[13]

And Peter said to her, "Let the remainder be distributed to the widows." . . . Peter had arranged to go to
Marcellus on the Lord's day, to see the widows as
Marcellus had promised, so that they should be cared
for by his own hands. So the boy who had returned to
life said, "I will not leave Peter." And his mother went
joyfully and gladly to her own house. And on the next
day after the sabbath she came to Marcellus' house
bringing Peter two thousand pieces of gold and saying
to Peter, "Divide these among the virgins of Christ
who serve him." (*Acts of Peter* 28-29)[14]

But Hermocrates <sold . . . . .> and brought the price to
the <widows>, and took it and divided it. . . . (*Acts of
Paul* 4)[15]

So all the people believed, and yielded their souls obe-
dient to the living God and to Christ Jesus, rejoicing in
the blessed works of the Most High and in his holy
service. And they brought much money for the service of the widows; for he [Thomas] had them gathered together in the cities, and to them all he sent what
was necessary by his deacons, both clothing and provision for their nourishment. (*Acts of Thomas* 59)[16]

That all this reflects (and encourages) almsgiving current in
the contemporary church is evident from a passage in the *Apostolic Tradition* of Hippolytus:

If there is anyone who takes it (the gifts) away, let him
bear it to the widows and the sick. And let him who is
occupied with the church take it away. And if he did
not take it away, on the morrow having added of that
which was with him, he shall take it away; for it
remained with him as bread of the poor (24).

But, applying the hermeneutic of suspicion even to these

13. Ibid., 301.
14. Ibid., 312-313.
15. Ibid., 367.
16. Ibid., 475.

passages, I suspect that the stories in the Apocryphal Acts reflect less the reality of the care for widows by the church, than the efforts of the widows to promote such care. They are prescriptive, not descriptive. And we may surmise that churchmen like the Pastor swatted these aside like the rest of the "old women's tales."

Cautionary Tales

I suspect they did more than disregard them. Just as the Pastor turned the widows' guns against them by, as MacDonald demonstrates, self-servingly fabricating his own Paul as the mirror opposite of theirs, so did the church authorities create their own stories in which widows were depicted as complaining nuisances censured by the apostles. We find one of them in *The Episodes from the Life of John the Beloved Disciple:*

> Now there were very many pious nuns, widows, and such holy persons following John, spending their lives listening to the splendid sermons which he used to deliver to the people. And they had no livelihood or substance, property or riches, save for whatever alms John received from the Christians. They complained constantly, and found fault often with John, because in their eyes, the amount of goods and alms which John got from the people was very ample and substantial, yet their share of it seemed meagre to them. They said, "What does he do with it, since we do not get it for food and clothing? He desires that he himself be rich, but that we should be poor. John heard this, yet he did not react with an angry outburst or uncontrolled rage, but went on with calmness and composure, until one day he chanced to be on a great wide bridge, where patient asses were drawing some hay. John drew out a good handful of the hay, and said: "O God whom I trust and follow, turn all of this into gold without delay." And John said to his companions: "Count all the gold." This was done, and there was found to be a hundred smooth rods of beautiful burnished gold. John said: "Beloved children, take the gold to the smelters." They took it to the nearest craftsman, and it was put over fire to smelt and refine it. They said that they had never found finer gold. Then the gold was handed to John, who dropped it into the deep waters and swift-flowing stream beneath the

bridge. Everyone was astonished at this. John said: "If I had wanted unlimited gold and riches, I would have received them from the Lord himself. But I freely prefer to be poor and lowly, for the kingdom of heaven belongs to the poor in spirit, as the Creator has said. And tell the hypocritical widows that the only thing I do with what I receive is to give it to them, and to other poor people." (12-13)[17]

Again, we may not doubt that this nasty tale reflects the annoyance felt by the ecclesiarchs who rejoiced to repeat it. In the third-century church order the *Didascalia Apostolorum* we read of

> widows in whom there is envy one toward another. For when thy fellow aged woman has been clothed, or has received somewhat from some one, thou oughtest, O widow, on seeing thy sister refreshed . . . to say: "Blessed be God, who hath refreshed my fellow aged woman." And to praise God; and afterwards him that ministered. (142)[18]

Gryson describes the situation of the widows' contentiousness according to *The Apostolic Constitutions*, from the next century, where the widows seem almost like a flock of vultures clawing at one another over the juiciest piece of carrion.[19] We will find some of this sentiment in Acts.

Episodes from the Life of John is a medieval text of uncertain date. It is said, in the colophon, to have been translated from an earlier Latin document by the Uighisdin Mac Raighin who is known to have died in 1405. It is possible, as Martin McNamara notes, that we should understand Mac Raighin to have composed a new Irish work on the basis of Latin sources, though as McNamara admits the plain sense would seem to be that the Irish work was a simple translation of a pre-existent whole.[20] In either case, the version we have just reviewed would seem ultimately to be based on one of two parallel Latin texts, *The Apostolic History of*

17. Maire Herbert and Martin McNamara, eds., *Irish Biblical Apocrypha* (Edinburgh: T & T Clark, 1989), 93.
18. Quoted in Thurston, *Widows*, 102.
19. Gryson, *Women*, 57-58.
20. Martin McNamara, *The Apocrypha in the Irish Church* ([Dublin:] Dublin Institute for Advanced Studies, 1975), 96.

Pseudo-Abdias (placed by M. R. James in the sixth century) or its nearly verbatim twin (in the relevant sections) *Pseudo-Mellitus* (Pseudo-Melito). As we have seen, James thinks the episode to represent part of the otherwise lost portions of the *Acts of John*. In this earlier version, interestingly, there is no mention of the consecrated women.

In the earlier version, the occasion for John turning reeds into gold (as well as pebbles into gemstones) is the rueful second thoughts of a pair of brothers from Ephesus, who have donated their wealth to the poor and followed John on into Pergamum where they are dismayed to see their former slaves parading around in what used to be their own finery. They imperil their new-won salvation by these second thoughts, but they do not actually complain to John. They need not voice their thoughts, since he can read them. John transforms the reeds and stones into treasure to restore the standing of the brothers but warns them that they have forfeited salvation. Eventually he persuades them to reconsider, whereupon the gold, silver, and precious stones revert again to wood, hay, and stubble.[21]

Note that somewhere in the process of transmission the story has substituted a group of consecrated women for the two brothers, and that unspoken regrets are turned into cantankerous complaints. I think we can see here just the sort of redactional agenda I am attributing to Luke in an earlier period.

The Widows of the Hellenists

Turning first to the story of the appointment of the Seven (Acts 6:1-6), we note that the problem posed by the neglect of the Hellenist widows is not the fact of their neglect but rather the stirring of the glassy smooth placidity of the halcyon Jerusalem church. The stomachs of widows might well rumble, but the peace of the archetypical church must not be disturbed. This much is evident from the conformity of the story to the pattern recurrent in Acts, delineated by Tyson, in which some issue or crisis arises to disturb the peace of the church, a means is found for restoring peace, and all is well again. For this, all specific people and issues are mere fodder.[22]

In the case of Acts 6:1-6 the widows' troubles are important simply as furnishing another example of the inner gyroscope of

21. M. R. James, *Apocryphal New Testament*, 258-262.
22. Joseph B. Tyson, "Dietary Regulations," 148-150.

the church whereby it automatically rights itself. In the other stories the problems range from heresy (8:9-12) and simony (8:18-19) to threats of persecution (5:17-18, 21b-33) and competition from Jewish magic (19:13-14). The grumbling of, or on behalf of, the widows is implicitly of the same character as these other problems: an invasive irritant from without. Its resolution is not so much a working out of the church's own kinks, but rather a fending off of another dart from Satan, as is the Ananias and Sapphira episode, which will claim our attention presently. So the complaining of the widows is implicitly one more diabolical stratagem, the hungry widows the instruments of Satan.

Commentators have not been slow to notice the pointed allusion in the "murmuring" (*goggusmos*) in this passage to that of the stubborn and rebellious Israelites in Numbers 11:1ff (LXX), where they are also complaining about food rations.[23] The food of angels, it seems, was not good enough for their gourmet palates. And though Yahweh eventually loses patience and, in a divine tantrum of his own, makes short work of his spoiled children, in the short run the murmuring does serve to put food on the table. The tale is told to commemorate, really to authorize, the institution of the system of seventy judges, extant in the writer's day.

This parallel to the Pentateuch points in two directions. First, we can see the same impatience with the complaints of the widows as we saw in the *Didascalia* and in *The Episodes from the Life of John:* beggars can't be choosers! Second, we can see that, as in Numbers, the complaining is made the occasion for legitimating a church office, local boards of seven men either to oversee food distribution to widows or, as I think more likely, to adjudicate disputes between widows or to hear their complaints of unfair treatment. The latter would certainly fit better the parallel with Numbers 11, where the issue of the matter is the appointment not of food service workers but rather of judges to hear complaints to take the burden off the prophet.

Note that Luke does not actually say that the Seven are to wait tables any more than the Twelve are willing to do. Nor, for that matter, does he say that the Seven are not to preach the word of God. The Twelve announce that they have no intention of giv-

23. C. S. C. Williams, *A Commentary on The Acts of the Apostles*, Black's New Testament Commentaries, ed., Henry Chadwick (London: Adam & Charles Black, 1978), 95-96; Rackham, *Acts*, 83-84.

ing up preaching to distribute food, but does this imply that the Seven chosen were to do nothing *but* distribute food? No, and there are three factors that lead me to believe this was not the task to which Luke meant to appoint them.

First, as is well known, two of the Seven are immediately said to have preached the word of God, and that rather aggressively. Scholars mark a gross contradiction here. But the contradiction only appears if we assume that the Seven are to wait tables to the exclusion of anything else. That v. 2 does not mean this should be evident from the hyperbolic coloring of exasperation in the words of the dodecade chorus: "It is not right that we should give up preaching the word of God to serve tables." Who's asking them to?

The words are a sarcastic suggestion that they are having to pause in their devotion to the sublime to waste a few moments on the ridiculous. Surely we are to think of Moses' bitter outburst back in Numbers 11:11-15,

> Why have you treated your servant so badly? And why have you looked askance at me, that you should lay the burden of the whole people on my back? Did I conceive this whole people? Did I give birth to the lot of them, that you should say to me, "Carry them in your bosom, as the nurse carries the suckling child ...."? Where am I supposed to find meat to give to the whole people? ... If you plan to deal with me this way, kill me right now and get it over with!

The Twelve speak with the same wounded sarcasm. Their words do not imply that someone else *will* be chosen to shoulder an unreasonable duty.

Second, the qualifications set forth for the Seven do not seem to be what we would expect for someone who is merely to serve food. They need to be full of the Spirit and wisdom—why? To sling hash? Luke shows Stephen using his equipment quite appropriately in preaching the word of God in v. 8. Haenchen rightly points to the similarity between this set of qualifications and those for bishops and deacons in 1 Timothy 3:1ff,[24] and it would seem that practical details are the least of their worries, though they are included (v. 4).

Third, the Twelve do not say that the Seven are to hand out

24. Haenchen, *Acts*, 262.

the food, but rather that they are to see to *tes chreias tautes,* "this business," i.e., what the Twelve did not wish to be bothered with: the adjudication of disputes like these. The Seven, as the Numbers parallel should have led us to see, are more like judges than food distributors. The Twelve are not so much rejecting the role of Jesus in Luke 22:27 as they are emulating his rejection of the role thrust upon him in Luke 12:13-14, "O man, who made me a judge or divider over you?"

I suspect Luke was attempting to inaugurate a system of seven-men appeal boards to deal with widow and charity affairs. Josephus extolled his own wisdom that he showed when, in power in Galilee during the rebellion against Rome, he "chose seven judges in every city to hear the lesser quarrels" (*Wars of the Jews* ii, 20, 5).

It is no argument against this view that no such system is known to have existed throughout the early church. I suggest only that Luke tried to establish it. It is well known that the ecclesiology of the Pastorals reflects no known period of church history either. Perhaps Luke did his work of retrojection all too well in both instances: readers may simply have assumed that such patterns as they found in the Pastorals and Acts had obtained in Paul's day but had long since passed away.

Though on the hypothetical pre-Lukan level we cannot press any of the details, it still seems that the basic function of the tale would have been the same: an ideal scene constructed in order to provide the imprimatur for a practical arrangement for church governance. Here I follow, tentatively, the analysis of Lienhard, who uses the Lukan vocabulary and thematic content of vv. 2-4 as a lever to displace the verses from the pericope as Lukan redaction of traditional material.[25]

He rather suspects that the mention of the apostles in v. 6 is Lukan also. It certainly seems to fit too well Luke's tendency to place all events in the unfolding of the church under the watchful and authenticating eyes of the Twelve. The rest, though, he deems pre-Lukan, partly because of *paratheoreisthai* and *kathemerinos,* which occur nowhere else in the New Testament, and partly because of the fact of the disharmony, something Luke certainly had no interest in showcasing if he didn't have to.

Earl Richard, seconded by Craig C. Hill, throws Lienhard's

25. J. T. Lienhard, "Acts 6:1-6: A Redactional View," *Catholic Biblical Quarterly* 37 (1975): 228-236.

analysis into some doubt by demonstrating that the Lukan redaction goes much deeper that he had thought.[26] Nonetheless, strikingly, Richard affirms the same basic pre-Lukan core of tradition suggested by Lienhard:

> That he has inherited various elements of this episode from tradition seems undeniable, e.g., the Hellenist-Hebrew conflict within the early community (v. 1b), the list, and probably the tradition of the Seven. However, other factors such as the role of the Twelve [or] apostles . . ., of the Seven, of the Spirit (in 1-7 and in relation especially to Stephen 6:10 and 7:55), and the various notions of "service" (and their function within 6:1-7) are so intimately related both to the structural and the thematic character of Acts 6:1-7 that one must consider these in terms principally of the author's purpose and theology.[27]

Lüdemann comes to the same basic assessment.[28]

In view of this analysis, I would like to point out the recurrence here of a very ancient tendency in the process of oral transmission. Martin Noth demonstrated how Pentateuchal pericopes which feature Moses flanked by superfluous characters must originally have put the latter at center stage, with no Moses in view at all. Moses was subsequently added when the redactor felt compelled, by virtue of Moses' later importance, to introject him into every episode of the Exodus, Sinai, and Wilderness history. The redactor, jealous of every ounce of sacred tradition, did not dare simply omit the old protagonists; he rather let Moses elbow them aside.

This, Noth reasoned, is the only way to understand the continued yet superfluous presence of characters like Nadab and Abihu in Exodus 24:1, 2, 9-11. In fact, Noth suggested, we really ought to view this story as having originally featured only the elders of Israel feasting with God atop his mountain, with Nadab and Abihu added later, then being pushed aside in turn by the later figure Moses, who himself comes, under the Priestly regime,

---

26. Earl Richard, *Acts 6:1 - 8:4: The Author's Method of Composition*, Society of Biblical Literature Dissertation Series 41 (Missoula: Scholars Press, 1978), 273-274; Craig C. Hill, *Hellenists and Hebrews: Reappraising Division Within the Earliest Church* (Minneapolis: Fortress Press, 1992), 89, 94.
27. Richard, *Author's Method*, 273-274.
28. Gerd Lüdemann, *Early Christianity*, 77-78.

to stand in the shadow of Aaron who now shoves his way to the front of the line.[29]

It is especially likely since, as it happens, one story, Exodus 5:15-21, seems somehow to have survived in nearly its original form: the story of the failed negotiation of the foremen with Pharaoh, during which Moses and Aaron, armed and ready with miracles of snakes and leprosy—wait out in the hall! "Well, what did he say?" Here Moses and Aaron have invaded the older story, like time-travellers in a science fiction novel, but they remain on the sidelines.

This seems to be exactly what has happened in Luke's redaction of the story of the Seven. The pre-Lukan traditional basis apparently had the community as a whole act to solve the dilemma. But Luke cannot have this! No democrat, he must have the Holy Apostles direct all the action, much like his near-contemporary Ignatius, who forbids the church mouse to eat a crumb of cheese without the supervision of the bishop.

I have already suggested that the invocation of Elijah in Luke 4:25-26 is a relic of the same dispute shown here. Then I also endorsed Tyson's reconstruction of the *Sitz-im-Leben* of the dispute as being a crisis very much like that in Antioch recorded in Galatians 2:11ff, where insistence on dietary restrictions eventuated in the severing of table fellowship with Gentiles. If we have truly been bequeathed the bare datum of a food dispute between Hellenist and Hebrew widows, then surely Tyson's is the best accounting for it.

So if we reconstruct the traditional report along the lines suggested by Lienhard, Richard, Hill, and Lüdemann, we come up with something like this:

> A dispute arose between the widows belonging to the Hellenists and the widows that were of the number of the Hebrews, for the cause that the widows of the Hellenists were passed by in the distribution of food. And the Hebrews said unto the Hellenists, "Let the children first be fed, for it is not right to take the children's bread and throw it to the dogs." But the Hellenists replied, saying, "Yet even the children's dogs under the table eat their crumbs."

---

29. Martin Noth, *A History of Pentateuchal Traditions*, trans. Bernhard W. Anderson (Englewood Cliffs, NJ: Prentice-Hall, 1972), 162.

> (Or perhaps they said: "There were many widows in Israel in the days of Elijah, when the heaven was shut up for three and a half years, when there came a great famine over all the land; and Elijah was sent to none of them but only to Zarephath, in the land of Sidon, to a woman who was a widow.")
>
> And this saying pleased the congregation, so they chose Stephen, and Philip, and Prochorus, and Nicanor, and Timon, and Parmenas, and Nicolaus, a proselyte of Antioch [—because the story originally took place there?].

It is striking that, once we eliminate the Lukan overlay, we have not a cautionary tale, but rather an episode like those in the Apocryphal Acts, which I suggest are widow traditions redactionally stitched into their present contexts. The core of Acts 6:1-6 is one more. Luke has added the murmuring, with its prejudicial Old Testament overtones, much as the redactor of the *Life of John* would later add an element of complaining widows to a story which first lacked it. The murmuring changes the sense completely, transforming the widow welfare story into a sarcastic put-down of the widows. None of this should surprise us by now.

Ananias and Sapphira

Acts 5:1-11, the tale of Ananias and Sapphira, seems certainly to be a cautionary tale after the manner of the crude priest-craft paradigms of the Old Testament. In these tales, hapless bumblers are smitten by the wrath of a peevish deity for offenses no less serious than gathering kindling on the sabbath (Numbers 15:32-36), asking for a promotion (Numbers 16:8-11), using the wrong incense recipe (Leviticus 10:1-2), seeking to democratize the clergy (Numbers 16:1-11), and trying to steady the ark without ritual preparation impossible in the circumstances (2 Samuel 6:6-7).

But what offense is the story of Ananias and Sapphira trying to discourage? What the doomed couple did is clear enough. They sold some property, claimed the reputation of big givers, and secretly kept back some of the proceeds of the sale for a rainy day. But is the nature of their deed after all so clear? The story seems to point in two directions at once, often a sign that both an original point and a secondary overlay can be identified.

First, the story points back unmistakably to the story of Achan (Joshua chapter 7), with its use of the word *nosphisasthai* in v. 3, the identical word used in the LXX for Achan secreting some of the booty that Yahweh (= the priests) had decreed go straight into the divine treasury. This is not missed by commentators.[30] But on the other hand it is no less clear from Acts 5:4 that it is not the only-partial donation, as if they had automatically owed the whole sum, but rather the fact of lying about it, that merits capital punishment.

Johnson cannot avoid seeing the heavy debt the story owes to the Achan prototype, but then he retreats behind a list of irrelevant non-parallels (the classic apologetical "the differences are greater than the similarities" evasion), and concludes that Luke used the Achan story "as a rough model" in order to teach a similar, but only vaguely similar, lesson about the misuse of possessions, an abstraction that would only occur to a harmonizer.[31]

Closer to the truth of the matter is Schuyler Brown who explains that "The obscurity arises from the fact that Luke has taken over an originally independent story and inserted it, no doubt with alterations, into his account of the conditions prevailing in the first Christian community in Jerusalem." But immediately he veers off the track:

> Traces of a pre-Lukan understanding of the story are found first of all within the pericope itself, in Peter's rebuke to Ananias (v. 4): "While it (the land) remained unsold, did it not remain your own? And after it was sold, was it not at your disposal?" The plain sense of these rhetorical questions is that Ananias was under no obligation *either* to sell his property *or* to give any part of the money to the apostles. His sin can therefore consist only in the fraudulent retention of a part of the proceeds, i.e., in pretending to give the full amount while secretly retaining a portion for his own private use.[32]

---

30. Haenchen, *Acts,* 327; Johannes Munck, *The Acts of the Apostles: A New Translation and Commentary,* rev. W. F. Albright and C. S. Mann, Anchor Bible, eds. William Foxwell Albright and David Noel Freedman, vol. 31 (Garden City, NY: Doubleday & Co., 1967), 40; Cadbury and Lake, "Commentary," *Beginnings* IV, 50; Seccombe, *Possessions,* 213; Williams, *Acts,* 88.

31. Johnson, *Literary Function,* 205-206; similarly in Johnson, *Acts,* 91-92.

32. Brown, *Apostasy,* 98-99.

Brown has it turned all the way round. It seems clear to me that it is precisely v. 4 that is the Lukan gloss, as Conzelmann sees.[33] We can see this from both formal and material considerations. As to the material, Peter's point-by-point explanation seems like what it is: an explanation for the reader that the rest of the story does not mean what it seems to mean, that contrary to appearances, there really isn't any parallel with the Achan story after all! That Ananias didn't owe the church a thing.

Note that the end of v. 4 merely repeats the end of v. 3, "to lie to the Holy Spirit" / "not lied to men but to God." This is a classic redactional seam: when one wants to insert new matter into a passage, one recaps the point at which the original left off, so as to be able to reattach the original continuation more smoothly. Without v. 4, the story fits the Achan prototype perfectly, the lying to the Spirit preparing for the embezzlement, not substituting for it as in v. 4.

Luke is trying to obscure the original Achan motif and to generalize the point. And that point Schuyler Brown correctly sees: "the attempt to circumvent the leaders of the community mean[s] an offence against the spirit itself."[34] Loisy is more forthright: "Whatever may be the source of it, the hair-raising story of Ananias and Sapphira is another invention intended to exalt the prestige of apostolic and ecclesiastical authority."[35]

Haenchen knows good and well that the essential point is the matter of withholding what belongs to God, not lying, and that it is a cautionary tale. He traces it back to the Jerusalem community, but since he has already, rightly, dismissed Luke's picture of early church communitarianism as a fiction, he must silently shift exegeses and make Acts 5:1-11 a lesson about vague "purity."[36] So he, like Johnson, is finally unwilling to give the Achan parallelism its due weight. Why? Because Haenchen realizes a story with such a point would presuppose something like the communism he has dismissed: "the total sacrifice of personal property is only called for when a celibate community is leading a monastic or semi-monastic existence. There was no question of this in the Christian community in Jerusalem."[37] For this reason he rejects the appeal by some scholars (e.g., recently Theissen)[38]

33. Conzelmann, *Acts*, 38.
34. Brown, *Apostasy*, 109.
35. Loisy, *Origins*, 199.
36. Haenchen, *Acts*, 239-241.
37. Ibid., 234.

to the rule in the Zadokite *Manual of Discipline* (1 QS VIII.20ff) that a member discovered to have lied about his property, withholding some of it when he joined, would suffer a severe reduction in food rations.[39]

Haenchen is prevented from seeing the solution to the problem by his vestigial attachment to the outmoded idea that the pericope represents Jerusalem tradition. Why should it, given what we know of Lukan proclivities? And if we may cast our net wider and, more importantly, *later*, we have precisely the milieu we need to provide the *Sitz-im-Leben* for such a community rule-miracle, or cautionary tale: the widow community. Here is Haenchen's celibate and semi-monastic community, ready-made.

Only where does Ananias fit into such a setting? Nowhere, admittedly, but then perhaps he does not fit into the original tradition either.

Haenchen, Conzelmann, and Lüdemann all make Sapphira a superfluous appendage to the story. It should have ended, and in effect did end, they say, after Ananias drops dead in v. 5, with the negative acclamation "And great fear came upon all who heard it."[40] These gentlemen critics can imagine no more than the phallocentric Luke himself that a woman might be central to a story. But Noth's redundancy principle ought to tip us off that it was originally only Sapphira, not Ananias, who was blasted like a fig tree. As the story now reads, she is indeed superfluous—so why is she there at all? She stands at the side, having been *shoved* aside, from an earlier position of centrality.

Paul Burns Brown regards the parallelism between husband and wife "as a literary means of showing emphasis."[41] This appears to me exceedingly limp. Noth's redundancy principle is more realistic in implying Sapphira's portion of the story is simply a left-over, which after all, is exactly how it strikes commentators. Only once it stood at center stage. When it was decided that a man must have been needed to mastermind the scheme, he was brought in to do it, and Sapphira was shunted aside. I will return to the reason for Ananias' inclusion.

Originally, then, Ananias had no role in this story at all.

---

38. Theissen, *Sociology*, 37.
39. Haenchen, 234.
40. Ibid., 241; Conzelmann, *Acts*, 38; Lüdemann, *Early Christianity*, 65.
41. Paul Burns Brown, "The Meaning and Function of Acts 5:1-11 in the Purpose of Luke-Acts" (Th.D. diss.: Boston University School of Theology, 1969), 109.

Once Luke created him, I should think the name Ananias came readily to mind. He must have had a liking for it, using it for two imaginary characters: both Paul's initiator (Acts 9:10ff; 22:12), another fabrication, since the Apostle himself denies that he was taught the gospel by any human agent (Galatians 1:1, 11-12), and the imaginary husband of Sapphira. But before the creation and insertion of Ananias, what was the function of the Sapphira story?

Though it is not directly stated, it seems implied in 1 Timothy 5 that if a widow was all alone but not destitute, and yet wanted to join the group of official church widows, she would have to turn over what means she possessed, in order that the church not be burdened (v. 16).

The *Didascalia* blamed widows for not turning over any excess funds to the bishop for him to dispense to the poor or to arriving travellers.[42] In the late fifth-century Syrian work *The Testament of Our Lord Jesus Christ* (1, 40, 2), we read that if a widow "possessed anything of value, she had to give it to the poor and the faithful; if she did not possess anything, the Church would assist her, just as it aided any widow."[43] I take this to mean that the funds the widow contributed would go to the church poor fund out of which she herself would henceforth be supported. It would be hard to see the point of any more complicated channeling of the money. And it was this way at Qumran.

I see no reason to doubt that the *Didascalia* and the *Testament* reflect an old rule inherited, like many of the others in the same documents, from centuries before. So my guess would be that the sin of the widow Sapphira was to keep back some of her inheritance from the church because perhaps she rightly did not trust the stewardship of the male authorities who thought a widow complained too much if she was not satisfied with a thread-bare coat.

The story is a narrative version of the rule, a cautionary tale illustrating the price for breaking the rule, especially in a case where the misdeed might not be discovered by any mortal: "Be sure your sin will find you out." That is why Peter is depicted as knowing of the scheme in a purely supernatural fashion. ("Simon bar-Jonah, flesh and blood hath not revealed it unto thee, but my Father in heaven.") God knows even if man does

---

42. Gryson, *Women*, 37.
43. Gryson's summary, ibid., 68.

not. The story's Peter is thus meant to stand for the widow-hearer's conscience which is told it ought to fear the invisible doom with which the reader of 1 Corinthians 11:30-31 is also threatened.

If the Sapphira story was concerned with matters of the common fund and the stipends paid out of it, then it is at least interesting to note that the word used for the "price" of the land sold is the same as that used for the widow stipend (as I have argued above) in 1 Timothy 5:3, *times*.

Who told this story? It is not impossible that it stemmed from the widows themselves, living in communal houses free of institutional control, as a stern warning to their prospective sisters to come clean and donate all to the house fund when they joined. But I doubt it. Somehow I see descending the mailed (maled) fist of age-old priestcraft which once smote Miriam with leprosy for daring to prophesy alongside Moses and which still man-dates that a priest must have a penis to mirror the celibate Christ at the altar. The story comes from the servants (henchmen) of the Christ who shall rule the nations with a rod of iron, the phallus of the Logos.

While the Sapphira story was by no means unamenable to Luke's sympathies, he changed it. Why? He obviously had other interests besides widow-bashing. There is no reason he should not rework one of his available polemical traditions for another purpose.

We have seen that both the present story and the story of the appointment of the Seven represent heavy Lukan redaction of earlier, simpler traditions. As it happens, Brodie argues convincingly that Luke used the story of Naboth's Vineyard (1 Kings 21:8-13 LXX) to supplement both the story of Ananias and Sapphira and that of the Martyrdom of Stephen, to which the story of the appointment of the Seven now serves as an introduction.

First, the parallels between the Naboth and Stephen stories: the witch-queen Jezebel writes to the elders and freemen (*eleutheroi*) to put forth Naboth during a feast and to produce lying witnesses against him (1 Kings 21:8-10a), while some members of the Synagogue of the Freedmen (*Libertinoi*) frame Stephen, soliciting false witnesses against him (Acts 6:9-11). Of poor Naboth the liars are to say that he had cursed both God and king, whereupon he should be stoned (1 Kings 21:10b). Stephen's accusers are told to say they heard him blaspheme both Moses and God (Acts 6:11). Both sets of false witnesses come forward and do as bidden by the villains (1 Kings 21:11-13a; Acts 6:12-13a). The charges are repeated in direct discourse (1 Kings 21:13b; Acts 6:13b-14). Each victim is similarly cast forth from the city and stoned to death (1 Kings 21:13c; Acts 7:58a). Once the deed is done, Ahab rends his garments either in mock horror or in self-reproach, while the witnesses to the mob-violence of the Sanhedrin pile their cloaks at the feet of the blood-thirsty Saul (1 Kings 21:14-16; Acts 7:58-8:1).[44]

We have already seen that the story of Ananias and Sapphira tips its hat visibly to the Achan story, but with a bit of work Luke made it resemble the Naboth story as well. Ahab and Jezebel conspire together to seize the coveted vineyard of Naboth (1 Kings 21:1-3, 5-7) just as Ananias and Sapphira scheme to liquidate a parcel of land and keep back part of the proceeds, while claiming that they have given all, having their cake and eating it (Acts 5:1-2).

Elijah confronts the miserable Ahab with knowledge of his deed (1 Kings 21:17-18), just as Peter confronts Ananias (Acts 5:3a), then Sapphira (v. 9a). Peter accuses each in turn of lying to the Holy Ghost (vv. 3b-4, 9b), echoing Ahab's disturbance in spirit (1 Kings 21:4). The prophet condemns Ahab and Jezebel to a shameful death sometime in the future (1 Kings 21:19-26), while Peter wastes no time in wasting the couple, as his reproach smites down each in turn (Acts 5:5a, 10a). Elijah's doom-oracle puts the fear of God into the spineless Ahab (1 Kings 21:27-29), while fear seizes all who hear the news of Peter's mighty word (Acts 5:5b, 11). In the next chapter of 1 Kings the young men of Israel defeat the greedy Syrians, while in Acts 5:6, 10b, the young men of the church take the graveyard shift, disposing of the corpses of the hell-bound couple.[45]

Perhaps Brodie has missed one more detail derived from the Naboth story, and that is the name "Barnabas," punningly understood as "Son of Naboth," a second Naboth, a man who sells a field and seemingly inspires the plot (of land) of Ananias and Sapphira.

---

44. Thomas Louis Brodie, "The Accusing and Stoning of Naboth (i Kgs. 21:8-13) as One Component of the Stephen Text (Acts 6:9-14; 7:58a)," *Catholic Biblical Quarterly* 45 (1983): 417-443; Thomas Louis Brodie, "Luke the Literary Interpreter: Luke-Acts as a Systematic Rewriting of the Elijah-Elisha Narrative in 1 and 2 Kings" (Ph.D. diss.: Pontifical University of St. Thomas Aquinas, 1981), 281-287.

45. Brodie, "Literary Interpreter," 272-281.

It seems to me that the original Sapphira story was more of a simple parallel to the Achan story. There need have been no reference to selling a field. It may simply have been assumed that she had some money, even a small amount. Even had she given one lepton and kept back the other, I have a hunch she would have ended up just as dead.

I assume that Peter's accusation about lying to the Spirit in order to keep the money is part of the original tale, and it is the most tenuous of all the points of contact with the Naboth story. Sapphira's death is closer to Achan's than to Ahab's or Jezebel's in that it happens then and there, not in the future. And the final note of fear seizing everyone as a result of her death is simply part of the furniture of a cautionary tale: it means to scare the reader with the possible consequences if she tries the same stunt. It needn't have come from the Naboth story.

The story of Acts 5:1-11 in its present form does present an impressive parallel with the Naboth story, but without what I have argued on other grounds are Lukan redactional features, the parallel really fades away. I agree with Brodie that Luke was shaping both the story of Stephen and that of Sapphira to conform to features of the Naboth story, and I would suggest that this was why he added Ananias: he needed an Ahab-analogue. With an Ahab in place he could make Sapphira a new Jezebel in tandem with him. He needed both for the sake of the parallel.

Exegetes, by the way, have continued gleefully to vilify Sapphira. E. M. Blaiklock says the sad tale "corresponds to the entrance of the serpent into Eden . . . the first fall from the ideal."[46] "Sapphira, for aught we know, may have suggested the deceit to her husband" (Bruce).[47] Derrett believes that "the kind of peculation she recommended and the role she was playing bore some resemblances to the episode of Eve and the apple."[48]

And her Eve-il deed in Derrett's estimation? Why, she had seen too much of male charitable treatment of women to trust her *ketubah*, or due inheritance as of her husband's death or divorce, to a collective treasury under the control of men.[49] Should, say,

46. E. M. Blaiklock, *The Acts of the Apostles: A Historical Commentary* (Grand Rapids: William B. Eerdmans Publishing Co., 1959), 70; cf. Rackham, *Acts*, 70.

47. Bruce, *Acts*, 112.

48. J. Duncan M. Derrett, "Ananias, Sapphira, and the Right of Property," *Downside Review* 89 (1971): 228.

49. Ibid., 227-228.

the Jerusalem church one day become insolvent thanks to the unwillingness of certain males to leave off preaching the word of God to waste time with mundane affairs, she didn't feel like waiting for Paul to round up a collection of Gentile alms before she could eat again. As it turned out, she didn't have to worry about that.

I have suggested that in two nearly adjacent stories in Acts Luke has once again employed for new purposes traditions which had as their first concern the conduct and welfare of the consecrated widows. The first of these was a widow welfare story in which benefactors were appointed to see to the needs of widows. The circulation of the story originally meant to remind future generations that the rights of Hellenist widows were not to be allowed to take a back seat to those of Hebrew widows. But Luke added certain Old Testament coloring, casting the widows as reincarnations of the murmurers in the wilderness who frayed the patience even of the meek Moses. Thus the focus shifted to the inconveniencing of men by the whining of women, a satire on the original widow welfare story. We found later parallels for such parody in the Apocryphal and Patristic literature.

In the case of the Ananias and Sapphira story we found that Luke's redaction had obscured a story which originally functioned as a cautionary tale and a community rule for widow households. A widow, Sapphira, was at the center of it, even though the story was unfriendly in its thrust and probably not a product of the widow communities. But even this story was not amenable to Luke in its prior form, since it gave center stage to a woman. Again, he supplied Old Testament coloring, making the story, with the convenient addition of a husband, into a parallel to the story of Naboths vineyard. Thus did Luke attempt to draw ever tighter the blanket of silence over the echo of women's voices in the church of his day.

CHAPTER ELEVEN

Partners in the Gospel:
Lydia and the Pythoness

Shall We Gather by the River?

In this chapter I occupy myself with Luke's account of the foundation of the Christian sect in Philippi (in Acts 16), focusing on the first Philippian convert. I will have little to say on the much discussed episode of Paul's miraculous jail-break and the cloud of improbabilities in which it is shrouded,[1] or of its possible literary models, including *The Bacchae* of Euripides.[2] My concern here, as elsewhere, is with Luke's treatment of the pre-Lukan traditions of consecrated women.

As Valerie Abrahamsen notes, we have another account (albeit fragmentary) of the foundation of the Philippian community by apostles and women in the *Acts of Paul*, in another chastity story centering on a virgin who is instrumental in the conversion of the Philippians.[3] She is Frontina, a convert to Paul's ascetic preaching. For this gross insubordination her own father orders her to be killed. Paul raises her from the dead, which prodigy persuades everyone to convert.

We will discover in the story of Paul and Lydia the vestiges of a similar chastity story. It is then hard not to place the story in the same tradition pool of "old women's tales"—the widow traditions.

Until very recently commentators on Acts 16 have been surprisingly blithe about the detail, which one would think quite remarkable, of there being a religious community composed altogether of women.[4] Usually commentators remark that there cannot have been enough Jewish males in the town to meet the minimum required for a recognized synagogue.

> Had there been ten male Jews permanently resident there, the quorum required by Jewish law, it would have been enough to constitute a synagogue. It was left to a number of women, probably Jewesses and proselytes, to maintain a limited form of worship and prayer.[5]

1. Baur, *Paul* I, 151-158; Haenchen, *Acts*, 500-504.

But this explanation fails to account for the oddity that there should be no males at all! Was the group *exclusively* female merely by default? I doubt it. The reference to "a place of prayer" is also unusual in Acts, which otherwise calls Jewish meeting places synagogues. Lüdemann takes this singularity to imply the use of a source.[6] I agree. Schaberg and O'Day speculate that this all-women group may well reflect similar groups known to Luke in his own day.[7] He is reworking the traditional foundation-story of one such group, that in Philippi.

I suspect that the story has retrojected the exclusively female character of the group into the time before Paul came to found the Christian sisterhood at Philippi. The traditional story already depicted the women as an organized cell of women before the conversion of its members, the tellers not being able to recall a time when they weren't together (much as the founding sagas of ancient Israel depicted events in the history of single component

---

2. Zeller (*Acts*, II, 324) thought Luke had taken the miraculous escape motif from Acts 12:10, a pre-Lukan legend, and multiplied the miracle throughout the Acts, including the occurrence in Acts 16:26. Otto Weinreich ("Gebet und Wunder: Türoffnung im Wunder-, Prodigien- und Zauberglauben der Antike, des Judentums und Christentums," in *Genetbliakon W. Schmid zum 70. Geburtstag*, Tübinger Beiträge zur Altertumswissenschaft 5 [Stuttgart: Kohlhammer, 1929], 334, quoted in A. Vögeli, "Lukas und Euripides," *Theologische Zeitschrift* 9 [1953]: 424) argued for direct literary dependence of Luke on Euripides.

Vögeli dismissed the notion of direct borrowing, preferring to picture Luke, so to speak, merely swimming through the Hellenistic motif-ocean with mouth open (see Vögeli, ibid., especially 423-424). Conzelmann (*Acts*, 94) and Haenchen (*Acts*, 501-502) yielded to Vögeli's arguments. Pervo (*Profit with Delight*) agrees that Luke was using general novelistic motifs, but admits that their original home in Euripides is evident, however indirect Luke's borrowing.

Lilian Portefaix (*Sisters Rejoice: Paul's Letter to the Philippians and Luke-Acts as Seen by First Century Philippian Women*, Coniectanea biblica. New Testament series, 20 [Stockholm: Almqvist & Wiksell, 1988], 170) has now shown that the Luke-Euripides parallels are much closer and more numerous than previous scholars seem to have noticed. It is hard to avoid her conclusion that Luke did after all make direct use of *The Bacchae*.

The clustering of Euripides parallels is especially thick in Acts 16, suggesting that here Luke is using a (probably written) source, just as the concatenation of instances of translation Greek or Septuagintalisms in the Infancy narrative suggested a pre-Lukan source there.

tribes as events befalling the whole amphictyonic league of which the respective tribes later became a part). The story was of the conversion "of our sisterhood," thus they are together at the beginning. Luke may have employed the same device, or used a tradition which did, in his depiction of a group of disciples of John the Baptist, conveniently meeting together when Paul encounters them to convert them (Acts 19:1-7).

It is noteworthy that in both cases Luke does not say that Paul's preaching divided the audience between believers and unbelievers as he often does. Again, this might mean that the traditional stories he is using were ones in which the events are inferred backwards from the state of things in the story-teller's own day, in which a whole community is envisioned as being converted en masse.

The first to respond to the preaching of the gospel in Philippi was Lydia, a seller of sumptuous purple cloth articles, a trade for which her homeland, Thyatira, had become renowned. Commentators have suggested that Lydia was a widow.[8] Only so, they reason, could she have been a wealthy, unattached woman in the purple trade. This is possible, but I will presently suggest a different explanation for her management of the business, as well as another sense in which she might have been considered a widow. To anticipate things a bit, it might be that Luke, dealing with another story of celibate women, intentionally reinterpreted Lydia's "widowhood" in a nonreligious sense. For Luke, to be sure, she is still a pious woman, even an exemplar of piety for women, but her exemplary piety consists in her readiness to provide hospitality to travelling missioners. But I suspect this was not originally the point.

Before we will be in a position to see just what Luke has done with the traditional figure of Lydia the first convert in Phil-

---

3. Valerie Abrahamsen, "Women at Philippi: The Pagan and Christian Evidence," *Journal of Feminist Studies in Religion* 3 (1987): 19-20.

4. D'Angelo, "Women in Luke-Acts," 459; Kraemer, "Monastic," 368; C. J. Barker, *The Acts of the Apostles, A Study in Interpretation* (London: Epworth Press, 1969), 145.

5. W. Derek Thomas, "Women in the Church at Philippi," *Expository Times* 83 (1976): 117.

6. Lüdemann, *Early Christianity*, 182.

7. Schaberg, "Luke," 287; O'Day, "Acts," 308.

8. Rackham, *Acts*, 282; Augustine Stock, "Lydia and Prisca," *Emmanuel* 94 (1988): 517; McNamara, *New Song*, 34-35.

ippi, we must turn our attention to the unnamed Pythoness of
16:16ff. One of the several oddities of the passage as it now
stands is that Luke has this woman pointing the way to Paul in
tones reminiscent of John the Baptist and yet doing so under
demonic afflatus! Something seems out of kilter here, a sign of an
incomplete job of rewriting.

And why should Paul silence the preaching of the gospel by
the inspired woman? That is in effect what she is doing. She
does not say, e.g., "Have you come to destroy us?" (Luke 4:34) or
"What have you to do with me? I beg you, do not torment me!"
(Luke 8:28) as in the most similar demonic "recognition" scenes
in Luke. Meyer makes the Pythoness's cry tantamount to the
demonic recognition in Mark 3:11 (or Luke 4:41), "You are the son
of God!", which, like the cry of the Pythoness, involves none of
the plaintive begging or hostile challenges by the demons in Luke
4:34 and 8:28.[9] But this is no true parallel because there can be no
question of a messianic secret that needs protecting while Paul is
preaching the messiahship of Jesus in Philippi. Thus why should
Paul silence the demon's voice, if that is really what it was?

This utterance is rather more in the nature of the later Christian Sibyllines, where pagan diviners are disingenuously called
to witness to the superior worth of the Christian religion. In fact,
the closest comparison might be to the Samaritan woman of John
4:29, "Come, see a man who told me all that I ever did! Can this
be the Christ?"

Johnson, oblivious of the implications of what he sees, correctly notes that "it is only the language used for Paul's response
that enables us to recognize in her proclamation the work of
demons, for Paul uses the formula of exorcism to command the
spirit's removal."[10] In other words, just this element is a redactional intrusion into a story that points in another direction
entirely.

Paul is "annoyed"! This will not do. It simply cannot have
been the way the tale was first told. I suggest that instead it is
Luke who in his patriarchalist ecclesiastical context feels annoyance at the prospect of a woman preaching or prophesying. My
guess is that the text before him depicted the Pythoness as a Philippian convert having joined Paul in his evangelistic activity
there—and that her name was Lydia.

---

9. Meyer, *Acts*, 313.
10. Johnson, *Acts*, 298.

How strange it is in Luke's version that Lydia, whom we expect, after her singling out and somewhat elaborate introduction, to be an important character, virtually vanishes after her conversion. Originally, I am saying, she didn't! Rather, she continued with Paul in partnership in the gospel from the first day (Philippians 1:5). A hint of this survives in the note in v. 17 that the Pythoness was daily following Paul to the place of prayer. This makes the most natural sense as the behavior of a convert or disciple.

I think Luke has split the original character of Lydia, the first Philippian convert and a preacher of the gospel, into two: he wanted to preserve the character of Lydia, but not as a prophetic preacher, rather merely as a generous patroness of male preachers. Recall that he did the same thing with Joanna. She, too, survives as but a shadow of her original character, employed only as a model for female supporters of male preachers. Luke wants Christian women to emulate Lydia (and Joanna) in the patroness role only.

It was not enough for Luke simply to silence Lydia. Instead he wanted to *show* women prophets *being silenced*. But the saintly Lydia cannot receive such treatment. She must be irreproachable as a Lukan/Pastoral model, not one who might have once "usurped authority" over men (1 Timothy 2:12). Hence Lydia has been cloned as the Pythoness, her own "evil twin." It is significant that Luke says she is possessed of a *pneuma Pythona*, not a *daimon*, a *pneuma akatharton*, or a *pneuma poneron*. In short, she is not quite a demoniac. She is a prophetess of sorts, an oracle like unto the Delphic oracle, in other words, a false prophetess, the only kind of prophetess there can ever really be for Luke, Anna and the daughters of Philip notwithstanding. We have already seen what he did to them.

It is common for commentators on the passage to note that Lydia's name denotes not only her origin in Asian Lydia, but also her possible status as a freed slave. This is so because geographical names were customarily given to slaves by their owners, not to children by their parents.[11]

But it is gratuitous to assume that Lydia had ever been freed. She could just as well have been a highly placed and trusted servant put in charge of her master's business.[12] Such

11. Rackham, Acts, 282; Portefaix, Sisters, 170.
12. Portefaix, Sisters, 144.

arrangements are familiar enough from the pages of Luke's gospel, where we read of a nobleman who gives great sums to his slaves to trade with in his name (19:12-13). Judith 8:10 depicts Judith's slave as in charge of all her property.

And if Lydia was still a slave, she may have been the same slave whose owners get Paul arrested. But what is the cause of the ire of the Pythoness's masters in Acts 16:19? As Luke has rewritten the story, the words "when her owners saw that their hope of gain was gone," seem obviously to refer to the sudden departure of the *pneuma Pythona*. But the words by themselves make no reference at all to her prophetic talents. I suggest that, in the pre-Lukan traditional version, her "owners' hope of gain" was her management of their purple-selling business, at which, as a Thyatiran, she was perhaps more adept than they. It is worth noting that Codex Bezae, as if sensing Luke's intention but thinking he had not made it sufficiently clear, adds the phrase "which they had through her" onto "gain," making her, not their purple wares, their stock-in-trade. Without these words, her commercial exploitation as a fortune-teller is not evident, and we gain a glimpse of the suppressed original.

Luke portrays Lydia as being baptized with her whole household. Is not this notice incompatible with Lydia being the slave of others? Not really: slaves could and did have families of their own. But at any rate, the reference to her family is Lukan redaction. The phrase is a favorite of Luke's, occurring also in 10:2; 11:14; 16:31, 32, 34; 18:8, always denoting household conversion. I assume Luke has simply added it here, to disguise what was originally going on in the story. If he is, or is like, the Pastor, we have a writer who vehemently rejects the celibacy gospel (1 Timothy 4:3) and prescribes the exact opposite: salvation by childbearing (2:15). Thus Lydia goes from a convert for celibacy (see below) to a *mater familias*, baptized with her whole brood, just the way Luke wants it.

A possible indication of the independent survival of the original version of the story in which Lydia was the one who followed Paul and preached may be tucked away in an old collection of Ethiopic Apocrypha called *Gadla Hawaryat*, or *The Contendings of the Apostles*, in which we read a complete rewrite of the story of Lydia. In it she is made the wife of a governor (remember, a constant feature of the chastity stories), and she is possessed of a devil whom not Paul, but Bartholomew, manages to exorcise! Here I suspect we see the unwieldy result of someone trying to harmonize the original version suppressed by Luke with the canonical version.[13]

The Chastity Story of Lydia

It may be that Lydia had also been the sexual property of her masters, as female slaves usually were. If so, we can understand all the more the outrage of the owners if she had "refused" (1 Corinthians 7:5) their advances like Thecla, Mygdonia, Maximilla, Drusiana, and the other celibate heroines of the chastity stories. Is there any hint of this in Acts 16? I think so.

When, freshly converted, Lydia invites Paul and his team to come enjoy her hospitality, she offers this condition, "If you have judged me to be faithful to the Lord, come to my house and stay" (v. 15). This is usually taken to mean, "Unless perhaps you think my profession of Christian faith to be a sham, do not insult me by refusing my hospitality." Perhaps rightly so. But I wonder if "pisten to kurio" does not rather refer to a pledge of celibacy, as in 1 Timothy 5:12.

In this case the point is that what would otherwise seem the grossest impropriety of a woman inviting a man to stay with her is in fact completely innocent given her new commitment to the continence gospel Paul had preached, just as in the chastity story of Frontina in Philippi. In precisely the same way that Maximilla provokes her husband to jealous fury by inviting Andrew into her home after her conversion, Lydia incurs the wrath of her masters by inviting Paul. And the hounding of Paul and his companions, their jailing, the earthquake—all this seems to be cut from the same bolt of (purple) cloth as the Apocryphal Acts.

Note also the complaint of the slave's owners: "These men are Jews and they are disturbing our city. They advocate customs which it is not lawful for us Romans to accept or practice." Cassidy remarks that "Remarkably, the charges which the girl's masters made against Paul and Silas went far beyond the deed of exorcism."[14] But it is not quite right to say that the charges "go beyond" the exorcism; in fact they have nothing to do with it! Here is a clue that, in the story as Luke himself read it, before he

---

13. E. A. Wallis Budge, ed. and trans., *The Contendings of the Apostles: Being the Histories of the Lives and Martyrdoms and Deaths of the Twelve Apostles and Evangelists, Vol. II. The English Translation* (London: Oxford University Press, 1901), 194-195.

14. Richard J. Cassidy, "The Non-Roman Opponents of Paul," in *New Views of Luke and Acts*, 151.

retold it, the accusations had nothing to do with exorcism because the story did not contain one! The reference to customs illegal to Romans would make much better sense as a reference to the encratite forbidding of marriage, indeed an abomination in the eyes of Roman law.[15]

Echoes in the Epistle to the Philippians

If I have read the implied pre-Lukan text correctly, I venture to say that the same scenario is reflected in the pseudonymous Epistle of Paul to the Philippians. I regard this text as virtually a fourth Pastoral Epistle. Though not written by the same hand, it seems to stem from the same ecclesiastical milieu, as verse 1's anachronistic "bishops and deacons" suggest.

The post-Pauline character of the epistle is evident, too, in the perspective from which Paul's martyrdom is implicitly viewed. As in Acts and the Pastorals, the reader is invited to read "Paul's" words about his martyr death with the irony and pathos of hindsight: Paul, thinking of others to the last, knows it might be time for Christ to call him home, but, selfless *bodhisattva* that he is, he is willing to postpone donning his prize (3:14) of the martyr's crown (4:1) for the continued use he may be to the Philippians (1:25), this last a wink to the reader, since it is through the device of epistolary pseudonymity that Paul's ministry among them will continue.

The reader of this "lost" epistle, as lost as the Book of the Covenant had been while Huldah, Hilkiah, and the rest were writing it, knows with sad irony that Paul did not survive his ordeal but went on to be made finally "perfect" in martyrdom after all, covering the final stretch of his race (3:12-14). Thus his words here assume the added gravity of a last testament, a common technique of pseudonymity.

There is little in the epistle by way of any explicit attempt to refute any "heretical" Christianity in Philippi, but we do hear of some vague preaching of the gospel by those considered by the writer to be his enemies, preaching which only stirs up trouble (1:15-17), just as the Pythoness's preaching "annoys" Paul. He urges two Philippian women who are remembered as co-workers

---

15. J. P. V. D. Balsdon, *Roman Women: Their History and Habits* (New York: John Day Company, 1963; New York: Barnes & Noble Books, a division of Harper & Row, Publishers, 1983), 222; McNamara, "Wives and Widows," 583-584.

of Paul, Evodia and Syntyche, to agree together—presumably with *him*.[16] Most exegetes have failed to see that this was no mere "tiff" (Marshall)[17] between "a couple of cantankerous old shrews" (Caird).[18] The Paul of Philippians is a mouthpiece for later patriarchy, precisely as in the Pastorals. The preaching by "some" that makes trouble for Paul is that of Philippian women who appeal to Paul as their patron, just as he functioned for Thecla. The trouble caused him is the embarrassment to the later church authorities who would claim the Pauline pedigree for themselves.

And Evodia and Syntyche? My guess would be that these two names represent, as D'Angelo says, a well-known female missionary team once active in Philippi[19] and remembered as leaders of the encratic Christianity along with Paul. The writer wishes their successors in Philippi to agree with the Paul who wrote the letter.

Why is Lydia not mentioned? It is nothing so innocent as her having left to pursue business interests elsewhere.[20] If she left for other parts then I suggest we look for her back home in Thyatira, under the epithet Jezebel. Ramsey cannot help but notice the naturalness of the identification:

> it is an interesting coincidence that the only two women of Thyatira mentioned in the New Testament are so like one another in character. The question might even suggest itself whether they may not be the same person, since Lydia seems to disappear from Philippian history (so far as we are informed of it) soon after St. Paul's visit to the city.[21]

But he cannot bring himself to credit it: "for it is utterly improbable that the hostess of St. Paul would ever be spoken about so

---

16. Abrahamsen, "Women at Philippi," 27.
17. I. Howard Marshall, *The Acts of the Apostles: An Introduction and Commentary,* Tyndale New Testament Commentaries, ed. R. V. G. Tasker (Leicester: Intervarsity Press; Grand Rapids: William B. Eerdmans Company, 1980), 264.
18. G. B. Caird, "Paul and Women's Liberty," *Bulletin of the John Rylands Library* 54 (1972): 281.
19. D'Angelo, "Women Partners," 75-77. Or perhaps we are to view the synonymous names "Successful" and "Lucky" as ideal figures like the "Beloved Disciple", and as Girardian doubles/rivals, split halves of the same character, just like Lydia and the Pythoness.
20. Stock, "Lydia," 517.

mercilessly and savagely as this poor prophetess is here."[22]   Yet Ramsey himself admits that John's vilification of "Jezebel" stems from a misunderstanding of her good intentions. A misunderstood Lydia might be as easily verbally abused as her misunderstood twin.

In any case, Lydia's memory has been silenced again, just as Luke, though willing to claim her as a precedent for wealthy patronesses of the church, tries to obliterate her gospel preaching. I believe that the story of Paul and Lydia in Philippi first read much like the chastity stories of Thecla and Frontina, the latter also set in Philippi and surviving only in fragments. In Lydia's story Paul entered the town, preached the continence-gospel, and reaped eager converts. Renouncing the embrace of mortal men for that of the Heavenly Bridegroom, they incurred the ire of masters, husbands, and fathers. One of these women was the high-ranking slave Lydia, valued by her masters as the steward over their dye business. She immediately heeded the preaching, inviting Paul into her quarters and refusing the advances of her owners. These latter, as is typical in such stories, had Paul imprisoned by the authorities, where, however, he was freed by an earthquake which even vibrated manacles loose and doors open. Paul exited unmolested, leaving behind a flock of Christian women who formed the nucleus of the Philippian church.

---

21. William M. Ramsey, *The Letters to the Seven Churches of Asia and Their Place in the Plan of the Apocalypse* (New York: A. C. Armstrong & Son, 1905), 336.
22. Ibid., 336-337.

CHAPTER TWELVE

The God of the Widows:
Anastasis and Artemis

Strange Gods

Following the episode at Philippi, Luke has Paul proceed to Athens, a puzzling choice from a later Christian viewpoint, given the lack of a church there. Perhaps the Athens scene is intended as a model for the Christian approach to the pagan intellectual, a lesson to be followed in the dawning age of the Apologists.[1] In any case, Plümacher claims the adventure of Paul in Athens as a prime specimen of Luke's literary art.[2] Here Luke pulls out all the stops. His Athens is that of contemporary writers, a gathering place for curious dilettantes ever hungering for a delectable new idea (who "will not endure sound teaching, but having itching ears . . . accumulate for themselves teachers to suit their own likings and will turn away from listening to the truth," 2 Timothy 4:3-4). Paul is put on trial before an Athenian jury just like his predecessor Socrates. I suspect that in this passage Luke includes a subtle polemic against one aspect of women's spirituality current in some circles of consecrated women known to him. I will indicate several touches in the Athens scene suggestive of such a Lukan agenda. He employs but alters traces of such traditions, and he makes a subtle but unmistakable criticism of such beliefs.

Luke has the skeptical Areopagites express a shallow view of Paul as propagating *xenon daimonon*, "foreign divinities" (17:18). Though this charge is no doubt meant to cast Paul in the role of Socrates, accused of the same offense, I believe Luke is thinking as well, as the whole scene shows, of Aristophanes' play *Horae*,

> in which Sabazius and certain other foreign gods were put on trial and sentenced to banishment from Athens; the complaint seems to have been chiefly directed, like Pentheus' complaint against Dionysus, to the celebration of women's rites under cover of darkness.[3]

1. Martin Dibelius, "Paul on the Areopagus," in *Studies in the Acts of the Apostles*, 63, 76-77.
2. Eckhard Plümacher, *Lukas als hellenistischer Schriftsteller: Studien zur Apostelgeschichte* (Göttingen: Vanderhoeck & Ruprecht, 1972), 97.

Just which foreign deities is Paul imagined to be preaching? As commentators starting with Chrysostom have recognized, in v. 18 two proper names are intended: Jesus and Anastasis.[4] Of course Luke's evident assumption is that the Areopagites, mere "debaters of this age" (1 Corinthians 1:20), know not whereof they speak. This is, for Luke, an amusing misconception soon to be set right. Jesus and the doctrine of the coming judgment (v. 31) have merely been distorted through the filter of Hellenistic superstition to sound as if Jesus were "simply another corn king" (C. S. Lewis),[5] accompanied by his divine consort, as Attis was by Cybele, Dionysus by Mother Rhea, Osiris by Isis, Adonis by Aphrodite, Baal by Anath, Tammuz by Ishtar.

But this makes me wonder if Luke had actually heard such a "misconception," and where. I suspect that what we have here is in fact another case of Luke trying to put down some "false" notion by attributing it to false witnesses, as many scholars think he is doing in the case of the charges against Stephen (Acts 6:11-14),[6] or the political nature of the charges against Jesus (Luke 23:2). Can this be another such instance? Does Luke perhaps know of an opinion widespread enough among Christians of some stripe that he feels he must use a forum like this to expose it as a misconception? I believe so. Interestingly, the redactor who produced the text preserved in Codex Bezae apparently felt Luke's treatment only kept the dangerous heresy available to readers who might not have thought of it otherwise, so he omitted the names entirely. His version reads, "He seemeth to be a setter forth of strange gods," period.

I nominate the consecrated widows as the prime candidates for the group that held the view Luke sought to dismiss as a simple mistake. Everything I suggested in Chapter 7 by way of their appropriation of mythemes from the lore of the dying and rising gods would lead us to suspect that Jesus must have had a divine

---

3. Dodds, *Euripides, Bacchae,* xxiv.
4. Haenchen, *Acts,* 518.
5. C. S. Lewis, *Miracles: A Preliminary Study* (New York: Macmillan Publishing Co., 1947, rpt. 1974), 117.
6. Marcel Simon, St. *Stephen and the Hellenists in the Primitive Church,* Haskell Lectures 1956 (New York: Longmans, Green & Co., 1958), 24; O'Neill, *Theology of Acts,* 74; Oscar Cullmann, "Dissensions within the Early Church," in *New Testament Issues,* ed. Richard Batey, Harper Forum Books, gen. ed. Martin E. Marty (New York: Harper & Row, Publishers, 1970), 122.

consort anyway. Why?

In virtually every instance, the slain god was raised to life, not by his father (even when, as in the case of Baal, his divine father figures into the myth), but *by his divine consort*. In fact it is precisely the mourning of the widowed goddess preliminary to her raising her lover in which the mourning women devotees of Attis, Adonis, Osiris, and the rest are joining by means of their rituals. That the female counterpart to Jesus in Acts 17:18 is named Anastasis (Resurrection) indicates that she played exactly this role. But this is not our only clue.

The Empty Tomb of Zeus

Paul is made to quote a line from the *Phainomena* of Aratus: "For we are indeed his offspring" (v. 28). Some have also considered the sentence in the same verse, "In him we live and move and have our being," as yet another quote, this time from Epimenides.[7] On the basis of a tradition preserved by the ninth-century Nestorian monk Ischodad of Merv, using lost commentaries of Theodore of Mopsuestia on the Pauline Epistles, it seemed to Kirsopp Lake and to Rendel Harris that this line of Epimenides originated as the concluding line of a quatrain which, astonishingly enough, also contained the slur against Cretans found in Titus 1:12. The whole would have read:

> They carve a tomb for thee, O high and holy one,
> The Cretans always liars, evil beasts, slow bellies;
> For thou art not dead for ever but alive and risen,
> For in thee we live and move and have our being.[8]

Max Pohlenz denied both that the lines had ever belonged together and that Luke had intended "In him we live and move and have our being" as a quotation at all. Pohlenz's arguments, remarkably weak in my opinion, shall have to be dealt with, as they have effectively determined the critical consensus, convincing Dibelius to withdraw his acceptance of the attribution of both New Testament lines to a single poem by Epimenides.[9] Haenchen

---

7. J. Rendel Harris, "St. Paul and Epimenides," *Expositor* 8th Series, 4 (1912): 348-353; Kirsopp Lake, "Your Own Poets," in *Beginnings* V, "Additional Notes to the Commentary," 246-251; Dibelius, "Paul on the Areopagus," 48-50.

8. Henry J. Cadbury, *The Book of Acts in History* (New York: Harper & Brothers, Publishers, 1955), 46-47.

and Conzelmann have both followed Pohlenz as well.[10] Some would thus consider the issue setttled. It is not.

The inclusion of the line from Acts 17 with that quoted in Titus, along with the rest, depends upon whether we can accept what Ischodad, admittedly a late source, tells us. Where does Pohlenz find the difficulty that so discredits Ischodad in his eyes? Pohlenz notes that the Titus quote, "Cretans are always liars, evil beasts, slow bellies," has been conflated by Epimenides from the *Hymn to Zeus* by Callimachus ("The Cretans always lie; for the Cretans, O Lord / Built your tomb. But you are not dead, you are eternal") and Hesiod's *Theogony* ("Shepherds dwelling in the fields, base reproaches [upon you], nothing but gluttons!").[11] Pohlenz congratulates Clement of Alexandria and Jerome for understanding that the Epistle to Titus is quoting Epimenides, and Jerome especially for knowing that Epimenides depends here on Callimachus.

But John Chrysostom and Theodore of Mopsuestia do not fare so well in Pohlenz's estimation.

> John Chrysostom has incredibly confused the matter in the third Homily on the Letter to Titus. . . . He names Epimenides as the poet of the verse cited by Paul, but appends as a motive the fact that the Cretans displayed the grave of Zeus. . . . He thus interprets Epimenides as well as the verse of Callimachus as a protest against the grave of Zeus.[12]

Here is the fatal mis-step, according to Pohlenz: all subsequent interpretation such as that which we find in Ischodad is based on a misreading. Pohlenz notes that what Callimachus means to dispute in the first instance is the Cretan claim that Zeus was born in Crete. The Cretans are judged inveterate liars because of this whopper which forever discredits them. But Chrysostom and Theodore seem to think the prevarication in question is the lie about having the tomb of the god. And insofar

9. Martin Dibelius, "Style Criticism of the Book of Acts," 18.
10. Haenchen, *Acts*, 524; Conzelmann, *Acts*, 145.
11. Translation of Helmut Koester in Dibelius and Conzelmann, *Pastoral Epistles*, 136.
12. M. Pohlenz, "Ischodad on Acts 17:28," trans. S. T. Joshi, rev. Robert M. Price (unpublished translation of section II, "Ischodad über Acts 17:28," of M. Pohlenz, "Paulus und die Stoa," *Zeitschrift für die Neutestamentliche Wissenschaft* 42 [1949]), 2.

as subsequent exegesis presupposes this error, Pohlenz concludes, it too is erroneous. Ischodad supplies the supposed circumstances for the building of the tomb of Zeus: "the Cretans maintained that Zeus had become an earthly lord, was torn apart by wild beasts and was entombed by them." Pohlenz regards this as an etiological mythopoeic explanation of the verse of Callimachus as misinterpreted by Chrysostom and Theodore.

But I think it is Pohlenz himself who has based his explanation on a misunderstanding. It seems fairly clear that Callimachus' characterization of the Cretans as "*always* lying" is meant to introduce *another* famous lie besides the one under consideration and so to show that one need not by any means take the latter seriously. Yes, the point at hand is to refute the absurd claim of having Zeus' birthplace in Crete, but Callimachus does also mean to refute the even bigger lie about the death and tomb so as to discredit the witness. It is no either/or proposition.

Pohlenz also argues that the sentence "In him we live and move and have our being" cannot have come from the Epimenides poem, as Ischodad thought, because he doubts "this kind of formulation of a pantheistic sentiment is at all possible for a man at the beginning of the 5th century."[13] But what makes it pantheistic? The dative with *en* might just as easily be taken as the dative of means as that of location. Indeed, it makes more sense to me to render it, even in Acts 17:28, "*By* him we live and move and have our being." The point is not about God the divine aether, but rather God the creator. And this could well have been said by Epimenides; we need not wait with Pohlenz for Poseidonis to come along. Pohlenz also doubts the likelihood that Paul would have granted so much ground to his heathen opponents at the Areopagus by quoting with approval a pagan poet singing the glories of Zeus. But if Paul (actually Luke) could do it with the Aratus quote, why not with one from Epimenides?

Cadbury remains unmoved in accepting the theory endorsed by his old friend Lake. He points out against Pohlenz that "In him we *live* . . ." would make a lot of sense as a pun if the poem quoted were about Zeus: *Zeus* and *zao*.[14] Similarly, Cadbury notes that the closest parallel we have to Luke's idea of an altar to whatever Unknown God might have been neglected comes from a story in which Epimenides delivers Athens from a

---

13. Ibid., 3.
14. Cadbury, *Book of Acts in History*, 47.

plague by propitiating the wrath of unknown gods neglected by the Athenians.[15] Hence it appears that Epimenides was on Luke's mind.

The Achilles' heel of Pohlenz's dismissal of Ischodad's report on the tomb of Zeus is that what Ischodad tells us fits in quite well with other information about the worship of Zeus on Crete: namely that it had been early mixed with that of Attis and Dionysus, and both of these deities are torn apart, Attis (like his variant-twin Adonis) by a wild boar.[16] W. K. C. Guthrie goes farther still: "the original identity . . . of Dionysos and the Cretan 'Zeus', seems certain."[17] W. Otto tells us of the grave of Dionysus shown to visitors in Delphi,[18] while Rohde says this was the same grave ascribed later to the Python killed by Apollo, explaining the link with Apollo's oracle and the Dionysiac Maenads.

For R. F. Willetts, the inscriptional and literary evidence, including that discussed here, points to the existence on Crete of

> an annual festival in celebration of a god like Adonis or Tammuz, at which this god was eaten in the form of a bull. For, although the evidence for tomb and epigraph is late, it proves that Cretan Zeus was conceived as a dying god; and it also carries the implication this god was one who died annually and was born again.[19]

Interestingly, one piece of evidence for a yearly rebirth is the mention of Zeus' complete maturation in a single year's time, found in Aratus' *Phainomena*, the same source Luke has mined for the line "For we are indeed his offspring."[20]

So I find myself willing, with Cadbury, to accept the ancient coupling of the lines found in Acts 17:28 and Titus 1:12 as part of a poem challenging the Cretan claim to have the remains of Zeus-Dionysus, not because he had not died, but because he had *risen* (*hestekas*). Accepting the identification of Luke as the writer of Titus, I see a connection, obviously a striking one, and not merely

15. Ibid.
16. Kroeger and Kroeger, *Suffer Not*, 54; E. R. Dodds, "Maenadism in the *Bacchae*," *Harvard Theological Review* 33 (July 1940): 155; R. P. Winnington-Ingram, *Euripides and Dionysus: An Interpretation of The Bacchae* (Amsterdam: Adolf M. Hakkert—Publisher, 1969), 150, 152.
17. W. Guthrie, *Greeks and Their Gods*, 156.
18. W. Otto, *Dionysus*, 190.
19. Willetts, *Cretan Cults*, 219.
20. Ibid.

a coincidence between the two passages. In any case, however, it seems to me that the line quoted by Luke in Acts 17:28 is the tip of the iceberg, and that Luke has Paul cite yet another piece of tradition concerning a dead and resurrected deity. But this is not all.

Dionysius and Damaris

Of the converts recruited by Paul on this occasion only two are named: Dionysius and Damaris. The first of these is obviously a Dionysian cult name. And probably the second is as well. "Damaris" means "heifer," an animal of strong associations with the religions of Dionysus and Baal. The sacred heifer was dismembered in ritual frenzy by crazed Maenads,[21] possibly in commemoration of the Orphic myth of Zagreus (another avatar of Dionysus, torn apart by the Titans, but reborn as Dionysus).[22] The heifer also stood for Dionysus' mother Semele, Dionysus being known as "the Ox-born."[23]

Baal's consort Anath mourns his death before she resurrects him: "As the heart of a cow for her calf / And the heart of a ewe for her lamb / So is the heart of Anat for Baal."[24] Before his ill-fated descent to the underworld to battle Mot the death-monster, Baal had, ahem, copulated with a heifer, in order to preserve his seed should he not survive the battle.[25] My guess is that this heifer is intended to stand for Anath. Why should only these two significant names, strangely redolent of the Dionysus myth, have been preserved in Acts 17? Nothing more is made of them in the story. Neither joins Paul on his way to Jerusalem, for example. I suspect Luke found both names in a source (some widow tradition) in a very different connection which made it impossible for him to say about Dionysius and Damaris what the source had said. And again, it is striking to note the redaction of Codex Bezae's text-form. It simply omits "and a woman named Damaris." Witherington imagines this deletion to be "anti-feminist,"[26]

---

21. Robert Graves, *The Greek Myths: Volume One* (Baltimore: Penguin Books, 1986), 105.
22. Martin P. Nilsson, *A History of Greek Religion*, trans. F. J. Fielden, 2nd ed. (New York: W. W. Norton & Company, 1964), 217.
23. W. Guthrie, *Greeks and Their Gods*, 163; W. Otto, *Dionysus*, 192-193.
24. Bronner, *Elijah*, 49, 114.
25. Ibid., 69.
26. Ben Witherington, "The Anti-Feminist Tendencies of the Western Text in Acts," *Journal of Biblical Literature* 103 (1984): 83-84.

which indeed it is, but not in the way he thinks. The redactor would have no reason to omit the note that a prominent woman converted; indeed, he adds such notes where they are lacking in the original (as earlier in the very same chapter, at Acts 17:12). Rather, Luke's successor decided to expunge the still-too-dangerous clues of Christian goddess-worship left by his predecessor.

If we put the pieces together, we find that in Acts 17, Luke has assembled fragments which have a peculiar consistency: first, reported preaching of Jesus and his divine consort Anastasis; second, an allusion to a poem affirming the resurrection of a slain pagan god; and, third, the names or epithets of the divine pair in a cognate myth. We can no longer discern the lines of the skeleton along which these fossils were once arranged, but I think we can pretty well deduce the nature of the beast. Here we have survivals of a tradition which unashamedly patterned Christ after analogous gods and their myths. Part of the pattern was his pairing with a mighty goddess who saved the savior.

Artemis of the Ephesians

I wonder if we may discern another echo of Christian goddess-worship in the story of the riot in Ephesus (18:23-41), another self-contained tradition like the preceding, as evidenced by its "Once upon a time" style of opening (v. 21).

MacDonald compares several close parallels between details of the *Acts of Paul* and the Pastoral Epistles; these, he argues, reflect the common use by both works of the same cycle of oral traditions about Paul, and these traditions depicted Paul as a preacher of the celibate Christianity taught in the circles in which these tales were told. The Pastor, he contends, retold these tales, against their original intent, to combat encratic Christianity. One such set of parallels is that concerning one Alexander, who opposes Paul. In the *Acts of Paul* he is a magistrate who falls in lust with Thecla, while in 2 Timothy 4:14, he is called "the coppersmith" and is said to have done Paul much harm.

There is precious little in common here. I venture to revise MacDonald's thesis at this point. I think the real connection is not between the *Acts of Paul* and the Pastorals, but rather between the canonical Acts and the Pastorals.

Acts 19's story features two characters, Demetrius the silversmith, a partisan of the worship of Artemis of the Ephesians, and a Jew named Alexander, who tries to make a speech against Paul but is shouted down. There may well be some connection between this story and the mention of "Alexander the copper-smith" in 2 Timothy 4:14, despite Haenchen's derision ("Fantasy can naturally establish a connection with the Alexander of I Tim. 1.20 and II. Tim. 4.14").[27] Haenchen has momentarily lapsed into the pedestrian skepticism of the apologist who will consider nothing not immediately obvious nor overwhelmingly documented.

E. L. Hicks, the editor of the Ephesian inscription in the British Museum, once noted there the attestation of one Demetrius as a *neopoios*, or temple-keeper, vestryman. He suggested, quite plausibly to my way of thinking, that Luke had misunderstood the title as that of a maker of temples, and since one could hardly make full-size temples single-handedly, Demetrius must have made miniature temples, votive or souvenir replicas.[28] I am suggesting that in a pre-Lukan version of the story Demetrius was a *neopoios*, a city official in charge of managing votive offering moneys and temple repairs, and that originally we would have seen him as none other than one of the Asiarchs (civic religious functionaries) friendly to Paul as well as identical to the municipal clerk who dispersed the crowd.

Originally the villain was the same one mentioned in 2 Timothy 4:14, Alexander, a Jewish coppersmith whose work had nothing to do with the temple of Artemis, but who opposed Paul's preaching of Jesus. In the extant version of the story Alexander plays but a puzzlingly vestigial role, again, a casualty of Noth's redundancy principle. He has been shunted aside in favor of Demetrius, also a smithy by Luke's mistaken reckoning, and something worse than a Jew: a pagan polytheist.

It was the original characterization of Alexander as a coppersmith that gave the nudge for Luke to misconstrue *neopoios*. Demetrius, too, he figured, was a metal-worker, and his work provided an economic motive for pagans to oppose Paul: he was losing money, like Lydia's owners, thanks to Paul's preaching!

The artificiality of the Lukan Demetrius is evident both from the apparent confusion of the meaning of *neopoios* and from the utter absence of any relics of the kind Luke posits as Demetrius' stock-in-trade. Images of Artemis and her variant-double Cybele have been found, but no little temple models.

27. Haenchen, *Acts*, 574.
28. E. L. Hicks, "Demetrius the Silversmith," *Expositor* Series 4, 1 (1890): 401-403, cited in Haenchen, *Acts*, 571-572.

Not only this, but the sheer extravagance of the occasion for Demetrius' ire marks it as clearly seconday. Can we really believe that Paul had won so many in the province of Asia to Christian monotheism that Artemis souvenirs were collecting dust on the shelves? This is as absurd as the roughly contemporary enormity of which we read in the spurious letter as by Pliny Secundus to the emperor Trajan in which some Christian apologist boasts that "the temples . . . had been almost entirely deserted for a long time; the sacred rites . . . had been allowed to lapse . . . and scarcely anyone could be found to buy sacrficial meat" (*Epistle* 2.405).[29] (Similarly we read that no true Christian could be made to renounce the faith even under torture, and that the Christians were guilty of no worse an offense than binding themselves with an oath to do no one any harm—all clearly the report Christians wanted people to think the Romans gave of them. Pliny was no more invulnerable to the indignities of Christian interpolators than was Josephus.)

Notice, too, that even in the canonical version of the story, there is a surprising pattern of enmities and allegiences. True, as we now read it, the worshippers of Artemis are opposed to Paul, but that is the issue of the Lukan apologetical fiction we have just noted. And this enmity ill-accords with the fact that both the Asiarchs and the municipal clerk clearly side with Paul. Alexander the Jew is solidly anti-Pauline, but then the crowd is opposed to Alexander! If we eliminate the suspicious-looking Lukan rallying of the crowd against Paul, we have left a story in which Jewish opponents accuse Paul before a popular assembly. And the sympathies of the crowd are with Paul. Now why should this be?

We must not quickly pass by the extraordinary statement of the clerk (originally Demetrius) that "these men . . . are neither sacrilegious *nor blasphemers of our goddess*" (v. 37). And the crowd accepts this verdict! How can it be that Paul's monotheistic preaching of "one God, the Father, . . . and one Lord, Jesus Christ" (1 Corinthians 8:6) did not smack of blasphemy to those who cherished a goddess for whom no space was left in such a narrow creed? In the original version of the story, in which Demetrius was the "noble pagan" and Alexander the villainous Jewish coppersmith, Paul preached no such thing. I suspect that the story had him preaching Jesus and Anastasis, a goddess readily

---

29. Cf. Conzelmann, *Acts*, 165.

assimilable to Artemis, just as she herself already represented a syncretic amalgam or twin with Cybele, the consort of resurrected Attis.[30] No, the preaching of Paul in this traditional story rang like blasphemy in the ears of Luke, which is perhaps why he has Paul strangely absent from the theatre during the melee: technically it is no longer Paul, but only his partners Gaius and Aristarchus, who are said not to have blasphemed the goddess.

---

30. Kroeger and Kroeger, *Suffer Not*, 106; Haenchen, *Acts*, 575.

Conclusion:
Vestigial Virgins

Recent studies of Luke-Acts have awakened an unwelcome realization that this New Testament work, long perceived as an important weapon in the arsenal of Christian feminism, might turn out instead to be a dangerous Trojan Horse smuggled into the camp by the enemy. If one dared look carefully, might one find the Lukan text harboring dangerous opponents? In the present dissertation I have sought to take as unblinking a look as I could at Luke to determine whether these fears were justified. I have brought to bear many recent insights of several courageous scholars who have done risky reconnaisance of strange new territory.

Stevan L. Davies showed how various stories in the Apocryphal Acts of the Apostles seem to champion the concerns of consecrated celibate women in the early church, manipulating the images of the New Testament apostles in order to preserve the fading influence of itinerant charismatics (first described for us by Gerd Thiessen) on the women's behalf as against the encroachment of the male ecclesiastical establishment. Dennis R. MacDonald then argued that such oral traditions (rather than whole written Acts, as Davies had suggested) might have been drawn upon to opposite ends by the authors of the *Acts of Paul* on the one hand and the Pastoral Epistles on the other.

Unique among these oral stories was the subgenre pinpointed by Ross S. Kraemer and Virginia Burrus, the chastity story in which women claim what measure they can of religious and social autonomy by abandoning the traditional family structure and embracing celibacy.

I found it possible to apply MacDonald's analysis to Luke-Acts in light of other scholarly developments: first, the insight of Richard I. Pervo that the canonical Acts are not so different from the Apocryphal Acts in which Davies, MacDonald, Kraemer, and Burrus had located the traditions of celibate women and, second, the new arguments of Stephen G. Wilson and Jerome D. Quinn that Luke and the author of the Pastoral Epistles are one and the same. The latter identification is not absolutley necessary for my thesis; even a mere similarity between the ecclesiastical outlooks of Luke-Acts and the Pastorals would facilitate the sort of comparison between the two that MacDonald had undertaken in the case of the Pastorals and the *Acts of Paul*.

The major difference between my approach and that of MacDonald was that I ranged the Pastorals and the Lukan redaction on the same side of the question. Where MacDonald had seen the redactor of the *Acts of Paul* as maintaining the radical emphases of the women's traditions, I found that Luke had already heavily redacted and rewritten them. This meant that I lacked MacDonald's advantage of seeing any of the traditions from both sides. Nevertheless it proved quite possible to identify several cases where it seemed that Luke had rewritten a story or other tradition from the circles of celibate women; he had left sufficient traces of the original version to enable the careful critic to restore the basic outlines as well as the polemical point of the pre-Lukan pericopae.

In discerning the thrust of the widow traditions it proved most helpful to place them against the background of the triangular relationship (Davies) obtaining between the bishops of the increasingly patriarchal church, the charismatic widows and virgins, some of whom lived on the church stipend and were therefore vulnerable to the restriction of their freedom by the bishops, and finally the itinerant charismatics who were gradually losing out to the routinized charisma of the bishops who claimed apostolic succession even as the itinerants did.

Many of the oral traditions in question seemed to proceed from a *Sitz-im-Leben* in which the consecrated women sought to manipulate one of the two other groups, the itinerants, against the other, the bishops. The widow communities might be seen simultaneously as clients of the bishops (at least those widows who received the stipend; not all did) and as patronesses of the itinerants, as they repaid their advocacy with hospitality and respect (and vice versa).

Luke sought to co-opt these traditions by heavily redacting them, in some cases turning them like captured weapons on the widow communities and their ministry (as in the cases of the Hellenist Widows, Martha and Mary, the silenced Anna, the daughters of Philip, Lydia, the persistent-cum-nagging widow, the woman in Simon's house), or else simply appropriating them for new and wholly different purposes (Joanna and Lydia as wealthy patronesses rather than as the subjects of chastity stories, the reference to Elijah ministering to Hellenist, not Hebrew widows, the Elijah-like resurrections on behalf of widows performed by Jesus and Peter). But the most dramatic discovery of all (bearing in mind that a "discovery," as Thomas Kuhn would remind us, is really a striking new configuration of the same old evidence) is that one of Luke's key redactional aims must have been to eradicate remaining traces of the Goddess-piety of the women's communities whose traditions he appropriated.

The devotion of the widows, including the mourning of their Passion vigil on the eve of the Easter Hilaria, was a participation in the bereftitude of Anastasis, a widow like them, who would fast in the day the Bridegroom was taken away and rejoice again when he was restored. (Recall again Jeremias's observation that the figure of the bridegroom was not yet used in Judaism as an image for Messiah,[1] whereas it had been familiar for centuries in the cults of the dying gods raised to life by their consorts.) This joyous reunion was symbolized by the women at the empty tomb in their Easter narratives, and their meeting with the Risen One.

I will conclude with the speculation, to which the arguments of this dissertation clearly point, but which would require much more extensive development, that the widespread diffusion of Dionysus and Tammuz motifs in Luke-Acts and John, even possibly in Mark (2: 2:20) and Q (Matthew 3:12/Luke 3:17, where Jesus is given the epithet of Dionysus, "Winnowing fan carrier"),[2] plus the attachment to all four canonical gospels of (carefully edited) versions of the empty tomb stories, all indicate that the cult of Jesus and Anastasis was widespread in Christianity very early on.

It seems to me, moreover, that no better origin for the legend of the resurrection of Jesus has been proposed than assimilation of the mythology of the dying and rising gods, especially now that text discoveries and archaeological finds have secured a pre-Christian date for the belief in their resurrections.[3] And if the resurrection mythology of Jesus is of a piece with that of Attis and the others, then the role of a resurrecting Goddess is necessitated as part of the package. But as far as I know, the only scholar to

---

1. Jeremias, Parables, 52.
2. Ross S. Kraemer, "Ecstasy and Possession: The Attraction of Women to the Cult of Dionysus," Harvard Theological Review 72 (1979): 61.
3. Pope, Song, 153; Maarten J. Vermaseren, Cybele and Attis: The Myth and the Cult, trans. A. M. H. Lemmers (London: Thames & Hudson, 1977), 114, 123; Hyam Maccoby, Paul and Hellenism (London: SCM Press; Philadelphia: Trinity Press International, 1991), 71-73.

see this has been Barbara G. Walker.[4] Here is the female savior in the period of formative Christianity sought with equivocal results by Gail Paterson Corrington.[5]

I suspect that the recovery of the role of women in earliest Christianity merges at this point with the recovery of the Goddess now being undertaken by feminist scholars.[6] It seems to me that in the beginning (or near the beginning, as soon as the resurrection mythology was applied to the figure of Jesus) the Easter kerygma was a gladful paean that Jesus had been raised from the dead by his divine widow Anastasis (whose very name might have reminded women of other divine consorts, Anath and Anahita, Baal's and Mithras's mates respectively). Perhaps Anastasis was even depicted as one of the women at the tomb (the spices with which they hope to anoint Jesus recall the substances brought by Isis in order to effect the resurrection of Osiris).

Soon, however, the regnant male monotheism began to reassert itself, as we see it doing in the Old Testament to erase every vestige of Asherah's worship as Yahweh's consort.[7]

> Popular religiosity, especially that of women, was always a source of concern to the authorities in antiquity, be they pagan, Jewish, or Christian. In the latter two cases, any devotion directed away from the one (male) deity and toward another was apostasy. (Gail Paterson Corrington)[8]

The clear traces of Dionysus, Attis and Cybele, and Tammuz

---

4. Barbara G. Walker, "Jesus Christ," in *Women's Encyclopedia of Myths and Secrets* (San Francisco: Harper & Row, Publishers, 1983), 468.
5. Corrington, *Her Image*, 34-35.
6. Carol P. Christ, *Laughter of Aphrodite: Reflections on a Journey to the Goddess* (San Francisco: Harper & Row, Publishers, 1988); Charlene Spretnak, *Lost Goddesses of Early Greece: A Collection of Pre-Hellenic Myths* (Boston: Beacon Press, 1984); Marija Gimbutas, *The Goddesses and Gods of Old Europe 6500-3500 BC: Myths and Cult Images,* new and updated ed. (Berkeley: University of California Press, 1982); Elinor Gadon, *The Once and Future Goddess: A Symbol for Our Time* (San Francisco: Harper & Row, Publishers, 1989); Naomi R. Goldberg, *Changing of the Gods: Feminism and the End of Traditional Religions* (Boston: Beacon Press, 1979); Riane Eisler, *The Chalice and the Blade: Our History, Our Future* (San Francisco: Harper & Row, Publishers, 1988).
7. Patai, *Hebrew Godess*, 38-39; Oiyan, *Asherah*, 70-74.
8. Corrington, *Her Image*, 172.

motifs associated with the Christianity of consecrated women in Acts 17, as well as in the reconstructed chastity story of Joanna (not to forget the similarity of the daughters of Philip to the groups of prophetic Dionysiac "daughters") all might seem to point to the conclusion that celibate women's Christianity was suspected and finally suppressed by church patriarchs because of its syncretic character. But we ought to pause before drawing such a conclusion.

After all, the close parallels between the miracle birth and resurrection of Jesus on the one hand and those of other Hellenistic gods were obvious enough to the early Christian polemicists as well as to their pagan opponents. These similarities proved to be no insurmountable stumbling block. The other, older deities were simply written off, as is well known, as diabolical counterfeits. The role of Anastasis, so similar to that of Isis and Cybele, need have occasioned no greater difficulty. So I do not think it was the origin of the mytheme in the general syncretic milieu that presented the scandal.

Rather it was the mere fact that the male savior had to share the glory with his female partner. In this respect the religion of Isis was less androcentric. Her consort Serapis had his own devotion, but so did she. Indeed, Isis was more popular than her mate. And no doubt this is what the increasingly patriarchal leaders of the churches feared, that a male symbol of the divine should be overshadowed by a female.

Now patriarchal monotheism sought to eradicate the role of the Christian Goddess as it had once eradicated that of the Hebrew Goddess. To that end the stories of the empty tomb were variously "sanitized," perhaps letting the mourning women behold the Risen Jesus (Matthew 28:9-10), perhaps letting them see only an angel (Mark 16:1-8; Luke 24:1-9) or nothing at all (John 20:1-2).

Not only so, but the credit for raising Jesus was stolen from his lover Anastasis and given instead either to Jesus himself (John 10:17) or to his Father (Acts 2:32; Romans 6:4, etc.), just as we would expect in an increasingly patriarchal religion. Ironically, because Luke preserved a single mention of the belief in the divine pair Jesus and Anastasis, albeit only to refute it, he made it possible to recognize one more widow tradition: the tradition of the widow of Jesus himself. Now she is dead, but if feminist scholars expand their reclamation of the history of the Goddess to include the New Testament, she, too, may rise again.

Bibliography

Abrahamsen, Valerie. "Women at Philippi: The Pagan and Christian Evidence." *Journal of Feminist Studies in Religion* 3 (1987): 17-30.

Achelis, H. "Agapetae." In *Encyclopaedia of Religion and Ethics*, eds. James Hastings, John A. Selbie and Louis H. Gray. New York: Charles Scribner's Sons, 1980.

Achtemaier, Paul J. "Jesus and the Disciples as Miracle Workers in the Apocryphal New Testament." In *Aspects of Religious Propaganda in Judaism and Early Christianity*, ed. Elisabeth Schüssler Fiorenza, 149-186. University of Notre Dame Center for the Study of Judaism and Christianity in Antiquity, no. 2. Notre Dame: University of Notre Dame Press, 1976.

Adams, Margaret G. "The Hidden Disciples: Luke's Stories About Women in His Gospel and in Acts." D.Min. diss.: San Francisco Theological Seminary, 1980.

Anderson, Hugh. "Broadening Horizons: The Rejection at Nazareth Pericope of Lk 4, 16-30 in Light of Recent Critical Trends." *Interpretation* 18 (1964): 259-275.

The Apostolic Fathers. Translated by Kirsopp Lake. Loeb Classical Library. Cambridge: Harvard University Press, Vols. 1 and 2, 1912, 1913.

Bacon, Benjamin W. "The Authoress of Revelation—A Conjecture." *Harvard Theological Review* 23 (July 1930): 235-250.

————. *The Gospel of Mark: Its Composition and Date*. New Haven: Yale University Press; London: Humphrey Milford: Oxford University Press.

Baker, Aelred. "One Thing Necessary." *Catholic Biblical Quarterly* 27 (February 1965): 127-137.

Balsdon, J. P. V. D. *Roman Women: Their History and Habits*. New York: John Day Company, 1963; reprinted, New York: Barnes & Noble Books, a division of Harper & Row, Publishers, 1983.

Barclay, William. *The Gospel of Luke*. Daily Bible Study Series. Revised ed. Philadelphia: Westminster Press, 1975.

Barker, C. J. *The Acts of the Apostles: A Study in Interpretation*. London: Epworth Press, 1969.

Barrett, C. K. *The Signs of an Apostle*. Cato Lecture, 1969. Introduction to American ed. by John Reumann. Philadelphia: Fortress Press, 1972.

Bassler, Jouette M. "The Widow's Tale: A Fresh Look at 1 Tim 5:3-16." *Journal of Biblical Literature* 103 (1984): 23-41.

Bauer, Walter. *Orthodoxy and Heresy in Earliest Christianity*. Ed. by Robert Kraft and Gerhard Kroedel. Translated by a team from the Philadelphia Seminar on Christian Origins. Philadelphia: Fortress Press, 1971.

Bauernfeind, Otto. *Kommentar und Studien zur Apostelgeschichte.* Wissen-schaftliche Untersuchungen zum Neuen Testament 22. Tubingen: J. C. B. Mohr (Paul Siebeck), 1980.

Baur, Ferdinand Christian. *Paul, the Apostle of Jesus Christ: His Life and Work, His Epistles and His Doctrine,* translated by A. Menzies. London & Edinburgh: Williams & Norgate, 1875. 2 vols.

Benjamin, D. C. "The Persistent Widow." *The Bible Today* 28 (April 1990): 213-219.

Berger, Peter L. *A Rumor of Angels: Modern Society and the Recovery of the Sacred.* Garden City, NY: Anchor Books, a division of Doubleday & Company, 1970.

Bergman, Ingmar. *The Seventh Seal.* In *Four Screenplays of Ingmar Bergman.* Translated by Lars Malmstrom and David Kushner, 125-202. New York: Touchstone Books, a division of Simon & Schuster, 1960.

Bernhard, T. "Women's Ministry in the Church: A Lukan Perspective." *St. Luke's Journal of Theology* 29 (April 1986): 261-263.

Blaiklock, E. M. *The Acts of the Apostles: A Historical Commentary.* Grand Rapids, MI: William B. Eerdmans Publishing Company, 1959.

Bloom, Harold. *Kabbalah and Criticism.* New York: Continuum Publishing Company, 1984.

Boswell, John. *The Kindness of Strangers: The Abandonment of Children in Western Europe from Late Antiquity to the Renaissance.* New York: Vintage Books, a division of Random House, Inc., 1990.

Bouman, Gilbert. *Das Dritte Evangelium.* Düsseldorf: Patmos Verlag, 1968.

Bovon, François, and Eric Junod. "Reading the Apocryphal Acts of the Apostles." *Semeia* 38 (1986): 161-171.

Bradley, F. H. *The Presuppositions of Critical History.* Edited with Introduction and Commentary by Lionel Rubinoff. Chicago: Quadrangle Books, 1968.

Brennan, Irene. "Women in the Gospels." *New Black Friars* 52 (July 1971): 291-299.

Brock, Sebastian P. "Early Syrian Asceticism." *Numen* 20 (1973): 1-19.

Brodie, Thomas Louis. "The Accusing and Stoning of Naboth (1 Kgs 21:8-13) as One Component of the Stephen Text (Acts 6:9-14; 7:58a)." *Catholic Biblical Quarterly* 45 (1983): 417-443.

————. "Luke-Acts as an Imitation and Emulation of the Elijah-Elisha Narrative." In *New Views of Luke and Acts,* ed. Earl Richard, 78-85. Collegeville, MN: Liturgical Press, 1990.

————. "Luke 7, 36-50 as an Internalization of 2 Kings 4, 1-37: A Study in Luke's Use of Rhetorical Imitation." *Biblica* 64 (1983): 457-485.

————. "Luke the Literary Interpreter: Luke-Acts as a Systematic

Rewriting and Updating of the Elijah-Elisha Narrative in 1 and
2 Kings." Ph.D. diss.: Pontifical University of St. Thomas
Aquinas, 1981.
————. "Not Q but Elijah." *Irish Biblical Studies* 14 (April 1992): 54-71.
Bronner, Leah. *The Stories of Elijah and Elisha as Polemics Against Baal
Worship.* Pretoria Oriental Series, ed. A. Van Selms, vol. VI.
Leiden: E. J. Brill, 1968.
Brooten, Bernadette J. "Early Christian Women and Their Cultural Con-
text." In *Feminist Perspectives on Biblical Scholarship,* ed. Adela
Yarbro Collins, 65-92. Society of Biblical Literature Centennial
Publications. Atlanta: Scholars Press, 1985.
Brown, Paul Burns. "The Meaning and Function of Acts 5:1-11 in the
Purpose of Luke-Acts." Th.D. diss.: Boston University School
of Theology, 1969.
Brown, Peter. *The Body and Society: Men, Women, and Sexual Renunciation
in Early Christianity.* New York: Columbia University Press,
1988.
————. *The Cult of the Saints: Its Rise and Function in Latin Christianity.*
Chicago: University of Chicago Press, 1981.
————. *Society and the Holy in Late Antiquity.* Berkeley: University of
California Press, 1989.
Brown, Raymond E. *The Birth of the Messiah: A Commentary on the Infancy
Narratives in Matthew and Luke.* Garden City, NY: Doubleday &
Company, 1977.
————. "Gospel Infancy Narrative Research from 1976 to 1986: Part II
(Luke)." *Catholic Biblical Quarterly* 48 (1986): 660-680.
Brown, Schuyler. *Apostasy and Perseverance in the Theology of Luke.* Ana-
lecta Biblica 36. Rome: Pontifical Biblical Institute, 1969.
Browning, W. R. F. *The Gospel According to Saint Luke, A Commentary.* A
Torch Biblical Commentary, gen. eds. John Marsh and Alan
Richardson. New York: Collier Books, 1962.
Bruce, F. F. *Commentary on the Book of Acts.* Grand Rapids, MI: William B.
Eerdmans Publishing Company, 1960.
Budge, E. A. Wallis, ed. and trans. *The Contendings of the Apostles: Being
the Histories of the Lives and Martyrdoms and Deaths of the Twelve
Apostles and Evangelists. Vol. II, The English Translation.* London:
Oxford University Press, 1901.
Bultmann, Rudolf. *History of the Synoptic Tradition.* Translated by John
Marsh. New York: Harper & Row, Publishers, 1972.
————. *Theology of the New Testament.* Volume 1. Translated by Ken-
drick Groebel. New York: Charles Scribner's Sons, 1951.
Burrus, Virginia. *Chastity as Autonomy: Women in the Stories of Apocryphal
Acts.* Studies in Women and Religion, Vol. 23. Lewiston and
Queenston, NY: Edwin Mellen Press, 1987.
Cadoux, C. J. *The Historic Mission of Jesus: A Constructive Re-examination
of the Eschatological Teaching in the Synoptic Gospels.* New York:

Harper & Brothers, Publishers, n.d.

Cadbury, Henry J. *The Book of Acts in History.* New York: Harper & Brothers, Publishers, 1955.

————. "The Hellenists." In *The Beginnings of Christianity, Part I: The Acts of the Apostles,* eds. F. J. Foakes Jackson and Kirsopp Lake. Vol. V, Additional Notes to the Commentary, ed. Kirsopp Lake and Henry Cadbury, 59-74. London: Macmillan & Co., 1933.

————. *The Making of Luke-Acts.* London: SPCK, 1958.

Cadbury, Henry, and Kirsopp Lake. "English Translation and Commentary." Vol. IV of *The Beginnings of Christianity, Part I: The Acts of the Apostles,* eds. F. J. Foakes Jackson and Kirsopp Lake. London: Macmillan & Co., 1933.

Caird, G. B. *The Gospel of St. Luke.* The Pelican New Testament Commentaries. Baltimore: Penguin Books, 1972.

————. "Paul and Women's Liberty." *Bulletin of the John Rylands Library* 54 (1972): 268-281.

Cameron, Averil. "'Neither Male Nor Female.'" *Greece and Rome* (1980): 60-68.

Camp, Claudia V. "1 and 2 Kings." In *The Women's Bible Commentary,* eds. Carol A. Newsom and Sharon H. Ringe. Louisville: Westminster/John Knox Press, 96-109.

Cartlidge, David R. Review of *The Revolt of the Widows: The Social World of the Apocryphal Acts,* by Stevan L. Davies. *Religious Studies Review* 7 (July 1981): 258.

Casey, Maurice. *The Son of Man: The Interpretation and Influence of Daniel 7.* London: SPCK, 1979.

Cassidy, Richard J. *Jesus, Politics, and Society: A Study of Luke's Gospel.* Maryknoll: Orbis Books, 1978.

————. "The Non-Roman Opponents of Paul." In *New Views of Luke and Acts,* ed. Earl Richard, 150-162. Collegeville, MN: Liturgical Press, 1990.

Castelli, Elizabeth. "Virginity and Its Meaning for Women's Sexuality in Early Christianity." *Journal of Feminist Studies in Religion* 2 (1986): 61-88.

Chance, J. Bradley. *Jerusalem, the Temple, and the New Age in Luke-Acts.* Macon: Mercer University Press, 1988.

Charlesworth, James H., ed. *The Old Testament Pseudepigrapha, Vol. 1: Apocalyptic Literature & Testaments.* New York: Doubleday & Company, 1983.

Chilton, Bruce. "Announcement in Nazara: An Analysis of Luke 4:16-21." In *Gospel Perspectives II,* 147-172. Sheffield: JSOT Press, 1981.

Christ, Carol P. *Laughter of Aphrodite: Reflections on a Journey to the Goddess.* San Francisco: Harper & Row, Publishers, 1988.

Clark, Elizabeth A. *Ascetic Piety and Women's Faith: Essays in Late Ancient Christianity.* Studies in Women and Religion, Vol. 20. Queenston and Lewiston, NY: Edwin Mellen Press, 1986.

—— —. Review of *Chastity as Autonomy: Women in the Stories of Apocryphal Acts,* by Virginia Burrus. *Religious Studies Review* 14 (July 1988): 256.

—— —— . Review of *The Revolt of the Widows: The Social World of the Apocryphal Acts,* by Stevan L. Davies. *Church History* 51 (1982): 335-336.

—— —— , ed. *Women in the Early Church.* Message of the Church Fathers Series 13. Collegeville, MN: Liturgical Press, 1983.

Clement of Alexandria. *Stromateis.* Translated by G. W. Butterworth. Loeb Classical Library.

Coker, H. E. "Women and the Gospel in Luke-Acts." Th.D. diss.: Southern Baptist Theological Seminary, 1954.

Collingwood, R. G. *The Idea of History.* New York: Galaxy Books, a division of Oxford University Press, 1957.

Combrinck, H. J. B. "The Structure and Significance of Luke 4:16-30." *Neotestamentica* 7 (1973): 27-47.

Conzelmann, Hans. *Acts of the Apostles.* Translated by James Limburg, A. Thomas Kraabel, and Donald H. Juel. Hermeneia Series, ed. Helmut Koester. Philadelphia: Fortress Press, 1987.

—— —— . *The Theology of St. Luke.* Translated by Geoffrey Buswell. New York: Harper & Row, Publishers. 1961.

Cooper, Kate. "Apostles, Ascetic Women, and Questions of Audience: New Reflections on the Rhetoric of Gender in the *Apocryphal Acts.*" Unpublished paper presented at Seminar on Intertextuality in Christian Apocrypha, Society of Biblical Literature, November 1992.

—— —— . "Insinuations of Womanly Influence: An Aspect of the Christianization of the Roman Aristocracy." *Journal of Roman Studies* 82 (1992): 150-164.

Cornford, Francis MacDonald. *The Origin of Attic Comedy.* Edited with a Foreword and Additional Notes by Theodor Gaster. Garden City, NY: Anchor Books, a division of Doubleday & Company, 1961.

Corrington, Gail Paterson. *Her Image of Salvation: Female Saviors and Formative Christianity.* Gender and the Biblical Tradition, eds. Ross S. Kraemer, Carol Meyers, and Sharon H. Ringe. Atlanta: Westminster/John Knox Press, 1992.

Cranfield, C. E. B. "The Parable of the Unjust Judge and the Eschatology of Luke-Acts." *Scottish Journal of Theology* 16 (1963): 297-301.

Creed, John Martin. *The Gospel according to St. Luke.* London: Macmillan & Co., 1950.

Crockett, Larrimore C. "Luke 4:25-27 and Jewish-Gentile Relations in Luke-Acts." *Journal of Biblical Literature* 88 (1969): 177-183.

Cross, Frank Moore, and David Noel Freedman. "The Song of Miriam." *Journal of Near Eastern Studies* 14 (1955) 237-250.

Crossan, John Dominic. *The Cross That Spoke: The Origins of the Passion Narrative*. San Francisco: Harper & Row, Publishers, 1988.

————. *The Historical Jesus: The Life of a Mediterranean Jewish Peasant*. New York: HarperCollins, Publishers, 1991.

Culler, Jonathan. *On Deconstruction: Theory and Criticism after Structuralism*. Ithaca: Cornell University Press, 1982.

Cullmann, Oscar. "Dissensions within the Early Church." In *New Testament Issues*, ed. Richard Batey, 119-129. Harper Forum Books, gen. ed. Martin E. Marty. New York: Harper & Row, Publishers, 1970.

————. *Peter: Disciple, Apostle, Martyr*. Translated by Floyd V. Filson. Philadelphia: Westminster Press, 1953.

Dammers, A. H. "Studies in Texts: A Note on Luke vii, 36-50." *Theology* 49 (1946): 78-80.

D'Angelo, Mary Rose. "Women in Luke-Acts: A Redactional View." *Journal of Biblical Literature* 109 (1990): 441-461.

————. "Women Partners in the New Testament." *Journal of Feminist Studies in Religion* 6 (1990): 65-86.

Danielou, Jean. *The Infancy Narratives*. Translated by Rosemary Sheed. London: Compass Books, a division of Burns & Oates, 1968.

————. *The Ministry of Women in the Early Church*. Translated by Glyn Simon. London: Faith Press, 1961.

Danker, Frederick W. *Jesus and the New Age: A Commentary on St. Luke's Gospel*. Revised Edition. Philadelphia: Fortress Press, 1988.

Davies, Stevan L. *The Revolt of the Widows: The Social World of the Apocryphal Acts*. Carbondale & Edwardsville: Southern Illinois University Press; London & Amsterdam: Feffer & Simons, 1980.

————. "Women, Tertullian and the Acts of Paul." *Semeia* 38 (1986): 138-143.

de Man, Paul. *Blindness and Insight: Essays in the Rhetoric of Contemporary Criticism*. 2nd ed. revised. Theory and History of Literature, vol. 7. Minneapolis: University of Minnesota Press, 1983.

Derleth, August W. "The Peabody Heritage." In *The Survivor and Others*. New York: Ballantine Books, 1962.

Derrett, J. Duncan M. "Ananias, Sapphira, and the Right of Property." *Downside Review* 89 (1971): 225-232.

————. "Law in the New Testament: The Parable of the Unjust Judge." *New Testament Studies* 18 (1971-1972): 178-191.

Derrida, Jacques. "Living On. Border Lines." In *Deconstruction and Criticism*, no editor. New York: Continuum Publishing Corporation, 1979.

Dibelius, Martin. *From Tradition to Gospel*. Translated by Bertram Lee Woolf. New York: Charles Scribner's Sons., n.d.

————. "Herodes und Pilatus." *Zeitschrift für die Neutestamentliche Wissenschaft* 16 (1915) 113-126.

————. *Studies in the Acts of the Apostles*. Ed. Heinrich Greeven. London: SCM Press, 1973.

————. "Zur Formsgeschichte des Neuen Testaments." *Theologische Rundschau* New Series 3 (1931): 207-242.

Dibelius, Martin, and Hans Conzelmann. *The Pastoral Epistles: A Commentary on the Pastoral Epistles.* Translated by Philip Buttolph and Adela Yarbro. Hermeneia Series, ed. Helmut Koester. Philadelphia: Fortress Press, 1983.

Dillon, Richard J. *From Eye-Witnesses to Ministers of the Word.* Analecta Biblica 82. Rome: Biblical Institute Press, 1978.

Dodd, C. H. *Historical Tradition in the Fourth Gospel.* New York: Cambridge University Press, 1963.

Dodds, E. R., ed. *Euripides, Bacchae.* Edited with Introduction and Commentary by E. R. Dodds. Second edition. Oxford: Clarendon Press, 1960.

————. "Maenadism in the *Bacchae.*" *Harvard Theological Review* 33 (July 1940): 155-176.

————. *Pagan and Christian in an Age of Anxiety: Some Aspects of Religious Experience from Marcus Aurelius to Constantine.* New York: W. W. Norton & Company, 1970.

Donahue, J. J. "The Pentitent Woman and the Pharisee: Luke 7:36-50." *American Ecclesiastical Review* 142 (1960): 414-421.

Douglas, Mary. *Natural Symbols: Explorations in Cosmology.* New York: Pantheon Books, 1982.

————. *Purity and Danger: An Analysis of Concepts of Pollution and Taboo.* London: Routledge & Kegan Paul, 1966; reprinted, Baltimore: Pelican Books, a division of Penguin Books, 1970.

Drury, John. *Luke.* J. B. Phillips New Testament Commentaries. New York: Macmillan Publishing Co., 1973.

————. *Tradition and Design in Luke's Gospel: A Study in Early Christian Historiography.* Atlanta: John Knox Press, 1977.

Dunn, James D. G. *Jesus and the Spirit: A Study of the Religious and Charismatic Experience of Jesus and the First Christians as Reflected in the New Testament.* Philadelphia: Westminster Press, 1975.

Easton, Burton Scott. *The Gospel According to St. Luke: A Critical and Exegetical Commentary.* New York: Charles Scribner's Sons, 1928.

————. *The Pastoral Epistles: Introduction, Translation, Commentary and Word Studies.* New York: Charles Scribner's Sons, 1947.

Eisenman, Robert, and Michael Wise, trans. and eds. *The Dead Sea Scrolls Uncovered.* Rockport, MA: Element, 1992.

Eisler, Riane. *The Chalice and the Blade: Our History, Our Future.* San Francisco: Harper & Row, San Francisco, 1988.

Eissfeldt, Otto. *The Old Testament: An Introduction.* Translated by P. R. Ackroyd. New York: Harper & Row, Publishers, 1965.

Elliott, J. K. "Anna's Age (Luke 2:36-50)." *Novum Testamentum* 30 (1988): 100-102.

————. "The Anointing of Jesus." *Expository Times* 85 (1973-1974):

105-107.

Ellis, E. Earle. *The Gospel of Luke*. The New Century Bible Commentary, general eds. Ronald E. Clements and Matthew Black. Grand Rapids. MI: William B. Eerdmans Publishing Company, 1987.

Epiphanius. *The Panarion of Epiphanius, Bishop of Salamis*. Selected Passages. Translated Philip R. Amidon. New York: Oxford University Press, 1990.

Esler, Philip Francis. *Community and Gospel in Luke-Acts: The Social and Political Motivations of Lucan Theology*. Society for New Testament Studies Monograph Series, ed. G. N. Stanton, 57. New York: Cambridge University Press, 1989.

Evans, C. F. *Saint Luke*. TPI New Testament Commentaries, general eds. Howard Clark Kee and Dennis Nineham. London: SCM Press; Philadelphia: Trinity Press International, 1990.

Evans-Wentz, W. Y., ed. *Tibet's Great Yogi Milarepa, A Biography From the Tibetan*. 2nd ed. Translated by Kazi Dawa-Samdup, with an Introduction and Annotations by W. Y. Evans-Wentz. London: Oxford University Press, 1951; reprint, 1974.

Farris, Stephen. *The Hymns of Luke's Infancy Narratives: Their Origin, Meaning and Significance*. Journal for the Study of the New Testament Supplement Series, ed. Stanley E. Porter, 9. Sheffield: JSOT Press, 1985.

Fee, Gordon D. *1 and 2 Timothy, Titus*. Good News Commentaries, ed. W. Ward Gasque. San Francisco: Harper & Row, Publishers, 1984.

————. "'One Thing Is Needful'?: Luke 10:42." In *New Testament Textual Criticism, Its Significance for Exegesis: Essays in Honor of Bruce M. Metzger*, eds. Eldon J. Epp and Gordon D. Fee, 61-75. Oxford: Clarendon Press, 1981.

Ferrar, F. W. *The Gospel According to Luke*. Cambridge Greek Testament for Schools and Colleges, ed. A. Carr. Cambridge: Cambridge University Press, 1912.

Finkel, Asher. "Jesus' Sermon at Nazareth (Luk. 4, 16-30)." In *Abraham Unser Vater: Juden und Christen im Gesprach über die Bibel, Festschrift für Otto Michel zum 60. Geburtstag*, eds. Otto Betz, Martin Hengel, Peter Schmidt, 106-115. Leiden: E. J. Brill, 1963.

Fitzmyer, Joseph A. *The Gospel According to Luke I-IX: A New Translation with Introduction and Commentary*. Anchor Bible, gen. eds. William Foxwell Albright and David Noel Freedman, 28. New York: Doubleday, a division of Bantam Doubleday Dell Publishing Group, 1981.

————. *The Gospel According to Luke X-XXIV: A New Translation with Introduction and Commentary*. Anchor Bible, gen. eds. William Foxwell Albright and David Noel Freedman, 28A. New York: Doubleday, a division of Bantam Doubleday Dell Publishing Group, 1981.

——. *Luke the Theologian: Aspects of His Teaching.* New York: Paulist Press, 1989.

Flanagan, Neal M. *The Acts of the Apostles: Introduction and Commentary.* 2nd ed. New Testament Reading Guide 5. Collegeville, MN: Liturgical Press, 1964.

——. "The Position of Women in the Writings of St. Luke." *Marianum* 40 (1978): 288-304.

Flender, Helmut. *St. Luke Theologian of Redemptive History.* Translated by Reginald H. Fuller and Ilse Fuller. London: SPCK, 1967.

Foakes Jackson, F. J. *The Acts of the Apostles.* The Moffatt New Testament Commentary, ed. James Moffatt. New York: Harper & Brothers, Publishers, 1931.

Freed, E. D. "The Parable of the Judge and the Widow." *New Testament Studies* 33 (1987): 38-60.

Fuller, Reginald H. *The Formation of the Resurrection Narratives.* New York: Macmillan Company, 1971.

——. *Interpreting the Miracles.* London: SCM Press, 1974.

Gadon, Elinor W. *The Once and Future Goddess: A Symbol for Our Time.* San Francisco: Harper & Row, Publishers, 1989.

Gelin, Albert. *The Poor of Yahweh.* Translated by Kathryn Sullivan. Collegeville, MN: Liturgical Press, 1964.

Georgi, Dieter. *The Opponents of Paul in Second Corinthians.* Philadelphia: Fortress Press, 1986.

Gerhardsson, Birger. *Memory and Manuscript: Oral Transmission in Rabbinic Judaism and Early Christianity.* Translated by Eric J. Sharpe. Uppsala: Almqvist & Wiksells, 1961.

Gimbutas, Marija. *The Goddesses and Gods of Old Europe 6500-3500 BC: Myths and Cult Images.* 2nd ed. Berkeley: University of California Press, 1982.

Glasson, Francis T. *The Second Advent: The Origin of the New Testament Doctrine.* London: Epworth Press, 1947.

Godet, F. *A Commentary on the Gospel of Luke.* New York: I. K. Funk & Co., 1881.

Goehring, James E. "Libertine or Liberated: Women in the So-Called Libertine Gnostic Communities." In *Images of the Female in Gnosticism,* ed. Karen L. King, 343-344. Studies in Antiquity & Christianity, ed. James M. Robinson. Philadelphia: Fortress Press, 1988.

Goldberg, Naomi R. *Changing of the Gods: Feminism and the End of Traditional Religions.* Boston: Beacon Press, 1979.

Goldziher, Ignaz. *Mythology Among the Hebrews and Its Historical Development.* Translated by Russell Martineau. New York: Cooper Square Publishers, 1967.

Goulder, Michael D. *Luke, A New Paradigm.* Vols. 1 and 2. Journal for the Study of the New Testament Supplement Series, ed. Stanley E. Porter, 20. Sheffield: JSOT Press, 1989.

Graves, Robert. *The Greek Myths: Volume One.* Baltimore: Penguin Books, 1986.

Gray, John. *I & II Kings: A Commentary.* 2nd ed. The Old Testament Library, general eds. Peter Ackroyd, James Barr, John Bright, G. Ernest Wright. Philadelphia: Westminster Press, 1970.

Grable, E. "The Anointing of Jesus." *Expository Times* 26 (1914-1915): 461-463.

Grundmann, Walter. *Das Evangelium nach Lukas.* Theologischer Handcommentar zum Neuen Testament III. Berlin: Evangelische Verlagsanstalt, 1966.

Gryson, Roger. *The Ministry of Women in the Early Church.* Translated by Jean Laporte and Mary Loise Hall. Collegeville, MN: Liturgical Press, 1980.

Gunkel, Hermann. *The Legends of Genesis: The Biblical Saga and History.* Translated by W. H. Carruth, with Introduction by William Foxwell Albright. New York: Schocken Books, 1964.

Guthrie, Donald. *New Testament Introduction.* Downers Grove, IL: Inter-Varsity Press, 1973.

————. *The Pastoral Epistles: An Introduction and Commentary.* Tyndale New Testament Commentaries, ed. R. V. G. Tasker. Leicester: Inter-Varsity Press; Grand Rapids, MI: William B. Eerdmans Publishing Company, 1957.

Guthrie, W. K. C. *The Greeks and Their Gods.* Boston: Beacon Press, 1955.

Haenchen, Ernst. *The Acts of the Apostles: A Commentary.* Translated by Robert McL. Wilson. Translation rev. by Bernard Noble, Gerald Shinn, Hugh Anderson. Philadelphia: Westminster Press, 1971.

Hahn, Ferdinand. *The Titles of Jesus in Christology: Their History in Early Christianity.* Translated by Harold Knight and George Ogg. New York: World Publishing Company, 1969.

Hamm, M. Dennis. "The Freeing of the Bent Woman and the Restoration of Israel: Luke 13.10-17 as Narrative Theology." *Journal for the Study of the New Testament* 31 (1987): 23-44.

Hannam, Wilfrid L. *Luke the Evangelist: A Study of His Purpose.* New York: Abingdon Press, 1936.

Hansen, Anthony Tyrell. *The Pastoral Epistles.* New Century Bible Commentary, gen. eds. Ronald E. Clements and Matthew Black. Grand Rapids, MI: William B. Eerdmans Publishing Company, 1982.

Hanson, Paul D. *The Dawn of Apocalyptic: The Historical and Sociological Roots of Jewish Apocalyptic Eschatology.* Philadelphia: Fortress Press, 1975.

Harnack, Adolf. *The Acts of the Apostles.* Translated by J. R. Wilkinson. Crown Theological Library XXVII. New York: G. P. Putnam's Sons, 1909.

————. *Luke the Physician: The Author of the Third Gospel and the Acts of the Apostles.* Translated by J. R. Wilkinson. Crown Theological

Library XX. London: Williams & Norgate, 1911.

Harris, J. Rendel. "St. Paul & Epimenides." *Expositor* 8th Series, 4 (1912): 348-353.

Harris, Xavier. "Ministering Women in the Gospels." *The Bible Today* 29 (March 1991): 109-112.

Harrison, P. N. *The Problem of the Pastoral Epistles.* Oxford: Oxford University Press, 1921.

Hausman, Robert. "The Function of Elijah as a Model in Luke-Acts." Ph.D. diss.: University of Chicago, 1975.

Heine, Susanne. *Women and Early Christianity: A Reappraisal.* Translated by John Bowden. Minneapolis: Augsburg Publishing House, 1988.

Helms, Randel. *Gospel Fictions.* Buffalo: Prometheus Books, 1989.

Hendrickx, Herman. *The Infancy Narratives.* Studies in the Synoptic Gospels. London: Geoffrey Chapman, 1984.

————. *The Parables of Jesus.* Studies in the Synoptic Gospels. San Francisco: Harper & Row, Publishers, 1986.

————. *The Passion Narratives of the Synoptic Gospels.* Revised ed. Studies in the Synoptic Gospels. London: Geoffrey Chapman, 1984.

Hengel, Martin. "Maria Magdalena und die Frauen als Keugen." In *Abraham Unser Vater: Juden und Christen im Gesprach über die Bibel, Festschrift für Otto Michel, zum 60. Geburtstag,* eds. Otto Betz, Martin Hengel, Peter Schmidt, 247-248. Leiden: E. J. Brill, 1963.

Hennecke, Edgar. *New Testament Apocrypha, Volume Two: Writings Relating to the Apostles, Apocalypses and Related Subjects.* Ed. Wilhelm Schneemelcher. English translation ed. Robert McL. Wilson. Philadelphia: Westminster Press, 1965.

Herbert, Maire, and Martin McNamara, eds. *Irish Biblical Apocrypha.* Edinburgh: T & T Clark, 1989.

Hicks, E. L. "Demetrius the Silversmith." *Expositor* Series IV, I (1890): 401-422.

Hicks, John Mark. "The Parable of the Persistent Widow (Luke 18:1-8)." *Restoration Quarterly* 33 (April 1991): 209-223.

Hiebert, Paul G. Review of *The Revolt of the Widows: The Social World of the Apocryphal Acts,* by Stevan L. Davies. *Sociology* 8 (May 1981): 82.

Hill, Craig C. *Hellenists and Hebrews: Reappraising Division Within the Earliest Church.* Minneapolis: Fortress Press, 1992.

Hill, David. "The Rejection of Jesus at Nazareth (Luke 4:16-30)." *Novum Testamentum* 13 (1971): 161-180.

Hill, Scott D. "The Local Hero in Palestine in Comparative Perspective." In *Elijah and Elisha in Socioliterary Perspective,* ed. Robert B. Coote, 37-74. Society of Biblical Literature Semeia Studies, ed. Edward L. Greenstein. Atlanta: Scholars Press, 1992.

Hippolytus. *The Apostolic Tradition of Hippolytus.* Translated by Dom

Gregory Dix. London: SPCK, 1960.

Hoehner, Harold W. *Herod Antipas.* Society for New Testament Studies Monograph Series, ed. Matthew Black, 7. New York: Cambridge University Press, 1972.

Holst, Robert. "The One Anointing of Jesus: Another Application of the Form-Critical Method." *Journal of Biblical Literature* 95 (1976): 435-446.

Holtzmann, Oscar. *The Life of Jesus.* Translated by J. T. Bealby and Maurice A. Canney. London: Adam & Charles Black, 1904.

Horsley, Richard A. *Jesus and the Spiral of Violence: Popular Jewish Resistance in Roman Palestine.* San Francisco: Harper & Row, Publishers, 1987; rpt., Minneapolis: Fortress Press, 1993.

————. *The Liberation of Christmas: The Infancy Narratives in Social Context.* New York: Crossroad Publishing Company, 1989.

————. *Sociology and the Jesus Movement.* New York: Crossroad Publishing Company, 1989.

Houlden, J. L. *The Pastoral Epistles, I and II Timothy, Titus.* Pelican New Testament Commentaries. Baltimore: Penguin Books, 1976.

Hughes, Sandra Boyd. Review of *The Revolt of the Widows: The Social World of the Apocryphal Acts,* by Stevan L. Davies. *Library Journal* 106 (February 1, 1981): 360.

Hunter, Archibald M. *Interpreting the Parables.* Philadelphia: Westminster Press, 1960.

James, Montague Rhodes. *The Apocryphal New Testament: Being the Apocryphal Gospels, Acts, Epistles, and Apocalypses with Other Narratives and Fragments Newly Translated by Montague Rhodes James.* Oxford: Clarendon Press, 1924, rpt. 1972.

Jeremias, Joachim. *The Parables of Jesus.* Revised ed. New York: Charles Scribner's Sons, 1972.

Jervell, Jacob. "The Daughters of Abraham: Women in Acts." In *The Unknown Paul: Essays on Luke-Acts and Early Christian History,* 146-157. Minneapolis: Augsburg Publishing House, 1984.

John, M. P. "Luke 2.36-37: How Old Was Anna?" *Bible Translator* 26 (February 1975): 247.

Johnson, Luke Timothy. *The Acts of the Apostles.* Sacra Pagina Series, ed. Daniel Harrington, vol. 5. Collegeville, MN: Liturgical Press, 1992.

————. *The Gospel of Luke.* Sacra Pagina Series, ed. Daniel Harrington, vol. 3. Collegeville, MN: Liturgical Press, 1991.

————. *The Literary Function of Possessions in Luke-Acts.* Society of Biblical Literature Dissertation Series no. 39. Missoula: Scholars Press, 1977.

Jüngst, Johannes. *Die Quellen der Apostelgeschichte.* Gotha: Perthes, 1895.

Juvenal. *The Sixteen Satires.* Translated by Peter Green. Baltimore: Penguin Books, 1974.

Kaestli, Jean-Daniel. "Response" [to Virginia Burrus]. *Semeia* 38 (1986):

119-131.

Karris, Robert J. *Invitation to Luke: A Commentary on the Gospel of Luke with Complete Text from the Jerusalem Bible.* Garden City, NY: Anchor Books, a division of Doubleday & Company, 1977.

—————. "Missionary Communities: A New Paradigm for the Study of Luke-Acts." *Catholic Biblical Quarterly* 41 (1979): 80-97.

—————. *What Are They Saying About Luke and Acts?: A Theology of the Faithful God.* New York: Paulist Press, 1979.

Käsemann, Ernst. "Sentences of Holy Law." In *New Testament Questions of Today*, translated by W. J. Montague, 66-81. Philadelphia: Fortress Press, 1979.

Kelly, J. N. D. *A Commentary on the Pastoral Epistles, Timothy I & II, and Titus.* Harper's New Testament Commentaries, ed. Henry Chadwick. New York: Harper & Row, 1960; rpt., Peabody, MA: Hendrickson Publishers, 1987.

Kilgallen, J. J. "John the Baptist, the Sinful Woman, and the Pharisee." *Journal of Biblical Literature* 104 (1985): 675-679.

Koenig, John. *New Testament Hospitality: Partnership with Strangers as Promise and Mission.* Overtures to Biblical Theology, eds. Walter Brueggemann and John R. Donahue. 17. Philadelphia: Fortress Press, 1985.

Koester, Helmut. *Ancient Christian Gospels: Their History and Development.* Philadelphia: Trinity Press International, 1990.

—————. *Introduction to the New Testament, Volume Two: History and Literature of Early Christianity.* Hermeneia Foundations and Facets, ed. Robert W. Funk. Philadelphia: Fortress Press; New York: Walter de Gruyter, 1982.

Koet, B. J. "'Today this Scripture has been fulfilled in your ears': Jesus' Explanation of Scripture in Luke 4:16-30." *Bijdragen* 47 (April 1986): 368-394.

Kopas, Jane. "Jesus and Women: Luke's Gospel." *Theology Today* 43 (February 1986): 192-202.

Kraemer, Ross S. "The Conversion of Women to Ascetic Forms of Christianity." *Signs: Journal of Women in Culture and Society* 6 (Winter 1980): 298-307.

—————. "Ecstasy and Possession: The Attraction of Women to the Cult of Dionysus." *Harvard Theological Review* 72 (1979): 55-80.

—————. "Monastic Jewish Women in Greco-Roman Egypt: Philo Judaeus on the Therapeutrides." *Signs: Journal of Women in Culture and Society* 14 (Winter 1989): 342-370.

Kramer, Samuel Noah. *The Sacred Marriage Rite: Aspects of Faith, Myth, and Ritual in Ancient Sumer.* Bloomington: Indiana University Press, 1969.

Kroeger, Catherine Clark. "1 Timothy 2:12—A Classicist's View." In *Women, Authority & the Bible*, ed. Alvera Mickelsen. Downers Grove, IL: InterVarsity Press, 1986.

Kroeger, Richard Clark, and Catherine Clark Kroeger. *I Suffer Not a Woman: Rethinking 1 Timothy 2:11-15 in Light of Ancient Evidence.* Grand Rapids, MI: Baker Book House, 1992.

Kuhn, Thomas S. *The Structure of Scientific Revolutions.* Chicago: University of Chicago Press, 1969.

Kümmel, Werner Georg. *Promise and Fulfillment: The Eschatological Message of Jesus.* Studies in Biblical Theology, eds. Peter R. Ackroyd, James Barr, C. F. Evans, Floyd V. Filson, and C. F. D. Moule, First Series 23. London: SCM Press, 1957.

Laffey, Alice L. *An Introduction to the Old Testament: A Feminist Perspective.* Philadelphia: Fortress Press, 1988.

Laland, Erling. "Die Martha-Maria-Perikope, Lukas 10, 38-42." *Studia Theologica* 13 (1959): 70-85.

Lake, Kirsopp. "The Communism of Acts." In *The Beginnings of Christianity, Part 1: The Acts of the Apostles,* eds. F. J. Foakes Jackson and Kirsopp Lake; Vol. V, Additional Notes to the Commentary, eds. Kirsopp Lake and H. J. Cadbury, 140-151. London: Macmillan & Co., 1933.

————. "Your Own Poets." In *The Beginnings of Christianity, Part 1: The Acts of the Apostles,* eds. F. J. Foakes Jackson and Kirsopp Lake; Vol. V, Additional Notes to the Commentary, eds. Kirsopp Lake and H. J. Cadbury, 246-251. London: Macmillan & Co., 1933.

Lampe, G. W. H. "Miracles in the Acts of the Apostles." In *Miracles: Cambridge Studies in their Philosophy and History,* ed. C. F. D. Moule, 165-178. London: A.R. Mowbray & Co., 1965.

Laverdiere, Eugene. "Women in the New Israel." *Emmanuel* 95 (1989): 34-41, 56.

Lawson, John Cuthbert. *Modern Greek Folklore and Ancient Greek Religion: A Study in Survivals.* Cambridge: Cambridge University Press, 1910.

Leaney, A. R. C. *A Commentary on the Gospel According to St. Luke.* Harper's New Testament Commentaries, ed. Henry Chadwick. New York: Harper & Brothers, Publishers, 1958.

Lefkowitz, Mary R., and Maureen B. Fant, eds. *Women's Life in Greece and Rome: A Source Book in Translation.* Baltimore: The Johns Hopkins University Press, 1987.

Legault, A. "An Application of the Form-Critique Method to the Anointings in Galilee (Lk 7, 36-50) and Bethany (Mt 26, 6-13; Mk 14, 3-9; Jn 12, 1-8)." *Catholic Biblical Quarterly* 16 (1954): 131-145.

Leipoldt, Johannes. "Zu den Auferstehungsgeschichten." *Theologisches Literaturzeitung* 73 (1948): 737-742.

Levine, Amy-Jill. "Ruth." In *The Women's Bible Commentary,* eds. Carol A. Newsom and Sharon H. Ringe, 78-84. Louisville: Westminster/John Knox Press, 1992.

Lewis, C. S. *Miracles: A Preliminary Study.* New York: Macmillan Publishing Co., 1947; reprinted 1974.

Liechty, Daniel. *Theology in a Postliberal Perspective.* London: SCM Press; Philadelphia: Trinity Press International, 1990.

Lienhard, J. T. "Acts 6:1-6: A Redactional View." *Catholic Biblical Quarterly* 37 (1975): 228-236.

Lindars, Barnabas. "Elijah, Elisha and the Gospel Miracles." In *Miracles: Cambridge Studies in their Philosophy and History,* ed. C. F. D. Moule, 63-79. London: A. R. Mowbray & Co., 1965.

Linnemann, Eta. *Jesus of the Parables.* With an Introduction by Ernst Fuchs. New York: Harper & Row, Publishers, 1966.

Lock, Walter. *A Critical and Exegetical Commentary on the Pastoral Epistles (I& II Timothy and Titus).* International Critical Commentary, eds. Charles Augustus Briggs, Samuel Rolles Driver, and Alfred Plummer. New York: Charles Scribner's Sons, 1924.

Lohfink, Norbert. "Von der 'Anawim-partei' zur Kirche der Armen: Die bibelwissenschaftliche Ahnentafel eines Hauptbegriffs der 'Theologie der Befreiung.'" *Biblica* 67 (1986): 153-176.

Loisy, Alfred. *Les Acts des Apôtres.* Paris: Emile Nourry, 1920.

————. *Les Evangiles Synoptiques.* Haute-Marne: Pres Montier-en-Der, 1907-1908.

————. *The Origins of the New Testament.* Translated by L. P. Jacks. London: George Allen & Unwin, 1950.

Lucian. *The Death of Peregrinus.* In *Selected Satires of Lucian,* ed. and translated by Lionel Casson. New York: W. W. Norton & Company, 1962.

Lüdemann, Gerd. *Early Christianity according to the Traditions in Acts: A Commentary.* Minneapolis: Fortress Press, 1989.

Maccoby, Hyam. *Paul and Hellenism.* London: SCM Press; Philadelphia: Trinity Press International, 1991.

MacDonald, Dennis Ronald. "Apocryphal and Canonical Narratives about Paul." In *Paul and the Legacies of Paul,* ed. William S. Babcock, 55-69. Dallas: Southern Methodist University Press, 1990.

————. *The Legend and the Apostle: The Battle for Paul in Story and Canon.* Philadelphia: Westminster Press, 1983.

————. "The Role of Women in the Production of the Apocryphal Acts of the Apostles." *Iliff Review* 41 (1984): 21-38.

MacDonald, Margaret Y. "Women Holy in Body and Spirit: The Social Setting of 1 Corinthians 7." *New Testament Studies* 36 (1990): 161-181.

MacHaffie, Barbara J. *Her Story: Women in Christian Tradition.* Philadelphia: Fortress Press, 1988.

Malina, Bruce J. *Christian Origins and Cultural Anthropology: Practical Models for Biblical Interpretation.* Atlanta: John Knox Press, 1986.

————. *The New Testament World: Insights from Cultural Anthropology.* Atlanta: John Knox Press, 1981.

Malina, Bruce J., and Jerome H. Neyrey. "Honor and Shame in Luke-Acts: Pivotal Values of the Mediterranean World." In *The Social World of Luke-Acts: Models for Interpretation,* ed. Jerome H. Neyrey, 25-66. Peabody. MA: Hendrickson Publishers, 1991.

Maly, Eugene H. "Women and the Gospel of Luke." *Biblical Theology Bulletin* 10 (1980): 99-104.

Manson, T. W. *The Sayings of Jesus.* London: SCM Press, 1937 as Part II of *The Mission and Message of Jesus;* issued as a separate volume, 1949; Study Edition, 1975.

Manson, William. *The Gospel of Luke.* Moffatt New Testament Commentary, ed. James Moffatt. New York: Richard R. Smith, 1930.

Marshall, I. Howard. *The Acts of the Apostles: An Introduction and Commentary.* Tyndale New Testament Commentaries, ed. R. V. G. Tasker. Leicester: Inter-Varsity Press; Grand Rapids, MI: William B. Eerdmans Publishing Company, 1980.

————. *Commentary on Luke.* New International Greek Testament Commentaries, eds. I. Howard Marshall and W. Ward Gasque. Exeter: Paternoster Press; Grand Rapids, MI: William B. Eerdmans Publishing Company, 1978.

Mattill, A. J. *Luke and the Last Things: A Perspective for the Understanding of Lukan Thought.* Dillsboro, NC: Western North Carolina Press, 1979.

Matura, Thaddée. *Gospel Radicalism: The Hard Sayings of Jesus.* Translated by Maggi Despot and Paul Lachance. Maryknoll: Orbis Books, 1984.

McKenna, Mary Lawrence. *Women of the Church: Role and Renewal.* With a Foreword by Jean Daniélou. New York: P. J. Kenedy & Sons, 1967.

McNamara, Jo Ann. *A New Song: Celibate Women in the First Three Christian Centuries.* Women in History Series, ed. Eleanor S. Riemer. New York: Institute for Research in History and Haworth Press, 1983.

————. "Sexual Equality and the Cult of Virginity in Early Christian Thought." *Feminist Studies* 3 (March/April 1976):145-158.

————. "Wives and Women in Early Christian Thought." *International Journal of Women's Studies* 2 (1979): 575-592.

McNamara, Martin. *The Apocrypha in the Irish Church.* [Dublin]: Dublin Institute for Advanced Studies, 1975.

Meyer, Heinrich August Wilhelm. *Critical and Exegetical Handbook to the Acts of the Apostles.* Translated by Paton J. Gloag; trans. rev. by William P. Dickson, with Preface and notes to American edition by William Ormiston. New York: Funk & Wagnalls, Publishers, 1883.

Moffatt, James. *An Introduction to the Literature of the New Testament.* International Theological Library, ed. Charles A. Briggs and Stewart D. F. Salmond. 3rd ed. New York: Charles Scribner's

Sons, 1918.

Mollenkott, Virginia Ramey. *Women, Men, and the Bible*. Nashville: Abingdon, 1977.

Moloney, Francis J. *Woman First Among the Faithful*. Notre Dame: Ave Maria Press, 1986.

Moltmann-Wendel, Elisabeth. *The Women Around Jesus*. New York: Crossroad Publishing Company, 1990.

Montefiore, C. G. *The Synoptic Gospels*. Vol. II; 2nd ed. London: Macmillan & Co., 1927.

Montefiore, C. G., and H. Lowe. *A Rabbinic Anthology*. New York: Schocken Books, 1974.

Moo, Douglas J. *The Old Testament in the Gospel Passion Narratives*. Sheffield: Almond Press, 1983.

Morris, Leon. *Luke: An Introduction and Commentary*. 2nd ed. Tyndale New Testament Commentaries, ed. Leon Morris. Leicester: Inter-Varsity Press; Grand Rapids, MI: William B. Eerdmans Publishing Company, 1989.

Moule, C. F. D. "The Problem of the Pastoral Epistles: A Reappraisal." *Bulletin of the John Rylands Library* 47 (1964-1965): 430-452.

Mowinckel, Sigmund. *The Psalms in Israel's Worship*. Translated by D. R. Ap-Thomas. Nashville: Abingdon Press, 1962.

Moxnes, Halvor. "Patron-Client Relations and the New Community in Luke-Acts." In *The Social World of Luke-Acts: Models for Interpretation*, ed. Jerome H. Neyrey, 241-268. Peabody, MA: Hendrickson Publishers, 1991.

Munck, Johannes. *The Acts of the Apostles: A New Translation with Introduction and Commentary*. Anchor Bible, eds. William F. Albright and David Noel Freedman, 31. Revised by W. F. Albright and C. S. Mann. Garden City, NY: Doubleday & Company, 1967.

Munro, Winsome. *Authority in Paul and Peter, The Identification of a Pastoral Stratum in the Pauline Corpus and 1 Peter*. Society for New Testament Studies Monograph Series, ed. G. N. Stanton, 45. New York: Cambridge University Press, 1983.

Murray, Robert. *Symbols of Church and Kingdom: A Study in Early Syriac Tradition*. New York: Cambridge University Press, 1975.

Neirynck, Franz. "The Miracle Stories in the Acts of the Apostles." In *Les Actes des Apôtres: Traditions, redaction, theologie*, ed. J. Kremer, 169-213. Bibliotheca Ephemeridum Theologicarum Lovaniensium XLVIII. Gembloux, Belgium: Leuven University Press, 1979.

Neyrey, Jerome H. "Ceremonies in Luke-Acts: The Case of Meals and Table Fellowship." In *The Social World of Luke-Acts: Models for Interpretation*, ed. Jerome H. Neyrey, 361-387. Peabody, MA: Hendrickson Publishers, 1991.

————. *The Passion According to Luke: A Redaction Study of Luke's Soteriology*. New York: Paulist Press, 1985.

————, ed. *The Social World of Luke-Acts: Models for Interpretation.* Peabody, MA: Hendrickson Publishers, 1991.

Nilsson, Martin P. *A History of Greek Religion.* 2nd ed. New York: W. W. Norton & Company, 1964.

Nock, A. D. *Conversion: The Old and the New in Religion from Alexander the Great to Augustine of Hippo.* New York: Oxford University Press, 1961.

Nolland, John. *Luke 1-9:20.* Word Biblical Commentary, gen. eds. David A. Hubbard and Glenn W. Barker, 35A. Dallas: Word Books, Publisher, 1989.

Norris, Christopher. *Deconstruction, Theory and Practice.* 2nd ed. New York: Routledge, a division of Routledge, Chapman, and Hall, 1991.

Noth, Martin. *A History of Pentateuchal Traditions.* Translated by Bernhard W. Anderson. Englewood Cliffs, NJ: Prentice-Hall, 1972.

Nugent, Rosamund M. *Portrait of the Consecrated Woman in Greek Christian Literature of the First Four Centuries.* Washington, DC: Catholic University of America Press, 1941.

O'Day, Gail. "Acts." In *The Women's Bible Commentary,* eds. Carol A. Newsom and Sharon H. Ringe, 305-312. Louisville: Westminster/John Knox Press, 1992.

O'Fearghail, Fearghus. "Rejection at Nazareth: Lk 4 22." *Zeitschrift für die Neutestamentlische Wissenschaft* 75 (1984): 60-72.

Olyan, Saul M. *Asherah and the Cult of Yahweh in Israel.* Society of Biblical Literature Monograph Series, ed. Adela Yarbro Collins, no. 34. Atlanta: Scholars Press, 1988.

O'Neill, J. C. *Paul's Letter to the Romans.* Baltimore: Penguin Books, 1975.

————. *The Theology of Acts in its Historical Setting.* London: SPCK, 1961.

O'Rahilly, A. "The Two Sisters." *Scripture* 4 (1949): 68-76.

Origen. *Contra Celsum.* 2nd ed. Translated by Henry Chadwick. Cambridge: Cambridge University Press, 1953.

————. *Fragment on 1 Corinthians.* Translated by Claude Jenkins. In Claude Jenkins, "Origen on 1 Corinthians." *Journal of Theological Studies* 10 (1908-1909): 41-42.

Osiek, Carolyn. "The Widow as Altar: The Rise and Fall of a Symbol." *Second Century* 3 (Fall 1983): 159-169.

Ott, W. *Gebet und Heil: Die Bedeutung der Gebetsparänese in der lukanishen Theologie.* Studien zur Alten und Neuen Testaments. Munich: Kösel, 1965.

Otto, Rudolf. *The Kingdom of God and the Son of Man: A Study in the History of Religion.* 2nd ed. Translated by Floyd V. Filson and Bertram Lee Woolf. Boston: Starr King Press, 1957.

Otto, Walter F. *Dionysus, Myth and Cult.* Translated with an Introduction by Robert B. Palmer. Bloomington: Indiana University Press, 1965.

Parker, Pierson. "Herod Antipas and the Death of Jesus." In *Jesus, the Gospels and the Church: Essays in Honor of William R. Farmer*, ed. E. P. Sanders, 197-208. Macon: Mercer University Press, 1987.

Parvey, Constance F. "The Theology and Leadership of Women in the New Testament." In *Religion and Sexism*, ed. Rosemary Radford Ruether, 139-146. New York: Simon & Schuster, 1974.

Patai, Raphael. *The Hebrew Goddess*. New York: Discus Books, a division of Avon Books, 1978.

Perkins, Judith. "The Apocryphal Acts of the Apostles and the Early Christian Martyrdom." *Arethusa* 18 (1985): 211-230.

Perkins, Pheme. Review of *The Revolt of the Widows: The Social World of the Apocryphal Acts*, by Stevan L. Davies. *America* 144 (June 6, 1981): 470.

Perrin, Norman. *Rediscovering the Teaching of Jesus*. New York: Harper & Row, Publishers, 1976.

Pervo, Richard I. *Profit with Delight: The Literary Genre of the Acts of the Apostles*. Philadelphia: Fortress Press, 1987.

Peterson, William L. "Tatian's Diatessaron." In *Ancient Christian Gospels* by Helmut Koester, 403-431. London: SCM Press; Philadelphia: Trinity Press International, 1990.

Philostratus. *The Life of Apollonius of Tyana*. I and II. Translated by F. C. Coneybeare. Loeb Classical Library.

Pilch, John J. "Sickness and Healing in Luke-Acts." In *The Social World of Luke-Acts*, ed. Jerome H. Neyrey, 181-209. Peabody, MA: Hendrickson Publishers, 1992.

Pliny Secundus. *The Letters of the Younger Pliny*. 2nd ed. Translated by Betty Radice. Baltimore: Penguin Books, 1969.

Plümacher, Eckhard. *Lukas als hellenistischer Schriftsteller: Studien zur Apostelgeschichte*. Göttingen: Vanderhoeck & Ruprecht, 1972.

Plummer, Alfred. *A Critical and Exegetical Commentary on the Gospel According to St. Luke*. International Critical Commentary, eds. Charles Augustus Briggs, Samuel Rolles Driver, and Alfred Plummer. New York: Charles Scribner's Sons, 1906.

————. *The Pastoral Epistles*. The Expositor's Bible, ed. W. Robertson Nicoll. New York: A. C. Armstrong & Son, 1888.

————. "The Woman That Was a Sinner." *Expository Times* 27 (1915-1916): 42-43.

Pohlenz, M. "Ischodad on Acts 17:28." Unpublished translation of section II, "Ischodad über Acts 17:28," 101-104, of M. Pohlenz, "Paulus und die Stoa." *Zeitschift für die Neutestamentlische Wissenschaft* 42 (1949): 69-104. Translated by S. T. Joshi, rev. by Robert M. Price.

————. "Paulus und die Stoa." *Zeitschrift für die Neutestamentlische Wissenschaft* 42 (1949): 69-104.

Pomeroy, Sarah B. *Goddesses, Whores, Wives and Slaves: Women in Classical Antiquity*. New York: Schocken Books, 1975.

Pope, Marvin H. *Song of Songs: A New Translation with Introduction and Commentary.* Anchor Bible, eds. William Foxwell Albright and David Noel Freedman, 7C. Garden City, NY: Doubleday & Company, 1977.

Portefaix, Lilian. *Sisters Rejoice: Paul's Letter to the Philippians and Luke-Acts as Seen by First Century Philippian Women.* Coniectanea biblica. New Testament series; 20. Stockholm: Almqvist & Wiksell, 1988.

Price, Robert M. "Mary Magdalene: Gnostic Apostle?" *Grail: An Ecumenical Journal* 6 (June 1990): 54-76.

Quesnell, Quentin. "The Women at Luke's Supper." In *Political Issues in Luke-Acts*, eds. Richard J. Cassidy and Philip J. Sharper, 59-79. Maryknoll: Orbis Books, 1983.

Quinn, Jerome D. "The Last Volume of Luke: The Relation of Luke-Acts to the Pastoral Epistles." In *Perspectives on Luke-Acts*, ed. Charles H. Talbert, 62-75. Perspectives in Religious Studies, Special Studies Series, ed. Watson Mills, no. 5. Danville, VA: Association of Baptist Professors of Religion, 1978.

Rackham, Richard Belevard. *The Acts of the Apostles: An Exposition.* Westminster Commentaries, ed. Walter Lock. London: Methuen & Co., 1901, rpt. 1951.

Rader, Rosemary. *Breaking Boundaries: Male/Female Friendship in Early Christian Communities.* Theological Inquiries: Studies in Contemporary Biblical and Theological Problems, ed. Lawrence Boadt. New York: Paulist Press, 1983.

Ramsey, William M. *The Letters to the Seven Churches of Asia and Their Place in the Plan of the Apocalypse.* New York: A. C. Armstrong & Son, 1905.

Ravens, D. A. S. "The Setting of Luke's Account of the Anointing: Luke 7.2-8.3." *New Testament Studies* 34 (1988): 282-292.

Reicke, Bo. "Instruction and Discussion in the Travel Narrative." In *Studia Evangelica: Papers Presented to the International Congress on "The Four Gospels in 1957" Held at Christ Church, Oxford, 1957*, eds. Kurt Aland, F. L. Cross, Jean Daniélou, Harald Riesenfeld, W. C. van Unnick, 206-216. Berlin: Akademie-Verlag, 1959.

Reitzenstein, Richard. *Hellenistic Mystery Religions: Their Basic Ideas and Significance.* Translated by John Steely. Pittsburgh Theological Monograph Series, ed. Dikran Y. Hadidian, 15. Philadelphia: Pickwick Press, 1978.

Reimarus, Hermann Samuel. *Reimarus: Fragments.* Translated by Ralph S. Fraser, ed. Charles H. Talbert. Lives of Jesus series, ed. Leander E. Keck. Philadelphia: Fortress Press, 1970.

Renan, Ernest. *The Life of Jesus.* New York: Modern Library, 1927.

Rengstorf, Karl Heinrich. *Das Evangelium nach Lukas.* Das Neue Testament Deutsch 3. Göttingen: Vandenhoeck & Ruprecht, 1969.

Rensberger, David. Review of *The Legend and the Apostle: The Battle for*

Paul in Story and Canon, by Dennis Ronald MacDonald. *Journal of Biblical Literature* 104 (1985): 363-365.

Rentería, Tamis Hoover. "The Elijah/Elisha Stories: A Socio-cultural Analysis of Prophets and People in Ninth-Century B.C.E. Israel." In *Elijah and Elisha in Socioliterary Perspective,* ed. Robert B. Coote, 75-126. Society of Biblical Literature Semeia Studies, ed. Edward L. Greenstein. Atlanta: Scholars Press.

Review of *The Revolt of the Widows: The Social World of the Apocryphal Acts,* by Stevan L. Davies. *Choice* 18 (March 1981): 968.

Richard, Earl. *Acts 6:1-8:4: The Author's Method of Composition.* Society of Biblical Literature Dissertation Series 41. Missoula: Scholars Press, 1978.

Robinson, James M., and Helmut Koester, eds. *Trajectories Through Early Christianity.* Philadelphia: Fortress Press, 1971.

Robinson, Neal. *Christ in Islam and Christianity.* Albany: State University of New York Press, 1991.

Rohde, E. *Der griechische Roman und seine Vorlaufer.* Hildesheim: Olms Verlag, 1960, rpt. of 1876 ed.

Roloff, Jürgen. *Die Apostelgeschichte.* Die Neue Testament Deutsch, eds. Gerhard Friedrich and Peter Stuhlmacher, 5. Göttingen: Vandenhoeck & Ruprecht, 1981.

Rordorf, Willy. "Tradition and Composition in the Acts of Paul and Thecla: The State of the Question." *Semeia* 38 (1986): 43-52.

Rossmiller, Celeste J. "Prophets and Disciples in Luke's Infancy Narrative." *The Bible Today* 22 (June 184): 361-365.

Rowland, Christopher. *The Open Heaven: A Study of Apocalyptic in Judaism and Early Christianity.* New York: Crossroad Publishing Company, 1982.

Ruether, Rosemary Radford. "Mothers of the Church: Ascetic Women in the Late Patristic Age." In *Women of Spirit,* eds. Rosemary Ruether and Eleanor Commo McLaughlin, 72-98. New York: Simon & Schuster, 1979.

————, ed. *Religion and Sexism: Images of Women in the Jewish and Christian Traditions.* New York: Simon & Schuster, 1974.

Ruether, Rosemary Radford, and Eleanor Commo McLaughlin, eds. *Women of Spirit.* New York: Simon & Schuster, 1979.

Ryan, Rosalie, "The Women from Galilee and Discipleship in Luke." *Biblical Theology Bulletin* 15 (1985): 56-59.

Ryrie, Charles Caldwell. *The Role of Women in the Church.* Chicago: Moody Press, 1978.

Salisbury, Joyce E. *Church Fathers, Independent Virgins.* New York: Verso, 1991.

Sanday, William, ed. *Oxford Studies in the Synoptic Problem by Members of The University of Oxford.* Oxford: Clarendon Press, 1911.

Sanders, Jack T. *The Jews in Luke-Acts.* Philadelphia: Fortress Press, 1987.

Sandmel, Samuel. "Parallelomania." *Journal of Biblical Literature* 81

(1962): 1-13.

Schaberg, Jane. "Luke." In *The Women's Bible Commentary*, eds. Carol A. Newsom and Sharon H. Ringe, 275-292. Louisville: Westminster/John Knox Press, 1992.

Schmeichel, Waldemar. "Christian Prophecy in Lukan Thought: Luke 4:16-30 as a Point of Departure." In *Society of Biblical Literature 1976 Seminar Papers*, ed. G. MacRae, 293-304. Missoula: Scholars Press, 1976.

Schmithals, Walter. *Das Evangelium nach Lukas.* Zürcher Bibelkommentare, eds. Georg Fohrer, Hans Heinrich Schmid and Siegfried Schulz. Zürich: Theologischer Verlag, 1980.

————. *Paul and James.* Translated by Dorothea M. Barton. Studies in Biblical Theology, eds. C. F. D. Moule, J. Barr, Peter Ackroyd, Floyd V. Filson, G. Ernest Wright, no. 46. Naperville, IL: Alec R. Allenson, 1965.

Scholem, Gershom. *Sabbatai Sevi: The Mystical Messiah 1626-1676.* Bollingen Series XCIII. Princeton: Princeton University Press, 1973.

Schottroff, Luise. "Sheep Among Wolves: The Wandering Prophets of the Sayings-Source." In *Jesus of Nazareth and the Hope of the Poor* by Luise Schottroff and Wolfgang Stegemann, 38-66. Translated by Matthew J. O'Connell. Maryknoll: Orbis Books, 1986.

————. "Women as Followers of Jesus in New Testament Times: An Exercise in Social-Historical Exegesis of the Bible." In *The Bible and Liberation: Political and Social Hermeneutics*, ed. Norman K. Gottwald, 418-427. Maryknoll: Orbis Books, 1989.

Schottroff, Louise, and Wolfgang Stegemann. *Jesus of Nazareth and the Hope of the Poor.* Translated by Matthew J. O'Connell. Maryknoll: Orbis Books, 1986.

Schürmann, H. *Das Lukasevangelium, Erster Teil: Kommentar zu Kap. 1,1-9,50.* Herders theologischer Kommentar zum NT. Freiburg: Herder, 1969.

————. "Zur Traditionsgeschichte der Nazareth-Perikope Lk 4, 16-30." In *Mélanges bibliques en homage au R. P. Beda Rigeaux*, eds. A. Descamps and A. de Halleuxi, 187-205. Gembloux, Belgium: Duculot, 1970.

Schüssler Fiorenza, Elisabeth. *Bread Not Stone: The Challenge of Feminist Biblical Interpretation.* Boston: Beacon Press, 1984.

————. *But She Said: Feminist Practices of Biblical Interpretation.* Boston: Beacon Press, 1992.

————. "A Feminist Critical Interpretation for Liberation: Martha and Mary: Luke 10:38-42." *Religion and Intellectual Life* 3 (1986): 21-36.

————. *In Memory of Her: A Feminist Theological Reconstruction of Christian Origins.* New York: Crossroad Publishing Company, 1984.

————. "Lk 13:10-17: Interpretation for Liberation and Transformation." *Theology Digest* 36 (1989): 303-319.

————. "Theological Criteria and Historical Reconstruction: Martha and Mary: Luke 10:38-42." In *Protocol of the Fifty-third Colloquy: 10 April 1986,* by the Center for Hermeneutical Studies in Hellenistic and Modern Culture, 1-12. Berkeley: Graduate Theological Union & University of California-Berkeley, 1986.

————. "Word, Power and Spirit: Women in the Early Christian Communities." In *Women of Spirit,* eds. Rosemary Radford Ruether and Eleanor Commo McLaughlin, 30-70. New York: Simon & Schuster, 1979.

Schweizer, Eduard. *The Good News According to Luke.* Translated by David E. Green. Atlanta: John Knox Press, 1984.

Schweitzer, Albert. *Paul and His Interpreters.* London: Adam & Charles Black, 1912.

Scroggs, Robin. "Paul and the Eschatological Woman: Revisited." *Journal of the American Academy of Religion* 42 (1974): 532-537.

————. Review of *The Legend and the Apostle, The Battle for Paul in Story and Canon,* by Dennis Ronald MacDonald. *Christian Century* 101 (August 1-8, 1984): 752.

Seccombe, David Peter. *Possessions and the Poor in Luke-Acts.* Studien zum Neuen Testament und seiner Umwelt, ed. Albert Fuchs, Series B, Band 6. Linz: Studien zum Neuen Testament und seiner Umwelt, 1982.

Selvidge, Marla J. *Daughters of Jerusalem.* Scottdale, PA: Herald Press, 1987.

Sharman, Henry Burton. *Son of Man and Kingdom of God: A Critical Study.* New York: Harper & Brothers, Publishers, 1943.

Sherwin-White, A. N. *Roman Society and Roman Law in the New Testament.* New York: Oxford University Press, 1963.

Sim, D. C. "The Women Followers of Jesus: The Implications of Luke 8:1-3." *Heythrup Journal* 30 (1 1989): 57-62.

Simon, Marcel. *St. Stephen and the Hellenists in the Primitive Church.* Haskell Lectures 1956. New York: Longmans, Green & Co., 1958.

Simpson, E. K. *The Pastoral Epistles: The Greek Text with Introduction and Commentary.* London: Tyndale Press, 1954.

Smith, B. T. D. *The Parables of the Synoptic Gospels, A Critical Study.* Cambridge: Cambridge University Press, 1937.

Smith, Ruth L. Review of *Chastity as Autonomy: Women in the Stories of Apocryphal Acts,* by Virginia Burrus. *Ethics* 99 (April 1989): 692.

Snell, Priscilla. "The Women from Galilee." *Sisters Today* 60 (1989): 483-485.

Soards, Marion L. "Tradition, Composition, and Theology in Jesus' Speech to the 'Daughters of Jerusalem' (Luke 23, 26-32)." *Biblica* 68 (1987): 221-244.

————. "Tradition, Composition, and Theology in Luke's Account of

Jesus before Herod Antipas." *Biblica* 66 (1985): 343-363.

Söder, Rosa. *Die Apokryphen Geschichten und die romanhafte Literatur der Antike.* Würzburger Studien zur Altertumswissenschaft 3. Stuttgart: Kohlhammer Verlag, 1932.

Sparks, H. F. D., ed. *The Apocryphal Old Testament.* Oxford: Clarendon Press, 1984.

Spittler, Russell P. "Introduction to *Testament of Job.*" In *The Old Testament Pseudepigrapha, Vol. 1: Apocalyptic Literature and Testaments,* ed. James H. Charlesworth, 829-838. New York: Doubleday & Company, 1983.

————. "The Testament of Job: A History of Research." In *Studies on the Testament of Job,* eds. Michael A. Knibb and Peter van der Horst, 7-32. Society for New Testament Studies Monograph Series, ed. G. N. Stanton, 66. New York: Cambridge University Press, 1989.

Spong, John Shelby. *Born of a Woman: A Bishop Rethinks the Birth of Jesus.* San Francisco: HarperSanFrancisco, a division of HarperCollins Publishers, 1992.

Spretnak, Charlene. *Lost Goddesses of Early Greece: A Collection of Pre-Hellenic Myths.* Boston: Beacon Press, 1984.

Stählin, Gustav. "Das Bild der Witwe." *Jahrbuch für Antike und Christentum* 17 (1974): 5-20.

Stegemann, Wolfgang. "The Following of Christ as Solidarity between Rich, Respected Christians and Poor, Despised Christians (Gospel of Luke)." In *Jesus of Nazareth and the Hope of the Poor* by Luise Schottroff and Wolfgang Stegemann, 67-120. Translated by Matthew J. O'Connell. Maryknoll: Orbis Books, 1986.

————. "Wanderradikalismus im Urchristentum? Historische und theologische Auseinandersetzung mit einer interessanten These." In *Der Gott den kleinen Leute: Sozialgeschichtliche Bibelauslegungen, Vol. 2: Neues Testament,* eds. Luise Schottroff and Wolfgang Stegemann, 94-120. Munich: Kaiser Verlag, 1979.

Stock, Augustine. "Lydia and Prisca." *Emmanuel* 94 (September 1988): 514-521, 525.

Stott, John R. W. *Basic Introduction to the New Testament.* Downers Grove, IL: InterVarsity Press, 1964.

Strahan, James. "Encratites." In *Encyclopaedia of Religion and Ethics,* 1981.

Strauss, David Friedrich. *The Life of Jesus Critically Examined.* Translated by George Eliot. Ed. Peter Hodgson. Lives of Jesus Series, ed. Leander E. Keck. Philadelphia: Fortress Press, 1972.

————. *The Life of Jesus for the People.* Vol II, 2nd ed. London: Williams & Norgate, 1879.

Strecker, Georg. "The Reception of the Book." Revised by Robert Kraft. Appendix 2 to Walter Bauer, *Orthodoxy and Heresy in Earliest Christianity,* 286-316. Translated by a team from the Philadelphia Seminar on Christian Origins, eds. Robert Kraft and Gerhard Kroedel. Philadelphia: Fortress Press, 1971.

Streeter, B. H. "On the Trial of Our Lord before Herod: A Suggestion." In *Studies in the Synoptic Problem by Members of the University of Oxford*, ed. William Sanday, 229-231. Oxford: Clarendon Press, 1911.

————. *The Four Gospels: A Study of Origins*. London: Macmillan & Co., 1951.

Stroebel, August. "Schreiben des Lukas? Zum sprachlichen Problem der Pastoralbriefe." *New Testament Studies* 15 (1968-1969): 191-210.

Sweetland, Dennis M. "Luke the Christian." In *New Views on Luke and Acts*, ed. Earl Richard, 48-66. Collegeville, MN: Liturgical Press, 1990.

Swidler, Leonard. *Biblical Affirmations of Women*. Philadelphia: Westminster Press, 1979.

Swift, Louis J. Review of *The Revolt of the Widows: The Social World of the Apocryphal Acts*, by Stevan L. Davies. *Classical Outlook* 60 (March 1983): 100.

Talbert, Charles H. *Luke and the Gnostics: An Examination of the Lucan Purpose*. New York: Abingdon, 1966.

————. *Reading Luke: A Literary and Theological Commentary on the Third Gospel*. New York: Crossroad Publishing Company, 1982.

Tannehill, Robert C. "The Mission of Jesus According to Luke iv 16-30." In *Jesus in Nazareth*, ed. W. Eltester, 51-75. Berlin: Walter de Gruyer, 1972.

————. *The Narrative Unity of Luke-Acts: A Literary Interpretation, Volume One: The Gospel According to Luke*. Philadelphia: Fortress Press, 1986.

————. *The Narrative Unity of Luke-Acts: A Literary Interpretation, Volume Two: The Acts of the Apostles*. Minneapolis: Fortress Press, 1990.

Taylor, Vincent. *Behind the Third Gospel: A Study of the Proto-Luke Hypothesis*. Oxford: Clarendon Press, 1926.

————. *The Formation of the Gospel Tradition*. London: Macmillan & Co., 1957.

————. *The Life and Ministry of Jesus*. New York: Abingdon Press, n.d.

————. *The Passion Narrative of St Luke: A Critical and Historical Investigation*. Ed. Owen E. Evans. Society for New Testament Studies Monograph Series, ed. Matthew Black, 19. Cambridge: Cambridge University Press, 1972.

Tertullian. *On the Veiling of Virgins*. In *The Ante-Nicene Fathers: Translations of the Fathers down to A.D. 325*, Vol. IV, eds. Alexander Roberts and James Donaldson, rev. by A. Cleveland Coxe, 27-38. Buffalo: Christian Literature Publishing Company, 1885.

Testament of Job. Translated by R. Thornhill. In *The Apocryphal Old Testament*, ed. H. F. D. Sparks. Oxford: Clarendon Press, 1984.

Tetlow, Elisabeth Meier. *Women and Ministry in the New Testament: Called to Serve*. New York: Paulist Press, 1980; rpt. as College Theology Society Reprints in Religion 1. New York: University Press of America. 1983.

Theissen, Gerd. *Social Reality and the Early Christians: Theology, Ethics, and the World of the New Testament*. Translated by Margaret Kohl. Minneapolis: Fortress Press, 1992.

————. *The Social Setting of Pauline Christianity: Essays on Corinth*. Edited and translated with Introduction by John H. Schutz. Philadelphia: Fortress Press, 1988.

————. *Sociology of Early Palestinian Christianity*. Translated by John Bowden. Philadelphia: Fortress Press, 1978.

Thomas, W. Derek. "Women in the Church at Philippi." *Expository Times* 83 (1976): 117-120.

Thurston, Bonnie Bowman. *The Widows: A Women's Ministry in the Early Church*. Minneapolis: Fortress Press, 1989.

Todd, Judith A. "The Pre-Deuteronomistic Elijah Cycle." In *Elijah and Elisha in Socioliterary Perspective*, ed. Robert B. Coote, 1-36. Society of Biblical Literature Semeia Studies, ed. Edward L. Greenstein. Atlanta: Scholars Press, 1992.

Tödt, H. E. *The Son of Man in the Synoptic Tradition*. Translated by Dorothea M. Barton. Philadelphia: Westminster Press, 1965.

Tolbert, Mary Ann. "Mark." In *The Women's Bible Commentary*, eds. Carol A. Newsom and Sharon H. Ringe, 263-274. Louisville: Westminster/John Knox Press, 1992.

————. *Perspectives on the Parables: An Approach to Multiple Interpretations*. Philadelphia: Fortress Press, 1979.

Tolkien, J. R. R. *The Fellowship of the Ring: Being the First Part of The Lord of the Rings*. New York: Ballantine Books, 1965.

Trevett, Christine. "Ignatius and the Monstrous Regiment of Women." In *Studia Patristica XXI: Papers Presented to the Tenth International Conference on Patristic Studies held in Oxford 1987. Second Century, Tertullian to Nicea in the West, Clement of Alexandria and Origen, Athanasius*, ed. Elizabeth A. Livingstone, 202-214. Leuven: Peeters Press, 1989.

————. *A Study of Ignatius of Antioch in Syria and Asia*. Studies in the Bible and Early Christianity, vol. 29. Lewiston, NY: Edwin Mellen Press, 1992.

Trible, Phyllis. "Bringing Miriam out of the Shadows." *Bible Review* 5 (February 1989): 14-25, 34.

————. *God and the Rhetoric of Sexuality*. Overtures to Biblical Theology, eds. Walter Brueggemann and John R. Donahue. Philadelphia: Fortress Press, 1978.

Tristam, Henry Baker. *Eastern Customs in Bible Lands*. London: Hodder & Stoughton, 1894.

Tuckett, C. M. "Luke 4, 16-30, Isaiah and Q." In *Logia: Les parables de*

Jesus—The Sayings of Jesus. Memorials Joseph Coppens, ed. Joel Delobel, 343-354. Bibliotheca Ephemeridum Theologicarum Lovaniensium LIX. Leuven: Leuven University Press, 1982.

Tyson, Joseph B. "Acts 6:1-7 and Dietary Regulations in Early Christianity." *Perspectives in Religious Studies* 10 (2 1983): 145-161.

————. *The Death of Jesus in Luke-Acts*. Columbia: University of South Carolina Press, 1986.

————. "The Lukan Version of the Trial of Jesus." *Novum Testamentum* 17 (1975): 249-258.

van der Horst, Pieter. "Images of Women in the Testament of Job." In *Studies on the Testament of Job*, eds. Michael A. Knibb and Peter W. van der Horst, 93-116. Society for New Testament Studies Monograph Series, ed. G. N. Stanton, 66. New York: Cambridge University Press, 1989.

van Manen, W. C. "Romans (Epistle)." In *Encyclopaedia Biblica: A Critical Dictionary of the Literary, Political and Religious History, the Archaeology, Geography, and Natural History of the Bible*, eds. T. K. Cheyne and J. Sutherland Black, 4127-4145. London: Adam & Charles Black, 1914.

Varela, A. T. "Luke 2. 36-37: Is Anna's Age What Is Really in Focus?" *Bible Translator* 27 (4 1976): 446.

Vermaseren, Maarten J. *Cybele and Attis: The Myth and the Cult*. Translated by A. M. H. Lemmers. London: Thames & Hudson, 1977.

Verrall, A. W. "Christ before Herod: Luke XIII 1-16." *Journal of Theological Studies* 10 (April 1909): 321-353.

Via, Dan Otto. "The Parable of the Unjust Judge: A Metaphor of the Unrealized Self." In *Semiology and the Parables*, ed. Daniel Patte, 1-32. Pittsburgh: Pickwick Press, 1976.

Via, E. Jane. "Women in the Gospel of Luke." In *Women in the World's Religions, Past and Present*, ed. Ursula King, 38-53. New York: Paragon House, 1987.

————. "Women, the Discipleship of Service, and the Early Christian Ritual Meal in the Gospel of Luke." *St. Luke's Journal of Theology* 29 (1985): 37-60.

Vielhauer, Philipp. "Gottesreich und Menschensohn in der Verkundigung Jesu." In *Festschrift für Günther Dehn*, ed. Wilhelm Schneemelcher, 57-79. Neukirchen: Verlag der Buchhandlung des Erziehungsvereins Neukirchen, 1957.

Vögeli, A. "Lukas und Euripides." *Theologische Zeitschrift* 9 (1953): 415-438.

Walaskay, Paul W. "The Trial and Death of Jesus in the Gospel of Luke." *Journal of Biblical Literature* 94 (1975): 81-93.

Walker, Barbara G. "Jesus Christ." In *The Women's Encyclopedia of Myths and Secrets*, 464-471. San Francisco: Harper & Row, San Francisco, 1983.

Walter, N. "Apostelgeschichte 6.1 und die Anfänge der Urgemeinde in

Jerusalem." *New Testament Studies* 29 (3 1983): 370-393.

Weinreich, Otto. "Gebet und Wunder: Türöffnung im Wunder-, Prodigien- und Zauberglauben der Antike, des Judentums und Christentums." In *Genetbliakon W. Schmid zum 70. Geburtstag*, 200-464. Tübinger Beiträge zur Altertumswissenschift 5. Stuttgart: Kohlhammer, 1929.

Wellhausen, Julius. *Das Evangelium Lucae.* Berlin: G. Reimer, 1904.

Wendt, Hans Heinrich. *Die Apostelgeschichte.* Kritisch-exegetischer Kommentar über des Neue Testament, ed. H. A. W. Meyer, part 3, ninth ed. Göttingen: Vandenhoeck & Ruprecht, 1913.

Whitney, Wayne Vohn. "The Liberation of the Kingdom of God: An Exegesis of Luke 10:38-42." *Paradigms* 3 (1987): 60-77.

————. "Women in Luke: An Application of a Reader-Response Hermeneutic." Ph.D. diss.: Southern Baptist Theological Seminary, 1990.

Wiens, Devon H. Review of *The Revolt of the Widows: The Social World of the Apocryphal Acts*, by Stevan L. Davies. *Journal of Biblical Literature* 101 (1982): 470-471.

Wilken, Robert L. *The Myth of Christian Beginnings: History's Impact on Belief.* Garden City, NY: Anchor Books, a division of Doubleday & Company, 1972.

Willetts, R. F. *Cretan Cults and Festivals.* London: Routledge & Kegan Paul, 1962.

Williams, C. S. C. *A Commentary on The Acts of the Apostles.* Black's New Testament Commentaries, ed. Henry Chadwick. London: Adam & Charles Black, 1978.

Willimon, William H. *Acts.* Interpretation series, ed. James Luther Mays. Atlanta: John Knox Press, 1988.

Wilson, J. M. *The Acts of the Apostles. Translated from the Codex Bezae with an Introduction on its Lucan Origin and Importance.* London: SPCK, 1923.

Wilson, Stephen G. *The Gentiles and the Gentile Mission in Luke-Acts.* Society for New Testament Studies Monograph Series, ed. Matthew Black, 23. New York: Cambridge University Press, 1973.

————. *Luke and the Pastoral Epistles.* London: SPCK, 1979.

Winnington-Ingram, R. P. *Euripides and Dionysus: An Interpretation of The Bacchae.* Amsterdam: Adolf M. Hakkert—Publisher, 1969.

Winterbotham, R. "Simon and the Sinner: St. Luke vii. 36-50." *Expositor* 1 (1877): 214-229.

Wire, Antoinette Clark. *The Corinthian Women Prophets: A Reconstruction through Paul's Rhetoric.* Minneapolis: Fortress Press, 1990.

————. "The Social Function of Women's Asceticism in the Roman East." In *Images of the Feminine in Gnosticism*, ed. Karen L. King, 308-323. Studies in Antiquity & Christianity, gen. ed. James M. Robinson. Philadelphia: Fortress Press, 1988.

————. "The Structure of the Gospel Miracle Stories and Their Tellers." *Semeia* 11 (1978): 83-113.

Witherington, Ben. "The Anti-Feminist Tendencies of the Western Text in Acts." *Journal of Biblical Literature* 103 (1984): 82-84.

————. "On the Road with Mary Magdalene, Joanna, Susanna, and Other Disciples—Luke 8 1-3." *Zeitschrift für die Neutestamentlische Wissenschaft* 70 (1979): 243-248.

————. *Women in the Ministry of Jesus*. Society for New Testament Studies Monograph Series, ed. G. N. Stanton, 51. New York: Cambridge University Press, 1987.

————. *Women in the Earliest Churches*. Society for New Testament Studies Monograph Series, ed. G. N. Stanton, 59. New York: Cambridge University Press, 1988.

Wojcik, Jan. *The Road to Emmaus: Reading Luke's Gospel*. West Lafayette, IN: Purdue University Press, 1989.

Zeller, Eduard. *The Contents and Origin of The Acts of the Apostles, Critically Investigated. To Which is Prefixed, Dr. F. Overbeck's Introduction to the Acts, from DeWette's Handbook.* Vols. I and II. Translated by Joseph Dare. London: Williams & Norgate, 1876.